OUR FIRM FOUNDATIONS

RESTORING THE POWER AND AUTHORITY OF THE FIRST CENTURY CHURCH

© 2011 Jubilee Enterprises Family Trust
Authors: James V. Potter, Ph.D. & Paula M. Potter, MA
Advocare Publishing Company
Redding, California ~ 96099

Our Firm Foundations: Restoring the Power and Authority of the First Century Church

ISBN 1-930327-57-9   EAN 13 9781930327573

Copyright © Jubilee Enterprises Family Trust
Authors: James V. Potter, Ph.D. & Paula M. Potter MA

All rights reserved. No portion of this book and/or cover may be copied or reproduced in any form or media, except for brief quotations, without the prior written permission from both the authors and publisher.

Unless otherwise noted, Biblical Scripture quotations in this volume are from the New International Version, Student Edition (NIV Study Bible), © 1985 by Zondervan Corporation, Grand Rapids, Michigan USA.

ISBN 1-930327-57-9   EAN 13 9781930327573

Published by: Advocare Publishing Co
Redding, California 96099-4114

Published in the United States of America

~ Introduction ~

We live in a difficult time – a time foretold long ago. Christ Jesus, when asked by his disciples, about the end of the age, responded: **"Watch out that no one deceives you.** For many will come in my name, claiming, 'I am the Christ,' and will deceive many. You will hear of wars and rumors of wars, but see to it that you are not alarmed. Such things must happen, but the end is still to come. **Nation will rise against nation, and kingdom against kingdom. There will be famines and earthquakes in various places**. All these are the beginning of birth pains" (Matt 24:4-8).

Another succinct prediction of our time can be found in the writings of the apostle Paul. "Do not become easily unsettled or alarmed by some prophecy, report or letter ... saying that the day of the Lord has already come. **Don't let anyone deceive you** in any way, for that day will not come until the rebellion occurs and the man of lawlessness is revealed, the man doomed to destruction; [and] ... **the secret power of lawlessness is already at work**" (1 Thessalonians 2:3 & 7).

Luke wrote that this time would be evidenced by: **"Men's hearts failing them for fear**, at the prospect of those things which are overtaking the world: for the powers of heaven shall be shaken" (Luke 21:26).

The result of these events is that people are – once again – beginning to turn to the church seeking answers. This sounds wonderful – fulfilling the hope of Christians worldwide. A pall of gloom hangs over this promising outlook. The reality is, we live in the church age foretold by the apostle John – the Laodicean age.

"To the angel of the church in Laodicea write: These are the words of the Amen, the faithful and true witness, the ruler of God's creation. I know your deeds, that you *are neither cold nor hot. I wish you were either one or the other! So, because you are lukewarm – neither hot nor cold – I am about to spit you out of my mouth. You say, 'I am rich; I have acquired wealth and do not need a thing.' But you do not realize that you are wretched, pitiful, poor, blind and naked"* (Rev 3:14-17).

The apostle Paul, speaking of this same era, wrote: *"There will be terrible times in the last days. People will be lovers of themselves, lovers of money, boastful, proud, abusive, disobedient to their parents, ungrateful, unholy, without love, unforgiving, slanderous, without self-control, brutal, not lovers of the good, treacherous, rash, conceited, lovers of pleasure rather than lovers of God –* **having a form of godliness but denying its power**" (2 Tim 3:1-5).

Many, seeking answers to the dilemma in the world and in their own life; have turned to the church seeking healing; but, have come away with the realization that the church has lost its power. They have read, or heard about, the miracles experienced in the first century church and have come seeking help; expecting the church today to exercise the same power.

Ask yourself: What did the first century church have that we do not? What did the apostles and first century Christians know that we do not? Why do we not see the same signs, wonders, miracles of healing [body, soul and spirit] that attended the first century church?

In these pages you will find answers to these questions. However, if you merely read it and put it with other good books on your library shelf, it will merely contribute to a powerless form of godliness. But, if the keys revealed here are put into practice, they will change your life, the life of your family, your ministry, your church, and your community. We challenge you to put the keys revealed here into action in your church!

~ Contents ~

Chapter	Title	Page
Intro.	Introduction	3
Ch. 1	A Spiritual Pilgrimage	7
Ch. 2	My Identity in Christ	35
Ch. 3	The Pilgrimage Continues	49
Ch. 4	Putting On Christ	65
Ch. 5	The Power of Faith	79
Ch. 6	Applied Rights	89
Ch. 7	God's Way	117
Ch. 8	Binding & Loosing	139
Ch. 9	Soul Healing	161
Ch. 10	Divine Editing of Memories	171
Ch. 11	The Battle For Your Soul	191
Ch. 12	Satan's Warfare Tactics	203
Ch. 13	Soul Healing & Discipleship	223
Ch. 14	The Complexities of Man [Body ~ Soul & Spirit]	229
Ch. 15	The Power of Imagination – Part 1	253
Ch. 16	The Power of Imagination – Part 2	271
Ch. 17	The Power of Imagination – Part 3	293
Ch. 18	Interior Redecorating	317
Ch. 19	Restoring Balance & Harmony	347
Ch. 20	Power in Our Hands	371
Ch. 21	Resolving Inner-Conflicts	381
Ch. 22	Restoring Inner-Peace	401

Ch. 23	Receive Ye The Holy Spirit	419
Ch. 24	Releasing Emotional Baggage	431
Biblio.	Bibliography & Resources	457
Bio.	Autobiography	459

Chapter 1 ~ A Spiritual Pilgrimage

Long ago – about 1000 BC – there lived in the Middle East, a very powerful, yet surprising gentle, king. His conquests were well known, his power feared, throughout the region. He conquered city-state after city-state, including the capital of the Canaanite kingdom -- the city of Salem, which he renamed New-Salem (or Jerusalem). He killed the last surviving giants living in the region, including Goliath, who practiced cannibalism, and were greatly feared – both far and near. Histories – sacred and secular – record his accomplishments. At the same time, this king was himself a chronicler, compiling the history of his people;

This king also wrote poems, songs and played the harpsichord – achievements one would hardly expect of a warrior king. It was in one of his poems that this king – whose name was **David** – described the spiritual journey we are all taking. He wrote: "O Lord of Hosts, my King and my God. how happy [blessed or fortunate, and to be envied] are those who dwell in Your house, and presence. And blessed [happy, fortunate] and to be envied, are those whose strength is in you; those who have set their hearts on a pilgrimage to find you. **Passing through the Valley of Baca [The Vale of Weeping] they make it a place of springs [living water]**; the early rains also filling the pools with blessings. They go from strength to strength, increasing in victorious power, till each of them appears before God in Zion" (Ps 84:3-7).

The Valley of Baca [the Vale of Weeping] is believed to be the valley that inspired another of David's poems -- perhaps the most well known of all: "Adonai is my shepherd; I lack nothing. He has me lie down in grassy pastures, he leads me to still waters, he restores my soul. He guides me in right pathways for his own name's sake. **And, even though I pass through death's dark ravine, I will fear no disaster, for you are with me; your rod and staff reassure me**. You prepare a table for me, even as my enemies look on; you anoint my head with oil from an overflowing vessel. Goodness, mercy and grace will pursue me every day of my life; and I will dwell with Adonai, in his house, forever and ever" (Ps 23 CJB).

The Valley of Baca, also known as the Valley of Hinnom (Jos 15:8; 18:6; 2 Ki 23:10; Jer 32:35; etc.), and as the Valley of Slaughter (Jer 7:32; 19:6), was a desert valley East of Jerusalem. Being near, but outside the city walls, it was the place where they took all of their dead and dying animals, including the remains from the sacrificial animals. Thus, it was rightly known as a place of slaughter and weeping. The original text suggests that pilgrims through this valley sometimes drank from the pools left by the autumn rains.

I'm sure you can imagine what that would be like! Stagnant pools contaminated by the nearby dead and dying animals. But, then – in the poetic imagery of King David – God appeared on the scene, to give the sojourners springs of living water [fresh cool water], and renew their strength from spring to spring, until they all appeared before Him – before His throne – in the city of Zion! The Valley of Baca, or Vale of Weeping, is an apt description of life on planet earth.

We are all on a pilgrimage through this Valley of Weeping -- a valley that ultimately passes through the dark ravine of death. None can escape the weeping associated with this pilgrimage, and none can escape death. The question we must all face is whether or not we fear this event; whether we view death as the end of all things, or worse yet, our entrance into hell; or whether we have embraced God's blessed assurance that He is preparing a table for us in the presence of our enemies – the principalities and powers of darkness (Eph 6:12).

The question is whether the grave is our final resting place, or whether – on the other side of death – God will anoint our head [mind] with the oil of His Spirit and say: *"The Spirit and the Bride say "Come!" Let everyone who hears me say, "Come!" Whoever is thirsty, let him come; and whosoever wishes, let him drink of the Water of Life, without cost"* (Rev 22:17).

Those who choose not to respond – or procrastinate in their decision-making until the grim-reaper calls – have a different fate. This same author, the apostle John describes their destiny.

"Outside the City are the dogs, those who practice the magical arts [alcohol, drugs and other things that induce

an altered state of consciousness], the sexually immoral [all expressions of sex outside of a monogamous, heterosexual marriage], murders [those who kill with malicious intent], idolaters [those who have put anyone, or anything on the throne of their heart (God's throne)], and everyone who loves and practices falsehood" (Rev 22:15). And what, I sense you asking, is the final destiny of those outside the City of Zion? Come with me to the Book of Jude – the next to last book in the Bible – where he describes their destiny.

"Dear friends, while I was busy at work, writing to you about the salvation we share, I felt it necessary to write, urging you to keep contending earnestly for the faith which was once and for all passed on to God's people. For certain **individuals; ones written about long ago as being meant for this condemnation**, *have wormed their way in -- ungodly people who pervert God's grace into a license for debauchery and disown our only Master and Lord, Yeshua the Messiah [Jesus the Savior]. ... These people, with their lying visions, defile their own flesh, despise godly authority and insult angelic beings. ... These people insult anything they don't understand naturally, without thinking, like animals -- by these things they are destroyed! ... They are* **waterless clouds carried along by the winds; trees without fruit even in autumn, and twice dead because they have been uprooted**; *[they are] savage sea-waves heaving forth their shameful deeds like foam,* **wandering stars for whom the blackest darkness has been reserved forever**" (Jude 1-13 CJB).

Twice Dead:
Taking this description and placing it alongside the apostle Matthew's warning: *"Don't fear those who can kill the body but are powerless to kill the soul. Rather, fear Him who can destroy both soul and body in hell"* (Mt 10:28), provides an much clearer understanding of the destiny of those outside the City of Zion. They are

twice dead: that is, not only do they die physically, but since **they failed to change their lifestyle**, God ultimately destroys their souls. However, this is not their end. Man is a spirit [made in the image of God, Who is Spirit (Jn 4:24)]. Spirit man has a soul [through which he thinks, feels and chooses how to express himself], and lives in a body [by which he carries out his chosen expression].

Even though we grow old and eventually die, our body thereafter decaying in the grave, and, if unredeemed, God destroys our soul; yet our spirit lives on. Our spirit is eternal; and it is in our spirit-being that we will live eternally in God's presence [in the City of Zion], or live alienated from God – one of the *"waterless clouds carried along by the winds ... wandering stars for whom the blackest darkness has been reserved forever"* (Jude 13)

The author of the Book of Hebrews wrote: *"Man is destined to die once, and after that to face the judgment"* (Heb 9:27). How, many ask, can one be judged after they are already dead? *"We must [in our soul] all appear before the judgment seat of Christ, that each one may receive what is due him for the things done while in the body, whether good or bad"* (2 Cor 5:10).

If the things we have done in the body are good [and the only good thing man can do is to accept Jesus Christ as our Lord and Savior], then – as the judge of the universe drops His gavel – we will hear the words: *"Excellent! You are a good, trustworthy servant. ...*

Come, enter in to the City and share in your master's happiness" (Mt 25:21 CJB). However, if we have failed to follow Jesus, we will hear the words: *"take from him what he has [his soul] ... and throw that worthless servant outside, into the darkness, where there is weeping and gnashing of teeth"* (vs 28-30). ... And the King will say, ... *"Depart from me, you who are cursed! Go – off into the fire prepared for the Adversary [of souls] and his angels"* (vs 41).

But, you may be saying, I'm a good person; I've never killed anyone, I don't steal or lie [much], or cheat [except on my taxes]. I don't curse or worship idols. I take care of my wife and kids, and I'm a good citizen. I even vote [most of the time.] What, beyond this, must I do to avoid this judgment – to be exiled from God and consumed in the everlasting fire? How can I pay for my sins? Must I give everything I have to the poor, or give my body to be burned – a human sacrifice for my own and my family's indiscretions? An apostle of Jesus, Paul – once named Saul of Tarsus, who before accepting Jesus as his Lord and Savior, committed many grevious sins, even hunting down and killing Christ's followers – answered this, writing:

"If I could speak in all the languages known to humans and angels alike, and did not love others, I would be nothing more than a noisy gong or clanging cymbal. If I could prophesy and understand all secrets and mysteries, and have all knowledge. If I had all this plus the faith that moved mountains, I would be nothing unless I loved others. Or, if I gave away all that I owned and gave my body to be burned alive as a sacrifice, it would gain me nothing, unless I loved others" (1 Cor 13:1-3).

In another place, Paul says" *"Let no debt remain outstanding [or unpaid] except the debt to love one another, for he who loves his fellowman has fulfilled the whole law ... Love your neighbor as yourself. Love does no harm to its neighbor. Therefore, love is the fulfillment of all law"* (Rom 13:8-10). Christ also said, love fulfills all law. *"Treat others as you want them to treat you. This is what the Law and the Prophets are all about"* (Mt 7:12). Compared to the many laws contained in the Old Testament Covenant, **Christ gave but law one to govern the New Covenant Church -- the law of love**.

The word, love, used in these Scriptures is the Greek word 'Agape' which is a word that is much more correctly translated as 'unconditional, irrevocable commitment.' It suggests – no demands – that we have a magnificent obsession for the well-being of others' souls.

This is soul-care elevated to the highest possible level. Were each person to care for others' souls in this manner, every person's deepest needs would be fulfilled. Sadly, this is impossible since man's ability to express this quality of love is – without a personal relationship with God [Father, Son and Holy Spirit] – an impossibility.

Born From Above

Let us explain. As mentioned earlier, man is a spirit, who has a soul, and lives in a body. One of the profound differences between a born-again (or born-from-above) Christian, and those who have not embraced Christ and experienced this change, is that a born-again Christian is indwelled by Holy Spirit. Paul spoke of this profound difference in his second letter to the Corinthians, saying:

"If any man be in Christ, he is a new creature: old things are passed away; behold, all things are become new" (2 Cor 5:17). ... *"In Him, bodily, lives the fullness of all God is, and it is in union [unified] with Him that you have been made complete – He is the head of all rule and authority"* (Col 2:9-10).

The Problem:
Notwithstanding this, many -- Christians and non-Christians alike – ask the question: *"If all the old things have passed away and all things have been made new"*, why do many born-again believers still act the way they did before accepting Christ as their Savior?" Since Scripture says, *"behold, all things are become new,"* are these people just 'wannabes' -- sinners, who aren't really saved at all? Or, have they lost their salvation, like some suggest, who apply Christ's parable of the sower's seed that fell among the rocks, springing up quickly but dying when the sun – representing trials – came out?

These are valid questions – questions that realistically demand answers, if in fact, born-again believers are to be seen as the salt of the earth, and a light for the lost to follow (Mt 5:13-14). As the apostle Peter said, we must: *"Always be prepared to give an answer to everyone who asks you to give the reason for the hope that you have. But do this with gentleness and respect"* (1 Peter 3:15-16).

The answers to these questions lie in the fact that we are a spiritual being who has a soul [giving us the ability to think, feel or sense, reason, choose and express ourselves], and live in a body [temporarily in a decaying body comprised of flesh and blood], created from the elements of the earth. How do we know this? Man was made in the image and likeness of God (Gen 1:26-27), and God is Spirit (Jn 4:24). God's Spirit originally indwelt man (Zech 12:1), but departed from man after he rebelled (W.S. 1:1-8), leaving man empty, creating that terrible void deep down inside, that is sensed by the unsaved.

Man's Misuse of Freewill:
Man was created to enjoy fellowship: with God, with one another, and with God's creation -- all other living things. But after man's rebellion and fall, his ability to fellowship was horribly disrupted. His spirit was alienated from God's Spirit; his fellowship with one another convoluted; and his designated role of ruler over creation terminated. Prior to his fall, man communed with God spirit to Spirit. But man's sins separated him from God so that He would not hear him (Is 59:2).

Before their rebellion, Adam and Eve enjoyed oneness and solidarity. After the fall, they immediately began blaming one another (Gen 3), and walking in spiritual darkness, their fellowship became strained (1 Jn 1:5-7). In the beginning, man was appointed ruler over all earthly creation (Gen 1:28). After their fall, Adam and

Eve and their progeny fell prey to the animals they once ruled (i.e., Lev 26:22). In all of this, God honored man created in His likeness, with the power of freewill choice.

Spiritual Consequences of the fall:
Created in the image and likeness of God, man had exchanged his glory for shame, cherishing delusions and seeking false gods (Ps 4:2). In so doing, his nature was altered: his empty spirit craved someone -- even something -- to worship. *"Although they knew God, they neither glorified him as God nor gave thanks to him, but their thinking became futile and their foolish hearts were darkened. Although they claimed to be wise, they became fools and exchanged the glory of the immortal God for images made to look like mortal man and birds and animals and reptiles"* (Rom 1:21-23). They made idols of metal (Ex 34:17), of stone (Lev 26:1), and of wood (Dt 29:17). And sadly, their idols were cast or carved in the shape of calves, goats, even serpents -- all creatures that once paid homage to them.

Relational Consequences of the fall:
Craving the solidarity of fellowship -- the oneness and intimacy they once shared with their spouse -- they turned to polygamy and prostitution. For example: Izban, one of the rulers of Bethlehem had multiple wives, thirty sons and thirty daughters. Not to be outdone, King Solomon had 700 wives of royal birth and 300 concubines (1 Ki 11:3). And, as one might expect, they led him astray. *"As Solomon grew old, his wives turned his heart after other gods, and his heart was not fully devoted to the LORD his God, as the heart of David his father had been. He followed Ashtoreth the goddess of the Sidonians, and Molech the detestable god of the Ammonites"* (1 Ki 11:4-6).

Physical Consequences of the fall:
Craving the intimate communication once enjoyed with his creator, man even consulted pieces of wood, calling them their diviner's wand (Hos 4:12), thinking that they

might convey his message to God! They examined animal and human organs, seeking to find some omen that might portend future events (Ezek 21:21-22). Becoming desperate to communicate with God, and vaguely aware of God's promised substitutionary sacrifice for man, that would resolve their alienation, *"They sacrificed their sons and daughters in the fire"* (2 Ki 17:17). ... *"They sacrificed their sons and their daughters to demons. They shed innocent blood, the blood of their sons and daughters, whom they sacrificed to the idols of Canaan"* (Ps 106:37-38). ... *"They committed adultery with their idols; they even sacrificed their children, whom they bore to me, as food for them"* (Ezek 23:37-38). ... [And] *"On the very day they sacrificed their children to their idols, they entered my sanctuary and desecrated it"* (Ezek 23:39).

As one might expect, instead of gaining access to God by these devious and unspeakable atrocities, *"the Lord was angry with his people and abhorred his inheritance. He handed them over to the nations, and their foes ruled over them"* (Ps 106:40-41). Yet, despite His great anger, God loved mankind -- His children -- with an incomprehensible love.

A Divine Solution:
"For God so loved the world that he gave [sacrificed] his one and only unique Son, so that everyone who trusts in him may have eternal life, instead of being utterly destroyed. For God did not send His Son into the world to judge the world, but rather so that through him, the world might be saved" (John 3:16-18).

To comprehend the full meaning of salvation, one needs to remember that when man sinned, indwelling Holy Spirit departed, alienating man from God. As a result, man -- who is a spirit, with a soul, living in a body -- lost his glorious body (his covering of the Shekinah glory), and began living as a body with a soul. In other words, part of him -- an essential part for fully functioning humans -- was missing. **Missing this critical element -- the indwelling of Holy Spirit --** man spiraled down into wickedness almost indescribable (Rom 1:18-32). Eventually -- in the fullness of time -- mankind bottomed out, thereafter being described as "children of the devil" (1 Jn 3:10). It was at this point that God reached down to save man. At that point, man needed far more than mere change: he needed to be saved.

Salvation ~ Making Whole Again:

The English word 'save', is translated from the Greek word, 'sode'-zo' which stems from a contraction that includes the obsolete word, 'saoz', which means 'to make safe' and another meaning to deliver or preserve. But the contraction conveys the more powerful concept of: healing, making whole, or putting back together. In other words, **through the sacrifice of God's one and only unique Son -- Jesus Christ -- man could be put back together**! As men and women embrace Christ, accepting His substitutionary sacrifice for their own sins, they are once again indwelled by Holy Spirit -- once more becoming whole. Praise God!

Fresh Promotions

Eternal Redemptive Provision:

God in His Great Love, made provision for this before the world was! The apostle Peter declared: *"You must know (recognize) that you were redeemed (ransomed) from the useless (fruitless) way of living inherited by tradition from [your] forefathers, not with corruptible things [such as] silver and gold, but [you were purchased] with the precious blood of Christ (the*

Messiah), like that of a [sacrificial] lamb without blemish or spot.

"It is true that **He was chosen and foreordained (destined and foreknown for it) before the foundation of the world**, but He was brought out to public view (made manifest) in these last days (at the end of the times) for the sake of you. Through Him you believe in (adhere to, rely on) God, Who raised Him up from the dead and gave Him honor and glory, so that your faith and hope are [centered and rest] in God" (1 Pe 1:18-21).

"For God says, "At the proper, propitious time I harkened to you; and in the time of salvation I provided aid for you: behold, now is the appointed season, behold now is the time for deliverance" (2 Cor 6:2).

Of those who embrace Jesus Christ, availing themselves of His substitutionary sacrifice and deliverance, Peter declared: "Though you have not seen him, you love him; and even though you do not see him now, you believe in him and are filled with an inexpressible and glorious joy, for you are receiving the goal of your faith, the salvation of your souls. Concerning this salvation, the prophets, who spoke of the grace that was to come to you, searched intently and with the greatest care, trying to find out the time and circumstances to which the Spirit of Christ in them was pointing when he predicted the sufferings of Christ and the glories that would follow.

"It was revealed to them that they were not serving themselves but you, when they spoke of the things that have now been told you by those who have preached the gospel to you by the Holy Spirit sent from heaven. Even angels long to look into these things. Therefore, prepare your minds for action; be self-controlled; set your hope fully on the grace to be given you when Jesus Christ is revealed. As obedient children, do not conform *to the evil desires you had when you lived in ignorance. But just as he who called you is holy, so be holy in all you do; for it is written: "Be holy, because I am holy"* (1 Pe 1:8-16).

Saved ~ Restored to Wholeness:
Our spirit is once again indwelled by Holy Spirit the moment we accept Jesus Christ as our Lord and Savior. From that moment on, we are never again the same -- spiritually. Our body -- both those of the saved and the lost -- will age, deteriorate and eventually return to the dust (elements) from whence it came (Gen 3:19). In fact, man's mortal body comprised of *"flesh and blood cannot inherit the kingdom of God, nor this perishable inherit the imperishable"* (1 Cor 15:50).

Embracing the fact that our spirit is once again indwelled by Holy Spirit, and our mortal body will be replaced with an immortal one, **there remains but one problem -- the transformation of our soul**. Scripture says: *"The soul who sins is the one who will die"* (Ezek 18:20); and, *"all have sinned and fallen short of the glory of God"* (Rom 3:32). We inherently know this, and King David clearly articulated man's plight, when he wrote: *"As the deer pants for streams of water, so my soul pants for you, O my God. My soul thirsts for God, for the living God. When can I go and meet with God? My tears have been my food day and night, while men say to me all day long, "Where is your God?"* (Ps 42:1-3).

Thankfully, *"the Son of man came to save* [from the penalty of eternal death] *that which was lost"* (Matt 18:11); and that which was lost just happened to be our souls (Ezek 18:20). But, when those who are lost embrace Christ, they do not at once become mature Christians. Jesus, explaining salvation to Nicodemus, a member of the Jewish council, said: *"you must be born again"* (Jn 3:5-8). Being born-from-above, when we accept Jesus as our Lord and Savior, is just the beginning of this process of salvation. This is our spiritual rebirth, but spiritual maturity -- like physical maturity -- is a process that takes time.

Explaining this to His disciples, *"Jesus said, "I praise you, Father, Lord of heaven and earth, because you have hidden these things from the wise and learned, and **revealed them to little children**"* (Matt 11:25-26). ... *"And he said: "I tell you the truth, **unless you change and become like little children**, you will never enter the kingdom of heaven. Therefore, whoever humbles himself like this child is the greatest in the kingdom of heaven"* (Matt 18:3-4).

King David grasped this concept and penned: *"My heart is not proud, O L*ord*, my eyes are not haughty; I do not concern myself with great matters or things too wonderful for me. But **I have stilled and quieted my soul; like a weaned child with its mother, like a weaned child is my soul within me**"* (Ps 131:1-2). The apostle Paul, likewise embraced the analogy between a baby and a new-born Christian, writing: *"As apostles of Christ we could have been a burden to you, **but we were gentle among you, like a mother caring for her little children**. We loved you so much that we were delighted to share with you not only the gospel of God but our lives as well, because you had become so dear to us"* (1 Thess 2:6-9).

Paul explaining this process of spiritual growth and maturation wrote: *"I urge you, brothers, in view of God's mercy, to **offer your bodies as living sacrifices**, holy and pleasing to God — this is your spiritual act of worship. Do not conform any longer to the pattern of this world, **but be transformed by the renewing of your mind**. Then you will be able to test and approve what God's will is — his good, pleasing and perfect will"* (Rom 12:1-2). ...

Removing our Blinders:

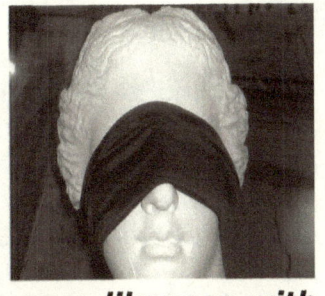

"Whenever anyone turns to the Lord, the veil [over their spiritual eyes] *is taken away. Now the Lord is the Spirit, and where the Spirit of the Lord is, there is freedom. And we, who with unveiled faces all reflect the Lord's glory, are* **constantly being transformed into his very own likeness with ever-increasing glory [from one degree of glory to another**], *which comes from the Lord, who is the Spirit"* (2 Cor 3:16-18).

Spiritual Rebirth, Growth and Maturation:

In summary, when one accepts Jesus Christ as their Lord and Savior, there is an immediate quantum-change that take place: [their spirit is indwelled by Holy Spirit]. **"We are [then] the temple of the living God"** (2 Cor 6:16), and **"our bodies are members of Christ himself"** (1 Cor 6:15). There are also other changes -- long-term changes -- that commence the moment one is born-anew, including [the transformation of the soul] -- which will be complete only when one enters glory [the transfiguration of their entire being]. There is another part of man that never experiences quantum-change [their body of flesh and blood]. It is destined to return to the elements of the earth.

From the moment one embraces Christ, to our transfiguration into glory, an inner struggle rages: a battle between our flesh and our spirit -- a battle between our body's physical deterioration and decay; and our spirit's growth and maturation, culminating in transfiguration, or glorification (1 Cor 15:53-54). The outcome of this battle, one's testimony to the unsaved world, and one's effectiveness -- or lack thereof -- **in the ministry of reconciliation that Jesus assigned each of us -- lies in the progress of our soulish transformation**. Thankfully, God provided us a road map to insure that we progress toward our final destination.

Concerning this, Paul wrote: *"I exhort you, therefore, brothers, in view of God's mercies, to make a decisive dedication of yourselves as a sacrifice [dedicating all your members and faculties], and live a life set apart for God. This will please him; it is your logical "Temple [spiritual, inner-being] worship." In other words, do not let yourselves be conformed [fashioned after or adapted to] the standards [customs] of this age. Instead, continue allowing yourselves to be transformed by the renewing [renovation or retrofitting] of your minds; so that you will know what God wants and will agree that what he wants is good, satisfying and something you are able [with His help] to achieve"* (Rom 12:1-2).

In these Scriptures, Paul sets forth the following steps:

1. Enter into a total covenant commitment with God: making a decisive dedication of every member of your body and every faculty of your soul (intellectual and emotional thoughts, beliefs, values and attitudes).

2. Commence living a life set apart for God in your inner-being (spirit).

3. Resist conforming to the world's standards and/or customs, through the indwelling Holy Spirit's aid.

4. Yield to Holy Spirit's continuing renovation and retrofitting of your mind, giving you an understanding of God's will.

5. Entering into an inner-agreement [between your spirit and Holy Spirit] that God's will is good -- and has at its center your best interest.

6. Acknowledge that with God in the Person of Holy Spirit -- Who testifies of Christ -- living in you; you can at all times, if you so choose, achieve Father God's will.

7. *"Clothing yourself in the Lord Jesus Christ, and not even thinking about how to gratify the desires of your sinful flesh"* (Rom 13:14).

8. Meditating on Father God's Will, knowing that *"those who live in accordance with the Spirit have their minds set on what the Spirit desires"* (Rom 8:5-6).

9. Resting in the fact that: *"[there is] now no condemnation (no adjudging guilty of wrong) for those who are in Christ Jesus, who live [and] walk not after the dictates of the flesh, but after the dictates of the Spirit. For the law of the Spirit of life [which is] in Christ Jesus [the law of my new being] has freed me from the law of sin and of death. For God has done what the Law could not do, [its power] being weakened by the flesh [the entire nature of man without the Holy Spirit]. [But] sending His own Son in the guise of sinful flesh and as an offering for sin, [God] condemned sin in the flesh [subdued, overcame, deprived it of its power over all who accept that sacrifice]. So that the righteous and just requirement of the Law might be fully met in us who live and move not in the ways of the flesh but in the ways of the Spirit [our lives governed not by the standards and according to the dictates of the flesh, but controlled by the Holy Spirit]"* (Rom 8:1-4).

Restoration In Process:
There is an old familiar saying that has been memorialized on bumper stickers, t-shirts and signs, that says: **"Don't judge: God isn't finished with me yet."** Concerning salvation -- the process of being put

back together -- Paul, in his letter to the believers in Thessalonica, wrote:

"May God himself, the God of peace, sanctify you through and through. May your whole spirit, soul and body be kept blameless at the coming of our Lord Jesus Christ. The one who calls you is faithful and he will do it" (1 Th 5:23-24). And, the author of the Book of Hebrews wrote: *"For the word of God is living and active. Sharper than any double-edged sword, it penetrates even to dividing soul and spirit, joints and marrow"* (Heb 4:12). God's Word, by which He called us into existence, is living and active (energizing and effective), capable of effecting healing of body, soul and spirit.

Man is one integral being -- body, soul and spirit. Only the Word of God is sharp enough to effect the divisibility of these features of humanity. Yet, when one contemplates such divisibility, interesting results become apparent:

- **Body** - Our body interacts with the physical features of creation,

- **Soul** - Our soul interacts with other human beings and the animal world through our thoughts, emotions, imaginations, attitudes, beliefs, values and choices. It is our vehicle of self-expression to the world around us in matters of relationships,

- **Spirit** - Our spirit interacts with other spirits in the unseen spiritual dimension we live in. Only a spirit can contact, or communicate with, another spirit. God is Spirit (Jn 4:24); as are God's angels (Heb 1:14), the angels who defected with Satan (Heb 2:16), and the demons -- spirits of the deceased Nephilim (Rev 16:14).

Man was created a spirit, with a soul for self-expression, living in a body of Shekinah Glory that after the fall was removed and replaced with an outer wrapper (a body) of flesh and blood. As Jesus explained to Nicodemus, *"Flesh gives birth to flesh, but the Spirit gives birth to spirit"* (Jn 3:6). Dwelling in this body of flesh and blood, which serves as the tabernacle, or tent of our spirit (2 Pe 1:13-14), man could no longer communicate directly with God. Man's sins created a separation between ourselves and God (Is 59:2).

Spirit Renewal:
When we are born again -- born of the Spirit (Jn 3:6) -- we are *"born-anew" not of perishable seed but of seed that is imperishable through the living and enduring Word of God"* (1 Pe 1:23). As natural-born humans we are born of perishable seed, making us perishable -- subject to decay, death and dying. Born-anew, of imperishable seed -- Divine seed -- we become once more members of God's Divine Family! *"If anyone is in Christ, he is a new creation; the old has gone, the new has come!"* (2 Cor 5:17-18). ... [For] *"he who unites himself with the Lord is one with Him in spirit"* (1 Cor 6:17).

Soul Transformation:
Although our sins are forgiven, our sin-record expunged, our guilt removed and our shame taken away, when we accept Jesus as our Lord and Savior, **our soul is not automatically renewed**. We still have soulish patterns that control our behavior, much like a computer program. If allowed, these will lead us back into sin. Paul illustrates this struggle in his letter to the Christians in Rome:

"We know that the law is spiritual; but I am unspiritual, sold as a slave to sin. I do not understand what I do. For what I want to do I do not do, but what I hate I do. And if I do what I do not want to do, I agree that the law is good. As it is, it is no longer I myself who do it,

but it is sin living in me. I know that nothing good lives in me, that is, in my sinful nature. For I have the desire to do what is good, but I cannot carry it out. For what I do is not the good I want to do; no, the evil I do not want to do — this I keep on doing. Now if I do what I do not want to do, it is no longer I who do it, but it is sin living in me that does it. So I find this law at work: When I want to do good, evil is right there with me. For in my inner being I delight in God's law; but I see another law at work in the members of my body, waging war against the law of my mind and making me a prisoner of the law of sin at work within my members" (Rom 7:14-24).

Since man's mind [psyche, or soul] is not automatically renewed when one is born-again, our soulish nature (mental processes) will dominate, directing our physical behavior. This will, as described by Paul in the Scripture cited above, result in ungodly behavior, making us a prime target of Satan. Moreover, our carnal nature is at enmity against God; a thing abhorrent to Him (Eze 35:11; Rom 8:8). **Satan is the father of legalism, the accuser of the brethren** (Rev 12:10), who will make accusation to God whenever our soulish nature is allowed to govern our behavior. He is our enemy, who *"prowls around like a roaring lion, looking for someone to devour"* (1 Pe 5:8). He maintains a dossier on each of us, giving him and the demons under his command a distinct advantage should we try to defend ourselves in our natural strength.

However, as God's redeemed children, we have access to spiritual weapons which are guaranteed to defeat every evil spirit! *"Although we do live in the world, we do not wage war in a worldly way; because the weapons we use to wage war are not worldly. On the contrary, they have God's power for demolishing strongholds. With them, we demolish arguments and every arrogance that raises itself up against the knowledge of God; we take every thought captive and make it obey the*

Messiah. And when we have become completely obedient [in Christ], then we will be able [ready] to punish every act of disobedience [the disobedient one]" (2 Cor 10:3-6).

A great deal of our inner-dialog [our self-talk] is negative and self-defeating. But, when we have *"offered ourselves [our entire being], as a sacrifice, living a life wholly set aside for God ... not allowing ourselves to be conformed to the standards and customs of this age, but rather, allowing ourselves to be continually transformed by the renewing of our minds [psyche or soul]"* (Rom 12:1-2); we will be ready and able to punish every act of the disobedient one [Satan] and the demons under his command.

"This is what the LORD Almighty says: ... These are the things you are to do: Speak the truth to each other, and render true and sound judgment in your courts; do not plot evil against your neighbor, and do not love to swear falsely. I hate all this," declares the Lord" (Zech 8:14-17).

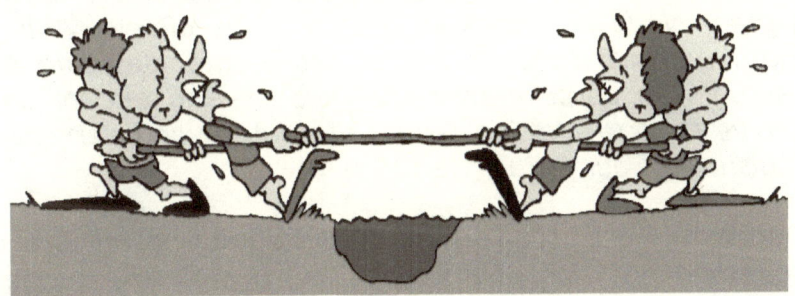

Winning vs. Losing:
"Those who identify with their old nature set their minds on the things of the old nature, but those who identify with the Spirit set their minds on the things of the Spirit. Having one's mind controlled by the old nature is death, but having one's mind controlled by the Spirit is life and peace. For the mind controlled by the old nature is hostile to God, because it does not submit itself to God's

Torah — indeed, it cannot. Thus, those who identify with their old nature cannot please God" (Rom 8:5-8). The carnal [fleshly-driven] mind is governed by our senses, or emotions and can never please God.

The author of the Book of Hebrews wrote: "God is coming soon! It won't be very long now. The people God accepts will live because of their faith. But he isn't pleased with anyone who turns back." We are not like those people who turn back and get destroyed. We will keep on having faith until we are saved. Faith makes us sure of what we hope for and gives us proof of what we cannot see. It was their faith that made our ancestors pleasing to God. Because of our faith, we know that the world was made at God's command. We also know that what can be seen was made out of what cannot be seen. ... Without faith no one can please God. We must believe that God is real and that he rewards everyone who searches for him" (Heb 10:37-11:6 CEV).

"Faith comes from hearing the message, and the message is heard through the word of Christ" (Rom 10:17-18). "Therefore, since we are surrounded by such a great cloud of witnesses, let us throw off everything that hinders and the sin that so easily entangles, and let us run with perseverance the race marked out for us. Let us fix our eyes on Jesus, the author and perfecter [finisher] of our faith" (Heb 12:1-2).

Our mind must be governed by our spirit, indwelled and governed by Holy Spirit, not by our fleshly senses [emotions]. To this end, we are instructed to: "clothe yourselves with the Lord Jesus Christ, and do not even think about how to gratify the desires of the sinful nature" (Rom 13:14).

Moreover, "Holy Spirit helps us in our weakness. We do not know what we ought to pray for, but the Spirit himself intercedes for us with groans that words cannot express. And he who searches our hearts knows the *mind of the Spirit, because the Spirit intercedes for the saints in accordance with God's will"* (Rom 8:26-27).

Remember: man is a spirit being, who has a soul [intellect and emotions] for self-expression, and temporarily lives in a corporeal [physical] body. The question is one of self-identification or self-image. What governs your self-image?

- **Body** - Physically focused self-image
- **Soul** - Soulish focused: centered on our emotions
- **Spirit** - Spirit to Spirit Union in Christ as God's Workmanship

Jesus did not put his self-identity in his soul. He said. *"My soul is overwhelmed with sorrow to the point of death"* (Mt 26:38; Mk 14:34), yet *"for the joy set before him endured the cross, scorning its shame, and sat down at the right hand of the throne of God"* (Heb 12:2).

David, the Psalmist, learned to overcome disabling depression by not putting his self-identity in his soul. He said: *"My soul thirsts for God, for the living God. ... My tears have been my food day and night. ... Why are you downcast, O my soul? Why so disturbed within me? Put your hope in God, for I will yet praise him, my Savior and my God"* (Ps 42:2-6).

The Prophet Isaiah also seems to have learned this lesson. He declared: *"Lord, walking in the way of your laws ... your name and renown are the desire of my heart. My soul yearns for you in the night; in the morning my spirit longs for you"* (Is 26:8-9).

Consider the following statements of self-identity:

- **Esau** *"Look, I am about to die"* (Gen 25:32).

- **Leah** *"I am not loved"* (Gen 29:33).

- **Jacob** *"Save me ... for I am afraid"* (Gen 32:11).

- **Moses** *"I am slow of speech and tongue"* (Ex 4:10).

- **Gideon** *"I am the least in my family"* (Judg 6:15).

- **Ezra** *"I am too ashamed & disgraced to lift my face"* (Ezra 9:6).

- **Job** *"I am full of shame and drowned in affliction"* (Job 10:15).

- **David** *"I am feeble and utterly crushed ... in anguish of heart"* (Ps 38:8).

- **Jeremiah** *"Look, O L*ord*, and consider, for I am despised"* (Lam 1:11).

In contrast to these expressions of self-identity, we will take up the next chapter, considering our true identity – who we are in Christ.

~ Questions, Concerns & Key Points ~

1. Are we – as the church – anointing new believers, like the first century church?

2. Are we teaching on Soul-Care and Soul-Cure?

3. Are we teaching about the transformation of the soul, and controlling self-talk or inner-dialogue?

4. Are we promoting wholeness through the indwelling Holy Spirit?

5. Are we teaching the Ministry of Reconciliation – model in the New Testament of High Priest and King?

6. Are we helping new converts surrender, allowing the indwelling Holy Spirit – Who testifies of Christ – do the work?

Chapter 2 ~ My Identity in Christ

Compared to the woefully negative statements of self-identity espoused by well known champions of faith in the Old Testament – that our last chapter ended with – consider who we are in God's eyes [How He sees us] – with our identity in Christ.

- *"With Christ in me, I am the hope of glory"* (Col 1:27).

- *"I am God's child, born of incorruptible seed, abiding forever"* (1 Pe 1:23).

- I am the temple of Holy Spirit (1 Cor 6:19).

- I am victorious (Rev 21:7).

- I am more than a conqueror (Rom 8:37).

- I am a co-inheritor and co-ruler in the Kingdom of God (Col 1:12).

- I am the light of the world (Mt 5:14).

- I am an ambassador for Christ (2 Cor 5:20).

- I am the apple of God's eye (Dt 32:10; Ps 17:8).

- I am beloved of God (Col 3:12; Rom 1:7; 1 Th 1:4)

These are just a few of many declarations of **our identity in Christ**. Which of these is true: 1] our self-identity? Or, 2] the identity God bequeaths upon us in His Son, Jesus Christ – our Lord and Savior? God's Word, of course! Concerning our identity, Jesus interceded for us with His Father, saying:

Just before his ascension, Jesus – interceding with His Father, prayed: *"My prayer is not that you take them out of the world but that you protect them from the evil one. They are not of the world, even as I am not of it. Sanctify them by the truth; your word is truth. As you sent me into the world, I have sent them into the world. For them I sanctify myself, that they too may be truly sanctified. "My prayer is not for them alone. I pray also for those who will believe in me through their message, that all of them may be one, Father, just as you are in me and I am in you"* (Jn 17:15-21).

Maintaining A Spirit Identity:
Do not find your self-identify in your body or soul! You may experience physical problems. Perhaps you may even suffer from soulish issues such as emotional trauma, but do not find your identity in these! Remember, *"God is Spirit and His worshipers must worship Him in spirit and in truth"* (Jn 4:24).

"All who are led by God's Spirit are God's sons. For you did not receive a spirit of slavery to bring you back again into fear; on the contrary, you received the Spirit, who makes us sons and by whose power we cry out, "Abba!" (that is, "Dear Father!"). The Spirit himself bears witness with our own spirits that we are children of God; and if we are children, then we are also heirs, heirs of God and joint-heirs with the Messiah" (Rom 8:14-17 CJB).

"Consider yourselves dead to sin, and your relationship with it broken, but alive to God in Christ Jesus, living in unbroken relationship with him. Do not let sin reign as king in your mortal body so that you yield to its evil desires. Do not yield any of the parts of your body, or your faculties, to sin, as instruments of wickedness. Instead, offer yourselves to God, yielding to Him as those who have been raised from the dead to enjoy eternal life. Yield your body members and faculties to

God, to be used as instruments of righteousness. For sin shall now longer be your master, because you are not under law, as slaves, but under grace [as subjects of God's mercy and unmerited favor]" (Rom 6:11-14).

"Don't you know that if you continually surrender yourselves to someone to do his will, you are slaves of him whom you obey — whether you are slaves to sin, which leads to death, or to obedience, which leads to righteousness? But thanks be to God that, though you used to be slaves to sin, you have wholeheartedly obeyed the standards of teaching in which you were instructed and to which you were committed. And having been set free from sin, you have become servants of righteousness -- conformed to the divine will in imagination, thought, purpose and action.

"I am putting this in familiar human terms, because of your natural limitations. Just as you previously yielded your body members and faculties as slaves to impurity and ever-increasing lawlessness; so now, yield your body members and faculties once for all times, as servants to righteousness, which leads to sanctification and holiness. For when you were slaves to sin, you were free with regard to the governance of righteousness. But, what benefit did you reap at that time from those things you are now ashamed of? Nothing! Those things result in death! But now that you have been set free from sin and have become slaves to God, the benefit you reap leads to holiness, and the end result is eternal life. For the wages of sin is death, but the gift of God is eternal life in union with Christ Jesus our Lord" (Rom 6:16-23).

In Union With Christ:
- We have governance over our life through indwelling Holy Spirit,

- As a child, rather than a slave, we have our power of choice restored,

- We surrender this mortal body as a living sacrifice, putting on Christ,

- We surrender our soul to the transforming power of Holy Spirit,

- We experience harmony with God -- spirit to Spirit in Christ.

- We may equal the total of our past choices, but our reaction is new.

- Thoughts may just come; emotions may be aroused; attacks may come from demons, the ungodly, or an errant brother in Christ; but

- In Christ, we can switch channels, choosing to give control to Holy Spirit!

The Natural Man:

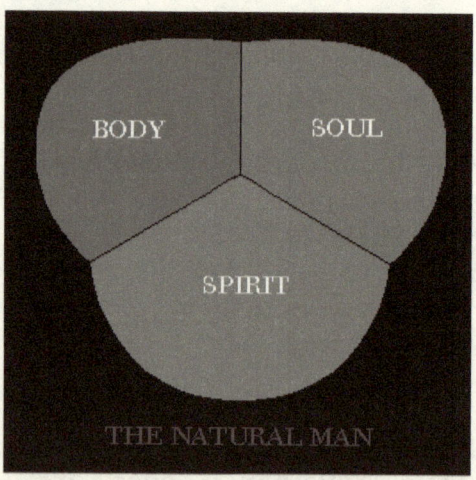

In the illustration above, the components of man's being -- body, soul and spirit -- are graphically illustrated. The sum of this represents our being, however, the interaction between these components is critical. Should a single component malfunction, our entire being malfunctions. When man rebelled and fell, this is exactly what happened – man's spirit malfunctioned. By divine design, man's spirit was indwelled by Holy Spirit, Who – through the interconnection between man's spirit and soul – directed man's body to fulfill God's commission for man: to exercise governance over the world. When Adam and Eve rebelled, Holy Spirit withdrew, leaving a profound void.

Spirit-Soul Link: The **link between our spirit and soul is our will**, exercised through the freewill God bestowed upon us. Some Scriptures that speak of this link include the following:

"I call on heaven and earth to witness against you today that I have presented you with life and death, the blessing and the curse. Therefore, ***choose life****, so that you will live, you and your descendants"* (Deut 30:19-20).

"Until I come and take you to a land like your own, a land of grain and new wine, a land of bread and vineyards, a land of olive trees and honey. ***Choose life and not death****!"* (2 Kings 18:32).

*"****Choose today whom you are going to serve****! Will it be the gods your ancestors served beyond the River? or the gods of the Emori, in whose land you are living?"* (Josh 24:15).

*"****Whosoever will save his life**** shall lose it: but whosoever will lose his life for my sake, the same shall save it"* (Luke 9:24).

"The Spirit and the bride say, Come. And let him that heareth say, Come. And let him that is athirst come. And ***whosoever will****, let him take the water of life freely"* (Rev 22:17).

Soul-Body Link: It should not surprise anyone to learn that **the link between the soul and the body is the tongue**. It is through our speech that we give expression to our soul [our thoughts, emotions, beliefs, etc.] Some Scriptures that speak of this link include the following:

"Make me savory meat, such as I love, and bring it to me, that I may eat; **that my soul may bless thee** before I die" (Gen 27:4).

"**I will not refrain my mouth**; I will speak in the anguish of my spirit; **I will complain in the bitterness of my soul**" (Job 7:11).

"**I will speak in the bitterness of my soul**" (Job 10:1).

"O **my soul, thou hast said unto the LORD**, Thou art my Lord" (Ps 16:2).

"You turned my mourning into dancing! You removed my sackcloth and clothed me with joy, so that **my inner-being can praise you and not be silent**; Adonai my God, I will thank you forever!" (Ps 30:12-13).

"A tree is known by its fruit. You snakes! How can you who are evil say anything good? For **the mouth speaks what overflows from the heart**. The good person brings forth good things from his store of good, and the evil person brings forth evil things from his store of evil. Moreover, I tell you this: on the Day of Judgment **people will have to give account for every careless word they have spoken; for by your own words you will be acquitted, and by your own words you will be condemned**" (Matt 12:33-37).

"**Mary said, My soul doth magnify the Lord**, and my spirit hath rejoiced in God my Savior" (Luke 1:46-47).

Spirit-Body Link: The **link between the human spirit and the body is the combination of will and tongue -- that is, the tongue controlled by the will**. Some of the Scriptures that speak of this link include the following:

"**The tongue has power over life and death**; *those who indulge it must eat its fruit*" (Pro 18:21).

"**The words of a man's mouth are deep waters**, *but the fountain of wisdom is a bubbling brook. It is not good to be partial to the wicked or to deprive the innocent of justice.* **A fool's lips bring him strife, and his mouth invites a beating. A fool's mouth is his undoing, and his lips are a snare to his soul. The words of a gossip are like choice morsels; they go down to a man's inmost parts**" (Pro 18:4-8).

"**Words from a wise man's mouth are gracious, but a fool is consumed by his own lips**. *At the beginning his words are folly; at the end they are wicked madness — and the fool multiplies words*" (Eccl 10:12-14).

"**My words come from an upright heart**; *my lips sincerely speak what I know. The Spirit of God has made me; the breath of the Almighty gives me life*" (Job 33:3-4).

"**The ear tests words as the tongue tastes food**. *Let us discern for ourselves what is right; let us learn together what is good*" (Job 34:3-4).

"**We all stumble in many ways. If anyone is never at fault in what he says, he is a perfect man, able to keep his whole body in check.** *When* **we put bits into the mouths of horses to make them obey us**, *we can turn the whole animal. Or take ships as an example. Although they are so large and are driven by strong winds, they are steered by a very small rudder* wherever the pilot wants to go. Likewise **the tongue is a small part of the body, but it makes great boasts**.

"Consider what a great forest is set on fire by a small spark. **The tongue also is a fire, a world of evil among the parts of the body. It corrupts the whole person, sets the whole course of his life on fire, and is itself set on fire by hell**. All kinds of animals, birds, reptiles and creatures of the sea are being tamed and have been tamed by man, but **no man can tame the tongue**. It is a restless evil, full of deadly poison. **With the tongue we praise our Lord and Father, and with it we curse men, who have been made in God's likeness. Out of the same mouth come praise and cursing. My brothers, this should not be**. Can both fresh water and salt water flow from the same spring?" (James 3:2-12).

Holy Spirit Control:
When our will is controlled by Holy Spirit, our spirit, soul and body are under Holy Spirit's control. This facilitates healing, transformation and restoration that is beyond our control. This change occurs as follows:

- Controlling my soul, Holy Spirit: *"Create(s) in me a clean heart, God; renew(s) in me a resolute spirit"* (Ps 51:12).

- With a clean heart, the words that come out of my mouth will be different. I will begin speaking life rather than death (Pro 18:21).

- As I -- through the guidance of indwelling Holy Spirit -- store up the Word of God in my heart, the words emanating from my mouth will change (Mt 12:34-36).

- And, with God's Word stored in my heart, my behavior changes. David said: *"Thy word have I hid in mine heart, that I might not sin against thee"* (Ps 119:11).

- As my words -- my tongue now controlled by indwelling Holy Spirit -- changes, my entire being will respond, like a ship that responds to a change in the rudder, and like a horse that changes direction with a slight pull on its reins (Jas 3:2-12).

- Through our spirit, indwelt by Holy Spirit, we are able to bring our will into agreement with Father God's will. The following Scriptures speak of this: *"Teach me to do thy will; for thou art my God: thy spirit is good; lead me into the land of uprightness. Quicken me, O Lord, for thy name's sake: for thy righteousness' sake bring my soul out of trouble"* (Ps 143:10-11). ... *"I delight to do thy will, O my God: yea, thy law is within my heart"* (Ps 40:8).

- Controlled by Holy Spirit, our life begins to change. *"If I pray in a tongue, my spirit prays, but my mind is unproductive. So, what about it? I will pray with my spirit, but I will also pray with my mind; I will sing with my spirit, but I will also sing with my mind"* (1 Cor 14:12-15). ... *"It is written: "I believed; therefore I have spoken." With that same spirit of faith we also believe and therefore speak"* (2 Cor 4:13-14).

- Controlled by Holy Spirit, we commence doing what is right, called righteousness. To better understand righteousness, consider the following words of Paul: *"Moses describes in this way the righteousness that is by the law: "The man who does these things will live by them." But the righteousness that is by faith says: "Do not say in your heart, 'Who will ascend into heaven?'" (that is, to bring Christ down) "or 'Who will descend into the deep?'" (that is, to bring Christ up from the dead). But what does it say? "**The word is near you; it is in your mouth and in** *your heart," that is, the word of faith we are proclaiming:*

"That if you confess with your mouth, "Jesus is Lord," and believe in your heart that God raised him from the dead, you will be saved. For it is with your heart that you believe and are justified, and it is with your mouth that you confess and are saved. As the Scripture says, "Anyone who trusts in him will never be put to shame." For there is no difference between Jew and Gentile — the same Lord is Lord of all and richly blesses all who call on him, for, "Everyone who calls on the name of the Lord will be saved" (Rom 10:5-13).

- **The tongue is the 'output channel' -- the vehicle of expression -- of our soul**. By the **"word of faith"** mentioned above, we call into existence things that are not. By confessing with our mouth that Jesus is Lord, we are saved. And, by confessing with our mouth the promises of God and fulfilling God's conditions, His promised blessings are ours.

- When we accept Jesus as Lord, Holy Spirit indwells our spirit, giving us the power -- by the words of our mouth -- to bring both our body and soul into subjection to our spirit. This, together with indwelling Holy Spirit, brings us into subjection to the will of Father God, effecting integration and harmony.

- When we confess that Jesus is Lord, we are redeemed from the household of bondage (Mic 6:4); and when Holy Spirit indwells us, our freewill is restored.

- Our spiritual maturity is from this moment on, dependent on our choices. These choices should not be that difficult, since we are given the mind of Christ! [*"For who has known the mind of the Lord that he may instruct him?" But we have the mind of*

Christ" (1 Cor 2:16).], but **we must choose to begin to think like Christ**. If Jesus is not the Lord of my thoughts, He will not be the Lord of my life.

- **We were seated with Christ in heavenly places** ["*God raised us up with Christ and seated us with him in the heavenly realms in Christ Jesus*" (Eph 2:6).].

- We must choose to experience life from Father God's perspective – **from the heavenly throne room**. This results in our problems – all of them – being under our feet. ["*He subdued peoples under us, and nations under our feet. He chose our inheritance for us*" (Ps 47:3-4).]

- **We must choose to be on God's Team** – having Him, not only 'by our side', but in us! ["*If anyone loves me, he will obey my teaching. My Father will love him, and we will come to him and make our home with him*" (John 14:23-24). ... "*On that day you will realize that I am in my Father, and you are in me, and I am in you*" (John 14:20).]

- With Father God, Christ Jesus and Holy Spirit living in us, God will -- if we permit -- be Adonai [the Lord] of every function of our life, through Holy Spirit. "*When the Counselor comes, whom I will send to you from the Father, the Spirit of truth who goes out from the Father, he will testify about me. And you also must testify, for you have been with me from the beginning*" (John 15:26-27).

Restored:
Remember, **salvation means to 'put back together'**. We are put back together – indeed, we are whole – when Jesus, Father God and Holy Spirit live in us and we in them. Paul wrote: "*This is a profound mystery — but I am talking about Christ and the church*" (Eph 5:32).

In [within] Christ we belong to: *"To the general assembly and church of the firstborn, which are written in heaven, and to God the Judge of all, and to the spirits of just men made perfect"* (Heb 12:23).

*"Adonai [the Lord] has proclaimed to the ends of the earth, "Say to the daughter of Zion [the church], '**Behold, your Salvation coming**! Behold, his reward is with him, his recompense accompanies him.'" They are called The Holy People, the Redeemed of Adonai [the Lord]. Your City will be sought after, known as a good place to live and full of people"* (Is 62:11-12).

Our Salvation is a Person: His Name is Jesus! In the Scripture referenced above, Jesus is named Salvation. Understanding this is vital. To be saved [put back together] we must be put back together with Christ. This is *"the mystery that has been kept hidden for ages and generations, but is now disclosed to the saints. To them God has chosen to make known among the Gentiles the glorious riches of **this mystery, which is Christ in you, the hope of glory**"* (Col 1:26-27).

Our New Identity:
Paul, the apostle to the Gentiles – to those who were not God's children but now are – wrote: *"If anyone is in Christ, he is a new creation; the old has gone, the new has come!"* (2 Cor 5:17-18). Echoing this, Peter declared: *"You are a chosen people, a royal priesthood, a holy nation, a people belonging to God, that you may declare the praises of him who called you out of darkness into his wonderful light. Once you were not a people, but now you are the people of God; once you had not received mercy, but now you have received mercy"* (1 Peter 2:9-10).

This is your true identity – a Child of God; born through the death of Christ, by which you – and I – have obtained mercy and become His people!

~ Questions, Concerns & Key Points ~

1. We must will to do Father God's will – it is a choice.

2. Are you teaching the Biblical concept of spirit-to-Spirit union with Father God, Christ Jesus and Holy Spirit?

3. Are you teaching the power of the tongue – the link between soul and body – and our speech?

4. Our tongue determines life or death. It is controlled by our will; the question is 'Who controls our will?'

5. When our will is controlled by Holy Spirit, our spirit, soul and body is under Holy Spirit control.

6. Our identity is in Christ – if we are encased within him.

7. Are you teaching the Throne Room perspective of Christian living? [Eph 2:6]

8. Are you teaching salvation and restoration as our being put back together, by and through the indwelling of Holy Spirit?

9. Salvation includes: Justification [title to a new life]; Sanctification [spiritual cleansing and being set-apart]; Transformation [restoration of the soul]; and Transfiguration [the final exaltation or glorification]. **Flesh and blood does not inherit the kingdom of God.**

10. Man is a spirit being: it is our spirit that must be restored through spirit-to-Spirit union with Christ. [Justification]

11.   Being indwelled by Holy Spirit is but a token [an earnest money or down payment] of all that God has for us in glory! [Sanctification]

12.   Holy Spirit, Who dwells within our spirit, writes on our heart God's laws of love, and transforms our soul. [Transformation]

13.   In a moment, in the twinkling of an eye; at the last trumpet sound, those who have been transformed by the indwelling Holy Spirit, will be glorified – this mortal body being exchanged for one immortal, [Transfiguration]

14.   Church of God – Do not miss the importance of the transformation of the soul!

Chapter 3 ~ The Pilgrimage Continues

Introduction:
Our world is in serious trouble today. There are wars and rumors of wars; financial woes, and organized international lawless gangs -- all signs of the end of this era. And, it's getting worse. There is, however, some Good News. Christ came to declare this good news: that God has a plan to redeem man and restore the earth to its Edenic perfection -- His original plan!

In The Beginning:
The Bible begins with these words: *"In the beginning God created the heavens and the earth"* (Gen 1:1). Throughout the rest of Genesis 1, the creative works of God are described, culminating in the creation of mankind (Gen 1:26.27). As God created each component and beheld His creation, He declared each feature *"very good"* (i.e., Gen 1:25). Even the environment was perfect.

After creating the family of man in the image and likeness of the God family [Father, Holy Spirit, Son (Jesus)], God placed this planet under the dominion of man, saying: *"Be fruitful and increase in number; fill the earth and subdue it. Rule over everything -- the fish of the sea, the birds of the air, every living creature that moves on the earth"* (Gen 1:28).

Having completed His creation and giving His children (mankind) dominion over the earth, it is recorded: *"And that is how it was. God beheld everything He had made and declared it very good" (Gen 1:30.31). Man – male and female (Adam and Eve) – were perfect, created in the mirror image and likeness of God himself, they were spirit beings, for *"God is Spirit: and they that worship Him must worship Him in spirit and in truth"* (Jn 4:24).

As God's children, created in His image, they were not only assigned dominion over the earth, they were given complete freedom of choice. They were also educated about the cosmos, the earth, and their environment – The Garden of Eden – also referred to as The Garden of God (Ezek 28:13; 31:8-9). They were informed concerning the presence of the fallen angels who were led by Satan, who, before his fall, had been Lucifer the arch angel, heavenly high priest, leader of the heavenly music ministry and bearer of the sacred colors.

God clearly explained to Adam and Eve that Satan's single avenue of access to them that was centered around a lone tree in the Garden of Eden. He fully explained the effects of eating from that tree, saying: *"You are free to eat from any tree in the garden; but you must not eat from the tree of the knowledge of good and evil, for when you eat of it you will surely die"* (Gen 2:16-17).

Rebellion ~ A Cosmic Tragedy:
How long Adam and Eve lived in the perfect environment of the Garden of God (the Garden of Eden) we don't know; but it must not have been long, since the first event that is recorded as occurring after their being expelled from Eden was Eve's conception with their first-born son, Cain (Gen 4:1).

The family of man's departure from Eden was part of a cosmic tragedy that profoundly effected not only themselves but their progeny - all mankind – even down to this day; all other living beings, and the earth itself. We begin reading about this tragedy in Genesis Chapter 3:

"Now the serpent was more crafty than any of the wild animals the LORD God had made. He said to the woman, "Did God really say, 'You must not eat from any tree in the garden'?" The woman said to the serpent, "We may eat fruit from the trees in the garden, but God did say, 'You must not eat fruit from the tree that is in the middle of the garden, and you must not touch it, or you will die.

"You will not surely die," the serpent said to the woman. "For God knows that when you eat of it your eyes will be opened, and you will be like God, knowing good and evil." When the woman saw that the fruit of the tree was good for food and pleasing to the eye, and also desirable for gaining wisdom, she took some and ate it. She also gave some to her husband, who was with her, and he ate it. Then the eyes of both of them were opened, and they realized they were naked; so they sewed a foreign substance together and made coverings for themselves" (Gen 3:1-7).

Prior to this tragic event, Adam and Even experienced complete solidarity and oneness: oneness with each other and with God. They not only lived in God's presence, they experienced complete oneness -- they in God and God in them. Following their rebellion, they were expelled from God's presence (Gen 3:23); and Holy Spirit, Who previously indwelled their spirits, withdrew, creating an unimaginable void, or emptiness within man's spirit (W.S. 1:1-8).

Following this horrendous episode, man was excluded from God's presence; and God -- Who cannot abide darkness (sin) -- was essentially excluded from man's inner-being (spirit).

Created as God's children, enjoying freedom of choice; Adam and Eve, following their rebellion, found themselves deprived of their freedom of choice. Before their rebellion, they were God's beloved children. Now, they were the slaves of Satan. After all, Satan has no children. His express purpose is to *"steal, kill and destroy"* (Jn 10:10). His objective is to destroy God's children, hoping thereby to regain his once coveted position – that of being the highest created being in the universe.

Tragedy of Tragedies:
Prior to their rebellion and fall, Adam and Eve were Children of God and were to reproduce 'after their kind' – after the image and likeness of God, their Creator. As a result of Adam and Eve's rebellion, everything on earth changed. They immediately began accusing and blaming each other, the serpent, Satan and even God (Gen 3). Their freedom of choice was materially impaired since their access to the Tree of Life was forbidden – even prevented by a cherub, positioned there to guard access to it. Moreover, their character, and that of their offspring became materially altered. There were two reasons for this: one genetic, the other environmental.

Genetic Mutation:
One of God's first universal laws concerning the earth, was that of "sowing and reaping" – that all living things bore seeds that dictated the nature of their reproduction. *"Then God said, "Let the land produce vegetation: seed-bearing plants and trees on the land that bear fruit with seed in it, according to their various kinds." And it was so. The land produced vegetation: plants bearing seed according to their kinds and trees*

bearing fruit with seed in it according to their kinds. And God saw that it was good" (Gen 1:11-12).

Prior to their rebellion, Adam's and Eve's 'seed' bore the image and likeness (the DNA programming) of God's character. Subsequent to their rebellion, their 'seed' passed on to their offspring, traits of rebellion. Indeed, their first-born son, Cain, manifest this DNA mutation, through rebellion that motivated him to murder his own brother, Abel. Cain did not inherit this nature from God, but from his earthly parents, Adam and Eve.

Environmental Modification:
Abel's death and Cain's banishment typified Adam's and Eve's spiritual death and their banishment from their heavenly home – the Garden of Eden. As tragic as this was, the cost of their rebellion was realized by Adam and Eve every day of their life. No longer having access to the Tree of Life, they had to till the ground for food. And, as a result of the curse brought on by their sin, the land no longer produced the same.

"To Adam God said, "Because you listened to your wife and ate from the tree about which I commanded you, 'You must not eat of it,' "Cursed is the ground because of you; through painful toil you will eat of it all the days of your life. It will produce thorns and thistles for you, and you will eat the plants of the field. By the sweat of your brow you will eat your food until you return to the ground, from whence you were taken" (Gen 3:17-19). Another result of their rebellion was that even the production of the ground was altered: *"Your strength will be spent in vain, because your soil will not yield its crops, nor will the trees of the land yield their fruit"* (Lev 26:20).

Even the climactic conditions were altered as a result of Adam's and Eve's rebellion. Prior to that time, *"the Lord God had not sent rain on the earth ... but mist came up from the earth and watered the whole surface of the ground. ... and, the Lord God ... planted a garden in the east, in Eden; and there he put the man he had formed. And the Lord God made all kinds of trees grow out of the ground – trees that were pleasing to the eye and good for food"* Gen 2:5-9). Subsequent to man's rebellion, and as a direct result thereof, God flooded the earth, broke up the surface of the earth, and sent rain, hail, snow, earthquakes, etc. (Gen 7; 10:25; 1 Ch 1:19; Am 1:1; Zech 14:5).

The High Cost of Rebellion:
Why, many ask, was God's punishment for man's rebellion so great? Wasn't it a bit extreme for all of mankind to suffer as the result of Adam's and Eve's rebellion? The cost is high – very high – but, keep in mind the principle of sowing and reaping. Whatever one sows, that also will he reap. God's Word says: **"Do not be deceived: God cannot be mocked. A man reaps what he sows.** *The one who sows to please his sinful nature, from that nature will reap destruction; the one who sows to please the Spirit, from the Spirit will reap eternal life"* (Gal 6:7-9).

Scripture says. *"For rebellion is like the sin of divination (witchcraft), and arrogance [pride] like the evil of idolatry. Because you have rejected the word of the Lord, he has rejected you"* (1 Sam 15:23). As Creator of the Cosmos, God is Sovereign. The prophet Ezekiel warned that *"You will suffer the penalty for your lewdness and bear the consequences of your sins of idolatry. Then you will know that I am the Sovereign Lord"* (Ezek 23:49). And in Exodus we read: *"For thou shalt worship no other god: for the Lord, whose name is Jealous, is a jealous God"* (Ex 34:14).

Satanic Worship:
Worship includes adoration, praise, devotion, reverence and obedience. One might at first think that Satan would be the last person we would worship. After all, he has made us his slaves, and his intent is to rob from us, kill and destroy us. But sadly, we *are* inclined to worship him. One of the aspects of adoration is to show respect, and if we are honest, we have all, often been guilty of respecting the alleged power and authority of Satan.

When we think of praising someone, we rarely think of Satan, yet how often we testify of his powers and abilities: one of the aspects of praise. We would hardly imagine being devoted to Satan, yet one of the aspects of devotion is fidelity, or loyalty; and when in rebellion against God, we are certainly being loyal to Satan, the archetypal rebel. None would consider reverencing Satan, yet one of the aspects of reverence is to crouch, bow or kneel before one whose authority they respect or fear. Finally, when we consider the fact that all rebellion originated from Satan, then we must acknowledge that when resisting God's lordship over our life, we are being obedient to Satan.

We are designed for 'hero-worship'. The one, or ones, we focus on, become our 'heroes'. King David understood this principle, and wrote: *"Incline my heart* to Your testimonies and not to covetousness (robbery, sensuality, unworthy riches. Turn away my eyes from beholding vanity (idols and idolatry); and restore me to vigorous life and health in Your ways. Establish Your word and confirm Your promise to Your servant, which is for those who reverently fear and devotedly worship You" (Ps 119:36-38).

"From men by Your hand, O Lord, from men of this world [these poor moths of the night] whose portion in life is idle and vain. Their bellies are filled with Your hidden treasure [what You have stored up]; their children are satiated, and they leave the rest [of their] wealth to their babes. **As for me, I will continue beholding Your face in righteousness** (rightness, justice, and right standing with You); I shall be fully satisfied, **when I awake [to find myself] beholding Your form [and having sweet communion with You]**" (Ps 17:14-15).

Deception:
One of the Scriptures quoted earlier says, "rebellion is like the sin of divination or witchcraft" (1 Sam 15:23). One of the principal aspects of divination, or witchcraft is sorcery, which includes: magic, witchery, spellbinding, enchantment, voodooism, omens and charms – all forms of trickery that entice us to both rebel against God and then unknowingly worship Satan.

Adam and Eve's descendants rebelled again and were even seduced into intermarriage with the fallen angels [the watchers] (Gen 6:1-4), giving birth to a breed of giants, called the Nephilim. The Watchers corrupted the seed of mankind even more, and their descendants, the Nephilim, became cannibalistic, devouring Adam's progeny. The effects of this rebellion, and God's merciful intervention once again materially altered man's nature and his environment. Moses, apparently quoting from the Book of Enoch, wrote:

"In time, when men began to multiply on earth, and daughters were born to them, the sons of God saw that the daughters of men were attractive; and they took wives for themselves, whomever they chose. Lord Adonai said, "My Spirit will not live in human beings forever, for they too are flesh; therefore their life span is to be 120 years." The Nephilim were on the earth in those days, and also afterwards, when the Watchers came in to the daughters of men, and they bore children to them; these were giants, the ancient heroes and men of renown" (Gen 6:1-4).

"Lord Adonai observed that the people on earth were very wicked, that all the imaginings of their hearts were always of evil only. Adonai regretted that he had made humankind on the earth; it grieved his heart. Lord Adonai said, "I will wipe out humankind, whom I have created, from the whole earth – not only human beings, but animals, creeping things and birds in the air; for I regret that I ever made them." But Noah found grace in the sight of Adonai" (Gen 6:5-8). God's covenant relationship with Adam was necessarily -- due to their rebellion -- coming to an end. To insure the preservation of the earth, indeed of man himself, God had to cleanse the earth.

"The earth was corrupt before God, the earth was filled with violence. God saw the earth, and, yes, it was corrupt; for all living beings had corrupted their ways on the earth. God said to Noah, "The end of all living beings has come before me, for because of them the earth is filled with violence. I will destroy them along with the earth. Make yourself an ark of gofer-wood; you are to make the ark with rooms

and cover it with pitch both outside and inside. Here is how you are to build it: the length of the ark is to be 450 feet, its width seventy-five feet and its height forty-five feet. You are to make an opening for daylight in the ark eighteen inches below its roof. Put a door in its side; and build it with lower, second and third decks. "Then I myself will bring the flood of water over the earth to destroy from under heaven every living thing that breathes; everything on earth will be destroyed. But I will establish my covenant with you; you will come into the ark, you, your sons, your wife and your sons' wives with you" (Gen 6:11-18).

The Nephilim (giants) were destroyed during Noah's Flood. We read about this from the prophet Isaiah, who wrote: "O Lord, our God, other lords besides you have ruled over us, but your name alone do we honor. **They are now dead, they live no more; those departed spirits do not rise**. You punished them and brought them to ruin; you wiped out all memory of them" (Is 26:13-14). The prophet Isaiah is the first one to mention the existence evil spirits, or demons in Scripture. He continues a few chapters later, saying:

"Therefore now, hear this, you who love pleasures and are given over to them, you who dwell safely and sit securely, who say in your mind, I am [the mistress] and there is no one else besides me. I shall not sit as a widow, nor shall I know the loss of children. But these two things shall come to you in a moment, in one day: loss of children and widowhood. They shall come upon you in full measure, in spite of the multitude of [your claims to] **power given you by the assistance of evil spirits**, in spite of the great abundance of your enchantments. For you [Babylon] have trusted in your wickedness; you have said, No one sees me. Your wisdom and your knowledge led you astray, and you said in your heart and mind, I am, and there is no one besides me" (Is 47:9-10).

Isaiah's reference to Babylon makes reference to the fact that the descendants of Ham – Noah's youngest son – who once more turned away from God. Noah had prophesied that Ham's progeny would serve the progeny of his brothers, Shem and Japheth. According to Enoch, they found evidence of the earlier invasion of the Watchers, and in their quest for power to avoid the manifestation of Noah's prophecy, they invoked the return of the Watchers. History tells us that the Watchers once more interbred with mankind, again producing giants, called the Anikim, or Annakites. Settling in the Plain of Shinar, Ham's descendants – including the Anikim – began building cities and towers for worshiping the cosmic bodies and demons. One of these was the infamous Tower of Babel.

There in the City of Babel – the chief city of the Babylonian Kingdom – Nimrod, the mighty hunter of men (a cannibal) and his Queen, Semiramis, founded the "Mystery Religions", the origin of all false religious systems on earth. It was here that the belief in reincarnation and transmutation originated. Babylon was the origin of the use of mind-altering substances. Here also was conceived the heresy of 'the Christ-consciousness' or 'inner-Christ', that is associated with the idea that one can, in and of themselves, attain divinity. It was this group who began to see themselves as of a higher form of creation than others, eventually leading once again to practice slavery, demon worship and cannibalism.

This divination, that began in the City of Babel, in the Plain of Shinar, shortly after Noah's Flood, has embraced the whole earth and will continue so until the end of this era. In revelation we read: *"One of the seven angels who had the seven bowls came and said to me, "Come, I will show you the punishment of the great prostitute, who sits on many waters. With her the kings of the earth committed adultery and the inhabitants of the earth were intoxicated with the wine of her adulteries."*

"Then the angel carried me away in the Spirit into a desert. There I saw a woman sitting on a scarlet beast that was covered with blasphemous names and had seven heads and ten horns. The woman was dressed in purple and scarlet, and was glittering with gold, precious stones and pearls. She held a golden cup in her hand, filled with abominable things and the filth of her adulteries. This title was written on her forehead: "Mystery, Babylon the Great: The Mother of Prostitutes and of the Abominations of the Earth" (Rev 17:1-5).

The Melchizdek Priesthood:
Abram was born about three hundred years after Noah's Flood, during the time that the Tower of Babel was being built. After God called him out of Ur of the Chaldees, He cut a covenant with Abram, after which Abram received mentoring by Melchizedek, of whom it was said: *"Melchizedek was king of Salem and priest of God Most High. He met Abraham returning from the defeat of the kings and blessed him, and Abraham gave him a tenth of everything. First, his name means "king of*

righteousness"; then also, "king of Salem" means "king of peace." Without father or mother, without genealogy, without beginning of days or end of life, like the Son of God he remains a priest forever" (Heb 7:1-3).

The Melchizdek Priesthood was based on the principles of Grace and Faith. Scripture says: "Abraham's faith was credited to him as righteousness. ... So then, he is the father of all who believe but have not been circumcised, in order that righteousness might be credited to them. And he is also the father of the circumcised who not only are circumcised but who also walk in the footsteps of the faith that our father Abraham had before he was circumcised" (Rom 4:9-12). "Therefore, the promise comes by faith, so that it may be by grace and may be guaranteed to all Abraham's offspring – not only to those who are of the law but also to those who are of the faith of Abraham" (Rom 4:16).

Bondage:
The Melchizedek Priesthood based on the Abrahamic Covenant, pf Faith and Grace, continued but a scant 215 years. It ended when the descendants of Jacob, after going down into Egypt during a famine, refused to leave after the famine, failing to trust in God's promises to care for them in Palestine.

At first, the children of Jacob (Israel) had been treated by the Egyptians – descendants of the Nephilim – as honored guests and provided the best home sites and pasturage, in the Land of Goshen. But, they overstayed God's purpose and became Egypt's slaves, building bricks for the Pharaoh.

Deliverance:
After another 215 years, God sent a deliverer named Moses. God's apparent intent was to take them back to the land He had promised them, and restore the Melchizdek Priesthood. During their exodus from Egypt, God appeared in their midst, manifesting his presence in signs and wonders – in a cloud by day, providing protection from the intense heat, and in a pillar of fire by night, providing an unusual light that protected them from their enemies.

However, due to the hardness of their hearts and their lack of faith, the Israelites spent forty years in the Sinai desert. And, when God asked them to meet Him on Mount Sinai, only Moses dared to step upon the mountain. And, while Moses was meeting with God and being given the seal of the covenant, Aaron succumbed to the entreaties of the people and built an idol to Baal.

Levitical Priesthood & Sacrifices
The result of their rebellion was that rather than the Melchizedek Priesthood being restored, God instituted the Levitical Priesthood and a system of sacrificial offerings that would serve as a shadow of things to come – the restoration of the Melchizedek Priesthood in and through Yeshua Messiah [Jesus Christ], nearly 2,000 years later! Approaching the promised land, the Children of Israel [descendants of Abram, a direct descendant of Shem, the eldest son of Noah] were again deceived. Listening to the ten spies, who returned from promised land with reports of giants, rather than listening to God, they spent forty years in the desert.

Once they finally crossed the Jordan River into the Land of Canaan – forty years later -- they were confronted by giants [the Annakites]: descendants of Anak, one of the Nephilim! **God had originally promised to remove the giants from the land by sending hornets to drive them out**.

One would think that after all the miraculous signs and wonders God had performed on their behalf in Egypt, they would have had faith in His promise, but they doubted. It was their lack of faith and their unwillingness to listen to, and trust, God; and carry out His direction, that cost them forty long years of wandering in the wilderness of Zin. They would spend forty years learning warfare to fight the giants whom God had originally promised to drive out ahead of them with hornets!

God's presence went with them – in the pillar of cloud by day and the pillar of fire by night. Once across the Reed Sea, they built the altar of the covenant and the tabernacle. God was with them, but not in them. They had a form of godliness, but denied God's power.

Out of the two to three million Hebrew people that began the pilgrimage from Egypt, only two individuals who left Egypt forty years earlier – Joshua and Caleb – would ever enter the promised land. They listened to, and obeyed God.

In the chapter four we will look at what we must do to enter the land that has been promised us; and, at the deception lurking about that we must be aware of.

~ Questions, Concerns & Key Points ~

1. Yielding to Satan, affects not only the individual concerned, but impacts that person's descendants for generations.

2. Faith and obedience also impact one's descendants for generations. After the fall, God limited the effect of evil to three to four generations, but said that one's righteousness would impact 1,000 generations!

3. Are you guarding those you minister to from the modern-day deception of the 'Christ-consciousness' or 'the Christ within' which stem from the mystery religions that originated in Babylon?

4. Mankind has had, every since the fall, a form of godliness yet he denies God's power – a weakness that we are warned of. We must listen, have faith, and obey.

Chapter 4 ~ Putting On Christ

Introduction:
Our last chapter ended with the Hebrews finally crossing the Jordan River into the promised land, after millions of them died in the wilderness due to their lack of faith in God's Word and His promises.

Using this catastrophe as an example for us, the author of the Book of Hebrews wrote: *"Who were they who heard and rebelled? Were they not all those Moses led out of Egypt? And with whom was he angry for forty years? Was it not with those who sinned, whose bodies fell in the desert? And to whom did God swear that they would never enter his rest if not to those who disobeyed? So we see that they were not able to enter, because of their unbelief. Therefore, since the promise of entering his rest still stands, let us be careful that none of you be found to have fallen short of it. For we also have had the gospel preached to us, just as they did; but the message they heard was of no value to them, because those who heard did not combine it with faith"* (Heb 3:16-4:2).

Ongoing Deception & Divination:
The effectiveness of deception – divination, sorcery or voodoo – stems in large part on the fact that the beings who are exerting the influence against us comprise the dark – normally invisible – forces that the apostle Paul refers to in Ephesians 6, where he warns us to: *"Put on the full armor of God so that you can take your stand against the devil's schemes. For our struggle is not against flesh and blood, but against the rulers, against the authorities, against the powers of this dark world and against the spiritual forces of evil in the heavenly realms"* (Eph 6:11-13).

Paul mentions more about this dark world, in his letter to the Philippians, saying: *"Do all things without grumbling and faultfinding and complaining [against*

God] and questioning and doubting [among yourselves], That you may show yourselves to be blameless and guileless, innocent and uncontaminated, children of God without blemish (faultless, unrebukable) in the midst of a crooked and wicked generation [spiritually perverted and perverse], among whom you are seen as bright lights (stars or beacons shining out clearly) in the [dark] world; Holding out [to it] and offering [to all men] the Word of Life, so that in the day of Christ I may have something of which exultantly to rejoice and glory in that I did not run my race in vain or spend my labor to no purpose. Even if [my lifeblood] must be poured out as a libation on the sacrificial offering of your faith [to God], still I am glad [to do it] and congratulate you all on [your share in] it" (Phil 2:14-16).

Substitutionary Sacrifice:
Paul, raised a Jew and trained in the Law, clearly understood the price of a substitutionary sacrifice. In his letter to the Philippians, he makes reference to the criteria set forth in Leviticus: *"For the life of a creature is in the blood, and I have given it to you to make atonement for yourselves on the altar; it is the blood that makes atonement for one's life"* (Lev 17:11-12).

Meditating on Paul's words, one may – in a small measure – begin to grasp the love of the Godhead [Father God, Holy Spirit and Yeshua (Christ)] for mankind, who had been duped by the arch-deceiver, Satan. *"For God so loved the world that he gave his only and unique Son, so that everyone who trusts in him may have eternal life, instead of being utterly destroyed. For God did not send the Son into the world to judge the world, but rather so that through him, the world might be saved. Those who trust in him are not judged; those who do not trust have been judged already, in that they have not trusted in the one who is God's only and unique Son"* (Jn 3:16-18).

The author of the Book of Hebrews, speaking of the plan of redemption, wrote: *"When Christ came as high priest of the good things that are already here, he went through the greater and more perfect tabernacle that is not man-made, that is to say, not a part of this [earthly] creation. He did not enter by means of the blood of goats and calves; but he entered the Most Holy Place once for all by his own blood, having obtained eternal redemption.*

"The blood of goats and bulls and the ashes of a heifer sprinkled on those who are ceremonially unclean sanctify them so that they are outwardly clean. How much more, then, will the blood of Christ, who through the eternal Spirit offered himself unblemished to God, cleanse our consciences from acts that lead to death, so that we may serve the living God!

"For this reason Christ is the mediator of a new covenant, that those who are called may receive the promised eternal inheritance — now that he has died as a ransom to set them free from the sins committed under the first covenant. In the case of a will, it is necessary to prove the death of the one who made it, because a will is in force only when somebody has died; it never takes effect while the one who made it is still

living. This is why even the first covenant was not put into effect without blood" (Heb 9:11-19).

Here, the author refers to the Levitical Priesthood and sacrificial system that prevailed in Israel for more than 2,000 years -- a system that was a foreshadowing of things to come, the reality of which was in the physical, substitutionary sacrifice of Jesus Christ. (Col 2:17). The Levitical Priests *"serve(d) at a sanctuary that is a copy and shadow of what is in heaven. This is why Moses was warned when he was about to build the tabernacle: "See to it that you make everything according to the pattern shown you on the mountain." But the ministry Jesus has received is as superior to theirs as the covenant of which he is mediator is superior to the old one, and it is founded on better promises"* (Heb 8:5-6).

Concerning the Old Testament tabernacle and Levitical Priesthood, it was prophesied that: *"The time is coming, declares the Lord, when I will make a new covenant with the house of Israel and with the house of Judah. It will not be like the covenant I made with their forefathers when I took them by the hand to lead them out of Egypt, because they did not remain faithful to my covenant, and I turned away from them, declares the Lord. This is the covenant I will make with the house of Israel after that time, declares the Lord. I will put my laws in their minds and write them on their hearts. I will be their God, and they will be my people. No longer will a man teach his neighbor, or a man his brother, saying, 'Know the Lord,' because they will all know me, from the least of them to the greatest"* (Heb 8:8-11).

Yeshua Messiah ~ The Substitutionary Sacrifice:
The substitutionary sacrifice of Christ was the only avenue for man's redemption since it was said of mankind: *"There is no one righteous, not even one! No one understands, no one seeks God, all have turned away and at the same time become useless; there is no one who shows kindness, not a single one!*

"Their throats are open graves, they use their tongues to deceive. Vipers' venom is under their lips. Their mouths are full of curses and bitterness. "Their feet rush to shed blood, in their ways are ruin and misery, and the way of peace they do not know. "There is no fear of God before their eyes" (Rom 3:10-18).

Following this statement, the author provides the legal justification for the redemption of mankind through Christ's substitutionary sacrifice, saying: "Moreover, we know that whatever the Law says, it says to those living within the framework of the Law, in order that every mouth may be stopped and the whole world be shown to deserve God's adverse judgment. For in his sight no one alive will be considered righteous on the ground of legalistic observance of Legal commands, because what the Law really does is show people how sinful they really are.

"But now, quite apart from the Law, God's way of making people righteous in his sight has been made clear — although the Law and the Prophets give their witness to it as well — and it is a righteousness that comes from God, through the faithfulness of Yeshua the Messiah, to all who continue trusting. For it makes no difference whether one is a Jew or a Gentile, since all have sinned and come short of earning God's praise. By God's grace, without earning it, all are granted the status of being considered righteous before him, through the act redeeming us from our enslavement to sin that was accomplished by the Messiah Yeshua.

"God put Yeshua forward as the substitutionary sacrifice for sin through his faithfulness in respect to his bloody sacrificial death. This vindicated God's righteousness; because, in his forbearance, he had passed over [with neither punishment nor remission] the sins people had committed in the past; and it vindicates his righteousness in the present age by showing that he is righteous himself and is also the one who makes people righteous on the ground of Yeshua's faithfulness" (Rom 3:19-26).

God's Plan for Satan's Defeat:
"For to **us a child is born, to us a son is given**, and the government will be on his shoulders. And he will be called Wonderful Counselor, Mighty God, Everlasting Father, Prince of Peace. Of the increase of his government and peace there will be no end. He will reign on David's throne and over his kingdom, establishing and upholding it with justice and righteousness from that time on and forever. The zeal of the LORD Almighty will accomplish this" (Is 9:6-7).

The prophet Isaiah foretold what has been named "**The Divine Exchange**" -- the substitutionary sacrifice of Jesus Christ: "Who has believed our message and to whom has the arm of the LORD been revealed? He grew up before him like a tender shoot, and like a root out of dry ground. He had no beauty or majesty to attract us to him, nothing in his appearance that we should desire him. He was despised and rejected by men, a man of sorrows, and familiar with suffering. Like one from *whom men hide their faces he was despised, and we esteemed him not"* (Is 53:1-4).

The Divine Exchange:

- *"Surely **he took up our infirmities and carried our sorrows**, yet we considered him stricken by God, smitten by him, and afflicted.*

- ***But he was pierced for our transgressions**,*

- ***He was crushed for our iniquities**;*

- *The punishment that brought us peace was upon him,*

- ***By his wounds we are healed**. We all, like sheep, have gone astray, each of us has turned to his own way; and*

- ***The** Lord **has laid on him the iniquity of us all**"* (vs. 5-6).

*"**He was oppressed and affl**icted, yet he did not open his mouth; **he was led like a lamb to the slaughter**, and as a sheep before her shearers is silent, so he did not open his mouth. **By oppression and judgment he was taken away**. And who can speak of his descendants? For **he was cut off from the land of the living**; for the transgression of my people **he was stricken**. **He was assigned a grave with the wicked, and with the rich in his death**, though he had done no violence, nor was any deceit in his mouth"* (vs. 7-9).

"Yet, it was the Lord's will to crush him and cause him to suffer, and though the Lord makes his life a guilt offering, he will see his offspring and prolong his days, and the will of the Lord will prosper in his hand. After

the suffering of his soul, he will see the light [of life] and be satisfied; by his knowledge my righteous servant will justify many, and he will bear their iniquities. Therefore I will give him a portion among the great, and he will divide the spoils with the strong, because he poured out his life unto death, and was numbered with the transgressors. For he bore the sin of many, and made intercession for the transgressors" (vs 10-12).

The Prophecy Fulfilled:
The apostle Paul describes the fulfillment of this prophecy, saying: *"For God has done what the Law could not do, [its power] being weakened by the flesh [the entire nature of man without the Holy Spirit]. Sending His own Son in the guise of sinful flesh and as an offering for sin, [God] condemned sin in the flesh [subdued, overcame, deprived it of its power over all who accept that sacrifice], so that the righteous and just requirement of the Law might be fully met in us who live and move not in the ways of the flesh but in the ways of the Spirit [our lives governed not by the standards and according to the dictates of the flesh, but controlled by the Holy Spirit]"* (Rom 8:3-4).

Son of God ~ Son of Man:
Jesus Christ -- Yeshua Messiah -- came to earth, incarnate in human flesh [sinful flesh] a Child of God, yet a child of man. As God's Own Divine son, concealed in human flesh, he restored God's spiritual DNA within the human race. But, to accomplish this, he must complete the blood atonement, fulfilling every dictate of the Law -- life for life and blood for blood.

The apostle Paul, a student of Jewish Law understood this and wrote: *"We ... speak a message of wisdom among the mature, but not the wisdom of this age or of the rulers of this age, who are coming to nothing. No, we speak of God's secret wisdom, a wisdom that has been hidden and that God destined for our glory before time began. None of the rulers of this age understood it, for if they had, they would not have crucified the Lord of glory. However, as it is written: "No eye has seen, no ear has heard, no mind has conceived what God has prepared for those who love him" – but God has revealed it to us by his Spirit"* (1 Cor 2:6-10).

In fulfilling every dictate of the Law, Jesus not only left heaven above and took on the form of a man, he became a servant to sinful man and died as a criminal on the cross – the innocent for the guilty. While hanging on the cross: *"From the sixth hour until the ninth hour darkness came over all the land. About the ninth hour Jesus cried out in a loud voice, "Eloi, Eloi, lama sabachthani?" – which means, "My God, my God, why have you forsaken me?"* (Matt 27:45-46).

During this time of absolute darkness, spiritually separated from His Father, Jesus – after suffering in agony for hours – *"cried out once again in a loud voice, and gave up his spirit. At that moment the curtain of the temple was torn in two from top to bottom. The earth shook and the rocks split. The tombs broke open and the bodies of many holy people who had died were raised to life"* (Mt 27:50-52). Jesus had one last dictate of the law that must be fulfilled. In death, with heaven looking on, he descended into hell and overcame the powers of darkness!

Victorious Over Hell:
"The Messiah himself died for sins, once and for all, a righteous person on behalf of unrighteous people, so that he might bring you to God. He was put to death in the flesh but brought to life by the Spirit; and in this form he went and made a proclamation to the imprisoned spirits, to those who were disobedient long ago, in the days of Noah, when God waited patiently during the building of the ark, in which a few people – to be specific, eight – were delivered by means of water" (1 Pe 3:18-21).

This was not imposed on him by Father God; and no man could – without his consenting – take his life. Jesus Christ chose to descend into hell and go through the Valley of the Shadow of Death, voluntarily -- for you and for me. Prior to the Passion Week, Jesus declared:

"I am the good shepherd; I know my sheep and my sheep know me — just as the Father knows me and I know the Father — and I lay down my life for the sheep. I have other sheep that are not of this sheep pen. I must bring them also. They too will listen to my voice, and there shall be one flock and one shepherd. The reason my Father loves me is that I lay down my life — only to take it up again. No one takes it from me, but I lay it down of my own accord. I have authority to lay it down and authority to take it up again. This command I received from my Father" (Jn 10:14-18).

Christ's Work of Redemption was now complete: having overcome the powers of darkness in hell, He declared: "I am the Living One; I was dead, and behold I am alive for ever and ever! And I now hold the keys of death and Hades" (Rev 1:15). After his resurrection, his "disciples went to Galilee, to the mountain to which Jesus had directed and made appointment with them. And when they saw Him, they fell down and worshiped Him; but some doubted. Jesus approached and, breaking the silence, said to them, All authority (all power of rule) in heaven and on earth has been given to Me" (Matt 28:17-18).

"God demonstrated His great love for us in this: that while we were still sinners, Christ died for us" (Rom 5:8). Yet, one thing remained to insure our salvation. "What does Scripture say? "The word is near you; it is in your mouth and in your heart," that is, the word of faith we are proclaiming: That if you confess with your mouth, "Jesus is Lord," and believe in your heart that God raised him from the dead, you will be saved. For it is with your heart that you believe and are justified, and *it is with your mouth that you confess and are saved"* (Rom 10:8-11).

Salvation is Nearer than When We First believed:
"The hour has come for you to wake up from your slumber, because our salvation is nearer now than when we first believed" (Rom 13:11-12). God has completed His part. Salvation is near: it is in our mouth and heart, but to have its desired effect in our life, it is essential that we confess with our mouth that Jesus is Lord – the Lord of our life – a nd believe in our heart that Father God raised Jesus from the dead. This is, as stated, **"the word of faith"** that we, and we alone, must proclaim.

If you – like many Christians – have accepted Christ as your Savior, but have never confessed that He is the Lord of your life, the power of redemption full and free, will never be yours until you do. To comprehend this, it is important to understand that the word 'confess' stems from the Greek word *'homologeo'* has do with covenant partners assenting, or coming into agreement, concerning declared promises.

Jesus said *"let every matter be established by the testimony of two or three witnesses"* (Mt 18:16). How does this apply? Consider the following:

- Father God declared that if we accept His Son, we would be saved.

- Jesus incarnated into human flesh, lived as a human, died as a human, went to hell, and was resurrected again – meeting all of the dictates of the Law. In doing so, he became the first witness.

- Holy Spirit indwelled all who accepted Jesus as their Lord and Savior, becoming the second witness.

- Our confession of faith – that Jesus is the Lord of our life, and that Father God raised him from the dead, provides the third witness.

Thus, our confession of faith – our agreement with Father God, Jesus Christ and Holy Spirit, insures our salvation and life eternal! Jesus said, *"According to your faith, it will be done for you"* (Mt 9:29); and the author of the Book of Hebrews, cautioned us, saying: *"Without faith it is impossible to please God, because anyone who comes to him must believe that he exists and that he rewards those who earnestly seek him"* (Heb 11:6).

Prayer of Agreement:
If you have never understood your part in making Jesus Christ your Lord and Savior – your confession of faith as a witness to Father God's declaration, or have – like many of us – obviated your confession of faith (your agreement) by making negative confessions, I encourage you to join me in the following prayer:

Father God, Holy Spirit, Yeshua Messiah, I come now as the third witness to the fulfilled plan of salvation that was established before the foundations of the earth, and confess (agree) with my mouth that Jesus Christ is my Messiah and Lord, who incarnated human flesh; was punished for me that I might be forgiven; wounded for me that I might be healed; made sin for me that I might have His righteousness imparted to me; died my death that I might share in His eternal life; was cursed that I might receive God's blessings; endured poverty that I might share in His prosperity; endured my shame that I might share in His glory; endured rejection and abandonment that I might share in His acceptance and approval. I invite you Holy Spirit, to indwell my spirit, and complete the Divine Exchange, erasing the laws of sin and death and writing on my heart God's immutable laws; and by my being born from above, exchanging DNA for DNA. I confess this now, as the third witness to Your plan of redemption for my soul.

~ Questions, Concerns & Key Points ~

1. Are you teaching spiritual warfare in your church – to protect your congregation from demonic attacks?

2. Do you and your congregation understand the significance of 'substitutionary sacrifice' – that Jesus is our substitute?

3. Do you understand and teach Christ's plan for Satan's defeat?

4. Have you embraced and taught the 'divine exchange'?

5. Are you teaching that Jesus Christ was fully divine [Son of God], and fully human [son of man]?

6. Jesus, after overcoming Satan and the powers of darkness, on the cross, descended into the netherworld to proclaim his victory.

7. Are you teaching your converts that to have victory in their lives, they not only need to recognize Jesus as their Messiah (Savior), but also, the Lord (Ruler) over their life?

Chapter 5 ~ The Power of Faith

Introduction:
The author of the Book of Hebrews, penned these striking words: *"There is so, so little time! The One coming will indeed come, he will not delay. But the person who is righteous will live his life by faithfully trusting, and if he shrinks back, I will not be pleased with him." However, we are not the kind who shrink back and are destroyed; on the contrary, we keep faithfully trusting and thus preserve our lives!*

"Trusting faith is being confident of what we hope for, being convinced about things we do not see. It was for this that Scripture attested the merit of the people of old. By trusting, we understand that the universe was created through a spoken word of God, so that what is seen did not come into being out of existing phenomena" (Heb 10:37-11:3 CJB).

Blind Faith:
Many will say, "I don't have the faith?"; or "Why is my faith is insufficient?" Saying this suggests that we don't really understand faith. We all know the classic Scriptural definition of faith: *"Faith is being confident of what we hope for, and convinced about things we do not see"* (Heb 11:1). This is what many refer to as "blind faith" and, suggest that this is the Christian's duty – to exercise blind faith. NO!

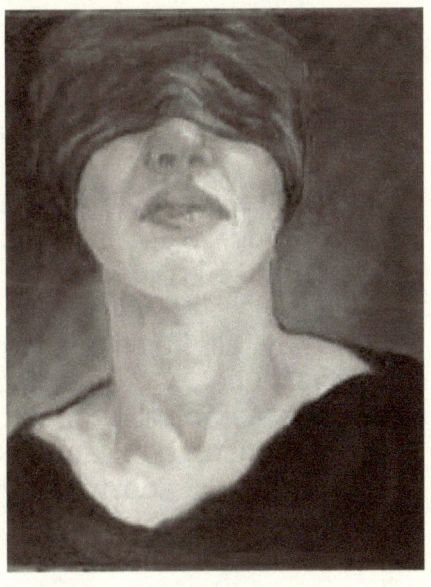

This is inconsistent with God's Word, which says: *"Come now, let us reason together, says the Lord"* (Is 1:18).

This strongly suggests that our God is a God of reason; One Who would have us make informed decisions. Otherwise, we make ourselves vulnerable to the divination of demons who practice magic and witchcraft, and demand 'blind faith'!

Informed Faith:
All of us have faith whether we realize it or not. We have faith that when we flip a light switch, the light will go on; we have faith that when we put s stamp on a letter and drop it in a postal pickup box, it will get to the addressee; and we have faith that the bank we deposit our checks in will honor the checks we write.

All of these illustrations involve faith – our being confident that the thing we cannot see, but put our hope, or expectation, in will produce the expected result. Each of these involves some very important principles concerning faith.

- First, there is a promise: i.e., the light will go on; the mail will reach its destination; and our check will be honored.

- They all involve an object – the promised thing.

- They all involve a higher authority – someone we put our trust in, relying on them to fulfill their promise.

- They all involve a conditioned response on our part: i.e., we must flip the light switch; we must put a stamp on the letter, address it and drop it in the postal box; and, we must deposit our funds in the bank, and then draft the checks to withdraw those funds.

Without our fulfilling the specified condition, nothing happens: the light doesn't go on; our letter never reaches its destination; and, we will live in poverty –

our needs going unmet – all because we fail to write a check!

God is certainly more reliable than your local electrical power supplier. All power supplies experience outages and damaged distribution lines. God is far more reliable than the post office. Some letters have been found in mail sacks fifty years after they were mailed, and some letters never arrive. God is far more reliable than your local banker. There were 140 bank failures in 2009, and 118 in the first six months of 2010. God's bank has never failed – His resources have never been insufficient to fulfill His promises. And, speaking of promises, His Word contains more than 8,000! And He says, *"my people are destroyed from lack of knowledge"* (Hos 4:6). Don't let your lack of knowledge destroy you – body, soul and/or spirit.

Now Faith:
"Now, faith comes by hearing [what is told], and what is heard comes by the preaching [of the message that came from the lips] of Christ (the Messiah Himself). But I ask, Have they not heard? Indeed they have; [for the Scripture says] Their voice [that of nature bearing God's message] has gone out to all the earth, and their words to the far bounds of the world" (Rom 10:17-18).

Notice that faith does not come automatically but by hearing (or reading) the Word of God. And, belief alone is not sufficient. We must act on it – committing our life to His loving care, demonstrating that we trust in God's promise: *"Casting all your cares upon him; for he careth for you"* (1 Pe 5:7).

We do not have the power, ability or resources to handle all of our problems or cares, and God does not expect us to. He invites us to cast, more literally to throw, all of our cares, or problems of life on Him! What an awesome truth! Jesus warned that Satan wants us to become so overloaded with *"the cares of this world, and the deceitfulness of riches, and the lusts of other things entering in, that choke the word, and we become unfruitful"* (Mark 4:19).

When we take our problems back [worrying and fretting about them, or trying once again to solve them ourselves], God cannot act, since we have exercised our freedom of choice – which He honors and respects. When we do this we have taken possession of the problem once again. We need to give our problems to God and leave them there with Him. He alone has the resources to solve them. He is infallible!

Jesus said again and again, *"With man this is impossible, but with God all things are possible"* (Mt 19:26). God can do anything we ask! And, equally exciting is the secret Jesus declared to his disciples: *"Everything is possible for him who believes"* (Mk 9:23). If we have confessed that Jesus Christ is our Lord and Savior, that Father God raised Him from the dead, and that Holy Spirit, Who testifies of Christ and acts on His and the Father's behalf, dwells within us, then we should expect miracles! After all, *"God is not a man, that he should lie, nor a son of man, that he should change his mind. Does he speak and then not act? Does he promise and not fulfill?"* (Num 23:19).

Taking Authority:
Jesus said, *"All authority in heaven and on earth has been given to me"* (Mt 28:18). He appointed those who had been with him *"to preach and have authority to drive out demons"* (Mk 3:15); *and "He gave them authority over evil spirits (demons)"* (Mk 6:7); *"He gave them power and authority to drive out all demons and to cure diseases, and he sent them out to preach the kingdom of God and to heal the sick"* (Luke 9:1-2); He gave them *"Authority to trample on snakes and scorpions and to overcome all the power of the enemy; nothing will harm you"* (Luke 10:19); Authority to build up the Body of Christ [the church] (2 Cor 10:8).

Exercising Our Faith:
Over and over again, Jesus declared that whatsoever those who believe in Him ask of the Father, it will be done [see (Mt 6:8-15; 18:19; 19:7; Mk 11:24; Lk 11:9; Jn 14:3; 15:7; 15:16; 16:23).] He went beyond this, declaring:

"If you have faith and do not doubt, not only can you do what was done to the fig tree, but also you can say to this mountain, 'Go, throw yourself into the sea,' and it will be done. If you believe, you will receive whatever you ask for in prayer" (Mt 21:21-22). However, we must be mindful that *"when one asks, he must believe and not doubt, because he who doubts is like a wave of the sea, blown and tossed by the wind. That man should not think he will receive anything from the Lord; he is a double-minded man, unstable in all he does"* (James 1:6-8).

The Power of Perseverance:
Our example of perseverance is the Abraham, the father of the faithful, of whom it is said: *"He is our father in the sight of God, in whom he believed –* **the God who gives life to the dead and calls things that are not as though they were***. Against all hope, Abraham in hope believed and so became the father of many nations, just as it had been said to him, "So shall your offspring be." Without weakening in his faith, he faced the fact that his body was as good as dead – since he was about a hundred years old – and that Sarah's womb was also dead.*

"Yet he did not waver through unbelief regarding the promise of God, but was strengthened in his faith and gave glory to God, being fully persuaded that God had power to do what he had promised. This is why "it was credited to him as righteousness." **The words "it was credited to him" were written not for him alone, but also for us, to whom God will credit**

*righteousness – **for us who believe in him who raised Jesus our Lord from the dead**"* (Rom 4:17-24).

Transference of Authority:
Jesus declared again and again that all authority in heaven and on earth had been given him, and that he was transferring this authority to those who believe in Him and make Him their Lord and Savior. Not only this, He commissioned us to go into all the world and exercise this authority. Failing to do so, is failing our Savior. We must remember that, *"The thief [Satan and his demonic forces] comes only to steal and kill and destroy; but I [Jesus] have come that they may have life, and have it to the full"* (John 10:10).

Exercising faith is NOT "mind over matter." It is "God's Word over Matter." He declared: *"Those who honor me I will honor, but those who despise me will be disdained"* (1 Sam 2:30). *"Not one word has failed of all the good promises he gave"* (1 Kings 8:56). *"As for God, his way is perfect; the word of the L*ORD* is flawless. He is a shield for all who take refuge in him"* (Ps 18:30).

"For the word of the Lord is right and true; he is faithful in all he does. The Lord loves righteousness and justice; the earth is full of his unfailing love. By the word of the Lord were the heavens made, their starry host by the breath of his mouth. He gathers the waters of the sea into jars; he puts the deep into storehouses. Let all the earth fear the Lord; let all the people of the world revere him. For he spoke, and it came to be; he commanded, and it stood firm. The Lord foils the plans of the nations; he thwarts the purposes of the peoples. But the plans of the Lord stand firm forever, the purposes of his heart through all generations" (Ps 33:4-11).

"Your word, O Lord, is eternal; it stands firm in the heavens. Your faithfulness continues through all generations; you established the earth, and it endures.

Your laws endure to this day, for all things serve you" (Ps 119:89-91).

Pleasing God:
We have spent some time studying the life of Enoch. The author of the Book of Hebrews mentions him, saying: *"By faith Enoch was taken from this life, so that he did not experience death; he could not be found, because God had taken him away. For before he was taken,* **he was commended as one who pleased God**. *And* **without faith it is impossible to please God**, *because anyone who comes to him must believe that he exists and that he rewards those who earnestly seek him"* (Heb 11:5-6).

Jesus, contrasting those of little faith with the faithful, said: *"O you of little faith? So do not worry, saying, 'What shall we eat?' or 'What shall we drink?' or 'What shall we wear?' For the pagans run after all these things, and your heavenly Father knows that you need them.* **But seek first his kingdom and his righteousness, and all these [other] things will be given to you as well**" (Mt 6:30-34).

"Ask and it will be given to you; seek and you will find; knock and the door will be opened to you. For everyone who asks receives; he who seeks finds; and to him who knocks, the door will be opened. "Which of you, if his son asks for bread, will give him a stone? Or if he asks for a fish, will give him a snake? If you, then, though you are evil, know how to give good gifts to your children, how much more will your Father in heaven give good gifts to those who ask him!" (Mt 7:7-12).

Entering the Holy of Holies:
In Jesus, we have access to Father God. We can personally make known our requests to Him. The author of the Book of Hebrews said: *"Brethren, since we have full freedom and confidence to enter into the [Holy of] Holies [by the power and virtue] in the blood of Jesus,*

By this fresh (new) and living way which He initiated and dedicated and opened for us through the separating curtain (veil of the Holy of Holies), that is, through His flesh, And since we have [such] a great and wonderful and noble Priest [Who rules] over the house of God, Let us all come forward and draw near with true (honest and sincere) hearts in unqualified assurance and absolute conviction engendered by faith (by that leaning of the entire human personality on God in absolute trust and confidence in His power, wisdom, and goodness), having our hearts sprinkled and purified from a guilty (evil) conscience and our bodies cleansed with pure water" (Heb 10:19-22).

"Let us then fearlessly and confidently and boldly draw near to the throne of grace (the throne of God's unmerited favor to us sinners), that we may receive mercy [for our failures] and find grace to help in good time for every need" (Heb 4:16). According to the apostle, Peter: *"the eyes of the Lord are on the righteous and his ears are attentive to their prayers"* (1 Peter 3:12).

Rights vs. Privileges:
As God's redeemed children, in covenant relationship with the Father, Son and Holy Spirit, we are co-inheritors of the Kingdom. We have prerogatives that the natural-born children of God do not. The unsaved have privileges: the saved have rights! Explaining this, the apostle John, said:

"He came to that which belonged to Him [to His own – His domain, creation, things, world], and they who were His own did not receive Him and did not welcome Him. But to as many as did receive and welcome Him, He gave the authority (power, privilege, right) to become the children of God, that is, to those who believe in (adhere to, trust in, and rely on) His name – Who owe their birth neither to bloods nor to the will of the flesh [that of physical impulse] nor to the will of man [that of

a natural father], but to God. [They are born of God!]" (John 1:11-14).

God has given us – His children – more than 8,000 promises, demonstrating what He is willing to do for those who are His covenant children. And, *"no matter how many promises God has made, they are "Yes" in Christ. ... He anointed us, set his seal of ownership on us, and put his Spirit in our hearts as a deposit, guaranteeing what is to come"* (2 Cor 1:20-22).

The rights granted us as covenant-children, with the Seal of Ownership [Holy Spirit indwelling our hearts], include access to the Tree of Life and the New Jerusalem. "Blessed are those who wash their robes, that they may have the right to the tree of life and may go through the gates into the city" (Rev 22:14-15).

~ Questions, Concerns & Key Points ~

1. Understand the difference between: a) Blind faith; b) Informed faith; and c) Now faith?

2. Is it a sin to worry?

3. Understand what Jesus gave us authority over!

4. Instead of living by 'mind over matter' Christians should live by 'spirit over matter.'

5. Understand Spiritual Rights vs. Privileges.

6. Are you teaching that, just as the Decalogue [10 Commandments] were the Seal of the Old Covenant [Testament]; receiving the indwelling of Holy Spirit is the Seal of the New Covenant [Testament]?

7. What must we, as Christians, do to ensure that we are prepared to enter our promised land – the New Jerusalem?

Chapter 6 ~ Applied Rights

Introduction:

As children of God – twice born: first of the flesh and second of the spirit – we have certain rights; the problem, however, is that most of us do not know our rights, and therefore, do not exercise them. God has given us more than 8,000 precious promises – promises that govern every aspect of life; even modifying our fallen nature into His divine nature. Most know but a few of these, and many have never even experienced any of these!

Purposeful Promises:

God's promises are designed not only to meet our felt needs, i.e., physical, emotional, financial and relational; they have been designed to conform us to God's character – His image and likeness. We read about this in the second epistle of Peter: *"His divine power has given us everything we need for life and godliness through our knowledge of him who called us by his own glory and goodness. Through these he has given us his very great and precious promises, so that through them you may participate in the divine nature and escape the corruption in the world caused by evil desires"* (2 Pe 1:3-4).

When we think of promises, we are inclined to focus on the gift, or benefit that is promised, but it is not this that changes us, enabling us to participate in God's divine nature. Rather than being the promised gift, per. se., it is our meeting the conditions – the prerequisites – for receiving the desired gift, that changes us. Jesus repeated numerous times, *"My Father will give you whatever you ask in mine name."*

We have explained in detail in our book, "God's Precious Promises, Advocare Publishing, 2010, that the Greek word used in these Scriptures, that has been translated, 'my name' really refers to one's character, or nature – in this instance, that of an obedient child. In this lesson, we want to examine specifically some of God's precious promises, appropriating them by using the "prayer of faith" sometimes called, "the prayer of reception."

We often hear people questioning why God allows diseases, sickness and suffering – often suggesting that a loving God would not do so. This is a reasonable question. Even Jesus' disciples posed it on more than one occasion. On one occasion, *"As he went along, he saw a man blind from birth. His disciples asked him, "Rabbi, who sinned, this man or his parents, that he was born blind? Neither this man nor his parents sinned," said Jesus, "but this happened so that the glory of God might be displayed in his life"* (Jn 9:1-4).

Notice that this was not just a 'healing' as we commonly think of healing; it was a creative miracle. This man had been blind since birth. Jesus healed those with physical illnesses, physical impairments, developmental disorders, mental and emotional disorders, spiritual disorders, and the demon possessed.

Claiming God's Promises for Healing:
The beloved apostle, John, said that he wished above all things that we experience prosperity and good health – even as our souls prosper (3 Jn 2). Peter declared: *"God does not show favoritism but accepts [all] who fear him and do what is right. You know the message God sent ... telling the good news of peace through Jesus Christ, who is Lord of all. You know that ... beginning in Galilee ... how God anointed Jesus of Nazareth by Holy*

Spirit and power, and how **he went around doing good and healing all who were under the power of the devil, because God was with him**" (Acts 10:34-38). *"He took our infirmities [to the cross] and carried our diseases"* (Mt 8:17); *"He forgiveth all [and[healeth all thy diseases"* (Ps 103:3-4).

The Origin of Sickness and Suffering:
People often blame God for their sickness, disease or disorder; but, according to the foregoing words of Peter (Acts 10:34-38), demons – under the direction of Satan – are responsible for all suffering – all illness and disease. Those suffers are, under the power of the devil. But there is hope.

Jesus, *"shared in our humanity so that by his death he might destroy him who holds the power of death – that is, the devil – and free those who all their lives have been held in slavery"* (Heb 2:14-16). And, *"through Christ Jesus the law of the Spirit of life set me free from the law of sin and death"* (Rom 8:2). Finally, *"If the Son [of God] sets you free, you are free indeed"* (Jn 8:36). *"It is for freedom that Christ has set us free. Stand firm, then, and do not let yourselves be burdened again by a yoke of slavery"* (Gal 5:1).

Paul says, Christ *"has rescued us from the dominion of darkness and brought us into the kingdom of the Son he loves, in whom we have redemption, the forgiveness of sins"* (Col 1:13-14).

The powers of darkness, including demons of illness, disease, disorders and addictions, no longer have a legitimate hold over us. We were redeemed from the power of sin and the curse of the law (Gal 3:13). Christ took all of our infirmities (diseases and disorders) to the cross (Is 53:4). Christ's testimony of Father God's restorative power and plan is complete. He became the first witness; Holy Spirit's indwelling presence and testimony of Christ, is the second witness.

The manifestation of God's restorative power is now contingent on our confession of faith – the third and essential witness.

Promissory Notes on Heaven's Bank:
It is imperative that we keep in mind the principle that all the promises in the Bible are promissory notes. That is, like promissory notes, they all have conditions attached to their fulfillment. One of the most important conditions involved when it comes to receiving God's blessings of heath and prosperity is found in Luke 6.

"Love your enemies, do good to them, and lend to them without expecting to get anything back. Then your reward will be great, and you will be sons of the Most High, because he is kind to the ungrateful and wicked. Be merciful, just as your Father is merciful. "*Do not judge, and you will not be judged. Do not condemn, and you will not be condemned. Forgive, and you will be forgiven. Give, and it will be given to you. A good measure, pressed down, shaken together and running over, will be poured into your lap. For with the measure you use, it will be measured to you"* (Luke 6:35-38).

If there are those whom we have judged or hold things against, this fact will block our reception of God's blessings. If such is the case, we need to *"cast all our*

cares on the Lord, and He will sustain you; never letting the righteous fall" (Ps 55:22). The Lord says: "Vengeance and payback belong to me" (Dt 32:35). The apostle Paul, referring to this Scripture, said: "Dearly beloved, avenge not yourselves, but rather give place unto wrath: for it is written, Vengeance is mine; I will repay, saith the Lord" (Rom 12:19).

Prayer for Healing:
If you have allowed unforgiveness, bitterness, resentment, anger, and/or similar negative feelings towards God's other children to block the channel of God's blessings, you may want to pray the following prayer with me:

Father God, in Jesus Christ, my Messiah and Lord, I now enter the Holy of Holies and bow before you at your throne of grace. I confess my sin of _____ (name the sin), toward _____ (name the person or persons). I forgive them, casting all the cares and concerns regarding them onto you. I renounce all bitterness, resentment, jealousy and criticism of them. I ask You to forgive them Father, and I ask your forgiveness Father, for all my wrong deeds, words and thoughts, relying on your promise, that: "If we confess our sins, he is faithful and just and will forgive us our sins and purify us from all unrighteousness" (1 John 1:9-10). According to Your Word, blot them out of Your Book of Remembrance by the precious blood of Jesus. I also ask you to erase them from Satan's record, so that he can no longer accuse me. And Father, through your indwelling Holy Spirit, cleanse my conscience, making my heart as white as snow.

I thank you, Father God, for your forgiveness and seek healing for _____ (name your illness or disorder) in and through Jesus Christ. In the authority of Jesus -- His precious body that was broken, and his blood that was shed for me, I now command you Satan and demons of _____ (name the various diseases and disorders you suffer from), to be bound (made ineffective). Satan and every demonic entity, my entire being -- body, soul and spirit -- belongs to God. I am His property and you have no rights to His property. Therefore, I command you, in the Name and blood of Jesus Christ, to take your hands off me, and I command you, and all the demons you have assigned to me, to be gone and placed under the captivity of Jesus my Lord and Savior, who came to "destroy the works of the devils" (1 Jn 3:8).

Solomon said: "For as man thinks within his heart, so he will be" (Pr 23:7). The word 'thinks' in this text is the Hebrew word that refers to the abstract, or creative, thoughts, i.e., visualization. [Visualization exercise: As you lift your hands toward heaven, pray the following prayer.] ~ Father, I lift my hands to you, releasing to you all those who have treated me unjustly, imploring You to *"Hear my cry for mercy as I call to you for help, as I lift up my hands toward your Most Holy Place"* (Ps 28:2). *"May my prayer be set before you like incense; may the lifting up of my hands be like the evening sacrifice"* [Amen] (Ps 141:2).

[Now, with one hand lifted heavenward, place the other where you need a healing touch, and pray the following prayer.] ~ Father, I ask You to restore every cell that has been damaged or destroyed. I breathe health and wholeness into my body, believing in my heart, and confessing with my mouth, that Jesus took my infirmities, and bore my sickness and pain, to the cross (Is 53:4-6; Mt 8:17). I am redeemed from the curse of the law (Gal 3:13). [Amen]

God has provided for those times that illness or disorders persist. His Word says: *"Is any one of you sick? He should call the elders of the church to pray over him and anoint him with oil in the name of the Lord. And the prayer offered in faith will make the sick person well; the Lord will raise him up. If he has sinned, he will be forgiven. Therefore confess your sins to each other and pray for each other so that you may be healed. The prayer of a righteous man is powerful and effective"* (James 5:14-16).

Calling on the elders of your fellowship to anoint you and pray for you, you will still want to be a witness, by your own confession of faith. You may want to pray a prayer similar to the following: Father God, Holy Spirit and Yeshua Messiah, I submit to the elders of your local body of believers, confessing my weaknesses and faults; and, having faith, I thank you for your healing promised in your Word I thank you Father God, Lord Jesus and Holy Spirit for your healing this hour – Amen.

Silencing Satan:

Satan is an aggressive enemy and must be silenced before the court of heaven, so that he can no longer accuse you. Asking Father God to blot out your sins from His Book of Remembrance, by the blood of Jesus Christ, enables you to be righteous in His sight, rather than your own. When you have prayed this prayer, Satan no longer has any unsettled claims against you, since Jesus has taken your sins, your guilt and your shame. Remember, healing is in the atonement: Jesus took upon himself every form of sickness, disease, disorder and curse, taking them to the cross, where they were vicariously put to death. You need no longer be affected by any of them.

Jesus said: *"Because I live, you also will live. On that day you will realize that I am in my Father, and you are in me, and I am in you. Whoever has my commands and obeys them, he is the one who loves me. He who loves me will be loved by my Father, and I too will love him and show myself to him"* (Jn 14:19-21); *"I will ask the Father, and he will give you another Counselor to be with you forever – the Spirit of truth. ... you know him, for he lives with you and will be in you"* (Jn 14:16-17). Praying to his Father, Jesus said: *"Father, just as you are in me and I am in you. May they also be in us so that the world may believe that you have sent me. I have given them the glory that you gave me, that they may be one as we are one: I in them and you in me"* (Jn 17:21-23).

Spirituality is boundaryless. We are in the Godhead – Father, Son and Holy Spirit; and they – each one of them – is within us! As God's children, we enjoy complete oneness: solidarity and intimacy with God. Feel God restoring your body: feel divine power infusing every cell of your body. Receive your healing. Continue expressing your confession of faith until God's miracle – His healing power – is manifest in your body.

Occasionally God may grant an instantaneous miracle; most of the time, however, healing is a process. Don't be disappointed if your healing isn't immediate. God knows what is best for each person under every circumstance. Our faith needs to be active, or continuing. *"The Word that God speaks is alive and full of power [making it active, operative, energizing, and effective]; it is sharper than any two-edged sword, penetrating to the dividing line of the breath of life (soul) and [the immortal] spirit, and of joints and marrow [of the deepest parts of our nature]"* (Heb 4:12).

Maintaining Active Faith:
God's Word is active, making it operative, energizing and effective. Christ's witness to the heavens, the world and the netherworld was active, making it operative, energizing and effective. Holy Spirit's witness is consistent with that of Jesus Christ (Jn 15:26), making it operative, energizing and effective. Our witness [the third witness] needs to be of the same nature – active [or continuing], making it operative, energizing and effective.

Matthew wrote: *"be cautious and active), watch and pray, that you may not come into temptation. The spirit*

indeed is willing, but the flesh is weak" (Matt 26:41). And, the apostle James cautioned us, saying: *"But he who looks carefully into the faultless law, the [law] of liberty, and is faithful to it and perseveres in looking into it, being not a heedless listener who forgets but an active doer [who obeys], he shall be blessed in his doing [his life of obedience]"* (Jas 1:25).

When you have carried out God's directives, summarized above, you may be assured that your healing is in progress. Having invited Holy Spirit to indwell your spirit, all Holy Spirit to take control of your thoughts and imagination, and through your thoughts and imagination, to control your body, that the will of Father God may become manifest, to His glory and honor.

To God Be The Glory:
Not only must we continue to claim God's healing until it becomes manifest; we must then give God all the glory and honor. Peter wrote: *"Praise be to the God and Father of our Lord Jesus Christ! In his great mercy he has given us new birth into a living hope through the resurrection of Jesus Christ from the dead, and into an inheritance that can never perish, spoil or fade – kept in heaven for you, who through faith are shielded by God's power until the coming of the salvation that is ready to be revealed in the last time. In this you greatly rejoice, though now for a little while you may have had to suffer grief in all kinds of trials. These have come so that your faith – of greater worth than gold, which perishes even though refined by fire – may be proved genuine and may result in praise, glory and honor when Jesus Christ is revealed"* (1 Pe 1:3-8).

Cleansing Your Record:
Should you slip, verbalizing a negative confession – and most of us do – merely ask God to forgive you according to His promised Word, and to clean your record: from His Book of Remembrance; from Satan's record; and from your own memory.

Following are just a few of the promises related to healing:

- "Abraham prayed to God, and God healed Abimelech, his wife and his slave girls so they could have children again" (Gen 20:17).

- "Worship the Lord your God, and His blessing will be on your food and water. He will take away sickness from among you" (Ex 23:25).

- "Heal me, O Lord, and I shall be healed; save me and I shall be saved, for You are the One I praise" (Jer 17:14).

- "O Lord my God, I called to You for help and You healed me" (Ps 30:2).

- "For you who revere My Name, the sun of righteousness will rise with healing in its wings" (Mal 4:2).

- "Go! It will be done just as you believed it would. And his servant was healed at that very hour" (Mt 8:13).

- "She said to herself, "If I only touch His cloak, I will be healed." Jesus turned and saw her. "Take heart, daughter," HE said, "your faith has healed you." And the woman was healed from that moment" (Mt 9:21,22).

- "By faith in the name of Jesus, this man ... was made strong. It is Jesus' Name and the faith that comes through Him that has given this complete healing to him ..." (Acts 3:16).

- "He Himself bore our sins in His body on the tree, so that we might die to sins and live for righteousness; by His wounds you have been healed" (1 Pe 2:24).

- "Therefore confess your sins to each other and pray for each other so that you may be healed. The prayer of a righteous man is powerful and effective" (Jas 5:16).

- "I am the Lord that healeth thee" (Ex 15:26).

- "...Who forgiveth all ... healeth all thy diseases..." (Ps 103:3-4).

Divine Protection:
"Blessed is the man whom God corrects; so do not despise the discipline of the Almighty. For he wounds, but he also binds up; he injures, but his hands also heal. From six calamities he will rescue you; in seven no harm will befall you. In famine he will ransom you from death, and in battle from the stroke of the sword. You shall be hidden from the scourge of the tongue, and need not fear when destruction comes.

"You will laugh at destruction and famine, and need not fear the beasts of the earth. For you will have a covenant with the stones of the field, and the wild animals will be at peace with you. You will know that your tent is secure; you will take stock of your property and find nothing missing. You will know that your children will be many, and your descendants like the grass of the earth. You will come to the grave in full vigor, like sheaves gathered in season" (Job 5:17-26).

Besides healing – body, soul and spirit – another of our greatest needs is divine protection: protection from the powers of darkness; from wicked people; from accidents; and from our own self. There are several important aspects in insuring divine protection:

- Claiming God's promises,

- Fulfilling all the conditions associated with these promises,

- Renouncing fear, which gives demons a foothold in our life (Eph 4:27),

- Putting on the full armor of God, and

- Resisting the demons until they flee.

- Praying for God's protection.

~ Specific Promises for Specific Needs ~

Claiming God's promises that are specific to our need, is of great importance. We urge you to obtain a copy of our book, "God's Precious Promises, Advocare Publishing, 2010 – or a similar book that tells you how to claim God's promises, and addresses the importance of **fulfilling the conditions**; as well as providing a good selection of the more than 8,000 scriptural promises.

Renouncing the fear of man. *"The fear of man brings a snare, but whoever leans on, trusts in, and puts his confidence in the Lord is safe and set on high"* (Pro 29:25). *"The Lord of hosts – regard Him as holy and honor His holy name [by regarding Him as your only hope of safety], and let Him be your fear and let Him be your dread [lest you offend Him by your fear of man and distrust of Him]"* (Is 8:13).

"Now all has been heard; here is the conclusion of the matter: Fear God and keep his commandments, for this is the whole [duty] of man" (Eccl 12:13); *"Fear God and give him glory, because the hour of his judgment has come. Worship him who made the heavens, the earth, the sea and the springs of water"* (Rev 14:7).

Putting on the armor of God. The apostle Paul counseled us to: *"be strong in the Lord and in his mighty power. Put on the full armor of God so that you can take your stand against the devil's schemes"* (Eph 6:10-12). ... *"The hour has come for you to wake up from your slumber, because our salvation is nearer now than when we first believed. The night is nearly over; the day is almost here. So let us put aside the deeds of darkness and put on the armor of light"* (Rom 13:11-13).

Resisting the demons! *"Submit yourselves, then, to God. Resist the devil, and he will flee from you. Come near to God and he will come near to you. Wash your hands, you sinners, and purify your hearts, you double-minded. Grieve, mourn and wail. Change your laughter to mourning and your joy to gloom. Humble yourselves before the Lord, and he will lift you up"* (Jas 4:7-10). .. *"Be self-controlled and alert. Your enemy the devil prowls around like a roaring lion looking for someone to devour. Resist him, standing firm in the faith, because you know that your brothers throughout the world are undergoing the same kind of sufferings"* (1 Pe 5:8-9).

Praying for Protection:
Father God, in Jesus, My Lord and Savior, I now enter the Holy of Holies and approach your throne of grace. Having cast all of my cares onto You, I now rest in Your protection, safe from all my enemies – human or demonic. Father, I thank you that, in Jesus my Lord, you did not give me a spirit of timidity, but a spirit of power, love and self-discipline (2 Tim 1:7), by which I

resist the demons, commanding them to flee (Jas 4:7). That I need not fear the enemy's attacks by day or night, and while the wicked may fall victims to demonic attacks, they will not come near me (Ps 91:5-7).

Lord, I have made you my dwelling place, even my refuge, and I am confident that no harm can befall me, no disaster come near my dwelling; for You have commanded angels concerning me, to guard me in all my ways, who will lift me up should I stumble, and protect me from every danger (vs. 9-13).

Father, according to Your word, I trust in you, to rescue me in troublous times, protecting me for Your Name's sake (vs 14-15). Father, as one of Your dear children, in the Name and Blood of Jesus Christ, I have overcome the powers of darkness because You are in me, and far greater than he who is in the world (1 Jn 4:4). I know, Father, according to Your Word, that Your angels encamp around me to deliver me. Therefore, in Jesus, I take refuge in you (Ps 34:7) – Amen.

Promises of Protection:
Following are a few of the many Scriptures pertaining to God's divine protection over His children:

- "In righteousness you will be established: Tyranny will be far from you; you will have nothing to fear. Terror will be far removed; it will not come near you. If anyone does attack you, it will not be my doing; whoever attacks you will surrender to you. "See, it is I who created the blacksmith who fans the coals into flame and forges a weapon fit for its work. And it is I who have created the destroyer to work havoc; no weapon forged against you will prevail, and you will refute every tongue that accuses you. This is the heritage of the servants of the Lord, and this is their vindication from me," declares the Lord" (Is 54:14-17).

- "You will be secure, because there is hope; you will look about you and take your rest in safety. You will lie down, with no one to make you afraid, and many will court your favor" (Job 11:18-19).

- "Let the beloved of the Lord rest secure in him, for he shields him all day long, and the one the Lord loves rests between his shoulders" (Deut 33:12).

- "But let all who take refuge in you be glad; let them ever sing for joy. Spread your protection over them, that those who love your name may rejoice in you. For surely, O Lord, you bless the righteous; you surround them with your favor as with a shield" (Ps 5:11-12).

- "The Lord is my light and my salvation – whom shall I fear? The Lord is the stronghold of my life – of whom shall I be afraid? When evil men advance against me to devour my flesh, when my enemies and my foes attack me, they will stumble and fall. Though an army besiege me, my heart will not fear; though war break out against me, even then will I be confident" (Ps 27:1-3).

- "Therefore let everyone who is godly pray to you while you may be found; surely when the mighty waters rise, they will not reach him. You are my hiding place; you will protect me from trouble and surround me with songs of deliverance" (Ps 32:6-7).

- "If you make the Most High your dwelling – even the Lord, who is my refuge – then no harm will befall you, no disaster will come near your tent. For he will command his angels concerning you to guard you in all your ways; they will lift you up in their hands, so that you will not strike your foot against a stone" (Ps 91:9-12).

- "Surely he will never be shaken; a righteous man will be remembered forever. He will have no fear of bad news; his heart is steadfast, trusting in the LORD. His heart is secure, he will have no fear; in the end he will look in triumph on his foes. He has scattered abroad his gifts to the poor, his righteousness endures forever; his horn will be lifted high in honor" (Ps 112:6-9).

- "The Lord will keep you from all harm – he will watch over your life; the Lord will watch over your coming and going both now and forevermore" (Ps 121:7-8).

- "You will go on your way in safety, and your foot will not stumble; when you lie down, you will not be afraid; when you lie down, your sleep will be sweet. Have no fear of sudden disaster or of the ruin that overtakes the wicked, for the Lord will be your confidence and will keep your foot from being snared" (Pro 3:23-26).

- [Meditate on Psalms 23, 84 and 91]

Divine Provision (Prosperity or Abundance):
Divine healing, protection and provision summarize God's care for His beloved children. Recognizing this, Gittith, one of the sons of Korah, penned these words: "Better is one day in your courts O Lord, than a thousand elsewhere; I would rather be a doorkeeper in the house of my God than dwell in the tents of the wicked. For the Lord God is a sun and shield; the Lord bestows favor and honor; no good thing does he withhold from those whose walk is blameless. O Lord Almighty, blessed is the man who trusts in you" (Ps 84:10-12).

Prayer for Provision:
You, Father, are the source for my every need. And, I am confident that you, my Father and my God, "will meet all my needs, according to Your glorious riches in Christ Jesus, my Lord and Savior" (Phil 4:19). I know that you "will provide pasturage for any cattle I may own, and that I will eat and be satisfied" (Dt 11:15); that my livestock – or other resources – will increase, and my storehouse will be filled with every kind of provision (Ps 144:13).

I know, Father, that You "will provide a place for Your people ... and will planting me them so that I may have a home of my own and no longer be disturbed" (2 Sam 7:10). I know, that when I seek you, though the wild animals may go hungry, I will lack no good thing (Ps 34:10). I know, Father, that you will provide for me in every circumstance and situation; that I will not be a victim of poverty or famine, nor bear the scorn of the wicked (Ezek 34:29).

I know, Father, that You are able to make all grace abound to [me], so that in all things at all times, having all that [I] need, [I] will abound in every good work. As it is written: "He has scattered abroad his gifts to the poor; his righteousness endures forever." Now, You who supplies seed to the sower and bread for food will also supply and increase [my] store of seed and will enlarge the harvest of [my] righteousness. [I know that I] will be made rich in every way so that [I[can be generous on every occasion, and through [me] your generosity will result in thanksgiving God" (2 Cor 9:8-11).

Therefore, I "fearlessly and confidently and boldly draw near to the throne of grace (the throne of Your unmerited favor to us sinners), that I may receive mercy [for my failures] and find grace to help in good time for every need [appropriate help and well-timed help, coming just when I need it]" (Heb 4:16). I know, Father, that "You bless the righteous and surround them with your favor as a shield (Ps 5:12); that with my life hidden (concealed) in my Lord and Savior, Jesus Christ, Your Beloved Son, I am eligible to receive Your Favor (Gal 2:21), and Your favor lasts a lifetime (Ps 30:5).

Father God, I put my life in Your hands and trust wholly in Your Word of Promise: "Therefore, I tell you, don't worry about your life – what you will eat or drink; or about your body – what you will wear. Isn't life more than food and the body more than clothing? Look at the birds flying about! They neither plant nor harvest, nor do they gather food into barns; yet your heavenly Father feeds them. Aren't you worth more than they are? Can any of you by worrying add a single hour to his life? "And why be anxious about clothing? Think about the fields of wild irises, and how they grow. They neither work nor spin thread, yet I tell you that not even Solomon in all his glory was clothed as beautifully as one of these. If this is how God clothes grass in the field – which is here today and gone tomorrow, thrown in an oven – won't he much more clothe you?" (Mt 6:25-30).

Father, by my confession of faith, I offer you my body, a living sacrifice (Rom 12:1), and into Your hands I commit my being, body, soul and spirit; in Jesus Name and through His blood – Amen.

God's Gift ~ Grace ~ His Empowerment:
In addition to healing, protection and provision, God's other foundational gifts are power, love and a sound

mind -- gifts which we receive by transference, through the laying on of hands. *"Wherefore I put thee in remembrance that thou stir up the gift of God, which is in thee by the putting on of my hands. For God hath not given us the spirit of fear; but of power, and of love, and of a sound mind"* (2 Tim 1:6-7).

These gifts are bestowed, not for our own pleasure, but to equip us for ministry. Continuing on in his letter to Timothy, Paul wrote: *"Be not thou therefore ashamed of the testimony of our Lord, nor of me his prisoner: but be thou partaker of the afflictions of the gospel according to the power of God; Who hath saved us, and called us with an holy calling, not according to our works, but according to his own purpose and grace, which was given us in Christ Jesus before the world began, but is now made manifest by the appearing of our Savior Jesus Christ, who hath abolished death, and hath brought life and immortality to light through the gospel: Whereunto I am appointed a preacher, and an apostle, and a teacher of the Gentiles"* (2 Tim 1:8-11).

Ambassadors for Christ:

"If anyone is in Christ, he is a new creation; the old has gone, the new has come! All this is from God, who reconciled us to himself through Christ and **gave us the ministry of reconciliation***: that God was reconciling the world to himself in Christ, not counting men's sins against them. And* **he has committed to us the message of reconciliation***.* **We are therefore Christ's ambassadors***, as though God were making his appeal through us"* (2 Co 5:17-20).

Christ selected twelve of His disciples and *"**called to Him the Twelve [apostles] and began to send***

them out [as His ambassadors] *two by two and* ***gave them authority and power over the unclean spirits***" (Mark 6:7). After His death and resurrection, *"the eleven disciples [Judas had betrayed Him] went to Galilee, to the mountain where Jesus had told them to go. When they saw him, they worshiped him; but some doubted. Then Jesus came to them and said,* "**All authority in heaven and on earth has been given to me. Therefore go and make disciples of all nations**, *baptizing them in the name of the Father and of the Son and of the Holy Spirit, and* **teaching them to obey everything I have commanded you**. *And surely I am with you always, to the very end of the age"* (Mt 28:16-20).

Mark reports Christ's commissioning of the apostles as ambassadors, as follows: *"He said to them, "Go into all the world and preach the good news to all creation. Whoever believes and is baptized will be saved, but whoever does not believe will be condemned. And* **these signs will accompany those who believe: In my name they will drive out demons; they will speak in new tongues; they will pick up snakes with their hands; and when they drink deadly poison, it will not hurt them at all; they will place their hands on sick people, and they will get well**" (Mk 16:15-18).

The Transfer of Power:
This power – the baptism of Holy Spirit for ministry – was acquired not by study, nor by prayer, although both are important – but by the laying on of hands. Most are familiar with the early church's practice of setting aside leaders, ordaining them with prayer and the laying on of hands. For example, Paul and Barnabas, during their missionary journeys, *"appointed and ordained elders for them in each church with prayer and fasting, they committed them to the*

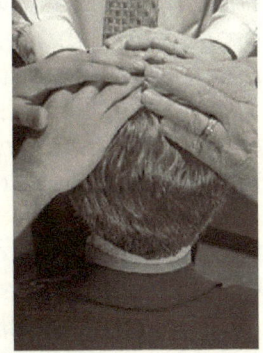

Lord in Whom they had come to believe [being full of joyful trust that He is the Christ, the Messiah]" (Acts 14:23).

In contrast to this, the practice of ordination, as it existed in the early church, has been obscured, and among many, obliterated. Consider the following Scripture: *"Now when the apostles (special messengers) at Jerusalem heard that [the country of] Samaria had accepted and welcomed the Word of God, they sent Peter and John to them, And they came down and prayed for them that the Samaritans might receive the Holy Spirit; For He had not yet fallen upon any of them, but they had only been baptized into the name of the Lord Jesus.* **Then [the apostles] laid their hands on them one by one, and they received the Holy Spirit**" (Acts 8:14-17).

Do you see what we see from this Scripture? All of the converts – **every one of them: not just the leaders, received the Baptism of Holy Spirit by the laying on of hands and prayer**! In other words, the authority that Jesus had transferred to His apostles was now being transferred to their converts – all of them!. No wonder the early church grew like wild fire. And conversely, it is no wonder that the present-day church is so powerless, so static – and in many instances withering and dying.

Paul in his letter to Timothy, said: *"Do not be in a hurry in the laying on of hands [giving the sanction of the church, too hastily in reinstating expelled offenders or in ordination in questionable cases], nor share or participate in another man's sins; keep yourself pure"* (1 Tim 5:22). This is excellent advice, however, it seems that the modern-day church may be carrying this admonition too far.

Paul – speaking to Timothy – illustrates the importance of continuing the practice, saying: *"I am calling up memories of your sincere and unqualified faith (the* leaning of your entire personality on God in Christ in absolute trust and confidence in His power, wisdom, and goodness), [a faith] that first lived permanently in [the heart of] your grandmother Lois and your mother Eunice and now, I am [fully] persuaded, [dwells] in you also. That is why I would remind you to stir up (rekindle the embers of, fan the flame of, and keep burning) the [gracious] gift of God, [the inner fire] that is in you by means of the laying on of my hands [with those of the elders at your ordination]" (2 Tim 1:5-6).

For Every Christian:
The author of the Book of Hebrews comments further on the fact that the laying on of hands, at the baptism of Holy Spirit, is something that should be given all who accept Jesus Christ as their Lord and Savior, saying:

"Therefore, let us go on and get past the elementary stage in the teachings and doctrine of Christ (the Messiah), advancing steadily toward the completeness and perfection that belong to spiritual maturity. Let us not again be laying the foundation of repentance and abandonment of dead works (dead formalism) and of the faith [by which you turned] to God, With teachings about purifying, the laying on of hands, the resurrection from the dead, and eternal judgment and punishment. [These are all matters of which you should have been fully aware long, long ago. If indeed, God permits, we will [now] proceed to advanced teachings]" (Heb 6:1-3).

Deeper Spiritual Teachings:
What are these deeper, advanced teachings? Continuing on, this author gives us a clue, writing: "Do grow disinterested and become [spiritual] sluggards, but imitators, behaving as do those who through faith (by their leaning on the entire personality on God in Christ in absolute trust

and confidence in His power, wisdom, and goodness) and by practice of patient endurance and waiting are [now] inheriting the promises" (Heb 6:12).

The apostle Paul provides an additional clue, saying: *"The man without the Spirit does not accept the things that come from the Spirit of God, for they are foolishness to him, and he cannot understand them, because they are spiritually discerned. The spiritual man makes judgments about all things, but he himself is not subject to any man's judgment: For who has known the mind of the Lord that he may instruct him?" But we have the mind of Christ"* (1 Co 2:14-16).

In another place, he says: *"With this in mind, we constantly pray for you, that our God may count you worthy of his calling, and that by his power he may fulfill every good purpose of yours and every act prompted by your faith. We pray this so that the name of our Lord Jesus may be glorified in you, and you in him, according to the grace of our God and the Lord Jesus Christ"* (2 Thess 1:11-12).

The Spirit of Truth:
What Jesus himself communicated to His apostles, is still clearer. Just prior to His ascension, He said: **"I have still many things to say to you, but you are not able to bear them or to take them upon you or to grasp them now. But when the Spirit of Truth (the Truth-giving Spirit) comes, you will be guided into all the Truth (the whole, full Truth)**. For the Spirit of Truth will not speak His own message [on His own authority]; but He will declare only what He hears [from the Father;

"He will declare the message that has been given to Him], and He will announce and declare to you the things that are to come [that will happen in the future]. He will honor and glorify Me, because He will take of (receive, draw upon) what is Mine and will reveal *(declare, disclose, transmit) it to you. Everything that the Father has is Mine. That is what I meant when I said that He [the Spirit] will take the things that are Mine and will reveal (declare, disclose, transmit) it to you"* (John 16:12-15).

Secrets and Mysteries:
On another occasion, He said: *"To you it has been given to know the secrets and mysteries of the kingdom of heaven, but to them it has not been given. For whoever has [spiritual knowledge], to him will more be given and he will be furnished richly so that he will have abundance; but from him who has not, even what he has will be taken away. This is the reason that I speak to them in parables: because having the power of seeing, they do not see; and having the power of hearing, they do not hear, nor do they grasp and understand"* (Mt 13:11-14 ~ see also Lk 8:10).

Speaking of these deeper things that are declared by Holy Spirit to those seekers of knowledge, Paul said: *"[For I always pray to] the God of our Lord Jesus Christ, the Father of glory, that He may grant you a spirit of wisdom and revelation [of insight into mysteries and secrets] in the [deep and intimate] knowledge of Him, by having the eyes of your heart flooded with light, so that you can know and understand the hope to which He has called you, and how rich is His glorious inheritance in the saints (His set-apart ones), [so that you can know and understand] what is the immeasurable and unlimited and surpassing greatness of His power in and for us who believe, as demonstrated in the working of His mighty strength, Which He exerted in Christ when*

He raised Him from the dead and seated Him at His [own] right hand in the heavenly [places]" (Eph 1:17-20).

Looking into the future, *"Jesus said, "I praise you, Father, Lord of heaven and earth, because you have hidden these things from the wise and learned, and revealed them to little children. Yes, Father, for this was your good pleasure. All things have been committed to me by my Father. No one knows the Son except the Father, and no one knows the Father except the Son and those to whom the Son chooses to reveal him"* (Matt 11:25-27).

Summary:
Holy Spirit was sent to us by Father God and Jesus Christ (Yeshua Messiah) to:

1. testify of Christ and remind us of everything He taught His apostles,

2. to tell us of things to come,

3. and to reveal the mysteries and secrets of the Father to seekers of knowledge.

Jesus came to be the propitiation for our sins – to pay a debt we could never pay – and to show us the way to the Father. Through His life, death and resurrection, the veil between the Holy and the Holy of Holies was rent (removed) so we may – in Jesus – enter the Holy of Holies, into the presence of our Heavenly Father. Here, before the Throne of Grace, God reveals His mysteries to His Children.

The gift God has given us in this last day is that of "power, love and a sound mind" (2 Ti 1:7). Christ gave the church but one law – the law of love. *"A new command I give you: Love one another. As I have loved you, so you must love one another. By this all men will know that you are my disciples, if you love one another"* (Jn 13:34-35). "God has qualified us [making us to be fit and worthy and sufficient] as ministers *and* dispensers of a new covenant [of salvation through Christ], not [ministers] of the letter (of legally written code) but of the Spirit; for the code [of the Law] kills, but the [Holy] Spirit makes alive" (2 Cor 3:6). Law brings death while love brings life. In love, God's power and a restored (sound) mind come together in His beloved children.

In the chapters ahead, we will share what we believe that God's Word reveals concerning our access to God's Throne in the Heavenly Holy of Holies, and the impact this has for you and for I – being God's Children.

~ Questions, Concerns & Key Points ~

1. What are the 'rights' that God has given mankind?

2. What is the key to claiming God's promises and receiving what He has promised?

3. What is the origin of sickness and suffering?

4. Promises are 'promissory notes' drawn on heaven's bank.

5. What are the 'three witnesses' to God's Word?

6. What is the significance of lifting one's hands to the Lord before administering the gift of healing?

7. How can one be certain that what they are asking of God is in accord with His will?

8. Where are our sins recorded?

9. What are those things one must we do to have this record erased?

10. How, specifically are we to cleanse our sin record from Satan's record and from our memory?

11. Understand how to pray Scripture for God's:
    1] Forgiveness;
    2] Protection; and,
    3] Provision

12. [Reread Ps 23; 30:5; 84; 91; and 144:13]

13. How are God's gifts and empowerment to be transferred to those in ministry?

14. How many of those in the First Century church, were empowered by the laying on of hands to receive the baptism of Holy Spirit for ministry?

15. What are the 'deeper things' the author of the Book of Hebrews speaks of that the church should be teaching? [reread Heb 6:12]

16. What does it mean that we have the 'mind of Christ?'

17. Understand God's New Covenant Gift and Law.

Chapter 7 ~ God's Way

God is a God of Order:
God's Universe – the cosmos, operates according to established principles and laws. Without laws such as gravity, centrifugal force, thermal dynamics, and light waves, the universe would not only experience chaos, it would self-destruct.

God's Unseen Laws:
God's entire universe is governed by unseen, immutable laws and principles. None of these laws can be seen, but they are discoverable – and many have been discovered. The reality of these laws and principles is based on the manifestation of their operation in and through those things which they rule or govern.

Our body – our very being – operates on unseen, universal laws and concepts. These are principles and laws one that must adhere to in order to survive and enjoy good health. Ignoring these principles and laws will deprive one of health, perhaps of their very life. Within our body, and the body of every other living, breathing thing on this planet – plant and animal – is DNA, an embedded code of principles and laws that governs the operation and reproduction of that plant or animal. Altering (mutating) that code creates genetic chaos, often spelling the death of that species or sub-species.

Considering this master design of the observable things within the universe, and its reliance on established laws and principles, shouldn't we expect that the unseen things also operate on established laws and principles? In fact, we know that they do. For example, the DNA mentioned is part of the unseen, as are the principles of gravity, centrifugal force, radiation, etc.

The operation of God's spiritual kingdom is no different: it also operates on established, immutable laws and principles. If these are complied with, the Kingdom of God – the church – functions well, and will experience growth and health. Denied, or violated, these same laws become manifest through waning spirituality and a lack of manifest spiritual powers within the church. Like the laws that govern the physical features of the cosmos, these laws cannot be seen, but they are discoverable; and if discovered and complied with, we can expect spiritual growth, health and maturity.

Discovering Spiritual Laws:
To discover and understand the laws and principles that govern a nation, city, state, school board, or business corporation, one needs to become acquainted with the person or persons who framed those principles and laws, and those who implement them. Discovering and comprehending the spiritual laws that govern the Kingdom of God are no different: we must become acquainted with the Lawgiver -- God, Creator, Messiah and Master.

To apply this, consider the following: There are a number of specific, established steps for discovering and applying laws and principles. These steps – applied to the discovery of spiritual principles, which are covered later in greater detail – include the following:

1. Entering into the presence of the lawgiver,

2. Removing everything and everyone undesirable,

3. Interviewing the lawgiver, to determine applicable laws and principles,

4. Giving thanks for the interview and information,

5. Implementing the laws and principles discovered.

Entering God's Presence:
To gain access to the lawmakers of a business corporation, a county, state or national government, one needs to make an appointment, and in most cases must have an introduction. Additionally, gaining an audience with leaders of states and nations involves an expectation that you – the visitor – will present the lawgiver with a gift of appreciation. Gaining access to The Lawgiver of the Universe – God our Creator – is no different: we need an appointment (or invitation), and we certainly need an introduction. And, when meeting with our Creator and God, the presentation of a gift of appreciation is certainly the appropriate protocol.

Putting on Garments of Righteousness:
In the Old Testament, only the High Priest had access to the Holy of Holies in the Tabernacle. Before entering, it was required that the High Priest cleanse himself, purify himself, and adorn himself with clean, priestly garments used only for that purpose. *"When they enter the gates of the inner court, they shall be clothed in linen garments"* (Ezek 44:17). This was symbolic of our position in Christ Jesus, which we read about in Paul's writings.

Removing the Barricade of Unforgiveness:
At one point in His earthly ministry, Jesus – teaching His disciples about spiritual warfare – we read: *"Peter came to Jesus and asked, "Lord, how many times shall I forgive my brother when he sins against me? Up to seven times?" Jesus answered, "I tell you, not seven times, but seventy-seven times.*

"Therefore, the kingdom of heaven is like a king who wanted to settle accounts with his servants. As he began the settlement, a man who owed him ten thousand talents was brought to him. Since he was not able to pay, the master ordered that he and his wife and his children and all that he had be sold to repay the debt.

"The servant fell on his knees before him. 'Be patient with me,' he begged, 'and I will pay back everything.' The servant's master took pity on him, canceled the debt and let him go. "But when that servant went out, he found one of his fellow servants who owed him a hundred denarii. He grabbed him and began to choke him. 'Pay back what you owe me!' he demanded.

"His fellow servant fell to his knees and begged him, 'Be patient with me, and I will pay you back.' "But he refused. Instead, he went off and had the man thrown into prison until he could pay the debt. When the other servants saw what had happened, they were greatly distressed and went and told their master everything that had happened.

"Then the master called the servant in. 'You wicked servant,' he said, 'I canceled all that debt of yours because you begged me to. Shouldn't you have had mercy on your fellow servant just as I had on you?' In anger his master turned him over to the jailers to be tortured, until he should pay back all he owed. "This is how my heavenly Father will treat each of you unless you forgive your brother from your heart" (Mt 18:21-35).

Our Sin Record Erased [Justification]:

When we follow God's Word, forgiving all whom we have held resentment and/or bitterness toward, and repent of this as sin, God forgives us and cancels, or eradicates the record thereof in His Book of Remembrance. John reminds us that:

"If we confess our sins, he is faithful and just and will forgive us our sins and purify us from all unrighteousness" (1 Jn 1:9-10). And, the apostle Paul says that God not only forgives us, He wipes our record clean, disarming the principalities and powers of darkness, and making them a public spectacle: "He forgave us all our sins, having canceled the written code, with its regulations, that was against us and that stood opposed to us; he took it away, nailing it to the cross. And having disarmed the powers and authorities, he made a public spectacle of them, triumphing over them by the cross" (Col 2:13-15).

Our Guilt Expunged:
"And when Jesus saw ... the paralyzed man's faith [confidence in God through Him], He said to, Son, your sins are forgiven [you] and put away [that is, the penalty is remitted, **your sense of guilt removed**, and you are made upright and in right standing with God]" (Mk 2:5). ... "He was betrayed and put to death because of our misdeeds and was raised to secure our justification (our acquittal), [making our account balance and **absolving us from all guilt before God**]" (Rom 4:25). ... "You were washed clean [purified by a complete atonement for sin and **made free from the guilt of sin**]" (1 Cor 6:11).

"If we [really] are living and walking in the Light, as He [Himself] is in the Light, we have [true, unbroken] fellowship with one another, and the blood of **Jesus Christ His Son cleanses (removes) us from all sin and guilt** [keeps us cleansed from sin in all its forms and manifestations]" (1 John 1:7). "When He had by offering Himself accomplished our cleansing of sins and riddance of guilt, He sat down at the right hand of the divine Majesty on high" (Heb 1:3).

Our Shame Exchanged for Glory:
"As it is written, Behold I am laying in Zion a Stone that will make men stumble, a Rock that will make them fall; but **he who believes in Him [who adheres to, trusts in, and relies on Him] shall not be put to shame** nor be disappointed in his expectations" (Rom 9:33). ... "Scripture says, **No man who believes in Him [who adheres to, relies on, and trusts in Him] will [ever] be put to shame** or be disappointed" (Rom 10:11). "Fear not, for **you shall not be ashamed;**

neither be confounded and depressed, for you shall not be put to shame" (Is 54:4).

"*Instead of your [former] shame you shall have a twofold recompense; instead of dishonor and reproach [your people] shall rejoice in their portion. Therefore in their land they shall possess double [what they had forfeited]; everlasting joy shall be theirs*" (Is 61:7).

"**Glory and honor and [heart] peace shall be awarded to everyone who [habitually] does good**" (Rom 2:10).

Changing Clothes [Sanctification]:
The prophet Isaiah said that when He, whom the Spirit of the Sovereign Lord would anoint, appeared, He would: "*provide for those who grieve in Zion — to bestow on them a crown of beauty instead of ashes, the oil of gladness instead of mourning, and a garment of praise instead of a spirit of despair*" (Is 61:3).

Paul says: "*Strip yourselves of your former nature [put off and discard your old unrenewed self] which characterized your previous manner of life and becomes corrupt through lusts and desires that spring from delusion; And be constantly renewed in the spirit of your mind [having a fresh mental and spiritual attitude], And put on the new nature (the regenerate self) created in God's image, [Godlike] in true righteousness and holiness*" (Eph 4:22-24).

[Transformation] "When Christ, Who is our life, appears, then you also will appear with Him in [the splendor of His] glory" (Col 3:4). ... "**He will transform and fashion anew the body of our humiliation to conform to and be like the body of His glory and majesty,** *by exerting that power which* enables Him even to subject everything to Himself" (Phil 3:21).

"And if we are [His] children, then we are [His] heirs also: heirs of God and fellow heirs with Christ [sharing His inheritance with Him]; only we must share His suffering if we are to share His glory. [But what of that?] For I consider that the sufferings of this present time (this present life) are not worth being compared with the glory that is about to be revealed to us and in us and for us and conferred on us!" (Rom 8:17-18).

Made Righteous:
"God made him who had no sin to be sin for us, so that in him we might become the righteousness of God" (2 Cor 5:21). ... "The eyes of the Lord are on the righteous and his ears are attentive to their prayer" (1 Pe 3:12). ... "I delight greatly in the LORD; my soul rejoices in my God. For he has clothed me with garments of salvation and arrayed me in a robe of righteousness, as a bridegroom adorns his head like a priest, and as a bride adorns herself with her jewels" (Is 61:10).

The author of the Book of Hebrews, continuing to employ the metaphor of the Levitical Priesthood, says: "Therefore, brothers, since we have confidence to enter the Most Holy Place by the blood of Jesus, by a new and living way opened for us through the curtain, that is, his body, and since we have a great priest over the house of God, let us draw near to God with a sincere heart in full assurance of faith, having our hearts sprinkled to cleanse us from a guilty conscience and having our bodies washed with pure water" (Heb 10:19-23). It is through Christ and in Christ alone that we have access to the Holy of Holies and the Throne of Grace.

Hidden Within Christ [spirit-to-Spirit Union]:
"For in Christ Jesus you are all sons of God through faith. For as many [of you] as were baptized into Christ [into a spiritual union and communion with Christ, the

Anointed One, the Messiah] have put on (clothed yourselves with) Christ" (Gal 3:26-27).

The High Priest in the Old Testament era, must – after putting on clean linen garments, put on the priestly vestments: these included a blue robe, called the Robe of the Ephod, that had a row of bells at the bottom; the Ephod itself, made of purple to represent royalty and containing two onyx stones worn on the shoulders, representing the two divisions of the people: Israel and Judah; over this he wore a breastplate containing twelve precious stones representing the twelve tribes of Israel; a sash, or girdle made of purple cloth intertwined with gold threads, representing purity; a miter of fine linen and a crown.

[Prepared for Battle]
Comparing our spiritual attire to this physical foreshadowing, the apostle Paul said: *"Put on God's whole armor [the armor of a heavy-armed soldier which God supplies], that you may be able successfully to stand up against [all] the strategies and the deceits of the devil. For we are not wrestling with flesh and blood [contending only with physical opponents], but against the despotisms, against the powers, against [the master spirits who are] the world rulers of this present darkness, against the spirit forces of wickedness in the heavenly (supernatural) sphere.*

"Therefore put on God's complete armor, that you may be able to resist and stand your ground on the evil day [of danger], and, having done all [the crisis demands], to stand [firmly in your place]. Stand therefore [hold your ground], having tightened the belt of truth around your loins and having put on the breastplate of integrity and of moral rectitude and right standing with God" (Eph 6:11-14).

"And having shod your feet in preparation [to face the enemy with the firm-footed stability, the promptness,

and the readiness produced by the good news] of the Gospel of peace. Lift up over all the [covering] shield of saving faith, upon which you can quench all the flaming missiles of the wicked [one]. And take the helmet of salvation and the sword that the Spirit wields, which is the Word of God" (Eph 6:15-17).

The High Priest in the Old Testament wore beneath the breastplate, in a special pocket, two precious stones, the Urim and Thummim. The word *'Urim'* means lights, or colors, and the word *'Thummim'* means perfections. Jewish tradition suggests that when the High Priest posed a question to the Lord, either the Urim or Thummim would illuminate, or flash, providing a positive or negative response. When God was displeased with His people in later history, He refused to permit the Urim and Thummim to function as a means of guidance.

The apostle John, speaking of our approaching God's Throne Room, says: *"I counsel you to buy from me gold refined in the fire, so you can become rich; and white clothes to wear, so you can cover your shameful nakedness; and salve to put on your eyes, so you can see"* (Rev 3:18).

Thus attired, we can be sure that we meet the criteria specified by the prophet Isaiah, who wrote: *"I will greatly rejoice in the Lord, my soul will exult in my God; for He has clothed me with the garments of salvation, He has covered me with the robe of righteousness, as a bridegroom decks himself with a garland, and as a bride adorns herself with her jewels"* (Is 61:9).

Encapsulated Within Christ:
Having put aside the deeds of darkness and adorned ourselves with the priestly garments; put on the armor of a warrior, He Who is light, enshrouds us within an armor of light [the

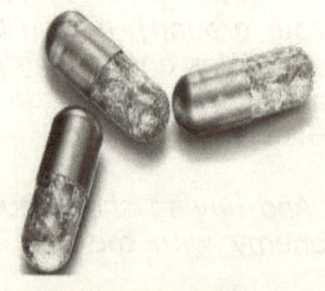

Shekinah Glory]: *"So putting aside the deeds of darkness, put on the armor of light"* (Rom 13:12-13); and put on Christ -- *"clothe yourselves with the Lord Jesus Christ, and do not think about how to gratify the desires of the sinful nature"* (Rom 13:14).

Paul described this state of being, saying: *"We know that if the tent which is our earthly home is destroyed (dissolved), we have from God a building, a house not made with hands, eternal in the heavens. Here indeed, in this [present abode, body], we sigh and groan inwardly, because we yearn to be clothed over [we yearn to put on our celestial body like a garment, to be fitted out] with our heavenly dwelling"* (2 Cor 5:1-2).

Prepared for Glory [Joining the Family of God]:
Clothed in light – the Shekinah Glory – we are prepared for intimate fellowship with the Father, the Son, Holy Spirit and with one another [the church]. John said: *"This is the message we have heard from him and declare to you: God is light; in him there is no darkness at all. If we claim to have fellowship with him yet walk in the darkness, we lie and do not live by the truth. But if we walk in the light, as he is in the light, we have fellowship with one another, and the blood of Jesus, his Son, purifies us from all sin"* (1 John 1:5-7).

It is those who are so adorned who John describes in the Book of Revelation, saying: *"I looked and there before me was a great multitude that no one could count, from every nation, tribe, people and language, standing before the throne and in front of the Lamb. They were wearing white robes and were holding palm branches in their hands. And they cried out in a loud voice: "Salvation belongs to our God, who sits on the throne, and to the Lamb"* (Rev 7:9-10).

"Then one of the elders asked me, "These in white robes – who are they, and where did they come from?" I answered, "Sir, you know." And he said, "These are they

who have come out of the great tribulation; they have washed their robes and made them white in the blood of the Lamb. Therefore, "they are before the throne of God and serve him day and night in his temple; and he who sits on the throne will spread his tent over them" (Rev 7:13-15). .. "Blessed are those who wash their robes, that they may have the right to the tree of life and may go through the gates into the city" (Rev 22:12).

The Psalmist speaking of this prophetically, wrote: "But I, by your great mercy, will come into your house; in reverence will I bow down toward your holy temple" (Ps 5:7). "Open to me the [temple] gates of righteousness; I will enter through them, and I will confess and praise the Lord. This is the gate of the Lord; the [uncompromisingly] righteous shall enter through it" (Ps 118:19-20).

Entering the Throne Room:
Having properly adorned ourselves and become part of the Family of God [the church] – through the Blood of Jesus – we now have access to the Throne Room of Father God, through the shed blood of Jesus Christ. "Therefore, brothers, since we have confidence to **enter the Most Holy Place by the blood of Jesus**, by a new and living way opened for us through the curtain, that is, his body, and since we have a great priest over the house of God, let us draw near to God with a sincere heart in full assurance of faith" (Heb 10:19-22).

Seated With Jesus on the Throne:
Of the faithful, Jesus said: "You are those who have stood by me in my trials. And I confer on you a kingdom, just as my Father conferred one on me, so that **you may eat and drink at my table in my kingdom and sit on thrones**, judging the twelve tribes of Israel" (Lk 22:28-30). And the apostle Paul, reflecting on this, wrote: "But God is so rich in mercy and loves us with such intense love that, even when we were dead because of our acts of disobedience, he brought us to

life along with the Messiah – it is by grace that you have been delivered. That is, **God raised us up with the Messiah Yeshua and seated us with him in heaven**, in order to exhibit in the ages to come how infinitely rich is his grace, how great is his kindness toward us who are united with the Messiah Yeshua" (Eph 2:4-8).

Gifts of Appreciation:
Having entered God's Holy Temple, the Psalmist described the gifts of appreciation we should have with us: "Know (perceive, recognize, and understand with approval) that the Lord is God! It is He Who has made us, not we ourselves [and we are His]! We are His people and the sheep of His pasture. **Enter into His gates with thanksgiving and a thank offering and into His courts with praise**! Be thankful and say so to Him, bless and affectionately praise His name! For the Lord is good; His mercy and loving-kindness are everlasting, His faithfulness and truth endure to all generations" (Ps 100:3-5).

"Sing to the Lord a new song; sing to the Lord, all the earth. Sing to the Lord, praise his name; proclaim his salvation day after day. Declare his glory among the nations, his marvelous deeds among all peoples. For great is the Lord and most worthy of praise; he is to be feared above all gods. For all the gods of the nations are idols, but the Lord made the heavens. Splendor and majesty are before him; strength and glory are in his sanctuary. Ascribe to the Lord, O families of nations, ascribe to the Lord glory and strength. **Ascribe to the Lord the glory due his name; bring an offering and come into his courts**. Worship the Lord in the splendor of his holiness; tremble before him, all the earth" (Ps 96:1-9).

The Throne-Room Perspective:
Seated by Jesus side in the Throne Room of the Holy of Holies, in the heavenly court, everything looks much different. Instead of being surrounded by the

principalities and powers of darkness; instead of being overwhelmed by the anxieties of life on earth (Lk 21:34), we are seated in the heavens, looking down on the spiritual battle below.

"God raised us up with Christ and seated us with Him in the heavenly realms" (Eph 2:6). We are, *"seated [with] him at his [Father's] right hand in the heavenly realms, far above all rule and authority, power and dominion"* (Eph 1:20-21). And, we realize that *"God [has] placed all things under his feet and appointed him to be head over everything for the church"* (Eph 1:22).

Under Our Feet:
In the beginning, before man's rebellion and fall, everything – on planet earth – was under man's feet: David penned: *"**What is man** that You are mindful of him, and the son of [earth-born] man that You care for him? Yet **You have made him but a little lower than***

God [or heavenly beings], and You have crowned him with glory and honor. You made him to have dominion over the works of Your hands; You have put all things under his feet" (Ps 8:4-6). In rebelling, thereby aligning himself with Satan, man lost his dominion over the earth and Satan acquired it through man's acquiescence.

Jesus came to earth and defeated Satan, thereby regaining dominion over the earth. Paul, commenting on this, wrote: *"And [so that you can know and understand] what is the immeasurable and unlimited and surpassing greatness of God's power in and for us who believe, as demonstrated in the working of His mighty strength, Which He exerted in Christ when He raised Him from the dead and seated Him at His [own] right hand in the heavenly [places], Far above all rule and authority and power and dominion and every name that is named [above every title that can be conferred], not only in this age and in this world, but also in the age and the world which are to come.* ***And He has put all things under His feet** and has **appointed Him the universal and supreme Head of the church [a headship exercised throughout the church]***" (Eph 1:19-22).

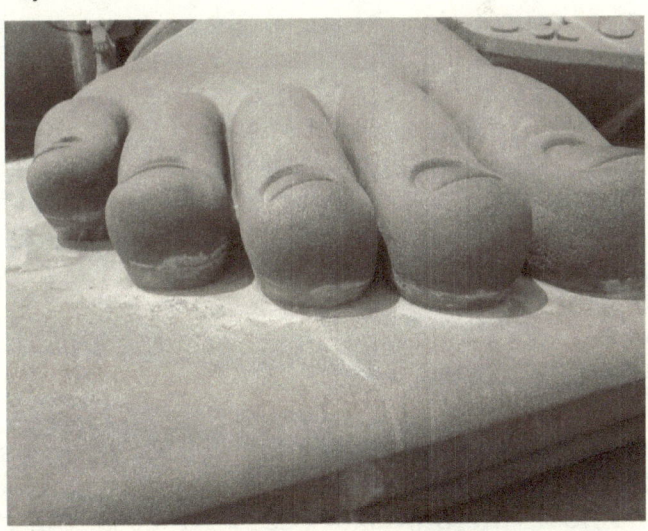

In and through Jesus, man's dominion over the earth – and everything thereon – was once more established. The author of the Book of Hebrews comments on this, saying: *"It was not to angels that God subjected the habitable world of the future, of which we are speaking. It has been solemnly and earnestly said in a certain place, What is man that You are mindful of him, or the son of man that You graciously and helpfully care for and visit and look after him? For some little time You have ranked him lower than and inferior to the angels; You have crowned him with glory and honor and set him over the works of Your hands"* [Ps 8:4-6.].

"For You have put everything in subjection under his feet. Now in putting everything in subjection to man, He left nothing outside [of man's] control. But at present we do not yet see all things subjected to him [man]. But we are able to see Jesus, Who was ranked lower than the angels for a little while, crowned with glory and honor because of His having suffered death, in order that by the grace (unmerited favor) of God [to us sinners] He might experience death for every individual person" (Heb 2:5-9).

Then, explaining the effect of Jesus' substitutionary death and resurrection, he says: *"In bringing many sons to glory, it was fitting that God, for whom and through whom everything exists, should make the author of their salvation perfect through suffering. Both the one who makes men holy and those who are made holy are of the same family. So Jesus is not ashamed to call them brothers. He says, "I will declare your name to my brothers; in the presence of the congregation I will sing your praises." And again, "I will put my trust in him." And again he says, "Here am I, and the children God has given me."*

"Since the children have flesh and blood, he too shared in their humanity so that by his death he might destroy him who holds the power of death – that is, the devil –

and free those who all their lives were held in slavery by their fear of death. For surely it is not angels he helps, but Abraham's descendants. For this reason he had to be made like his brothers in every way, in order that he might become a merciful and faithful high priest in service to God, and that he might make atonement for the sins of the people. Because he himself suffered when he was tempted, he is able to help those who are being tempted" (Heb 2:10-18).

Long ago, one of the Sons of Korah declared prophetically: "Clap your hands, all you nations; shout to God with cries of joy. How awesome is the Lord Most High, the great King over all the earth! He subdued nations under us, peoples under our feet. He chose our inheritance for us, the pride of Jacob, whom he loved. God has ascended amid shouts of joy, the Lord amid the sounding of trumpets. "Sing praises to God, sing praises; sing praises to our King, sing praises. For God is the King of all the earth; sing to him a psalm of praise. God reigns over the nations; God is seated on his holy throne. The nobles of the nations assemble as the people of the God of Abraham, for the kings of the earth belong to God; he is greatly exalted" (Ps 47).

Spiritual Exercise:
With your eyes closed, invite Holy Spirit to guide you as you visualize yourself being in the Holy of Holies, approaching the Throne of Grace in reverence. Now, see yourself seated with Christ by Father God's right hand. Experience Father God calling you His child (Heb 12:5). Now, from this perspective, look down on the earth. Equipped with the Sword of the Spirit – the Word of God – visualize yourself beginning to do battle with principalities and powers of darkness.

[As you approach Father God on His throne, He beholds you as Jesus, in whom you are encased: then, as you turn around and face the powers of darkness, they to will behold you as Jesus, and flee from your presence!

Always look down from the Throne Room of God, not up from the fox hole on the battlefield when engaged in spiritual warfare.]

Hear the Voice of Jesus reminding you: *"All authority in heaven and on earth has been given to me"* (Mt 28:18). ... *"I have given you authority to trample on snakes and scorpions and to overcome all the power of the enemy; nothing will harm you"* (Lk 10:19). ... *"Have faith in God,"* ... *"I tell you the truth, if anyone says to this mountain, 'Go, throw yourself into the sea,' and does not doubt in his heart but believes that what he says will happen, it will be done for him"* (Mk 11:22-24).

"These signs will accompany those who believe: In my name they will drive out demons; they will speak in new tongues; they will pick up snakes with their hands; and when they drink deadly poison, it will not hurt them at all; they will place their hands on sick people, and they will get well" (Mk 16:17-18).

Now, hear Christ tell you: *"I will give you the keys of the kingdom of heaven; whatever you bind on earth will be bound in heaven, and whatever you loose on earth will be loosed in heaven"* (Mt 16:19-20). ... [Go] *"enter the strong man's house and carry off his possessions ... [but] first tie up the strong man. Then [you] can rob his house"* (Mt 12:29).

Eliminating Your Problems:
Identify the specific situations, circumstances, events, objects, persons that seem to be giving you problems. You may wish to categorize them, using the following divisions: a) Spiritual; b) Relational; c) Environmental (housing, home locale, etc.); d) Financial; e) Emotional; f) Physical (the last two suggesting a need for healing). Keep in mind as you carry out this assignment, that: *"Our struggle is not against flesh and blood, but against the rulers, against the authorities, against the powers of this dark world and against the spiritual forces of evil in the heavenly realms"* (Eph 6:12-13). And, remember that whatever your problem it is under the authority of Jesus Christ, who has designated the authority over demons to you.

"Therefore God exalted him to the highest place and gave him the name that is above every name, that at the name of Jesus every knee should bow, in heaven and on earth and under the earth, and every tongue confess that Jesus Christ is Lord, to the glory of God the Father" (Phil 2:9-11). ... *"He raised him from the dead and seated him at his right hand in the heavenly realms, far above all rule and authority, power and dominion, and every title that can be given, not only in the present age but also in the one to come"* (Eph 1:20-22).

Now, once again visualize yourself looking down on your problems from the Throne of Grace [Divine Empowerment.]

Focus on the ruling magistrates, not on the minor minions. They and the people whom they oppress are Satan's unwilling retainers. Focusing from the heavenly realm, envision cut off Satan's lines of authority – his transmission lines, if you please – disabling the

'Rulers, Authorities, and Cosmic Powers that govern the kingdom of darkness – the spiritual forces of evil – in the heavenly realm' (Eph 6:12) .

Remember, "With man this is impossible, but with God all things are possible" (Mt 19:26). Jesus declared that: "Everything is possible for him who believes" (Mark 9:23).

Summary:
The church – Christ's Bride and Body; Father God's Family – must come to understand and respect the order and power of God within the universe; the plan of salvation [of putting back together] His children; learn to listen to the Spirit of Truth; and step out in the authority that Jesus transferred onto us, commissioning us to take the Ministry of Reconciliation to the world.

To accomplish this, we must learn not only how to put on the Armor of God, but how to use the weapons He has provided [praying His truths] effectively to defeat the powers of darkness. Learning to live within the order of God, we are to manifest the image and likeness of the fullness of the Godhead, through Christ Jesus – our High Priest and King.

"He who is able to hear, let him listen to and give heed to what the Spirit says to the assemblies (churches). To him who overcomes (is victorious), I will grant to eat [of the fruit] of the tree of life, which is in the paradise of God" (Rev 2:7). ... *"He who overcomes (is victorious) shall in no way be injured by the second death"* (vs. 11).

"He who overcomes (is victorious) and who obeys My commands to the [very] end [doing the works that please Me], I will give him authority and power over the nations" (Rev 2:26). ... *"He who conquers (is victorious) be clad in white garments, and I will not erase or blot out his name from the Book of Life"* (Rev 3:5).

"He who overcomes (is victorious), I will make him a pillar in the sanctuary of My God" (Rev 3:12). ... *"He who overcomes (is victorious), I will grant him to sit beside Me on My throne, as I Myself overcame (was victorious) and sat down beside My Father on His throne"* (Rev 3:21).

"Then I saw what seemed to be a glassy sea blended with fire, and those who had come off victorious from the beast and from his statue and from the number corresponding to his name were standing beside the glassy sea, with harps of God in their hands. And they sang the song of Moses the servant of God and the song of the Lamb, saying, Mighty and marvelous are Your works, O Lord God the Omnipotent! Righteous (just) and true are Your ways, O Sovereign of the ages" (Rev 15:2-3). ... *"He who is victorious shall inherit all these things, and I will be God to him and he shall be My son"* (Rev 21:7).

God is sifting and sorting – separating the sheep [His children]; from the goats [those who have turned away, (Heb 4:12; Jn 10:14). He calls His own sheep by name (Jn 10:3), and they follow Him (vs. 27).

~ Questions, Concerns & Key Points ~

1. God is a God of order, not chaos, understanding and cooperating with His order is essential to effective living, transformation and ministry.

2. Jesus is the Law-giver: the origin, or source, of all spiritual, physical and moral laws.

3. Salvation [putting mankind back together] is a process, including: Justification, Sanctification, Transformation, and Transfiguration (Exaltation or Glorification).

4. Justification and Sanctification are prerequisites for entering the heavenly Holy of Holies in Christ.

5. Only when we – in Christ – enter the heavenly realms, can we conduct spiritual warfare as a victor instead of a victim.

6. Understand the significance of the 'throne room perspective' to successful Christian living.

7. From the heavenly throne room – everything in the physical [phenomenal] and spiritual [pneumenal] realms are under our feet. Therefore, we can – in Christ – pray confidently.

8. God's order governs not only persons individually, but corporately, as the church.

Chapter 8 ~ Binding and Loosing

Introduction:
One of the essential teachings concerning our exercising dominion over the powers of darkness is Jesus' teaching concerning binding and loosing. Jesus' said: *"Whatever you bind on earth will be bound in heaven, and whatever you loose on earth will be loosed in heaven"* (Mt 18:18); and, *"your will be done on earth as it is in heaven"* (Mt 6:9).

This together with Solomon's words that: *"the tongue has power over life and death"* (Pr 18:21), make it apparent that God's will is already being done in heaven, and it is now our responsibility to see that His will is done on earth. We have the privilege of participating in this by speaking-out (declaring) God's words.

From our spiritual position in the Holy of Holies – in the heavenly temple – we have the awesome privilege and responsibility of **declaring God's will into the world**. From this perspective, we now get to view the problems of we identified earlier, from God's perspective. From this perspective, we have access to every spiritual weapon, and all power and all authority – authority assigned to us by Christ, to resolve these problems.

Paul understood this and declared: *"The weapons we fight with are not the weapons of the world. On the contrary, they have divine power to demolish strongholds. We demolish arguments and every pretension that sets itself up against the knowledge of God, and we take captive every thought to make it obedient to Christ"* (2 Cor 10:4-5).

"By speaking the Word of truth, in the power of God; with weapons of righteousness in the right hand [to attack] and in the left hand [to defend]; amid honor and dishonor, in defaming and evil report and in praise and good report. [We are branded] as deceiver [impostors], yet vindicated as truthful and honest" (2 Cor 6:7-8).

Binding and loosing in the spirit realm is two-fold; that is, they both apply to the principalities and powers of darkness, and to God's holy angels – those He commands to *"guard you in all your ways"* (Ps 91:11). Those who have been previously trained in spiritual warfare understand well the principles of binding the powers of darkness and loosing the Spirit of God, but this does not begin to embrace the full meaning of Matthew 18:18. We will endeavor to make this as clear as possible.

Managing Principalities and Powers of Darkness:
On one occasion, *"Jesus was driving out a demon that was mute. When the demon left, the man who had been mute spoke, and the crowd was amazed. But some of them said, "By Beelzebub, the prince of demons, he is driving out demons." Others tested him by asking for a sign from heaven.*

"Jesus knew their thoughts and said to them: "Any kingdom divided against itself will be ruined, and a house divided against itself will fall. If Satan is divided against himself, how can his kingdom stand? I say this because you claim that I drive out demons by Beelzebub. Now if I drive out demons by Beelzebub, by whom do your followers drive them out? So then, they will be your judges. But if I drive out demons by the finger of God, then the kingdom of God has come to

you. *"When a strong man, fully armed, guards his own house, his possessions are safe. But when someone stronger attacks and overpowers him, he takes away the armor in which the man trusted and divides up the spoils"* (Luke 11:14-22).

Matthew and Mark record Jesus' words a bit different, saying: *"Or again, how can anyone enter a strong man's house and carry off his possessions unless he first ties up the strong man? Then he can rob his house"* (Matt 12:29; Mk 3:27).

The principles Jesus imparts here are these:

Binding ~ *tying-up, binding or confining.*
- The strong [boisterous mighty] men [principalities and powers of darkness] are fully armed [equipped] and [although isolated] guard(s) [watches over] their [his] own house [sheep-fold], making [sure] their [his] possessions [are] safe [at peace, or enjoying prosperity]. The implications here are that the strong man [the rulers of darkness] directed by Satan, who although isolated [confined to the abyss], watches over/directing them. The rulers of darkness then direct the principalities [magistrates or potentates], who are fully equipped with subordinates [demons], whom they dispatch to make sure that Satan's possessions [the souls of men] are 'safe' [enjoying the pleasures of sin and their temporary prosperities].

- For our spiritual warfare to be effective, it is important that we first tie up, or bind, the "strong man" [Ruler of Darkness]. Attacking individual demons can be a never-ending task, as we bind one, only to have another -- even up to seven as Jesus described in the parable of Mark 12 and Luke 11 -- return to make *"the final condition of that man is worse than the first"* (Lk 11:45).

- Binding the strong-man first, enables one to *take away the armor [incapacitating the demons, defusing their lies in which the [strong] man trusted by declaring God's truths]* (Lk 11:14); after which one can *"enter the strong man's house and carry off his possessions [the souls of men]. Then he can rob his house [sheep-fold] {the principalities and powers}"* (Mt 12:29).

Loosing ~ untying, releasing or freeing
- Once the strong-man's house has been plundered, his possessions [the souls of men] may be recovered. We have the right to claim the following promise on their behalf: *"God made you alive with Christ. He forgave us all our sins, having canceled the written code, with its regulations, that was against us and that stood opposed to us; he took it away, nailing it to the cross. And having disarmed the powers and authorities, he made a public spectacle of them, triumphing over them by the cross"* (Col 2:13-15). This looses, or removes, the spiritual assignments against that person or persons.

It is common when engaged in spiritual warfare for the release of souls that the powers of darkness will come to remind the intercessor of their past sins, suggesting that they are in no position spiritually to pray for another, having committed similar or worse sins themselves. We know that *"there is no condemnation for those who are in Christ Jesus"* (Rom 8:1), yet there are times when the accuser of the brethren can make us wonder. Thankfully, our Lord provided us the answer for this accusation.

In a parable, Jesus said: *"Two men owed money to a certain moneylender. One owed him five hundred denarii, and the other fifty. Neither of them had the money to pay him back, so he canceled the debts of both. Now which of them will love him more?"*

Simon replied, "I suppose the one who had the bigger debt canceled." "You have judged correctly," Jesus said" (Luke 7:41-43). By the confession of your faith, Jesus has canceled you debts; and according to His promise, *"he bore the sin of many, and made intercession for the transgressors"* (Is 53:12).

Engaging the Heavenly Host:
Having eliminated the attacks of the powers of darkness, and having canceled their assignments for oppression and/or infestation, it is now time for us to turn our attention to establishing favorable conditions by engaging the host – the righteous heavenly angels.

Determining The Father's Will:
In the majority of instances, the Father's will has already been expressed. His Word provides clear direction for most areas of living. His Word contains more than eight thousand (8,000) promises, or promissory agreements, which specify what the Father will do for us, or provide us, if we will fulfill the covenant conditions. Therefore, the majority of the time, Christ's words: *"Ye do err, not knowing the Scriptures, nor the power of God"* (Mt 22:29) apply.

Claiming God's Promises:
Acquainting ourselves with the Scriptures – specifically God's promises – and actively practicing the confession of faith, provides the solution to most of life's problems. To aid 'seekers' we have recently published a little book that categorizes many of God's promises and illustrates how to fulfill these promissory covenant agreements,

thereby receiving the promised blessing. ["God's Precious Promises", Advocare Publishing Co., Redding, CA, 2010).

Even where there are not clearly articulated covenant promises, there are clear directions for discovering God's express will. Consider the following Scriptures: *"In that day you will no longer ask me anything. I tell you the truth, my Father will give you whatever you ask in my name. Until now you have not asked for anything in my name. Ask and you will receive, and your joy will be complete"* (John 16:23-24).

Prayers of Agreement:
"I tell you, whatever you ask for in prayer, believe that you have received it, and it will be yours" (Mark 11:24-25). ... *"Again, I tell you that if two of you on earth agree about anything you ask for, it will be done for you by my Father in heaven. For where two or three come together in my name, there am I with them"* (Mt 18:19-20).

While memorizing – or at least becoming familiar with – God's promises is critical to successful spiritual warfare, asking Father God in confidence, when your request is beyond His declared promises, is equally important. This area of spiritual warfare [prayers of agreement] includes asking for creative miracles – i.e., the restoration of bodily organs, and the creation of those that never existed, such as the blind man who Jesus healed, who had been blind from birth; and the deaf mute that had been that way all of his life.

Another application of this is asking for divine resources – the creation of resources out of what is not visible. Speaking of this type of God's provision, the author of the Book of Hebrews, wrote: *"By faith we understand that the universe was formed at God's command, so that what is seen was not made out of what was visible"* (Heb 11:3).

Wielding the Sword of the Spirit:
Paul tells us to: *"Take the helmet of salvation and **the sword of the Spirit, which is the word of God**. And pray in the Spirit on all occasions with all kinds of prayers and requests"* (Eph 6:17-18). God's Word is the sword of the Spirit, but to be effective we must wield it. Only when angels hear God's Word emanating from our mouth will they hearken to us. Only then is it effective against the enemy of our souls. We must guard our hearts (Pr 4:23) since unbelief will stifle God's power (Mk 3:4-6).

Ministry of Holy Spirit:
Just prior to His ascension, Jesus called His disciples together, and after teaching them many things, elaborated on His soon departure, saying: *"I will ask the Father, and he will give you another comforting Counselor like me, [Holy Spirit] the Spirit of Truth, to be with you forever. The world cannot receive him, because it neither sees nor knows him. You know him, because he lives with you and will soon be in you -- united with you"* (John 14:15-18). ...

"Those controlled by the sinful nature cannot please God. You, however, are controlled not by the sinful nature but by the Spirit, because the Spirit of God lives in you" (Rom 8:8-9). ... [And] *"The Spirit himself testifies with our spirit that we are God's children. Now if we are children, then we are heirs — heirs of God and co-heirs with Christ"* (Rom 8:16-17).

[Moreover], *"the Spirit helps us in our weakness; for we don't know how to pray the way we should. But Holy Spirit himself pleads on our behalf with groanings too deep for words; and the one who searches hearts knows exactly what the Spirit is thinking, because his pleadings for God's people are in accord with God's will"* (Rom 8:26-27). [And] *"This is the confidence we have in his presence: if we ask anything that accords with his will, he hears us. And if we know that he hears us – whatever we ask – we then know that we have what we have asked from him"* (1 John 5:14-15).

God honors the Sovereign dominion of mankind. **Holy Spirit does not initiate but responds to our requests that are spoken according to the perfect will of the Father.** When we ask in Jesus' Name and according to God's will, then we know that we have our petition. *"This is the confidence that we have in him, that, if we ask any thing according to his will, he heareth us: And if we know that he hear us, whatsoever we ask, we know that we have the petitions that we desired of him"* (1 Jn 5:14-15).

Ministry of Angels:
Angels are God's messengers, created as ministering servants to His household -- of which you and I are, in Christ, members. Angels serve us at the direction of Father God and Holy Spirit, and convey messages between heaven and ourselves. They also watch over, or guard, us. Scripture says: *"He will command his angels concerning you to guard you in all your ways"* (Ps 91:11).

God's angels do God's bidding, carrying out assignments. *"The Lord has established His throne in heaven, and His kingdom rules over all. Praise the Lord, you His angels, you mighty ones who do His bidding, who obey His word. Praise the Lord, all His heavenly hosts, you his servants who do his will"* (Ps 103:19-21).

Similarly, **angels do our bidding, provided it is in accord with God's will**: *"To which of the angels did God ever say, "Sit at my right hand until I make your enemies a footstool for your feet"?* **Are not all angels ministering spirits sent to serve those who will inherit salvation**?*"* (Heb 1:13-14). ... At God's direction, they immediately come to our aid. Jesus said: **"Do you think I cannot call on my Father, and he will at once put at my disposal more than twelve legions of angels?"** (Mt 26:53-54).

That is 72,000 angels! But, to receive this aid, we must ask. In Jesus, we have the same standing with the Father. He said: *"I tell you, whoever acknowledges me before men, the Son of Man will also acknowledge him before the angels of God"* (Luke 12:8).

Our guardian angels – the one(s) God has appointed to watch over us and guard us – have direct access to our heavenly Father! *"See that you do not look down on one of these little ones. For I tell you that **their angels** in heaven always see the face of my Father in heaven"* (Matt 18:10).

They do spiritual warfare on our behalf. *"And there was war in heaven. Michael and his angels fought against the dragon, and the dragon and his angels fought back. But he was not strong enough, and they lost their place in heaven. The great dragon was hurled down – that ancient serpent called the devil, or Satan, who leads the whole world astray. He was hurled to the earth, and his angels with him"* (Rev 12:7-9).

"Since the children have flesh and blood, he too shared in their humanity so that by his death he might destroy him who holds the power of death – that is, the devil – and free those who all their lives were held in slavery by their fear of death. For surely it is not angels he helps, but Abraham's descendants. For this reason he had to be made like his brothers in every way, in order that he might become a merciful and faithful high priest in service to God, and that he might make atonement for the sins of the people" (Heb 2:14-18).

Angels – on God's behalf – hold us accountable for the vows we make. "When thou vowest a vow unto God, defer not to pay it; for he hath no pleasure in fools: pay that which thou hast vowed. Better is it that thou shouldest not vow, than that thou shouldest vow and not pay. Suffer not thy mouth to cause thy flesh to sin; neither say thou before the temple angel, that your vow was an error: wherefore should God be angry at thy voice, and destroy the work of thine hands?" (Eccl 5:4-6).

Even God's Law was implemented by angels. "You who have received the law that was put into effect through angels but have not obeyed it" (Acts 7:52-53). Angels, like we who have accepted Jesus, are members of the Church of the firstborn – the Body of Christ – "You have come to Mount Zion, to the heavenly Jerusalem, the city of the living God. You have come to thousands upon thousands of 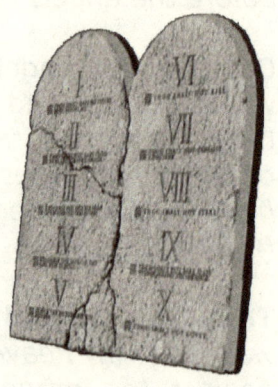 angels in joyful assembly, to the church of the firstborn, whose names are written in heaven. You have come to God, the judge of all men, to the spirits of righteous men made perfect, to Jesus the mediator of a new covenant" (Heb 12:22-24).

We also share eternity with the angels: *"Then I looked and heard the voice of many angels, numbering thousands upon thousands, and ten thousand times ten thousand. They encircled the throne and the living creatures and the elders. In a loud voice they sang: "Worthy is the Lamb, who was slain, to receive power and wealth and wisdom and strength and honor and glory and praise!"* (Rev 5:11-12).

And, we may – from time to time – entertain them without knowing it. The author of the Book of Hebrews cautions us about this, saying: *"Do not forget to entertain strangers, for by so doing some people have entertained angels without knowing it"* (Heb 13:2).

Binding and Loosing Messengers of God:
When eliminating the attacks of the powers of darkness, we bind, or tie up, the strong man [the Rulers of Darkness], thereby making impotent both them and those that serve them [principalities and powers of the air, the cosmic powers and the demons on earth. After that, we enter the strongman's house and steal his possessions -- the souls of men.

Establishing the desired conditions through our fulfilling of God's promises and God subsequently granting our petitions for things beyond or outside of His declared promises, we essentially reverse the process employed when dealing with the powers of darkness:

- We ask the Father to release [loose] whatever number of His Holy angels He deems sufficient to carry out the task we petitioned of Him.

- We then ask Holy Spirit to dispatch [loose] these angels and, according to the authority of Jesus, our Lord and Savior, to place them at our disposal.

- Having now been dispatched to help us, we than assign them [binding them] to the task at hand.

[Remember, these *"angels [are] ministering spirits sent to serve those who will inherit salvation?"* (Heb 1:13-14). They are commanded to insure that you keep your word (vows), fulfilling the conditions associated with the promises you claimed. Keep in mind that they are messengers, who have direct access to Father God (Mt 18:10); and will report back to Him (Eccl 5:4-6).

Thank God ~ Your Petition has been Granted:
Jesus said: *"I tell you, whatever you ask for in prayer, believe that you have received it, and it will be yours"* (Mark 11:24-25). After we have presented our petitions to Father God, that are in accord with His will; have fulfilled any specified conditions; have asked God to release [loose]; and Holy Spirit to dispatch [loose] the ministering servants [angels], we can be assured that the fulfillment of our petition is in motion.

Our attitude should now be that recommended by the apostle Paul: *"Rejoice in the Lord always. I will say it again: Rejoice! Let your gentleness be evident to all. The Lord is near. Do not be anxious about anything, but in everything, by prayer and petition, with thanksgiving, present your requests to God. And the peace of God, which transcends all understanding, will guard your hearts and your minds in Christ Jesus"* (Phil 4:4-7).

An example of one who understood this – there was a Roman Centurion who came to Jesus asking for help. *"When Jesus had entered Capernaum, a centurion came to him, asking for help. "Lord," he said, "my servant lies at home paralyzed and in terrible suffering." Jesus said to him, "I will go and heal him." The centurion replied, "Lord, I do not deserve to have you come under my roof. But just say the word, and my servant will be* healed. For I myself am a man under authority, with soldiers under me. I tell this one, 'Go,' and he goes; and that one, 'Come,' and he comes. I say to my servant, 'Do this,' and he does it." When Jesus heard this, he was astonished and said to those following him, "I tell you the truth, I have not found anyone in Israel with such great faith" (Matt 8:5-11).

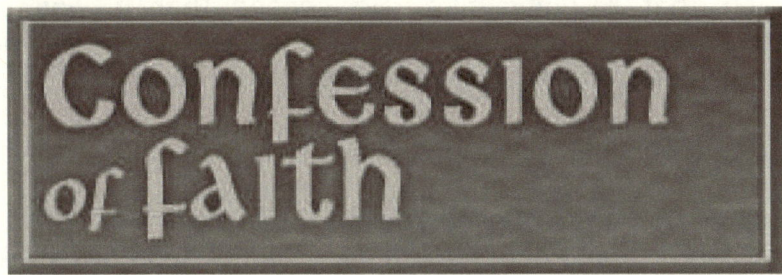

Maintaining Your Confession of Faith:
Don't cancel the manifestation of your confession of faith before comes to maturity. Verbalize it again and again. Remember, *"God gives life to the dead and calls nonexistent things into reality"* (Rom 4:17).

Once we have fulfilled all requisites and have expressed our thanks to Father God, it is common for the accuser of the brethren to dispatch demons, assigned to sow seeds of doubt. **This is a critical time. What happens during this interval largely determines whether or not God's promised provision, His answer to your petition, is received.** The apostle James addresses this issue, saying:

*"Consider it pure joy, my brothers, whenever you face trials of many kinds, because you know that the testing of your faith develops perseverance. Perseverance must finish its work so that you may be mature and complete, not lacking anything. If any of you lacks wisdom, he should ask God, who gives generously to all without finding fault, and it will be given to him. But **when he asks, he must believe and not doubt, because he who doubts is like a wave of the sea, blown and***

tossed by the wind. That man should not think he will receive anything from the Lord; *he is a double-minded man, unstable in all he does"* (Jas 1:2-8).

There is a battle raging in the unseen spiritual realm during this interval. A story in the Book of Daniel describes this in graphic detail. Daniel had received a vision that troubled him. He sensed that it was of utmost importance and was praying for Divine interpretation. Day after day he continued to pray, even fasting and praying until he had no strength left and fell into a deep sleep (Dan 10:8-9).

Finally: *"A hand touched me and set me trembling on my hands and knees. He said, "Daniel, you who are highly esteemed, consider carefully the words I am about to speak to you, and stand up, for I have now been sent to you." And when he said this to me, I stood up trembling"* (Dan 10:10-11).

"Then the angel continued, "Do not be afraid, Daniel. Since the first day that you set your mind to gain understanding and to humble yourself before your God, your words were heard, and I have come in response to them. But the prince of the Persian kingdom resisted me twenty-one days. Then Michael, one of the chief princes, came to help me, because I was detained there with the king of Persia. Now I have come to explain to you what will happen to your people in the future, for the vision concerns a time yet to come" (Dan 10:12-14).

For three weeks, this battle raged in the unseen realm – a battle between the angels of God and the principalities and powers of darkness, while the prophet Daniel waited and prayed. What if he had given up? The length and intensity of this battle is no match for that which must have occurred in an effort to prevent God from fulfilling His covenant of promise with mankind. Our petition can be repeated over and over, without negating our faith. Holy Spirit who indwells us will match our inner-reality –

the belief of our heart (Pr 23:7 KJV) - with our outer-reality - the physical manifestation.

Consider the covenant promise between God and Abraham. *"Therefore, the promise comes by faith, so that it may be by grace and may be guaranteed to all Abraham's offspring - not only to those who are of the law but also to those who are of the faith of Abraham. He is the father of us all. As it is written: "I have made you a father of many nations. "He is our father in the sight of God, in whom he believed - the God who gives life to the dead and calls things that are not as though they were.*

"Against all hope, Abraham in hope believed and so became the father of many nations, just as it had been said to him, "So shall your offspring be." Without weakening in his faith, he faced the fact that his body was as good as dead - since he was about a hundred years old - and that Sarah's womb was also dead. Yet he did not waver through unbelief regarding the promise of God, but was strengthened in his faith and gave glory to God, being fully persuaded that God had power to do what he had promised. This is why "it was credited to him as righteousness." (Rom 4:16-23).

While the battle in the unseen rages, we are instructed to: *"Trust in the Lord with all your heart and lean not on your own understanding; in all your ways acknowledge him, and he will make your paths straight"* (Pro 3:5-6). ... *"My son, pay attention to what I say; listen closely to my words. Do not let them out of your sight, keep them within your heart; for they are life to those who find them and health to a man's whole body. Above all else, guard your heart, for it is the wellspring of life. Put away perversity from your mouth; keep corrupt talk far from your lips. Let your eyes look straight ahead, fix your gaze directly before you. Make level paths for your feet and take only ways that are firm. Do not swerve to the right or the left; keep your foot from evil"* (Pro 4:20-27).

Providing the Raw Material for the Physical Manifestation of Petitions:
In the well known definition of faith [*"Now faith is the substance of things hoped form the evidence of things not seen"* (Heb 11:1)], the word *'substance'* is in the Greek, the word, *'hupostasis'*, which literally means *'the essence of'*; and the word evidence, is the Greek word, *'elegchos'*, which refers to a *'conviction based on evidence'*; and the words 'things not seen', stems from the Greek word, referring to *'unseen business matters.'*

This is an apt description of our covenant agreement with unseen Divine Ones. The important thing to note here is that we provide the substance (our petition) relying on our evidence-based conviction developed through our relationship with Father God, Holy Spirit and our Lord and Savior, Jesus Christ.

Don't Limit the Possible:
"Trust in the Lord with all your heart, lean not on your own understanding" (Pro 3:5). ... *"My son, pay attention to what I say; listen closely to my words. Do not let them out of your sight, keep them within your heart; for they are life to those who find them and health to a man's whole body. Above all else, guard your heart, for it is the wellspring of life"* (Pro 4:20-23).

If we allow our focus [our thoughts] to shift from God's promised provision back to our problem, we have allowed the Word of God [His promise] to departed from our eyes and heart.

Abiding Faith:
Jesus said: *"I am the vine; you are the branches.* **If a man abides [remains] in me and I in him, he will bear much fruit**; *apart from me you can do nothing.* **If anyone does not abide [remain] in me, he is like a**

branch that is thrown away and withers; such branches are picked up, thrown into the fire and burned. If you abide [remain] in me and my words abide [remain] in you, ask whatever you wish, and it will be given you. *This is to my Father's glory, that you bear much fruit, showing yourselves to be my disciples"* (Jn 15:5-8).

The word *'abide'* used here is translated from the Greek word, *'meno'* which means to tarry, to endure, to remain, stand still, or to dwell. Tie implications are obvious: after we have made our petition to the Father, met the conditions, asked Holy Spirit to dispatch angels and have given them their assignment, we are to dwell in Christ, tarrying in prayer, standing still, and enduring until God's promise is fulfilled. *"Jesus said, "If you hold fast onto what I have said, you are really my disciples. Then you will know the truth, and the truth will set you free"* (Jn 8:31-32).

Concerning this, the author of the Book of Hebrews, wrote: *"Let us continue holding fast to the hope we acknowledge, without wavering; for the One who made the promise is trustworthy. And let us keep paying attention to one another, in order to spur each other on to love and good deeds, not neglecting our own congregational meetings, as some have made a practice of doing, but, rather, encouraging each other"* (Heb 10:23-25).

Here are additional keys for receiving God's promised blessings:

- Continuing to hold fast to our hope (expectation) without wavering, allowing God time to orchestrate His perfect solution.

- Pay attention to one another to spur each other on to love and good deeds.

- Maintain corporate worship, encouraging one another.

The apostle James gives us specific guidelines for dealing with problems of life. He says:

- *"Is any one of you in trouble? He should pray.*

- *Is anyone happy? Let him sing songs of praise.*

- *Is any one of you sick? He should call the elders of the church to pray over him and anoint him with oil in the name of the Lord. And the prayer offered in faith will make the sick person well; the Lord will raise him up.*

- *If he has sinned, he will be forgiven.*

- *Therefore confess your sins [cracks, faults problems] to each other and pray for each other so that you may be healed.*

- *The prayer of a righteous man is powerful and effective"* (Jas 5:13-16).

After this, James reveals just how powerful and effective the prayer of a righteous man is by making reference to the prophet Elijah: *"Elijah was a man just like us. He prayed earnestly that it would not rain, and it did not rain on the land for three and a half years. Again he prayed, and the heavens gave rain, and the earth produced its crops"* (Jas 5:17-18).

The Power of Our Testimony:
John says: *"They [the overcomers] overcame (conquered) him [Satan] by the blood of the Lamb (Christ Jesus our Lord -- the Lamb of God); and by the word of their testimony. They did not love and cling to life even when faced with death"* (Rev 12:11).

In his letter to Timothy, Paul wrote: *"So **don't be ashamed of bearing testimony to our Lord** or to me, his prisoner. On the contrary, **accept your share in suffering disgrace for the sake of the Good News. God will give you the strength for it, since he delivered us and called us to a life of holiness as his people**. It was not because of our deeds, but because of his own purpose and the grace which he gave to us who are united with the Messiah Yeshua. He did this before the beginning of time, but made it public only now through the appearing of our Deliverer, the Messiah Yeshua, who abolished death and, through the Good News, revealed life and immortality"* (2 Tim 1:8-10).

Summary:
We are indeed in the process of transformation. Recognizing this, we must rest in God's promise that *"there is no condemnation for those who are in Christ Jesus"* (Rom 8:1).

We must continue to share our testimony, knowing that *"the accuser of our brothers, who accuses [us] before our God day and night, has been hurled down. They **[we] overcome him by the blood of the lamb and by the word of our testimony**"* (Rev 12:10-11).

We need to keep in mind that Christ came *"that we might have life and have it more abundantly"* (Jn 10:10). God the Father, Christ, and Holy Spirit live within us to insure the manifestation of God's likeness in and through us.

At the same time, we must keep in mind that Holy Spirit's transformational power can be inhibited, our manifestation of God's likeness, expressed through our testimony – verbal and non-verbal tarnished; and our enjoyment of the promised abundant life in Jesus, inhibited through unresolved soulish issues. This is why the apostle Paul counseled us:

"Do not let yourselves be conformed to the standards of the present age and culture. Instead, continue allowing yourselves be transformed by the renewing (renovation or retrofitting) of your minds; so that you will know what God wants and will agree that what he wants is good, satisfying and will enable you to succeed" (Rom 12:2-3 CJB).

Looking Forward:
This process of soul-healing, or transformation, is the focus of the next lesson.

~ Questions, Concerns & Key Points ~

1. Understand the principle of Binding and Loosing [Matthew 18:18].

2. Father God wills [desires] to protect us, to provide for us and to heal us.

3. Satan and the demons under his command are intent to block God's care of man, and to destroy our bodies and souls.

4. Christ transferred to us the authority to wage a victorious warfare against Satan and the demons.

5. We must understand the weapons of spiritual warfare: our words. Every time we speak, we are doing spiritual warfare – the question is, whose bullets we are using and who or what our target is.

6. Holy Spirit is not the initiator in our warfare, but the responder – responding to our requests that are in accord with Father God's will.

7. If we ask in humility, God will assign as many as 72,000 angels to help us (Matt 26:53-54).

8. Angels sent to minister to those who will inherit salvation (Heb 1:13-14).

9. Angels guard, or watch over us (Matt 18:10).

10. Angels administer God's Laws (Heb 12:22-24).

11. Angels hold us accountable for our vows (Eccl 5:4-6).

12. Angels do spiritual warfare on our behalf (Rev 12:7-9).

13. We often entertain angels without knowing it (Heb 13:12).

14. Angels, as God's messengers, bind the strongmen at our request, reversing the situation – and they report back to Father God (Eccl 4:5-6).

15. Angels will share eternity with us (Rev 5:11-12).

16. Claiming God's promises includes our [A] – asking; [B] believing; [C] claiming specific, applicable promises; and [D] giving thanks that our petition has been granted.

17. Perseverance in prayer is often essential – praying until the answer is manifest.

18. Abide in faith – giving God time to answer.

19. Our victory is through the Blood of the Lamb, combined with the power of our testimony. [Jesus is our victory!]

Chapter 9 ~ Soul Healing

Introduction:
Reflecting on our last lesson concerning the transformation of our soul, it is important for us to realize that the process of transformation is active and ongoing. As such, there are things that can facilitate the transformation, or healing, of our soul; and there are things that can wound our souls, hindering the process of transformation. Jesus came to save (heal) our souls but Satan, and the demons under his command, are determined to wound our souls – hopefully beyond recovery. But, to materially wound our souls, they must gain access, and they can only do so if we – intentionally or unintentionally – provide an open doorway.

Soul Wounding:

The apostle Paul warns us about this, providing a list of things we can do that provide such a doorway. *"Therefore, **stripping off all falsehood**, let everyone **speak truth** with his neighbor, because we are intimately related to each other as parts of a single body (the body of Christ, the church). Be angry, but don't sin — **don't let the sun go down before you have dealt with the cause of your anger; otherwise you leave room [make place, or leave an open doorway] for the Adversary**. The thief must **stop stealing**; instead, he should make an honest living by his own efforts. This way he will be able to **share with those in need**.*

"**Let no harmful language come from your mouth**, only good words that are helpful in meeting the need, words that will benefit those who hear them. **Don't cause grief to God's Ruach HaKodesh (Holy Spirit)**, for he has stamped (sealed) you as his property until the day of final redemption. **Get rid of all bitterness, rage, anger, violent assertiveness and slander, along with all spitefulness**. Instead, **be kind to each other, tenderhearted; and forgive each other, just as in the Messiah God has also forgiven you**" Eph 4:25-32 CJB).

In his letter to the Galatians, Paul mentioned a similar but more comprehensive list, writing: *"The acts of the sinful nature are obvious: **sexual immorality, impurity** and **debauchery; idolatry** and **witchcraft; hatred, discord, jealousy, fits of rage, selfish ambition, dissensions, factions** and **envy; drunkenness, orgies, and the like**. I warn you, as I did before, that those who live like this will not inherit the kingdom of God"* (Gal 5:19-21 NIV).

In addition to these things that we do that can cause further soul wounding, there are things outside of our control that can inflict wounds, creating doorways for demons. These include: rejection, abandonment and neglect; abuse – whether spiritual, mental, emotional, physical or relational; unresolved soulish wounds that were sufficient in intensity to cause Post Traumatic Stress flash-backs; as well as multi-generational predispositions to sinful patterns of behavior.

All of these things can create footholds, doors or passageways through our spiritual armor into our soul (Eph 6:11-18), and our armor of light (Rom 13:12). This gives demons access to our soul who will then draw us back into the kingdom of darkness. For most Christians, one of the more common and more serious passageway is the issue of unforgiveness.

Unforgiveness blocks our access to God, leaving us vulnerable to satanic and demonic attack.

"Jesus said: 'Don't judge others, and God won't judge you. Don't be hard on others, and God won't be hard on you. Forgive others, and God will forgive you. If you give to others, you will be given a full amount in return. It will be packed down, shaken together, and spilling over into your lap. The way you treat others is the way you will be treated'" (Luke 6:37-38 CEV).

In another place it is recorded that he said: *"if you forgive men when they sin against you, your heavenly Father will also forgive you. But if you do not forgive men their sins, your Father will not forgive your sins"* (Matt 6:14-15).

Whether our unforgiveness is directed toward the living or the dead, the effect is the same – it blocks our access to God, and insures that we receive precisely what we hoped to avoid; being once again treated in an abusive manner.

Unforgiveness also binds us to the party or parties we refuse to forgive. This gives those whom we desire most to be free from, control over our soul (our mind: intellect, emotions, attitudes, beliefs, values, etc.). And, since the soul-wounding we refuse to forgive centers on past incidents of injustice, unforgiveness keeps us bound to the past. This must be applied multi-generationally, taking in familial curses, any occult involvement, multi-generational sins.

This is why Jesus said: *"I tell you, whatever you ask for in prayer, believe that you have received it, and it will be yours. And when you stand praying, if you hold anything against anyone, forgive him, so that your Father in heaven may forgive you your sins"* (Mark 11:24-25).

The apostle Paul said: *"Brothers, I do not consider myself yet to have taken hold of perfection. But one thing I do: Forgetting what is behind and straining toward what is ahead, I press on toward the goal to win the prize for which God has called me heavenward in Christ Jesus. All of us who are mature should take such a view of things"* (Phil 3:13-15).

The Power of Forgiveness:
In contrast to the effects of unforgiveness mentioned above; forgiveness achieves the following:

- It provides access to Father God,

- It allows God to forgive us our sins,

- It alters the way we will be treated by others,

- It breaks others bondage of, and control over, us,

- It enables us to let go of the past and move on in life,

- It opens the doorway to God's bountiful blessings,

- It opens our soul to receive God's healing presence and power.

Forgiveness is a Choice:

The English word *forgive* literally means 'to give as before', suggesting that when we have forgiven one, we will treat them like we did before the incident, or incidents, of injustice. This does not accurately reflect the meaning of the Hebrew, Aramaic and Greek words thus translated; and giving as we did before the incident may – in certain cases – result in our being wounded the way we were, once more. To understand this, let's look at the various words translated 'forgive' and determine their meanings.

Forgive

Hebrew	English
Naw-saw	to absolve
Saw-kaw	to pardon
Shoob	to turn back
Aw-bar	to cover
Naw-kah	to cleanse
Kaw-far	to make atonement for

Greek	English
Aphiemi	lay aside, or let go
Charizomai	grant a pardon -- as a favor

Aramaic	English
Khayaw	untie
Sabaq	forsake

Forgiving might seem to be as complex as the many words indicate, however, when we remember that we are under the New Covenant, rather than the Old, it limits our consideration to the Greek and Aramaic root words.

Taking all of this into consideration, one can see that the Greek 'aphiemi' (lay aside or let go) and the Aramaic 'khayaw' (untie) have basically the same meaning. Similarly the Greek word 'charizomai' (grant a pardon) and the Aramaic 'sabaq' (forsake), meaning to forsake one's course of action, have approximately the same meaning.

Bringing this all together, we get: **untie/let-go (of the perpetrator/abuser); and forsake action against him/her, granting them a pardon full and free**. This translation enables us to comprehend Jesus' admonition: *"If you forgive men when they sin against you, your heavenly Father will also forgive you. But if you do not forgive men their sins, your Father will not forgive your sins"* (Matt 6:14-15).

Spiritual vs. Soulish
Forgiveness is a spiritual issue. As born-anew beings we are in spirit-to-spirit union with Jesus, making us the one who is to 'let go and let God' and Him the one who grants them a pardon full and free. *"For as many [of you] as were baptized into Christ [into a spiritual union and communion with Christ, the Anointed One, the Messiah] have put on (clothed yourselves with) Christ"* (Gal 3:27 AMP).

In contrast to this, the injustices we have suffered, the emotional wounds inflicted, and our memories, are all soulish issues. And, unlike our spirit that is renewed in a moment -- the moment we embrace Jesus as our Lord and Savior -- our soul must be transformed by the renewing (or retrofitting) of our mind: the work of a lifetime.

Spirit/Soul Connection:
The following texts demonstrate the connection between spirit and soul: *"The human spirit is a lamp of Adonai (the Lord); it searches one's inmost being"* (Pr 20:27 CJB). ... *"You are my lamp, O Lord; You turn my darkness into light. With your help I can advance against a troop; with You my God, I*

can scale a wall" (2 Sam 22:29-30). ... "The Lord is my light and my salvation – whom shall I fear?" (Ps 27:1).

"Do not fret because of evil men or be envious of the wicked, for the evil man has no future hope, and the lamp of the wicked will be snuffed out" (Pr 24:19-20). ... "The lamp of the wicked is snuffed out; the flame of his fire stops burning. The light in his tent becomes dark; the lamp beside him goes out. The vigor of his step is weakened; his own schemes throw him down" (Job 18:5-7). "The light of the righteous shines brightly, but the lamp of the wicked is snuffed out" (Pr 13:9).

When the lamp of the Lord [our human spirit] is lit, our deep inner-being [our soul] is illuminated. King David no doubt understood this when he wrote: "Look deep into my heart, O God, and find out everything I am thinking. Don't let me follow evil ways, but lead me in the way that time has proven true" (Ps 139:23-24 CEV). It is this **spirit/soul connection that facilitates the healing and transformation of our soul**. The apostle Paul referenced this, saying:

"We are communicating a secret wisdom from God which has been hidden until now but which, before history began, God had decreed would bring us glory. Not one of this world's leaders has understood it; because if they had, they would not have executed the Lord from whom this glory flows. But, as the Tanakh (law) says, "No eye has seen, no ear has heard and no one's heart has imagined all the things that God has prepared for those who love him."

"It is to us, however, that God has revealed these things. How? Through the Spirit. For **the Spirit probes all things, even the profoundest depths of God. For who knows the inner workings of a person except the person's own spirit inside him**? So too no one knows the inner workings of God except God's Spirit.

"Now we have not received the spirit of the world but the Spirit of God, so that we might understand the things God has so freely given us. These are the things we are talking about when we avoid the manner of speaking that human wisdom would dictate and instead use a manner of speaking taught by the Spirit, by which we explain things of the Spirit to people who have the Spirit.

*"**Now the natural man does not receive the things from the Spirit of God – to him they are nonsense**! Moreover, he is unable to grasp them, because they are evaluated through the Spirit. **But the person who has the Spirit can evaluate everything**, while no one is in a position to evaluate him"* (1 Cor 2:7-15 CJB).

*"**If anyone is united with Jesus Christ, the Messiah, he is a new creation – the old has passed; behold, what has come is fresh and new**! ... God in Christ, the Messiah, is reconciling mankind to himself, not counting their sins against them, and entrusting to us the message of reconciliation. Therefore **we are ambassadors of the Messiah; in effect, God is making his appeal [to the world] through us**. ...*

"Be reconciled to God! God made this sinless one become a sin offering on our behalf, so that in spirit to spirit union with him we might fully share in God's righteousness" (2 Cor 5:17-21). ... *"Do you not know that your bodies are members of Christ himself?... he who unites himself with the Lord is one with him in spirit"* (1 Cor 6:15-17).

Only God and our own spirit knows what is in our subconscious mind, or soul. When we accept Jesus as our Lord and Savior, and are once again indwelt by Holy Spirit, Holy Spirit once again has access to our spirit and soul. This enables the process of soul transformation to begin. Here is what God Himself says concerning this process:

*"**This is what the Lord says**, he who made the earth, the Lord who formed it and established it – the Lord is his name: **'Call to me and I will answer you and tell you great and unsearchable things you do not know**. ... **I will bring health and healing** to it; **I will heal my people** and will let them enjoy abundant peace and security. I will bring [them] back from captivity and will rebuild them as they were before. **I will cleanse them from all the sin they have committed against me and will forgive all their sins of rebellion against me**. Then this [people] will bring me renown, joy, praise and honor before all nations on earth that hear of all the good things I do for it; and they will be in awe and will tremble at the abundant prosperity and peace I provide"* (Jer 33:2-9).

God has promised to cleanse our souls – which means He can and will edit our memories, forgive our sins, and heal our souls.

~ Questions, Concerns & Key Points ~

1. Unforgiveness blocks God's blessings; it prevents God from working in our life, and the life of those who we hold accountable to us; and contributes to our becoming like those we refuse to forgive.

2. Unforgiveness opens passageways into our soul, giving access to the powers of darkness.

3. Forgiveness is both a choice of our will, and our experientially releasing the injustices, and our wounded emotions, to God.

4. Understand the true meaning of forgiveness, based on the original languages.

5. We are to be Christ's Ambassadors to the world. We are to do the works of Christ. First, our soul [subconscious mind] must be cleansed; our spirit redirected (2 Cor 5:17-21).

Chapter 10 ~ Divine Editing of Memories:

Introduction:

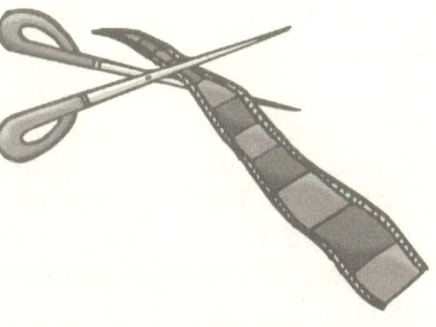

We closed the last chapter introducing the concept of the divine editing of our memories. Concerning this, David wrote: *"Have mercy on me, O God, according to your unfailing love; according to your great compassion blot out my transgressions.* **Wash away all my iniquity and cleanse me from my sin.** *Cleanse me with hyssop, and I will be clean; wash me, and I will be whiter than snow"* (Ps 51:1,2 & 7).

The author of the Book of Hebrews speaks of this, saying: *"When Christ came as high priest of the good things that are already here, he went through the greater and more perfect tabernacle that is not man-made, that is to say, not a part of this creation. He did not enter by means of the blood of goats and calves; but* **He entered the Most Holy Place once for all by his own blood, having obtained eternal redemption.**

"The blood of goats and bulls and the ashes of a heifer sprinkled on those who are ceremonially unclean sanctify them so that they are outwardly clean. **How much more, then, will the blood of Christ, who through the eternal Spirit offered himself unblemished to God, cleanse our consciences from acts that lead to death, so that we may serve the living God!"** (Heb 9:11-14).

Christ is eternal – He is not limited by time nor space – but is the Lord of all time, and Lord of the Universe. We are in Him and He is in us (Jn 14:20). We need only practice His presence – inviting Him into our present-moment affairs. The author of the Book of Hebrews mentions this concept, saying:

"Therefore, brothers, since we have confidence to enter the Most Holy Place by the blood of Jesus, by a new and living way opened for us through the curtain, that is, his body, and since we have a great priest over the house of God, **let us draw near to God with a sincere heart in full assurance of faith, having our hearts sprinkled to cleanse us from a guilty conscience** and having our bodies washed with pure water" (Heb 10:19-22).

God even promises that He will heal our backsliding! "Return, faithless people; **I will cure you of backsliding**" (Jer 3:22). ... "They will no longer defile themselves with their idols and vile images or with any of their offenses, for **I will save them from all their sinful backsliding, and I will cleanse them**. They will be my people, and I will be their God" (Ezek 37:23).

Divine editing does not remove one's memory of the injustices against them, but it does remove the sting. Jabez may have understood this principle since: *"his mother called his name Jabez, saying, [it is] because I bare him with sorrow. But, Jabez called on the God of Israel, saying, Oh that thou wouldest bless me indeed, and enlarge my border, and that thy hand might be with me, and that thou wouldest keep me from evil, that it be not to my sorrow! And God granted him that which he requested"* (1 Ch 4:9-10).

Jabez' blessings made him forget his pain and Jesus said this is how it will be for us as well. *"When a woman is giving birth, she is in pain; because her time has come. But when the baby is born, she forgets her suffering out of joy that a child has come into the world. So you do indeed feel grief now, but I am going to see you again. Then your hearts will be full of joy, and no one will take your joy away from you"* (John 16:21-22).

The Psalmist certainly grasped this concept. Consider his words: *"The cords of death entangled me, the anguish of the grave came upon me; I was overcome by trouble and sorrow. Then I called on the name of the L<small>ORD</small>: "O L<small>ORD</small>, save me!" The L<small>ORD</small> is gracious and righteous; our God is full of compassion. The L<small>ORD</small> protects the simplehearted; when I was in great need, he saved me. Be at rest once more, O my soul, for the L<small>ORD</small> has been good to you. For you, O L<small>ORD</small>, have delivered my soul from death, my eyes from tears, my feet from stumbling, that I may walk before You L<small>ORD</small>, in the land of the living"* (Ps 116:3-10).

God promised through the prophet Jeremiah: *"I will turn their mourning into gladness; I will give them comfort and joy instead of sorrow"* (Jer 31:13).... And, the apostle Paul assured is that: *"Godly sorrow brings repentance that leads to salvation and leaves no regret, but worldly sorrow brings death. See what this godly sorrow has produced in you: what earnestness, what eagerness to clear yourselves, what indignation, what alarm, what longing, what concern, what readiness to see justice done"* (2 Cor 7:10-11).

The more traumatic our memories, the more profound God's healing. Whether our trauma is grief-based, stemming from the loss of a loved one; violation-based, stemming from childhood abuse; rejection, or any other form of trauma – God can heal, and has promised to do so.

Regarding rejection, God promised: *"As I was with Moses, so I will be with you; I will never leave you nor forsake you"* (Josh 1:5). Concerning grief, we are promised that: *"God shall wipe away all tears from their eyes; and there shall be no more death, neither sorrow, nor crying, neither shall there be any more pain: for the former things are passed away"* (Rev 21:4).

Perhaps even more fascinating than God's ability to heal any and every form of trauma, is the fact that time is not a factor with God – He can bring healing in our life, as well as in our genetic stream! Isaiah wrote: *"the Lord shall be unto thee an everlasting light, and thy God thy glory. Thy sun shall no more go down; neither shall thy moon withdraw itself: for the LORD shall be thine everlasting light, and the days of thy mourning shall be ended"* (Is 60:19-20).

God is eternal. Everyone and all time, exists in His presence at all times. And, since we are in God, and He is in us (Jn 14:17-20; 15:4' 17:21), He has been with us every moment of our life. He has shared both the good times and the painful times, those times we felt loved and those when we experienced rejection. He was also there when we were being nurtured and when we were abused. He has never left us nor forsaken us. Why then, has He not intervened to protect us from harm; to prevent our sorrow and shame?

Freewill Guarantee:
He created us in His own image and likeness (Gen 1:26-27) including: His self-ownership, self-direction and freewill. As His children, God loves us so much, is so jealous of us, He honors and protects our freewill, even when doing so causes Him much sorrow and grief. God is all powerful, yet out of love and respect for us -- His children -- He chose to self-limit his power, to constrain His rights in this area; yielding to us even though it might cost us our life, and His. Jesus -- God in the flesh

-- came to earth, lived as a man, died in our stead and entered the netherworld [the abyss] to overcome Satan whose intent and purpose was, and is, to exterminate mankind, God's image and likeness.

Overcoming Satan, Jesus Christ arose from the grave, gaining victory over death for you, me, and all our descendants who will choose to embrace Him as their Savior and their Lord. In an effort to grasp the significance of this, consider the words of the author of the Book of Hebrews, who wrote:

*"**There is so, so little time**! The One coming will indeed come, he will not delay. But the person who is righteous will live his life through faith, but if he shrinks back, I will not be pleased with him. However, we are not the kind who shrink back and be destroyed; on the contrary, **we keep expressing faith and thus preserve our lives**! Faith is being confident of what we hope for, convinced about things we do not see. It was for this that Scripture attested the merit of the people of old. In faith, we understand that the universe was created through a spoken word of God, so that what is seen did not come into being out of existing phenomena"* (Heb 10:37-11:3).

Soul Restoration:
Jesus is not limited by time; neither is our spirit or our subconscious. If they were, we would not be able to remember past events nor dream about the future. To experience soul transformation and restoration, we must both, exercise our faith and use our imagination. In fact, faith and imagination are intertwined in the word 'hope'. Remember, *"faith is being confident of that which we*

hope for, convinced about things we do not see" (Heb 11:1). In other words, the realization of our soul healing, as well as the fulfillment of any of the other 8,000 plus promises in Scripture is dependent on our imagination plus faith.

Imagination alone is not sufficient. In fact, it can be very dangerous. We read about man's imagination gone wild in Genesis: *"The Lord saw that the wickedness of man was great in the earth, and that every **imagination** and intention of all human thinking was only evil continually"* (Gen 6:5). ... *"They hearkened not, nor inclined their ear to God, but walked in the counsels and in the **imagination** of their evil heart, and went backward, and not forward"* (Jer 7:24). But, with Christ everything is different. We are: *"Looking unto **Jesus the author and finisher of our faith**"* (Heb 12:2). This is why Scripture says, *"without faith it is impossible to please God, because anyone who comes to him must believe that he exists and that he rewards those who earnestly seek him"* (Heb 11:6).

Faith ~ Hope ~ Love:
The apostle Paul records the functional tie between our faith, our imagination and our action, that resuts in our creativity, saying: *"Three things last — trust, hope, love; and the greatest of these is love"* (1 Cor 13:13 CJB).

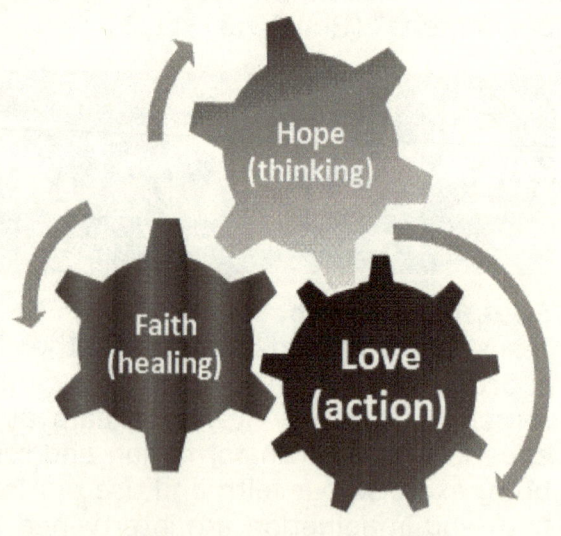

To grasp the difference between man's imagination run-a muck, vs., man's imagination combined with faith [hope], consider the following Scriptures:

*"You will surely forget your trouble, recalling it only as waters gone by. Life will be brighter than noonday, and darkness will become like morning. You will be secure, because there is hope [**imagination + faith**]; you will look about you and take your rest in safety. You will lie down, with no one to make you afraid, and many will court your favor"* (Job 11:16-19).

"The eyes of the L̲ord *are on those who fear him, on those whose hope [**imagination + faith**] is in his unfailing love, to deliver them from death and keep them alive in famine"* (Ps 33:18-19).

*"Evil men will be cut off, but those who hope [**imagination + faith**] in the* L̲ord *will inherit the land. A little while, and the wicked will be no more; though you look for them, they will not be found. But the meek will inherit the land and enjoy great peace"* (Ps 37:9-11).

The Psalmist understood this, relying on it as he commanded his soul concerning his state of being, or emotional state: *"Why are you downcast, O my soul? Why so disturbed within me? Put your hope [**imagination + faith**] in God, for I will yet praise him, my Savior and my God"* (Ps 42:5-6).

What does the Lord think of us using our imagination in this manner? *"The* L̲ord *delights in those who fear him, who put their hope [**imagination + faith**] in his unfailing love"* (Ps 147:11). ... *"I know the plans I have for you," declares the* L̲ord*, "plans to prosper you and not to harm you, plans to give you hope [**imagination + faith**] and a future. Then you will call upon me and come and pray to me, and I will listen to you"* (Jer 29:11-12).

Abraham, the father of the faithful, certainly understood this. *"Against all hope [**imagination +faith**], Abraham in hope [**imagination +faith**] believed and so became the father of many nations, just as it had been said to him, "So shall your offspring be." Without weakening in his faith, he faced the fact that his body was as good as dead – since he was about a hundred years old – and that Sarah's womb was also dead. Yet he did not waver through unbelief regarding the promise of God, but was strengthened in his faith and gave glory to God, being fully persuaded that God had power to do what he had promised"* (Rom 4:18-22).

The apostle Paul certainly understood the power of hope [**imagination + faith**], writing: *"And we rejoice in the hope [**imagination + faith**] of the glory of God. Not only so, but we also rejoice in our sufferings, because we know that suffering produces perseverance; perseverance, character; and character, hope [**imagination + faith**]. And hope [**imagination + faith**] does not disappoint us, because God has poured out his love into our hearts by the Holy Spirit, whom he has given us"* (Rom 5:2-5) ...

*"But hope [**imagination + faith**] that is seen is no hope [**imagination + faith**] at all. Who hopes [exercises **imagination + faith**] for what he already has? But if we hope [**imagination + faith**] for what we do not yet have, we wait for it patiently"* (Rom 8:24-25). ... *"Be joyful in hope [**imagination + faith**], patient in affliction, faithful in prayer"* (Rom 12:12-13). ...

Paul employs this concept to draw our hearts and minds heavenward: *"May the God of hope [**imagination + faith**] fill you with all joy and peace as you trust in him, so that you may overflow with hope [**imagination + faith**] by the power of the Holy Spirit"* (Rom 15:13). ... *"I pray also that the eyes of your heart may be enlightened in order that you may know the hope [*imagination + faith*] *to which he has called you, the riches of his glorious inheritance in the saints, and his incomparably great power for us who believe"* (Eph 1:18-19).

"The author of the Book of Hebrews even describes hope [*imagination + faith*] as the anchor of our soul: *"We have this hope [imagination + faith] as an anchor for the soul, firm and secure. It enters the inner sanctuary behind the curtain, where Jesus, who went before us, has entered on our behalf"* (Heb 6:19-20).

Soul Transformation Through Hope:
Relying on the Scriptures above, it is time to put this into practice in your own life. If you can remember -- remember anything -- you have an active imagination; and if you have a relationship with Jesus -- even though it may be a brand new relationship -- you have faith, for He is the author and perfecter of our faith (Heb 12:2). Having established that you have both an imagination and faith, the ingredients for hope, through which we lay claim to God's precious promises -- including His promises for healing, **it is now time to seek His face.**

For the very best results, you may wish to record the prayers that follow in your own voice, so that you can play them back while you rest in Jesus' arms. Why record these prayers in your own voice? Your own voice is the one most trusted by your subconscious mind, the voice that you have the least resistance to and are most likely to agree with and follow.

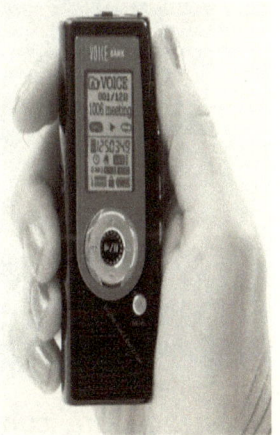

A Private Healing Session With Jesus:
Set aside at least an hour or so to meet with Jesus -- alone and undisturbed. find a chair, or couch, where you will be comfortable and can relax. You will probably want

to have a bottle or glass of water, and a box of tissues handy so that you won't need to interrupt your session with Jesus to go and get them. You may also wish to kick off your shoes and loosen your collar so you will be comfortable. And be sure to turn off your radio, CD player, TV and your telephone. You surely wouldn't want these to disturb your private session with Jesus.

Now, snuggle down in your chair, with your feet on the floor and your hands on your knees, palm down. Close your eyes to help shut out the world around you, and begin to relax. With your eyes still closed, take a few deep breaths and as you exhale, purse your lips and blow gently through your lips. This will force more oxygen into your blood stream, helping you relax even deeper.

When you are comfortably relaxed, with your eyes still closed, invite Father God and Jesus to join you. Remember, as a born-again Christian, Holy Spirit is already with you – in fact, in you. Jesus said: *"If anyone loves me, he will obey my teaching. My Father*

will love him, and we will come to him and make our home with him" Jn 14:23-24). ...
"On that day you will realize that I am in my Father, and you are in me, and I am in you" (Jn 14:20-21). Jesus prayer is: *"Father, just as you are in me and I am in you. May they also be in us"* (John 17:21). ... [Shh] *"Listen!"* Jesus said. *"I am standing and knocking at your [heart's] door. If you hear my voice and open the door, I will come in and we will eat [fellowship] together"* (Rev 3:20).

Quiet your intellect and then – linking your imagination with your faith, listen as Jesus speaks to you – spirit to spirit. Sense His presence. You may – many do – even smell His presence; catching a fresh, almost indescribable fragrance in the air. You may – some have – even felt His touch. Should doubt arise, you may hear Him whisper *"Why are you troubled, and why do doubts rise in your minds? ... Touch me and see; a ghost does not have flesh and bones, as ... I have"* (Luke 24:38-39).

Long ago David said: *"Taste and see [trust in your perceptions] that the Lord is good; blessed is the man who takes refuge in him. Fear the Lord, you his saints, for those who fear him lack nothing"* (Ps 34:8-9). ... *"Cast your cares on the Lord and he will sustain you"* (Ps 55:22).

Jesus said: *"If you are tired of carrying heavy burdens, come to me and I will give you rest. Take the yoke I give you. Put it on your shoulders and learn from me. I am gentle and humble, and you will find rest for your soul. For my yoke is easy to bear, and my burden [the one I will give you] is light"* (Matt 11:28-30).

Healing Prayers:
Following are typical prayers you may wish to use in future private sessions with Jesus. To optimize their effectiveness, you will want to record them in your own

voice – since your voice is the most acceptable to your subconscious mind. Today, however, join me as we pray these prayers together – inviting the Lord to come and edit our painful, destructive memories. Information contained in brackets [such as these] provides clarification or directions that you need to follow in order to realize the greatest release, and receive the fullness of all that God has promised.

Warning!
If you are one who has been subjected to ritualistic and/or satanic abuse, be certain that you have an experienced pastoral counselor – one experienced in spiritual warfare and deliverance with you during your prayer sessions.

Otherwise, your visualization of past horrendous events could give the Adversary of our souls an opportunity to vex you, inflicting more fear, anxiety and pain.

Prayer:
Father God, Lord Jesus and Holy Spirit; I know you have promised that you will be with me at all times, and I invite your presence now. Through the finished work of Your Beloved Son, Yeshua Messiah, and shrouded with His Robe of Righteousness, I enter Your Holy of Holies, and approach Your Throne of Grace.

I know, Father God, that You are not bound by time or space – that all time [past, present and future] is before you this moment, within the spirit realm. Holy Father, in Jesus' Name, and through the power of indwelling Holy Spirit, I ask You to illuminate my soul, and walk with me back in time, enabling me to remember the events that caused my soul-wounding; and to momentarily re-experience the sensory information concerning that incident [what I saw, heard, smelled, tasted and felt];

enabling You to edit the pain out of my memory of the incident; while maintaining the memory so that I may learn thereby.

[Allow yourself to engage your imagination, envisioning yourself being the age when the incident Holy Spirit illuminated, occurred. Envision yourself becoming that little girl/boy again. Remember what kind of a day it was – was it clear or cloudy? Warm, cool, or downright cold? Take time to identify those who were there with you, or around you. In your mind's eye, see the people, the environment – all of the details that you can see.

Listen, recalling all that was said, and all other pertinent sounds. Smell all the scents, aromas and/or stenches that filled the air. If you were eating or drinking, or even tasting anything – pleasant or otherwise – allow yourself to sense those flavors once again. Allow yourself to feel any physical touch associated with the incident. It may help for you to visualize the incident as though it were being displayed on a movie screen or on your television set. Finally, if during the incident, you sensed any demonic presence, allow yourself to very briefly re-experience this sensation – knowing that you are perfectly safe in God's presence.

Now, hold your hands out in front of you and cup them – like you were going to catch something. As we pray together, allow all the hurt – all the emotional pain – to flow up and out of your soul – out through your arms into your cupped hands.]

Now, praying together: *Heavenly Father, in Jesus' Name, I release all of this pain, all who were responsible for it, and all the incidents of injustice, to you. I trust completely in Your Word – that Your Son, Jesus: "anointed to announce good news to the poor, ... to heal the brokenhearted, to proclaim freedom to captives [those bound in chains as well as those bound by emotional wounds], to bring light to those bound in spiritual darkness, to proclaim ... the favor of the Lord ... to comfort all who mourn ... to provide for them, giving them ... the oil of gladness in place of their mourning, a cloak of praise in place of their heavy, weighted down spirit"* (Is 61:1-3).

[Now, holding up your outstretched arms visualize all of your hurt, all your pain, all of those who inflicted any injustice against you, and all of the incidents themselves, being taken from you by Jesus, and handed to His Father. Then, when your hands are empty, see and feel, Father God filling your cupped hands with the oil of gladness. When your cupped hands begin overflowing with the oil of gladness, pull your arms toward you and press your cupped hands to your chest, allowing God's oil of gladness – His love, joy and peace – to permeate your entire being, flooding your soul, filling your spirit, and invigorating your body.]

Now, praying together once again: *Jesus, I know, and trust in Your Word – that You "bore all [my] diseases, all the pains from which we have suffered ... [that You were] wounded for [my] crimes, crushed because of [my] sins; the discipline due [me – that makes us whole] fell on You, and by Your bruises, I am healed"* (Is 53:4-5).

Father God, Lord Jesus, Holy Spirit, forgive my sins, take my wounds, take my emotional pain. Erase the record of this event from Your Book of Remembrance; take away all of the pain; apply the Balm of Gilead (Jer 8:22; 46:11).

[See – in your imagination (the eyes of your spirit) – Father God (Abba, or Daddy God), applying the Balm of Gilead to your spirit (to the inner-core of your being). Seated with Christ in the Holy of Holies – in heavenly places (Eph 2:6); look down on the incident and see it as God sees it. Identify the Principality of this dark world (the demonic spirit ruling over the geographic region); identify the Ruling Power – the demonic Strongman, that rules over the type of injustice you suffered; finally, identify the cosmic forces influencing the person or persons who are abusing you.]

Now, praying with me: *In Jesus' Name and authority, I command you Principality of (name the area); Strongman of (name the type of injustice); and the cosmic forces influencing (name the person or persons); I bind you and break the power you have exercised over me. And now, through the power of Indwelling Holy Spirit, I compel you to depart my soul, to leave my presence, being cast away – into outer darkness – where you will be made a part of Christ Jesus' footstool, until He return to exercise judgment against you.*

[Now, in Jesus' Name and Authority, renounce all of your negative thoughts, emotions, attitudes, beliefs and life-commandments that developed in your soul as a result of the incident or incidents Holy Spirit has illuminated. This may include things such as anger, rage, hostility, bitterness, resentment, hate, self-hate, homicidal and/or suicidal thoughts.

It may also involve pride, rebellion, arrogance, obstinacy, defiance, rejection, abandonment, accusations, blaming, mocking, lying, betraying, deceiving, fear, anxiety, panic, sadness, depression, lust, incest, pedophilia, bestiality, and many other things.]

Praying with me: *Father God, in Jesus' Name, and through the empowerment of Holy Spirit, Who indwells me, I now renounce all the [identified] demons of darkness in my life, commanding them to flee! Holy Spirit, I invite You to fill the voids created in my soul by the departure of the demons of darkness; I implore You to fill these voids with Your Holy presence and write on the walls of my heart, the will of Father God.*

In Jesus' Name, and through His intercession, I now address my abuser, or abusers, recognizing that they are – in their spirits, and by the will of Jesus – present this very moment. [Speaking out their names], In Jesus' Name, I now forgive you, releasing you to Father God, simultaneously setting myself free from you, and all that you subjected me to.

Father God, in the Name of my Lord and Savior, Jesus Christ, I ask that You direct Holy Spirit to edit my memory of this event; removing the sting, the pain, and any influence over my life. I know that Your "Word is living and active; sharper than any double-edged sword – cutting through to where [my] soul meets [my] spirit .. and it is quick to judge [my] inner reflections and attitudes ... [For] Before You, nothing created is hidden" (Heb 4:12-13).

Father God, through the blood of Jesus, "Cleanse me with hyssop, and I will be clean; wash me, and I will be whiter than snow; let me [my soul] hear the sound of joy and gladness ... Turn away Your face from my sins and blot out all of my crimes. Create in me a clean [pure] heart, O God, and renew in me a resolute spirit.

... Restore my joy in Your salvation, and let a willing spirit uphold me" (Ps 51:7-12).

Thank you, Father God, Lord Jesus and Holy Spirit, for healing me ["Heal me, O Lord, and I will be healed" (Jer 17:14).]*; Thank You for "purifying my conscience"* (Heb 9:14)*; for editing my memories, for restoring my soul* (Ps 23:3). *I now receive the freedom You were sent to proclaim, Lord Jesus* (Lk 4:18).

I invite You, Holy Spirit, to restore my soul, repairing all the chinks in my spiritual armor. Quicken my spirit and remind me to forgive quickly and not internalize the injustices of others. Help me not to take offense, but to "Cast my cares on the Lord, trusting that He will sustain me" (Ps 55:22). *I henceforth invite You, Jesus, to be the Lord of my life, governing (controlling and directing) every function of my being, and every activity in my life.*

According to Your promise, I now take a stand against the Adversary of my soul, and resist all demons, knowing that they must flee from me (Jas 4:7). *Thank You, Father God, that You have made known to me the glorious riches of the mystery of salvation, through Your Beloved Son, Jesus Christ, which is in me, my hope of glory in the coming age – Amen!* (Col 1:27).

As King David penned long ago: *"Taste and see that the Lord is good; blessed is the man who takes refuge in Him"* (Ps 34:9). ... *"The Lord helps and delivers them from the wicked and saves them, because they take refute in Him"* (Ps 37:40).

Jesus said: *"I am the vine; you are the branches; if a man remain in me and I in him, he will bear much fruit; apart from me you can do nothing. ... If you remain in me and my words remain in you, [you may] ask whatever you desire, and it will be given you"* (Jn 15:5). The apostle Paul said: *"In Him we live, and move, and have our being"* (Acts 17:28).

[Engaging your imagination, and exercising your faith in God's precious promises, see yourself encased within your Lord Jesus; wearing His Robe of Righteousness. See yourself encapsulated within Him, standing before the throne of Father God – Lord Almighty – Creator of the Cosmos. Hear Him say: *"Well done, my good, trustworthy and faithful child"* (Mt 25:21). Feel the presence of Holy Spirit – within your spirit – reconciling you to Father God, in and through Christ Jesus (2 Cor 5:19).

~ Questions, Concerns & Key Points ~

1. God is eternal – not limited by time or space. All events occurring everywhere and at any time in earth's history, are always in God's present-moment view.

2. Christ – being a part of the eternal Godhead – is not limited by time or space.

3. Born-again Christians, being in God and having God in us, are not limited by time or space.

4. Soul transformation occurs through hope, which is the combination of imagination plus faith.

5. Man is designed so that the movement of his hands stimulates specific brain functions – a feature called 'neurolinguistic programming.'

6. For those who have backslidden and are bound by guilt and shame, God has promised to heal our backsliding.

Chapter 11 ~ The Battle For Your Soul

Introduction:

Virtually every Christian understands that Satan is the Adversary of our souls. However, many do not understand who his messengers and helpers are. Many have been taught, and therefore believe, the fallen angels are the forces of evil against which we are to contend. But, Jesus made it clear that Satan's compatriots are the demons – which Christ gave us authority over.

Mark, the author of the earliest Gospel, said: *"He appointed twelve – designating them apostles – that they might be with him and that he might send them out to preach and to have authority to drive out demons"* (Mark 3:14-16). Reporting on their ministry, Mark wrote: "They went out and preached that people should repent. They drove out many demons and anointed many sick people with oil and healed them" (Mark 6:12-13).

Matthew, one of the later authors, wrote: *"These twelve Jesus sent out with the following instructions: "Do not go among the Gentiles or enter any town of the Samaritans. Go rather to the lost sheep of Israel. As you go, preach this message: 'The kingdom of heaven is near.' Heal the sick, raise the dead, cleanse those who have leprosy, drive out demons"* (Matt 10:5-8).

And Luke – the physician on a team of seventy-two whom Jesus had commissioned – wrote: *"When Jesus had called the Twelve together, he gave them power and authority to drive out all demons and to cure diseases, and he sent them out to preach the kingdom of God and to heal the sick"* (Luke 9:1-2). He also records the results of this assignment, saying: *"The seventy-two returned with joy and said, "Lord, even the demons submit to us in your name"* (Luke 10:17).

Some have asserted that this authority was restricted to the twelve mentioned by Mark and Matthew; others claim it was limited to the seventy-two that Christ sent to the Israelites. However, in what has come to be known as "The Great Commission" Jesus gave His disciples specific instructions concerning their ministry after His departure, saying: *"All authority in heaven and on earth has been given to me. Therefore go and make disciples of all nations, baptizing them in the name of the Father and of the Son and of the Holy Spirit, and teaching them to obey everything I have commanded you. And surely I am with you always, to the very end of the age"* (Matt 28:18-20).

Clearly, Jesus intended the transfer of authority to extend to those the disciples taught as wells as themselves. And, there are some who believe that this is where our authority over demons and the power to heal, etc., came to an end – with the death of those who the apostles discipled. However, this is not what the apostles themselves indicated. For example, Peter – speaking to those he was ministering to – said:

"Repent and be baptized, every one of you, in the name of Jesus Christ for the forgiveness of your sins. And you will receive the gift of the Holy Spirit. The promise is for you and your children and for all who are far off — for all whom the Lord our God will call" (Acts 2:38-39). Or, as the Jewish Version says: *"For **the promise is for you, for your children, and for those far away — as many as Adonai our God may call!**"*

This sounds like the authority Christ transferred onto His apostles is pretty inclusive – including themselves, their families, and even for those far away [or far off in the future] – a many as the Lord our God calls out of darkness into His glorious light.

Peter, speaking of this, said: *"You are a chosen people, a royal priesthood, a holy nation, a people belonging to God, that you may declare the praises of him who called you out of darkness into his wonderful light. Once you were not a people, but now you are the people of God"* (1 Peter 2:9-10).

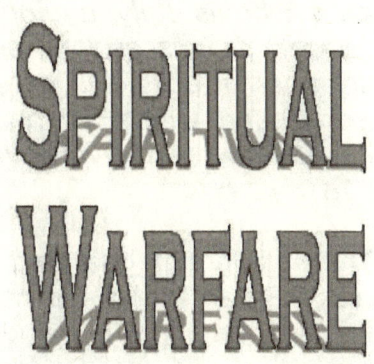

We are in a spiritual battle – a battle for the souls of men: your soul and mine. Jesus, speaking in parable to the Scribes and Pharisees, said: *"How can Satan expel Satan? If a kingdom is divided against itself, that kingdom can't survive; and if a household is divided against itself, that household can't survive.*

"So if Satan has rebelled against himself and is divided, he can't survive either; and that's the end of him. Furthermore, no one can break into a strong man's house and make off with his possessions unless he first

ties up the strong man. After that, he can ransack his house"* (Mark 3:23-28 CJB).

King David, caught up in this battle long before Mark wrote his Gospel, said: *"He makes me swift and sure-footed as a deer and enables me to stand on my high places. He trains my hands for war until my arms can bend a bow of bronze; You give me your shield, which is salvation; your answers make me great. You lengthen the steps I can take, yet my ankles do not turn.*

"I pursued my enemies and wiped them out, without turning back until they were destroyed. I destroyed them, crushed them; they can't get up; they have fallen under my feet. "For you braced me with strength for the battle and bent down my adversaries beneath me. You made my enemies turn their backs in flight, so that I could destroy those who hate me" (2 Sam 22:34-41 CJB).

Doctor Luke – Paul's contemporary and companion – who it id believed used Mark's Gospel to write his, provides a bit of clarification, saying: *"When a strong man who is fully equipped for battle guards his own house, his possessions are secure. But when someone stronger attacks and defeats him, he carries off all the armor and weaponry on which the [strong] man was depending, and divides up the spoils"* (Luke 11:21-23 CJB).

The strongman guarding his house in Christ's parable, was Satan. His armor and weaponry are the Principalities, Powers and Cosmic Forces that rule over the Kingdom of Darkness. The possessions being guarded are the souls of men that they have taken into bondage. The stronger man, in Christ's parable, who carries off the inferior strongman's possessions, is Christ himself, who redeems us, setting us free.

Concerning this, the apostle Peter, said: *"For Christ died for sins once for all, the righteous for the unrighteous, to bring you to God. He was put to death in the body but made alive by the Spirit, through whom also he went and preached to the spirits in prison who disobeyed long ago when God waited patiently in the days of Noah while the ark was being built"* (1 Peter 3:18-20).

Our Victorious Savior:

The proclamation Jesus made to the imprisoned spirits was a proclamation of victory! He had overcome Satan, the fallen angels Satan had deceived, and the horde of demons – the spirits of the Nephilim – under his command. The apostle Paul, commenting on this, said: "Not one of this world's leaders has understood it; because if they had, they would not have executed the Lord from whom this glory flows" (1 Cor 2:8-9 CJB).

Following His declaration of victory, before the demonic forces, Jesus told His disciples: *"Be brave! I have conquered the world!"* (John 16:33). He also revealed to them: *"I saw Satan fall like lightning from heaven. Remember, I have given you authority; so you can trample down snakes and scorpions, indeed, all the Enemy's forces; and you will remain completely unharmed. Nevertheless, don't be glad that the spirits submit to you; be glad that your names have been recorded in heaven"* (Luke 10:18-20 CJB).

Transfer of Authority:
Jesus Christ transferred His authority over all demonic forces onto His apostles, and them whom they would subsequently transfer it to – even to them who were far off [or far removed in time.] The apostle Paul, speaking of this transfer of authority, wrote:

"Each one of us, however, has been given grace to be measured by the Messiah's bounty. This is why it says, "After he went up into the heights, he led captivity captive and he gave gifts to mankind."

"Now this phrase, "he went up," what can it mean if not that he first went down into the lower parts, that is, the netherworld? The one who went down is himself the one who also went up, far above all of heaven, in order to fill all things. Furthermore, he gave some people as Emissaries [Ambassadors, Missionaries], some as Prophets, some as Proclaimers of the Good News [Evangelists], and some as Shepherding-Teachers [Pastoral-Counselors].

"Their task is to equip God's people for the work of service that builds the body of the Messiah, until we all arrive at the unity implied by trusting and knowing the Son of God, at full manhood, at the standard of maturity set by the Messiah's perfection.

"We will then no longer be infants tossed about by the waves and blown along by every wind of teaching, at the mercy of people clever in devising ways to deceive. Instead, speaking the truth in love, we will in every respect grow up into him who is the head, the Messiah.

"Under his control, the whole body is being fitted and held together by the support of every joint, with each part working to fulfill its function; this is how the body grows and builds itself up in love" (Eph 4:7-16 CJB).

Satan is Defeated!
Satan is defeated, his demise is sure. None the less, we must – as Peter warned: *"Stay sober, stay alert! Your enemy, the Adversary, stalks about like a roaring lion looking for someone to devour. Stand against him, firm in your trust, knowing that your brothers throughout the world are going through the same kinds of suffering. You will have to suffer only a little while; after that, God, who is full of grace, the one who called you to his eternal glory in union with the Messiah, will himself restore, establish and strengthen you and make you firm"* (1 Peter 5:8-11 CJB).

The Mop-up Task:
Knowing that Satan – the Adversary of our souls – is roaring about seeking to devour us is one thing; understanding the tricks of his trade is another; and it is our comprehension of this that will help us wage a winning war in the spirit realm. Christ's victory over Satan determined the final outcome of this Conflict of the Cosmos, but there is still mop-up work to be done; and this task has been assigned to the church.

In 1944, Lt. Hiroo Onoda, of the Japanese Army, was dispatched to the remote Philippine island of Jubang. His mission – conduct guerrilla warfare against the Allied Forces. As Onoda and his comrades were preparing to debark their ship, to carry out their individual missions, their company commander gave them this order:

"You are absolutely forbidden to die by your own hand. It may take three years, it may take five, but whatever happens, we'll come back for you. Until then, so long as you have one soldier, you are to continue to lead him. You may have to live on coconuts; if that's the case, live

on coconuts! Under no circumstance are you to give up your life voluntarily."

Onoda took these words far more seriously than his commander had ever imagined. He was at his assigned post just a time, when on September 2, 1945, Japan surrendered. Unfortunately, Lt. Hiroo was never officially notified that the war had ended; so for the next twenty-nine (29) years, Onoda lived in the jungle, hiding out, awaiting further instructions.

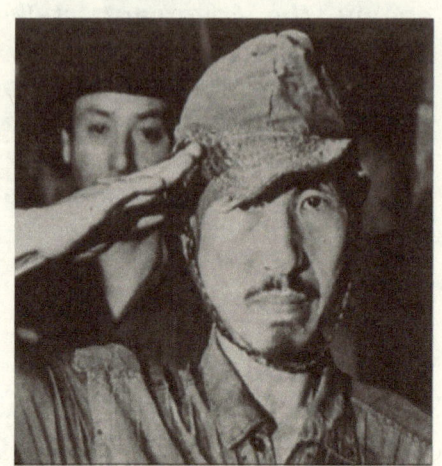

Surviving on coconuts and bananas, he managed to evade searching parties, who he believed were enemy scouts. If Onoda had made an effort to carry out the guerrilla warfare he had been charged with, he would have soon learned of his country's defeat and the victory of the Allied Forces. But, Onoda was more concerned for his own life, than for the outcome of his guerrilla warfare mission. The consequence for this was his hiding out in the jungle until the prime of his life was past. Even worse, his service for his Emperor and Country, had been totally obviated by his compulsion to save his own life.

When finally found and convinced the war had indeed ended, Mr Onoda, now 83, wept uncontrollably as he agreed to lay down his rifle, unaware that Japanese forces had surrendered 29 years earlier. He returned to Japan the same year, but was unable to adapt to the changed life in his home country, so he emigrated to Brazil in 1975.

Defeated Christians:
Many people – professing to be Christians – have a great deal in common with Lt. Hiroo Inoda. But, unlike him, they are on the winning side. None the less, they seem totally unaware that their enemy has been defeated and is on the run. Thus, instead of living a victorious life, they are running from him! They are proud to be known as Christians, and may even hold an office, or serve on the staff of their local church; but when it comes down to carrying out warfare in the spirit realm – against Satan, the Adversary of their soul – they hide, being more concerned for the pleasures of this life, than they are about defeating the enemy.

As a result, these Christians live a defeated life, even though their side is victorious. They miss out on the abundant life Christ promised His disciples; and in the end, they stand to lose their own life – their spirit life – and share the lake of fire and brimstone with the Adversary whom they refused to fight.

What a sad, sad situation, when Christ has provided all the weaponry we will ever need, both to insure our success in battling the Enemy, and for saving our own – and others' souls. Paul describes this sad situation, saying:

"Although we do live in the world, we do not wage war in a worldly way; because the weapons we use to wage war are not worldly. On the contrary, they have God's power for demolishing strongholds. We demolish arguments and every arrogance that raises itself up against the knowledge of God; we take every thought

captive and make it obey the Messiah. And when you have become completely obedient, then we will be ready to punish every act of disobedience" (2 Cor 10:3-6 CJB).

Think of it: we have all the power needed to demolish the strongholds – those we;;-guarded houses of the strong men [Principalities, Rulers and Cosmic Forces of the Kingdom of Darkness.] In contrast, our Adversary, the devil, is confined to the Abyss and must rely on the demons to do his bidding – the same demons over whom Christ gave his disciples, and the church, authority! Knowing that he has been conquered, Satan – from his prison – dispatches demons, to carry out his guerrilla warfare against Christ's victorious church and His disciples.

Satan's Scheme"
Satan has – through the demons – mobilized an organized attack against the church, designed to make Christians a reproach before the world that they are commissioned to reconcile to Christ. By thus oppressing us, he endeavors to make Christians' evangelistic efforts ineffective, thus deferring his own final annihilation.  Not allowed by God to destroy our spirits, Satan dispatches his demons to torment our souls; continually bombarding our conscious and subconscious thought processes: our thoughts, imaginations, emotions, beliefs, values, attitudes, defense-mechanisms, etc.

If successful, these demons will keep us from experiencing God's love; from sharing in God's abundant provision; from enjoying God's protection. Unfettered, they will also damage, or destroy, our relationships, socioeconomic status and environment. They seek to prevent us from manifesting God's likeness to the world, from experiencing, and sharing, His magnificent love with others.

~ Questions, Concerns & Key Points ~

1. As born-again Christians we are automatically a warrior in the greatest battle of all time – spiritual warfare between God's holy angels vs. Satan and the demons.

2. Satan's battle plan is to take dominion of mens' souls.

3. Yeshua Messiah [Jesus Christ] fought the battle against Satan for us and was victorious, winning authority over all spiritual principalities, powers and cosmic forces.

4. Jesus transferred His authority over these spirit entities to His apostles, and through them to all born-again believers.

5. In Christ, we are already victorious; we need only learn to identify Satan's schemes of spiritual oppression, and engage him and the demons in battle, for we are promised that if we resist, they will flee.

Chapter 12 ~ Satan's Warfare Tactics:

Satanic & Demonic Warfare Tactics:
This section continues the identification of Satan's and the demons' warfare tactics against us; followed with a section designed to facilitate soul healing, restoration and transformation.

1. **Deception** ~ i.e., *"Now the serpent – Satan – was more **crafty** (**deceptive**) than any of the wild animals the Lord God had made"* (Gen 3:1). *"The great dragon was thrown out, **that ancient serpent, also known as the Devil and Satan** [the Adversary], **the deceiver of the whole world**. He was hurled down to the earth, and his angels were hurled down with him"* (Rev 12:9 CJB).

   *"**The Adversary who had deceived** them was hurled into the lake of fire and sulfur, where the beast and the false prophet were"* (Rev 20:10 CJB).

2. **Lies** ~ i.e., *"You belong to your father, Satan, and you want to carry out your father's desires. **From the start he was a murderer**, and **he has never stood by the truth, because there is no truth in him**. When he tells a lie, he is speaking in character; because **he is a liar — indeed, the inventor of the lie!**"* (John 8:44-45 CJB).

3. **Threats and intimidation** ~ *"They scoff and speak with malice, they loftily utter threats. They set their mouths against heaven; their tongues swagger through the netherworld"* (Ps 73:8-9 CJB).

4. **Inciting conflict and quarrels** ~ *"Keep reminding people of this, and charge them solemnly before the Lord not to engage in word-battles. They accomplish nothing useful and are a catastrophe for the hearers!"* (2 Tim 2:14-15 CJB).

5. **Temptation** ~ When Satan was tempting Him, Jesus responded, saying: *"It is written also, You shall not tempt, test thoroughly, or try exceedingly the Lord your God"* (Matt 4:7). And, the apostle Paul gave instructions to help us avoid being tempted by Satan. Speaking primarily to married couples, he wrote:

"Do not refuse and deprive and defraud each other [of your due marital rights], except perhaps by mutual consent for a time, so that you may devote yourselves unhindered to prayer. But afterwards resume marital relations, lest Satan tempt you [to sin] through your lack of restraint of sexual desire" (1 Cor 7:5).

Temptations is apparently one of Satan's favorite ploys for in His Model Prayer, Jesus prayed: *"And lead us not into temptation, but deliver us from the evil one"* (Matt 6:13).

Satan's Warfare Objective:
Satan's objective is to regain, and exercise, dominion over mankind, claiming the world as his own. He commands the demons under his authority to lie, threaten, deceive, intimidate, instigate conflicts and quarrels; and anything else they believe might work, seemingly attempting to entice mankind to join them. However, demonic forces have no human allies. *"The thief comes only to steal, kill and destroy"* (Jn 10:10).

Satan's Warfare Methodology:
Satan and his demonic forces seek to obstruct our freewill. Their methodology for gaining control over mankind is eightfold:
1. Developmental and Relational Trauma
2. Substance Abuse and Other Compulsions & Addictions
3. Illicit and/or Deviant Sexual Activity
4. Involvement in the Occult
5. Audiovisual Over-stimulation
6. Physical and Psychological Illnesses
7. Cultist Religious Activities
8. Trans-generational Predispositions for Psychological, Physiological, Relational and Behavioral Disorders

Let's look at each of these carefully, to understand how they can entrap us; and to develop strategy to defend ourselves in this spiritual battle.

Developmental & Relational Trauma ~ Severe or prolonged trauma – either developmental or relational – can create sufficient emotional stress to inhibit the body's production of the essential reward hormones. When this happens, it results in the onset of **Reward Deficiency Syndrome**; the precursor for numerous psychological and physiological disorders that are more fully enumerated below. This trauma results in one focusing on their soulish well-being rather than the well-being of their spirit; which gives the demons a foothold, or passageway, into their soul.

Substance Abuse, Addictions and Obsessive-compulsive Disorders ~ Substance abuse, as well as other addictions and compulsive behaviors [i.e., pornography, sexual addictions, gambling, compulsive spending, etc.] as well as compulsive behaviors [i.e., running exercise, television, shopping, etc.] all create an altered state of consciousness, artificially stimulating, or inhibiting, certain of the body's essential reward hormones. The result is that they all turn one's focus from one's inner-man and spiritual things, to carnal things [desires of the flesh.] Any altered state of consciousness, however achieved, provides a foothold, or passageway, into our soul for demons.

Sexual addiction and compulsive behaviors have the ability to artificially stimulate the excessive production of certain reward hormones, while inhibiting others. In the truest sense, pornography, sex addiction and activity addictions are psychoactive substance addictions, created by one's own internal chemistry. Over time, the abuse of psychoactive substances, and/or one's involvement in compulsive activities, will contribute to the onset of **Reward Deficiency Syndrome**, contributing to relational conflict, chaos, and catastrophe – and will cause serious physical and psychological disorders.

Illicit & Deviant Sexual Activities ~ In addition to contributing to the onset of Reward Deficiency Syndrome, illicit and deviant sexual practices and fantasies – including fantasizing and masturbating – contribute directly to relational conflict, chaos and catastrophe, by fostering a sense of dissatisfaction, promoting instrumental sex – where one uses his/her sexual partner as an instrument or tool, to achieve orgasmic fulfillment without meeting the spiritual, emotional and physical needs of their partner.

Sexual activity of any variety that occurs outside the marriage bed is illicit, involving two forms of spiritual violation: porneia and molcheia. Porneia includes all forms of sexual perversion and deviancy including prostitution, sexual fantasy and masturbation. Molcheia speaks to the double-bonding that occurs through extra-marital affairs. Being spiritual violations, these activities provide an open doorway into our soul for demons.

Illicit and deviant or perverted sexual activity also contributes to Erectile Dysfunction and Premature Ejaculation in males and orgasmic problems in females. They contribute to the spread of Sexually Transmitted Diseases (STD's), of which there are about twenty-five (25) varieties.

God designed mankind in such a way that partners – who have taken time bonding before achieving sexual fulfillment – develop antibodies to protect them against any bacteriological or viral disorder the other may carry. But, when insufficient time was invested in the bonding process, or steps within the process were skipped, these important antibodies are not developed, increasing the likelihood for passing STD's.

If one has multiple sexual partners, not only does the risk of passing STD's back and forth occur; there are additional, more worrisome complications. Because the protective antibodies are lacking, males are far more likely to develop prostatitus and prostate cancer; and females are far more likely to develop endometriosis and cervical dysphasia.

Involvement in the Occult ~ Occult involvement includes one's participation in clandestine, or hidden, things such as idol worship, divination, fortune-telling, curses, casting spells, astrology, spiritualism, litohmancy (spirit-writing), numerology, alchemy, extra-sensory perception (ESP), necromancy, rituals involving aberrant sex, and the sacrifice of animals – and sometimes humans.

Occult activities are efforts to achieve extra-human power by defying God or trying to usurp powers reserved unto God Himself. As such, all occult involvement provides a direct doorway into our soul for demons. A few of the Scriptures that mention occult involvement, prohibiting one's involvement therein, include the following:

- *"Let no one be found among you who sacrifices his sons or daughters in the fire, who practices divination or sorcery, interprets omens, engages in witchcraft, or casts spells, or who is a medium or spiritist, or who consults the dead. Anyone who does these things is detestable to the Lord"* (Dt 18:10-12).

- *"When you look up into the sky and see the sun, the moon and the stars – all the heavenly array – do not be enticed into bowing down to them and worshiping things the Lord your God has apportioned to all the nations under heaven"* (Dt 4:19).

- *"The images of their [other nations'] gods you are to burn with fire. Do not covet the silver and gold on them, and do not take it for yourselves, or you will be ensnared by it, for it is detestable to the Lord your God. Do not bring a detestable thing into your house, or you – like it – will be set apart for destruction"* (Dt 7:25-26).

- *"Disaster will befall you, and you won't know how to charm it away; calamity will come upon you, and you won't be able to turn it aside; ruin will overcome you, suddenly, before you know it. So for now, keep on with your powerful spells and your many occult practices; from childhood you have been working at them; maybe they will do you some good, maybe you will inspire terror! You are worn out with all your consultations – so let the astrologers and stargazers, the monthly horoscope-makers, come forward now and save you from the things that will come upon you!"* (Isa 47:11-13 CJB).

- *"It is perfectly evident what the old nature does. It expresses itself in sexual immorality, impurity and indecency; involvement with the occult and with drugs"* (Gal 5:19-20 CJB).

- *"The cowardly, the untrustworthy, the vile, the murderers, the sexually immoral, those involved with the occult and with drugs, idol-worshipers, and all liars — their destiny is the lake burning with fire and sulfur, the second death"* (Rev 21:8 CJB).

Some other common satanic techniques or rituals engaged in that are mentioned in Scripture, include the following:

- Voodoo, employed to 'snatch away' portions of one's soul, replacing those portions of one's thoughts, imaginations, emotions, attitudes, beliefs, memories, etc., with those of demonic spirits.

    "As heat and drought snatch away the melted snow, so the grave [the dead] snatches away those who have sinned" (Job 24:19).

- Fortune-telling ~ *"Son of man, turn your attention to the daughters of your people. What they prophesy comes out of their own minds (imagination). So prophesy against them. Tell them, 'The Lord and King says, "How terrible it will be for you women who sew magic charms to put around your wrists! You make veils of different lengths to put on your heads. You do those things to trap people. You trap my people. But you will also be trapped. ...*

    "You told lies to my people. They like to listen to lies. You killed those who should have lived. And you spared those who should have died." "'So the Lord and King says, "I am against your magic charms. You use them to trap people as if they were birds. I will tear them off your arms. I will set free the people you trap like birds. I will tear your veils off your heads. I will save my people from your powerful hands. They will no longer be under your control. Then you will know that I am the Lord" (Ezek 13:17-21 NirV).

- Ekankar, or soul-travel. The Hebrew word *'uwph'* that has been translated 'fly away' literally means to wax faint or break away. Soul travel literally breaks away one's soul – piece by piece. This technique is so effective the Soviets and Iranians are investigating using the tactics of witches to gain dominance over people, enabling them to control them – particularly political leaders of countries they consider their enemies.

- Sexual Encounters with Demons ~ Giving one's self sexually to demons is a practice common among those deeply involved in the occult. Sexual orgasms with demonic forces results in soul bondage, causing soul-pairing, or bonding, with demons.

Audio Visual Over Stimulation ~

Satan, prior to his rebellion and fall, was named Lucifer, meaning Light-bearer, or the Standard-bearer of the sacred colors. *"You put the seal on perfection; you were full of wisdom and perfect in beauty; you were in 'Eden, the garden of God; covered with all kinds of precious stones – carnelians, topaz, diamonds, beryl, onyx, jasper, sapphires, green feldspar, emeralds; your pendants and jewels were made of gold, prepared the day you were created. You were a cherub, protecting a large region; I placed you on God's holy mountain. You walked back and forth among stones of fire. You were perfect in your ways from the day you were created, until unrighteousness was found in you"* (Ezek 28:12-15).

Lucifer was also leader of the heavenly choir. *"The workmanship of thy tabrets and of thy pipes was prepared in thee in the day that thou wast created"* (Ezek 28:13). The term 'tabrets and pipes' refers to musical instruments [see Gen 31:27; 1 Sam 10:5; Is 5:12; Is 30:12; etc.).

Fallen, Lucifer – now Satan, the Devil or the Serpent – still had the same characteristics, even though they were now perverted. He was – and is – still capable of using music and colors (art) to captivate his audience. He still applies these abilities, but now uses them for destructive, rather than constructive purposes – for wickedness rather than for righteousness.

Music and art [audio and visual effects] enter one's soul through their subconscious mind, rather than through their conscious mind. The subconscious mind 'thinks' in pictures and symbols, but is not capable of analyzing. Thus, what comes into our subconscious mind is just accepted as fact. Therefore, music and art have a much greater effect on one – for good or for ill.

Both music and art – particularly video art – have found their way into the healing arts. Sounds and pictorial symbols, when presented in low intensity, produce a state of calm, reflective meditation. In contrast, heightened intensities of both music and video-art create headaches, dizziness, disorientation, and fatigue, resulting in neurological distress.

Similarly, colors have an effect on one's psyche, and through one's mind-body connection, they actually affect one's physical well-being. The more subtle tones create soothing emotions, while more intense colors, and more complex patterns of colors and shapes, create confusion, agitation and a host of other negative emotions and attitudes.

Understanding this, there has developed both music and art therapies and professional therapists. While promising, there is a word of caution: know your therapist well; since music and video-art are passageways into your soul.

Physical and Psychological Illnesses ~ Whether one realizes it or not, we are all caught up in spiritual warfare – the conflict of the cosmos. The Old Testament Psalmist suggests that even babies and infants are engaged in spiritual warfare, long before they can intellectually comprehend it: *"Adonai! Our Lord! How glorious is your name throughout the earth! The fame of your majesty spreads even above the heavens! From the mouths of babies and infants at the breast you* *established strength because of your foes, in order that you might silence the enemy and the avenger"* (Ps 8:2-3 CJB).

Another translation of this Scripture says: *"Our Lord and Ruler, your name is wonderful everywhere on earth! You let your glory be seen in the heavens above. With praises from children and from tiny infants, you have built a fortress. It makes your enemies silent, and all who turn against you are left speechless"* (Ps 8:1-2 CEV).

James, the brother of our Lord, Jesus Christ, wrote: *"Do you suppose the Scripture speaks in vain when it says that there is a spirit in us which longs to envy? But the grace he gives is greater, which is why it says, "God opposes the arrogant, but to the humble he gives grace." Therefore, submit to God. Moreover, take a stand against the Adversary, and he will flee from you"* (James 4:5-8 CJB).

Both physical and psychological disorders impair one's full functionality, and can weaken one's ability to effectively conduct spiritual warfare if that person focuses on their impairment, rather than carrying out – within their ability – aggressive spiritual warfare.

<u>Physical Illnesses</u> ~ Physical illnesses weaken our constitution and entice us to focus on our problem rather than on God's power to heal, thereby impairing our ability to carry out spiritual warfare. Since demons actually cause disease, our focus on our physical health, may provide a passageway into our soul. Luke, a physician himself, wrote:

"Yeshua was teaching in one of the synagogues on the Sabbath and, a woman came up [to him] who had a spirit which had crippled her for eighteen years; she was bent double and unable to stand erect at all. On seeing her, Yeshua called her and said to her, "Lady, you have

been set free from your weakness!" He put his hands on her, and at once she stood upright and began to glorify God" (Luke 13:10-13 CJB).

There are numerous other Scriptures that record Jesus' affirming that all illness is demonic – not that the ill person is evil, but that they are being demoniacally oppressed. For example: *"When evening came, many who were demon-possessed were brought to him, and he drove out the spirits with a word and healed all the sick. This was to fulfill what was spoken through the prophet Isaiah: "He took up our infirmities and carried our diseases"* (Matt 8:16-17).

On another occasion, *"As Jesus and his disciples were on their way, some people brought to him a man who could not talk because a demon was in him. After Jesus had forced the demon out, the man started talking. The crowds were so amazed that they began saying, "Nothing like this has ever happened in Israel!"* (Matt 9:32-33 CEV). ... *"Some people brought to Jesus a man who was blind and could not talk because he had a demon in him. Jesus healed the man, and then he was able to talk and see. The crowds were so amazed that they asked, "Could Jesus be the Son of David?"* (Matt 12:22-23 CEV).

<u>Emotional Disorders and/or Mental Illness</u> ~ Demonic possession is a rare phenomenon in our culture and our day, although it occurs more often than most people realize. Many illnesses once considered to be manifestations of demonic possession [i.e., Schizophrenia, Tourettes Syndrome, Manic-Depressive Disorder, etc.], have been reclassified by medical science as being manifestations of biological or neurological malfunctions.

We have, in some ways, distanced ourselves too far from the idea of demonic involvement in these illnesses. It is true that we see few instances of demonic possession [where one has surrendered the control of their spirit to a demon or demons], but instances of demonic infestation are still quite common. After all, any aberrant thinking – all thought process disorders – are influenced by the powers of darkness who have come to steal, kill and destroy (Jn 10:10).

Examples of this demonic involvement can be seen in the following Scriptures: *"Suddenly a man with an evil spirit in him entered the meeting place and yelled, "Jesus from Nazareth, what do you want with us? Have you come to destroy us? I know who you are! You are God's Holy One." Jesus told the evil spirit, "Be quiet and come out of the man!" The spirit shook him. Then it gave a loud shout and left. Everyone was completely surprised and kept saying to each other, "What is this? It must be some new kind of powerful teaching! Even the evil spirits obey him"* (Mark 1:23-28 CEV).

This man quite obviously was not possessed since he still had his faculties – choosing to enter the synagogue. He was in control of his physical faculties, but his soul was infested – resulting in him manifesting demonic activity, both emotionally and mentally.

One of Satan's favorite ploys is for two or more demons under his command to infest one of God's children. This creates mental confusion, contributing to: identity disturbance, often manifest through sexual identity disorders [i.e., homosexuality, bisexuality and bestiality]; to what scientists call Disassociative Identity Disorder (DID), Ego-state Disorder (ESD), Multiple Personality Disorder (MPD), Bipolar or Manic-Depressive Disorders, and a host of other mental or emotional illnesses.

Severe illness – whether physical, emotional or mental – compromises one's ability to effectively conduct spiritual warfare [to resist the powers of darkness]. This creates chinks or cracks in one's spiritual armor – a break in their wall of defense, providing demons a passageway into their soul.

Cultic Religious Activities ~ Cults differ from the occult in that the occults are secret societies that are openly opposed to Christ and Christianity, while cults are organized groups of individuals who call themselves Christians. We refer to them as religions. Cultism practices – compared to activities encouraged in the Scriptures, or the personal faith of believers – encompasses the totality of externalized religious practice and observance.

A 'cult' quite literally refers to the care one gives – the worship one directs – to anything or anyone not specifically embodied in, and directed by, Scripture. Cults can be recognized by their established, often rigid, religious disciplines, rules and regulations. Thus, in a sense, any group of individuals who believe in our Lord and Savior, Jesus Christ, and follow the Scriptures to the best of their ability, yet draw distinctions between themselves and other Christians, is a cult.

Cultist activities include: established rituals, rules, regulations, ceremonies and liturgy [or form of worship.] They often embrace icons, such as idols, shrines, 'holy' pictures or venerated sites, where visions are said to be received, or where healing occurs. Dedicated centers of religious pilgrimage are also indicative of cultist practice.

These activities inhibit the move of Holy Spirit on the one hand, and tend to separate believers into disassociated bands that foster prejudice. As such, they provide passageways for demonic forces to penetrate the souls of their adherents.

Trans-generational Predispositions for Psychological, Physiological and Behavioral Disorders ~ The apostle Paul, speaking of those things that keep us in bondage, wrote: *"We know that the Law is spiritual. But I am merely a human, and I have been sold as a slave to sin. In fact, I don't understand why I act the way I do. I don't do what I know is right. I do the things I hate. Although I don't do what I know is right, I agree that the Law is good. So I am not the one doing these evil things. The sin that lives in me is what does them.*

"I know that my selfish desires won't let me do anything that is good. Even when I want to do right, I cannot. Instead of doing what I know is right, I do wrong. And so, if I don't do what I know is right, I am no longer the one doing these evil things. The sin that lives in me is what does them.

"The Law has shown me that something in me keeps me from doing what I know is right. With my whole heart I agree with the Law of God. But in every part of me I discover something fighting against my mind, and it makes me a prisoner of sin that controls everything I do. What a miserable person I am. Who will rescue me from this body that is doomed to die?

"Thank God! Jesus Christ will rescue me. So with my mind I serve the Law of God, although my selfish desires make me serve the law of sin. If you belong to Christ Jesus, you won't be punished. The Holy Spirit will give you life that comes from Christ Jesus and will set you free from sin and death.

"The Law of Moses cannot do this, because our selfish desires make the Law weak. But God set you free when he sent his own Son to be like us sinners and to be a sacrifice for our sin. God used Christ's body to condemn sin. He did this, so that we would do what the Law commands by obeying the Spirit instead of our own desires" (Rom 7:14 – 8:4 CEV).

The Law of Moses stated: *"I am the Lord your God, and I demand all your love. If you reject me, I will punish your families for three or four generations. But if you love me and obey my laws, I will be kind to your families for thousands of generations"* (Ex 20:5-6 CEV (See also 34:7; Num 14:8; Dt 5:9).].

The Law of Sowing and Reaping: [*"Don't delude yourselves: no one makes a fool of God! A person reaps what he sows. Those who keep sowing in the field of their old nature, in order to meet its demands, will eventually reap ruin; but those who keep sowing in the field of the Spirit will reap from the Spirit everlasting life"* (Gal 6:7-9 CJB)] is the law of the flesh mentioned by Paul in Romans 7. It is the law of genetics, from which only the substitutionary sacrifice of Christ Jesus could liberate us.

This law of genetics is the trans-generational passageway that enable demons that have oppressed – and infested – our ancestors [familial spirits or demons] to oppress us. They have one distinct advantage over us – unlike us, they have greater longevity, giving them a multi-generational understanding of the weaknesses in the spiritual defenses of one's genetic stream. These result in chinks or cracks in the walls of our soul, providing passageways for demons.

Demons of Disease ~ There are many more 'tricks of the trade' that Satan and his demons employ against the children of God, including: all diseases – bacteriological, viral, fungal, genetic, addictions, and on and on. Satan and his horde of demons are accurately described as being like ravenous lions skulking about unseen – or roaring if it better suits the occasion – as they seek whom they may devour.

Consistent with these unseen demonic beings, are the unseen attacks against, and holds over, God's children. Their objective in all of this is to steal, kill and destroy the souls of men (Jn 10:10). To accomplish this, while avoiding detection, and their victims' defensive counter-attacks, they focus their attacks on the deep parts of man's soul – his subconscious mind, which is outside the control of one's conscious, analytical mind.

Jekyll & Hyde: Hot Buttons & Triggering Mechanisms The idea of someone 'pushing your buttons' or Visa. Versa., activates subconscious triggering mechanisms – triggering one's subconscious defense mechanisms. When triggered, these produce an incongruence or dissonance between one's conscious (analytical) and

subconscious (symbolic) thought processes. This dissonance is manifest through a reactive lifestyle – often referred to as the "Dr. Jekyll/Mr. Hyde Dual Personality."

This dissonance in thought processes contributes to a form of Post-traumatic Stress Disorder (PTSD), manifest through hypersensitivity to certain conditioned responses, similar to persons with biological mental disorders termed Organic Brain Syndrome – meaning they have certain deficits in their 'wiring.'

Their habitual patterns of aberrant thinking and reactive behaviors produce what has been called 'triggering mechanisms' or 'hot-buttons.' Once established, these develop subconscious life-commandments (or directives) triggering negative behaviors – behaviors the person usually tries to excuse by saying: "I just couldn't help it." Little do they – or others whom they offend – realize that they are being attacked by demons.

This duality of thoughts creates relationship havoc, contributing to parent/child conflict, spousal conflicts, extra-marital affairs, marital separations, divorces, workplace conflict, loss of jobs and financial distress, obsessive compulsive disorders (OCD), substance abuse and addictions, plus a host of other relational issues and stressors. These stressors in turn, contribute to a host of mood and personality disorders – which, in turn, contribute to psychosomatic ailments and a host of physical disorders – all triggered by demonic attacks.

Mind-Body Medicine:
Many people, seeking healing – emotional (psychological) and/or physical – through prayer, medical approaches, alternative therapies, or any combination thereof – without realizing any significant relief, do not, and can

not, respond to these approaches until their soul is healed [freed from demonic infestation, restored and transformed.]

Medical report after medical report, and book after book, have been written on the subject of 'mind-body medicine' – focusing on the mind-body connections and associated illnesses. Out of this extensive research has grown a new medical approach called "Mind-Body Medicine" which uses the power of the patient's own thoughts to influence their health. While an excellent approach, it often fails, either because the underlying demonic influence has not been dealt with, or because occult meditation is taught rather than biblical meditation.

~ Questions, Concerns & Key Points ~

We have listed only two key points, but each of them has several aspects, or components – each one very important for you to be aware of:

1. Identify Satan's warfare tactics?

2. Identify Satan's warfare methodology?

Chapter 13 ~ Soul Healing & Discipleship

Introduction:
The New Testament Church was, by Christ's design, to be a healing community. He commissioned His disciples to go forth into all the world, teaching others what He had taught them; healing the sick, casting out demons,  and raising the dead. Jesus' own ministry clearly demonstrated the relationship between healing [body, soul and spirit] and discipleship.

The word 'disciple' – and, as Christians, we are all called to be disciples – stems from a word meaning 'teacher-learner.' Neither of these roles – in and of itself – makes one a disciple: it takes both. Disciples of Christ must always be learning [seeking to know God at a deeper level, and understand His will for their life], and always be teaching [imparting to others, what the Lord has revealed to them.] Anything less than this, is not discipleship.

During our years of clinical counseling, we have worked with scores of individuals suffering from physical ailments, afflicted with psychological disorders, struggling with addictions and other life-controlling compulsivities, experiencing occupational disorders, struggling under relationship woes and financial distress, all because of unresolved – unhealed – soul wounds.

Recognizing this, we developed a one year – fifty-two lesson – discipleship program. The first half of the program was tailored to the person's presenting problem

– i.e., addictions, domestic violence, shop-lifting, voyeurism, etc. This was followed by an in-depth Insight and Reality Therapeutic approach, designed to help the person gain new insights into their life experiences, by bringing them into the light and then testing the reality of their beliefs about them.

This technique – which incorporates forgiveness [or letting-go] of the past, helped them resolve past injustices they had suffered, facilitating soul restoration, healing and transformation. The efficacy of this approach was measured, by administering standardized psychometric assessments, at the time of their enrollment, at the half-way, and upon their completion of the program.

Employing this therapeutic approach, the outcomes [results] were phenomenal. At the time of enrollment, nearly ninety percent (90%) of our clients – most of whom were court ordered participants – met the diagnostic criteria for one or more psychological disorders, and were experiencing a collage of physical ailments.

At the half-way point in the therapeutic [discipleship] program, their assessment results were often more alarming than the findings with entering the program; but this was merely the result of them becoming less defensive and guarded – and more open and honest – than when enrolling. In proof of this, upon their completion of the program, more than eighty-five percent (85%) of those who had met the diagnostic criteria for multiple psychological disorders, evidenced no psychological problem whatsoever.

In addition to resolving their psychological disorders, and mitigating their presenting problem, many of their physical ailments were healed, or were in remission; many spontaneously decided to complete long deferred educational objectives; others made significant occupational changes; and still others gave up their illegal activities [such as Marijuana cultivation] and entered the competitive job market, applying their skills in honest employment.

Marriages were restored; parent/child, employer/employee, sibling, and other relationships were healed, and a host of other issues in their lives – outside the primary focus of their program – were resolved, remedied, or eliminated altogether. Issues that had seemed hopeless to these clients responded to discipleship soul restoration and transformation.

To better understand the effects of demonic attacks against our souls, and to better comprehend soul transformation, the following chapters examine some of the marvelous – God ordained – complexities of the human spirit and soul, from a medical, or scientific viewpoint.

Healing Prayers:
In the last chapter we identified Satan's eightfold warfare strategy against mankind, the church and the family. Here we include guidelines for prayers to address each technique in Satan's strategy. To gain the most from this, you will want to use a recorder and after praying make a CD or continuous tape that will enable you to listen to your prayers over and over again, while you sleep.  While asleep, your subconscious mind is fully awake and alert – yet, your

defense-mechanisms are not deployed, allowing your prayers to effect meaningful changes.

James, the brother of our Lord, provided us admonition that seems most appropriate here: He said: *"Submit to God. Moreover, [resist] – take a stand – against the Adversary, [Satan and the demons] and he [they] will flee from you. Come close to God, and he will come close to you. Clean your hands, sinners; and purify your hearts, you double-minded people! Wail, mourn, sob! Let your laughter be turned into mourning and your joy into gloom! Humble yourselves before the Lord, and he will lift you up [exalt you"* (James 4:7-10 CJB).

The apostle Paul's comments supports this: *"God causes everything to work together for the good of those who love God and are called in accordance with his purpose; because those whom he knew in advance, he also determined in advance would be conformed to the pattern of his Son, so that he might be the firstborn among many brothers; and those whom he thus determined in advance, he also called; and those whom he called, he also caused to be considered righteous; and those whom he caused to be considered righteous he also glorified!"* (Rom 8:28-30 CJB).

First, let us enter the heavenly Holy of Holies, and, covered with Christ's Robe of Righteousness, approach Father God's Throne of Grace. *Father God, in the Name of Your Beloved Son, Yeshua Messiah, and covered with His Robe of Righteousness, I humbly approach Your Throne of Grace; and praying in my spirit, I ask Holy Spirit, Who indwells my spirit, to convey to you my thoughts and emotions, in words I cannot utter. Thank You, that through the sacrifice of Your Son, I can now stand in Your presence, Father God.*

[Looking at the typical prayers that follow, pray into each area that has been a struggle in your life]:

- <u>Addictions</u> ~ Father God I renounce any and all past involvement in: substance abuse and other addictions, compulsive behaviors, and poor impulse-control that has manifest itself in episodes of anger and rage;

- <u>Sexual Issues</u> ~ Father, I renounce all past illicit, deviant and perverted sexual activities, all pre-marital and/or extra-marital affairs, sexual fantasies and masturbation;

- <u>Overstimulating Activities</u> ~ Father, I renounce my involvement in music and/or audiovisual activities that were over-stimulating – creating an altered mood state;

  I ask you, Father God, to cut-off the effect of these activities on my soul and to heal any chink or crack in my soul caused by these, so there be no passageway for demons into my soul, and no place for them to gain a foothold to oppress me;

- <u>Aberrant Behaviors</u> ~ Father God, I renounce and and all aberrant behaviors, such as explosive anger, a-motivational behavior, poor-impulse control, or other aberrant behavior;

- <u>Developmental Trauma</u> ~ Father, I come before You in the Name of Your Son, Jesus Christ – Who died for me – to seek healing in my soul caused by past developmental trauma, and all trans-generational predispositions for psychological and/or physiological diseases [genetic mutations];
- <u>Relationship Wounds</u> ~ Father, I renounce all those things I have done – intentionally or unintentionally – that have wounded my relationships with my spouse, children, parents, brothers and sisters, employers, employees,

business proprietors, neighbors, and others, and I seek forgiveness for my wounding acts, and express forgiveness for those who have wounded me; and I seek healing and restoration in my relationships;

- *Cultic Religious Practices ~ Father, I renounce all the distorted doctrines and beliefs that I have assimilated in the cults I have been involved in and I ask You to wash away all false doctrines and inappropriate practices from my soul; I ask You to forgive the leaders of these cults and, to cut my soul loose from theirs. Father, I ask that You open my spirit and soul to receive Your truths and, close my soul and spirit to falsehood and errors, and grant me the discernment to tell the difference between spiritual truths and cultic teachings.*

- *Closing Prayer ~ Father God, I stand in Your presence – before Your Throne of Grace – and ask you to commission a sufficient number of angels to guard me and join me in spiritual warfare against the powers of darkness that oppress me; to insure that I become an overcomer; so that when man's work on earth is done, I will hear You say, ""Excellent! You have been a good and trustworthy servant. ... Come, join in your Master's joyfulness, as one of my beloved children" – Amen (Matt 25:23 CJVP).*

~ Key Points ~

1. Identify issues that have been shown to respond to heaking prayer?

2. What is the relationship between discipleship, soul transformation, and soul-healing?

Chapter 14 ~ The Complexities of Man
(Body ~ Soul ~ Spirit)

Our Amazing Body:
As humorous as it is, the booklet cover depicted right, is about where we need to begin in oder to understand relationships between body, mind and spirit: mind vs. soul; spirit vs. heart; and the so called 'mind-body' connection. The human body is comprised of about 100 trillion cells, over 600 muscles, and 22 internal organs.

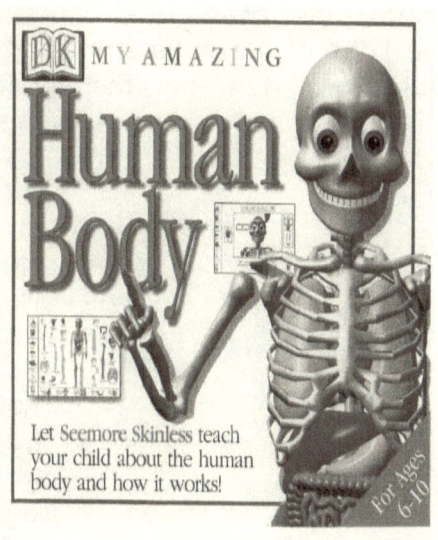

Every square inch of the human body exhibits about 19 million skin cells. Every hour, about one billion cells in the human body die and are replaced. The average human has approximately 100,000 hairs on his/her head. Our circulatory system – comprised of arteries, veins and capillaries – is about 60,000 miles long.

The circulatory system is unbelievable. The human heart beats more than 2.5 billion times in an average lifetime. It develops enough pressure to spurt blood thirty feet! While the entire length of the circulatory system approaches 60,000 miles in length, a red blood cell, dispatched from the heart, completes its circumnavigation of the body, and returns in less than 20 seconds!

The tongue is the strongest muscle in the body, and on its surface and in the throat, and on the roof of the mouth, there are about 9,000 taste buds. The human – the most complex organ, other than the brain, is composed of more than two million working parts. The eye blinks more than ten billion times each year, and can process more than 36,000 bits of information every hour. Under the right circumstances, the eye can discern the light of a candle from a distance of fourteen miles. During the average lifespan, it will bring one about 24 million pictures – images of the world around us.

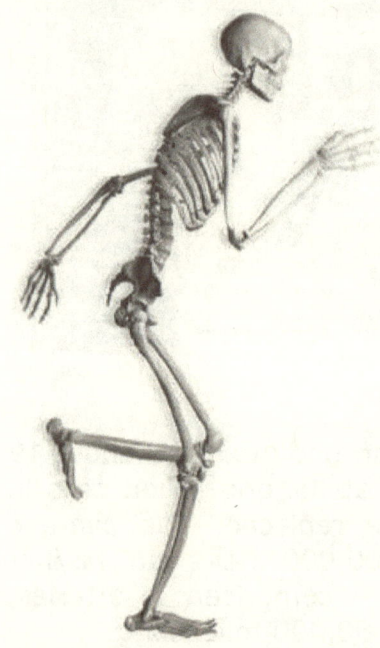

The skeletal system is just as amazing. One-fourth of the bones in the entire body are located in one's feet. When born, we have nearly 350 bones, but as we mature, some of these – e.g., those in the cranium and the pelvis – fuse together, leaving adults only 206. Bones are, in themselves, living organisms that can repair themselves when injured or broken. The design of bones – being hollow – makes them stronger and lighter than if they were solid. And, their hollow center is not empty: it is a beehive of activity, creating red and white blood cells that carry oxygen and a collage of nutrients to each and every cell in the body.

The human ear and auditory system is equally astounding. The folds of cartilage surrounding the ear, called the pinna begin attenuating (changing) the sound waves; these changes providing

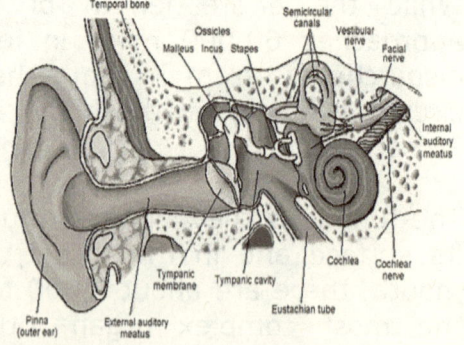

additional information that help the brain determine the direction from which the sounds came. The ear canal amplifies sounds and at the far end of the ear canal is the eardrum (or tympanic membrane), which marks the beginning of the middle-ear.

Sound wave information travels across the air-filled middle-ear cavity via a series of delicate bones called the hammer, the anvil and stirrup. These act as a kind of a teletype, converting the lower-pressure sound vibrations into higher-pressure sound vibrations, transmitting these to the cochlea, located in the inner-ear.

Connected to the cochleas is the cochlear duct which contains an extracellular fluid similar in composition to the fluid usually found inside of cells. The organ of Corti is located at the end of this duct, which transforms the mechanical waves into electric signals in neurons. The Corti forms a ribbon of sensory epithelium which runs lengthwise the cochlea's entire length. Its hair cells transform the fluid waves into nerve signals. From here, further processing leads to a panoply of auditory reactions and sensations that are conveyed to, and interpreted by, the brain.

These are just a few of the wondrous facts that describe a few of the many complex systems within the human body. All of these systems, such as the circulatory, respiratory, excretory, urinary, digestive, reproductive, immune, skeletal, muscular, endocrine and immune systems, are governed from one, quite small, command center – the brain, which is, in itself, an amazingly complex organ.

The Human Brain:
The human brain weighs a mere three pounds – about half the weight of our skin. The cerebrum, the largest part of the brain, makes up nearly eighty-five percent (85%) of its weight. What's in the brain that weighs so

much? Water! That's right – water comprises up to seventy-five percent (75%) of the total weight of your brain. Then, there is the oft referenced 'gray matter' and the less notable 'white matter.' Of the two, the white matter accounts for approximately sixty percent (60%), while the more well known gray matter makes up only forty percent (40%).

The brain contains nearly one hundred billion (100,000,000,000) neurons, and each neuron has between one thousand (1,000) to ten thousand (10,000) synapses [junctions that permit each neuron to pass an electrochemical signal (or charge) on to adjacent cells.] The human brain, which comprises only one to two percent (1% to 2%) of an individual's body weight, is the largest of all species. The elephant's brain, in comparison, weighs a mere fifteen hundredths of one percent (0.15%) of its body weight.

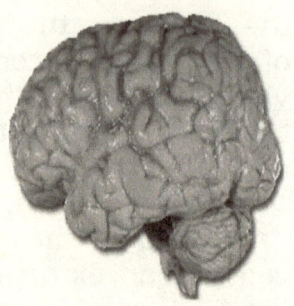

There are more than one hundred thousand (100,000) miles of blood vessels within the brain. During one's intrauterine experience, brain neurons develop at the rate of two hundred fifty thousand (250,000) each minute. A newborn baby's brain grows to about three times its size by the time the child reaches three, then grows more slowly, reaching its full size when one is about eighteen (18).

Even then, structural changes occur within the brain until one is about twenty-six (26); and new neurons continue to grow throughout one's lifetime in direct response to one's mental activity. Each time one has a new thought, or recalls a memory, he or she is creating new neural connections within their brain. The capacity for feeling emotions, such as happiness, joy, fear, embarrassment, etc., are already well developed at birth; however, the brain itself feels no pain, since there are no pain receptors within the brain.

The average number of thoughts one has during a day exceeds seventy thousand (70,000), which is nearly three thousand (3,000) per hour, or fifty (50) each minute. During the average lifetime of seventy (70) years, this would equate to approximately one billion, eight hundred million (1,800,000,000) thoughts! During one's wakeful hours, the brain generates somewhere between ten and 23 watts of power – enough electrical energy to illuminate a light bulb.

Our brain is tremendously flexible, capable of processing information at the rate of one-half (0.5) to one hundred twenty (120) meters per second [or about 268 miles per hour], and adjusting this speed automatically to meet the present need. Whenever we blink our eyes – about twenty thousand (20,000) times a day – our brain kicks in, keeping our environment illuminated within our imagination, thereby keeping our inner-world from becoming dark.

Inside the Brain:

Taking a closer look at the brain, you can see that the precen[tral gyrus, or motor cortex] makes [up the area where we percei]ve [temper]ature; and fr[om where] [vol]untary moven[ts of] [every] our ho[rmone] [bod]y part, the mo[ve].

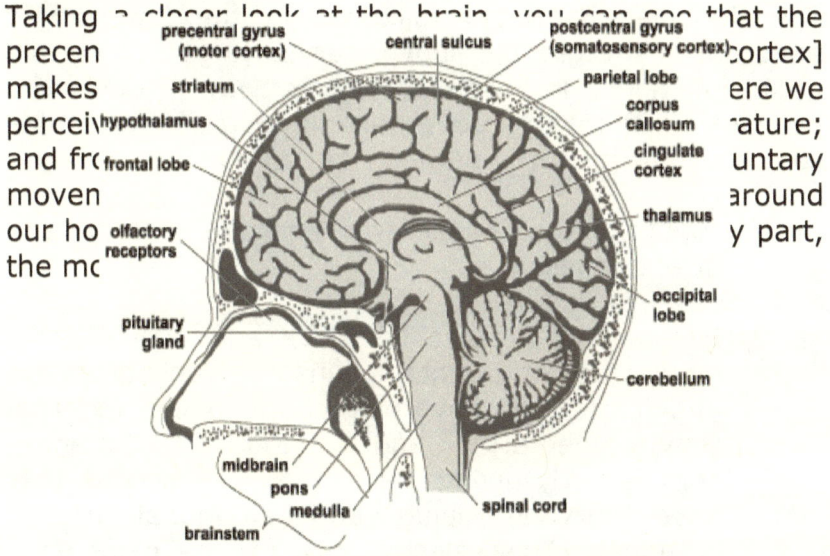

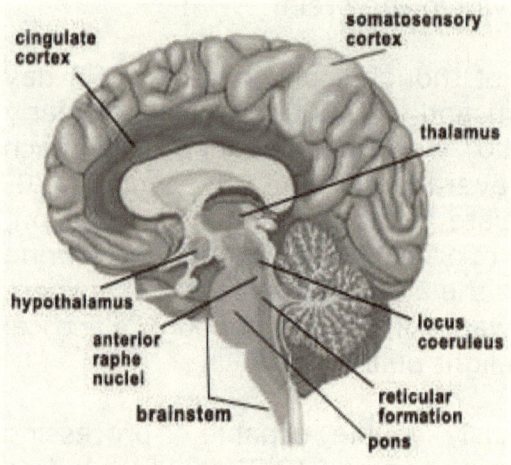

Pictured left, one can see that the Somatosensory and Cingulate Cortex lies the Limbic System. This center governs five major drives: fear, anger, hunger, love and sex. The Limbic System can be activated in two ways: [1] extremal stimuli through our five senses; and [2] internal stimuli through our own imagination and self-talk or inner dialog. The external stimuli represents only fifteen to eighteen percent (15% to 18%) of an experience – the other eighty-two to eighty-five percent (82% to 85%) stemming from our own imagination and inner-dialog. These in turn, are governed by the Reticular Formation.

The Reticular Formation:
The Reticular Formation pictured in the lower right quadrant of the graphic above, serves to govern certain brain functions, in much the same way – but more complex – than the governor on a gasoline engine controls it. It has three primary functions:

1. Maintaining general wakefulness and attentiveness;

2. Maintaining a selective focus and activation of intellectual thoughts, sensory feelings, and imagination – governing both one's external [environmental] and internal [imagery stimulation]; giving preference to functions that have survival value and emotional impact potential. [This selectivity is, for the most part,

an automatic, semi-conscious function; however, the will is also activated giving rise to deliberate decision-making.

3. Maintaining internal homeostasis; limiting what one accepts or rejects by what they consider normal. It accomplishes this through:
    - Resisting any information outside the bounds of what one considers normal,
    - Restraining one from behaving in a manner outside the limits of that considered safe and normal,
    - Rejecting information and opportunities not consistent with one's belief systems, that have been under construction since conception,
    - Dictating what one believes they can or cannot be and/or do,
    - Determining what one believes they do, or do not deserve,
    - Contributing to what one believes about their capabilities and limitations, abilities and disabilities,
    - Affecting the outcomes of everyday situations, circumstances and events, such as the outcome based on the above limitations one has established.

System Control:
As complex as our brain is, it is governed by yet an even more complex network of neurons. One computer governing the operation of another isn't as easy as it may sound, but it is often essential. During the years while I was working in the field of engineering, I was associated with the firm that designed the Bay Area Rapid Transit System [BART].

While with them, there was an incident involving a computer

glitch that allowed one train to crash into the rear of another. To resolve this systemic weakness, a second, smaller but very complex, computer was installed to govern the operations of the main computer; that managed the integral movement of many trains over miles and miles of track.

The Enteric, or Belly, Brain:
Compared to the design of our anterior brain, the enteric, or belly brain, is comprised of a thin sheath of extremely sensitive neural cells lining the gastrointestinal tract [our esophagus, stomach, upper intestine, pancreas, and gallbladder.]

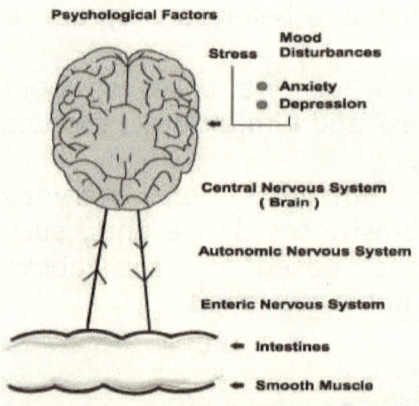

This enteric brain contains about one billion neurons – that is (1,000,000,000) – about the same number as our spinal cord, or the front lobe of our brain. It operates pretty much independently from our central nervous system – the (CNS). Disruptions in the enteric brain create little, if any, impairment in the gastrointestinal tract, pancreas or gallbladder. However, congenital and/or acquired derangements within the enteric system are well recognized causes of digestive tract disorders.

The health and well-being of our enteric brain dictate, to a large degree, our overall health and well-being, and govern the manner in which our thought processes function. The majority of our essential reward hormones

– those that govern our moods and thought processes – originate within the enteric brain. Ninety-five percent (95%) of the body's Serotonin – the hormone that keeps us from becoming depressed, that enables us to get up and get going in the morning, that controls our anger and impulse-control, is created within the enteric brain.

One hundred percent (100%) of the body's GABA, our body's own endogenous Benzodiazapam – a chemical, similar to Valium or Xanax – that prevents anxiety, panic attacks and paranoia, is made in the belly brain; as is seventy percent (70%) of the body's Dopamine – the hormone that enables us to feel pleasure, enjoy a sense of well-being, and prevent disorders such as Parkinson's Disease and Tourette's Syndrome, is made in the belly brain. Finally, almost eighty percent (80%) of the body's Acetylcholine – the hormone that contributes to our energy, our mental focus, our ability to concentrate, reason and remember, originates in the enteric system.

The enteric brain is connected to our anterior brain by a special group of neurons depicted in the adjacent graphic. These neurons are designed to selectively send about nine messages to the anterior brain for every one it receives back. Why this difference? Consider for a moment the words of Jesus, when speaking to the Samaritan woman at the well. He told her:

"Everyone who drinks this water will be thirsty again, but whoever drinks the water I give him will never thirst. Indeed, **the water I give him will become in him a spring of water welling up to eternal life***"* (John 4:13-14). Our Lord believed this principle – which he conveyed to this woman to be of such import, he repeated it.

"On the last day of the Great Festival – Hoshana Rabbah – Yeshua stood and cried out, "If anyone is thirsty, let him keep coming to me and drinking! Whoever puts his trust in me, as the Scripture says, rivers of living water will flow from his inmost being!" [Now he said this about the Spirit, whom those who trusted in him were to receive later – the Spirit had not yet been given, because Yeshua had not yet been glorified]" (John 7:37-39 CJB).

Jesus was no doubt referring to the words of Jeremiah, the prophet, who wrote: *"My people have committed two evils: they have abandoned me, the fountain of living water, and dug themselves cisterns, broken cisterns, that can hold no water!"* (Jer 2:13 CJB). ... *"All who abandon you will be ashamed, those who leave you will be inscribed in the dust, because they have abandoned Adonai, the source of living water"* (Jer 17:13 CJB).

The Hebrew word, *'mah'-yim'*, that Jeremiah used in these texts, that has been translated 'water', is elsewhere more correctly translated 'juice,' 'urine,' or 'semen.' Taken in the context that Jeremiah used it; and as referenced by Christ, it refers to life-giving streams of fluids. The source of these streams, according to Jeremiah, stems from the Hebrew word, *'maw-kore'*, that has been translated *fountain*, however, a more correct translation would be *'umbilical cord.'*

This is consistent with the word Christ used for the source of these streams, that has been translated, 'inmost-being.' It stems from the Greek words, [ek tee's 'koilias'], meaning 'out of his belly,' or 'out of the womb.'

How, pray tell, do the umbilical cord and the womb relate to what Christ was explaining to the Samaritan woman at the well, and that he proclaimed from the temple steps on that last day of the Great Feast, *Hoshana Rabbah?* The answer, no doubt, lies in the title of that feast itself – *Hoshana Rabbah* – which means "Judgment is Delivered," or "Awakening to Judgment."

Consider the fact that unborn babes are kept alive and nourished through the umbilical cord – nourished from another source [other being] – that they are part of, and that is a part of them. Was not Jesus explaining to his listeners on both occasions, that they much be nourished spiritually through a source that they must be a part of, and that must be a part of them? Thus seems to be the case since the apostle John explains: *"[Now he said this about the Spirit, whom those who trusted in him were to receive later – the Spirit had not yet been given, because Yeshua had not yet been glorified]"* (Jn 7:39).

Jeremiah states that the Israelites rejected this life-giving source, developing sources of their own that could not hold this life-giving essence [Holy Spirit]. Israel had enjoyed the actual presence of God: in the cloud that covered them by day, protecting them from the desert heat, and hiding them from their enemies; and in the pillar of fire by night, that provided them light and guidance.

Later, God's presence rested between the Covering Cherubs above the Mercy Seat on the Ark of the Covenant. They were in God, and He was in them; but in their rebellion, they created idols – first a golden calf, then gold, silver, stone and wooden idols. In their rebellion, they finally reduced themselves to worshiping the idols they had carved on their staffs (walking sticks)!

They had gods all around them, but not within them; and worse, none of them were life-giving.

Their idols were, like the prophet, Jeremiah, declared – empty, broken cisterns – like their own spirits, which (because of their rebellion) were no longer indwelled by Holy Spirit. Being without Holy Spirit's indwelling presence, they spiraled downward into every imaginable evil. Worshiping idols, *"Whereof the Lord had said unto them, "Ye shall not do this thing"* (2 Ki 17:12); they offered their own sons and daughters as burnt offerings to some of these horrendous gods [demons] (2 Ki 17:17).

The Downward Spiral:
Spiraling downward further and further, they alas even turned to cannibalism, eating their own sons and daughters! During a particularly distressing time, when the city was under siege, a woman approached the king to lodge a complaint against her neighbor.

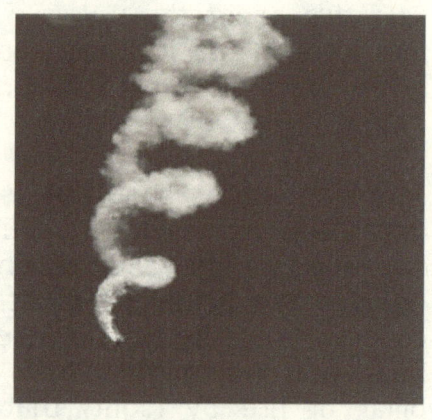

"This woman said to me, "Give up your son so that we may eat him today, and tomorrow, we will eat my son." So, we cooked my son and ate him. The next day, I said to her, "Give up your son so we may eat him," but she had hidden him away" (2 Ki 6:27-29).

Detached from the 'umbilical cord' to God [God's indwelling presence], mankind does unimaginable things. Thus, even our enteric system, or belly brain, that directs our anterior brain, is not – in and of itself – sufficient.

Just as the governing computer on the BART system, installed to control the main computer, still needed an operator for the system to function properly; so we must be indwelled, and directed, by Holy Spirit, thereby connected, through Yeshua Messiah, to Father God.

In the words of Christ himself: *"On that day you will realize that I am in my Father, and you are in me, and I am in you"* (John 14:20-21). ... *"If you remain in me and my words remain in you, ask whatever you wish, and it will be given you"* (John 15:7). Connected thus to God [Father, Son and Holy Spirit] we can be assured of receiving proper guidance for our life.

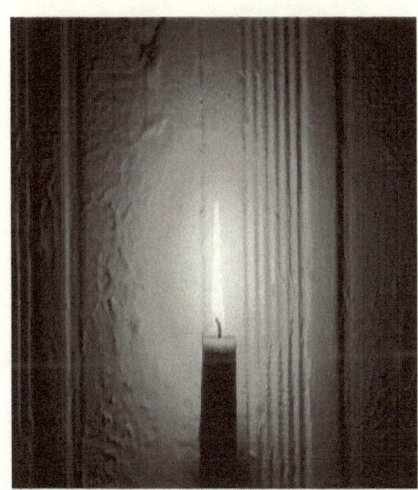

Consider the words of Solomon, who wrote: *"The spirit of man is the candle [lamp] of the Lord, searching all the inward parts of the belly [inner-being]"* (Prov 20:27). ... *"The blueness of a wound cleanseth away evil: so do stripes the inward parts of the belly"* (Prov 20:30). It was in fulfilling this that Jesus proclaimed:

"Whoever believes in me, as the Scripture has said, streams of living water will flow from within him." By this he meant the Spirit, whom those who believed in him were later to receive. Up to that time the Spirit had not been given, since Jesus had not yet been glorified" (John 7:38-39).

As profound as this is, consider the words of the Psalmist, who wrote: *"Adonai, my assigned portion, my cup: you safeguard my share. Pleasant places were measured out for me; I am content with my heritage. I bless Adonai, my counselor; Who instructs me at night in my inmost being"* (Ps 16:5-7 CJB). ... *"In the night I remember my songs, I commune with myself, my spirit inquires [of Adonai]"* (Ps 77:7 CJB).

And, long before this, the patriarch Job, declared: *"But no one asks, 'Where is God my maker, who causes glad songs to ring out at night, who teaches us more than he teaches wild animals and makes us wiser than the birds in the air?' They may cry out, but no one answers, because of evil men's pride. For God will not listen to empty cries; Shaddai pays no attention to them"* (Job 35:10-13 CJB).

When speaking of the spirit of man being the candle of his soul, and God instructing one's heart in the secret watches of the night; of giving them songs in the night; these ancient authors – quite obviously knew through revelation – what modern man is just beginning to realize.

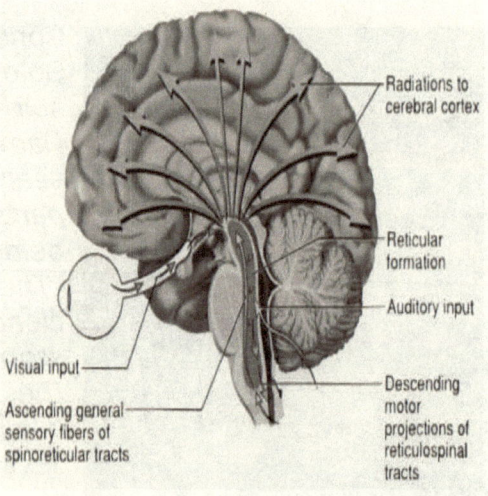

Scientists tell us that when sleeping the Reticular Formation in our brain is open, allowing new information to pass through, into the deepest recesses of our memory – the Amygdala; an almond sized gland, from which we generate our life-commandments and social norms.

When Holy Spirit indwells us, and we make Yeshua Messiah Lord over our life, surrendering every function of our being; giving God permission to instruct our heart and give us songs in the night; then the prayer of Christ, recorded in (John 17), will become a reality. Then, and only then, can we overcome the prince of this world [the thief who comes to steal, kill and destroy (John 10:10); that *"the world must learn that I love the Father and that I do exactly what my Father has commanded me"* (John 14:31).

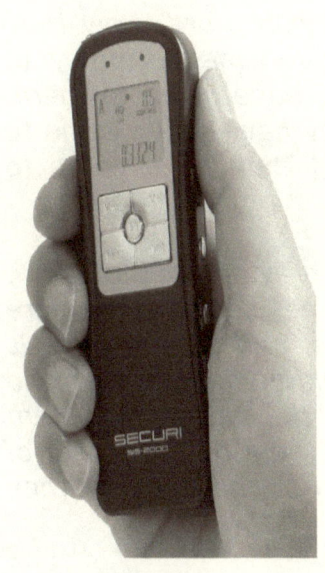

To gain the fullest possible appreciation of Christ's prayer, invest the small amount of funds for a digital recorder that will interconnect with your computer; then record the prayer in your own voice – which is the voice most acceptable to the subconscious. Once your recording is complete, copy it onto the hard-drive of your computer. Next copy your sound recording onto a CD or DVD that can be played from your DVD player, CD player or computer.

Once you have prepared your CD, find a quiet place, sit down, relax and close your eyes. Remembering that in the the causal realm – in the presence of God – time as we know it, does not exist. So, in your imagination, see yourself seated with Christ in heavenly places (Eph 2:6). Now, as you quiet your intellect ... relax ... more, and more ... and more. Now, quickened in your spirit and imagination, listen carefully to the still small voice within – of Christ as he communicates his love for you to his Father:

"Father, the time has come. Glorify your Son, so that the Son may glorify you – just as you gave him authority over all mankind, so that he might give eternal life to all those whom you have given him. And eternal life is this: to know you, the one true God, and him whom you sent, Yeshua the Messiah.

"I glorified you on earth by finishing the work you gave me to do. Now, Father, glorify me alongside yourself. Give me the same glory I had with you before the world existed. "I made your name known to the people you gave me out of the world. They were yours, you gave them to me, and they have kept your word. Now they know that everything you have given me is from you, because the words you gave me I have given to them, and they have received them. They have really come to know that I came from you, and they have come to trust that you sent me.

"I am praying for them. I am not praying for the world, but for those you have given to me, because they are yours. Indeed, all I have is yours, and all you have is mine, and in them I have been glorified. Now I am no longer in the world. They are in the world, but I am coming to you. Holy Father, guard them by the power of your name, which you have given to me, so that they may be one, just as we are.

"When I was with them, I guarded them by the power of your name, which you have given to me; yes, I kept watch over them; and not one of them was destroyed (except the one meant for destruction, so that the Tanakh might be fulfilled). But now, I am coming to you; and I say these things while I am still in the world so that they may have my joy made complete in themselves.

"I have given them your word, and the world hated them, because they do not belong to the world – just as I myself do not belong to the world. I don't ask you to take them out of the world, but to protect them from the Evil One. They do not belong to the world, just as I do not belong to the world. Set them apart for holiness by means of the truth – your word is truth. Just as you sent me into the world, I have sent them into the world. On their behalf I am setting myself apart for holiness, so that they too may be set apart for holiness by means of the truth.

"I pray not only for these, but also for those who will trust in me because of their word, that they may all be one. Just as you, Father, are united with me and I with you, I pray that they may be united with us, so that the world may believe that you sent me. The glory which you have given to me, I have given to them; so that they may be one, just as we are one – I united with them and you with me, so that they may be completely one, and the world thus realize that you sent me, and that you have loved them just as you have loved me.

"Father, I want those you have given me to be with me where I am; so that they may see my glory, which you have given me because you loved me before the creation of the world. Righteous Father, the world has not known you, but I have known you, and these people have known that you sent me. I made your name known *to them, and I will continue to make it known; so that the love with which you have loved me may be in them, and I myself may be united with them"* (John 17 CJB).

Now, slowly leaving the heavenly holy of holies, and returning to earth with me, travel forward a bit in time, to those moments just preceding Jesus' ascension into heaven. We are gathered – with Christ's eleven apostles and other disciples, on the slopes of the Mount of Olives – right where he told us he would meet us. *"So the eleven talmidim [disciples] went to the hill in the Galilee, where Yeshua had told them to go. When they saw him, they prostrated themselves before him; but some hesitated"* (Matt 28:16-17 CJB).

In the eye of your soul, see yourself expectantly sitting there with the other disciples, waiting for Jesus to come. See him approaching now, and see yourself, spontaneously prostrating yourself before him, and worshiping him – the King of Kings and Lord of Lords. As you quiet your intellect and emotions, but quickened in your spirit and imagination, hear him say:

"All authority in heaven and on earth has been given to me. Therefore, go and make people from all nations into talmidim [disciples], immersing [baptizing] them into the reality of the Father, the Son and Ruach HaKodesh [Holy Spirit], teaching them to obey everything that I have commanded you. And remember! I will be with you always, yes, even until the end of this age" (Matt 28:18-20 CJB).

Should the thought enter your mind, "I don't know everything that Jesus taught his disciples – I've even forgotten a good deal of what I have been taught – how can I teach others?" Don't despair! Travel with me just a little further back in time, and hear Jesus' promise to his disciples:

"The Counselor, the Holy Spirit, whom the Father will send in my name, will teach you all things and will remind you of everything I have said to you. Peace I leave with you; my peace I give you. I do not give to you as the world gives. Do not let your hearts be troubled and do not be afraid" (John 14:26-27). ...

"I am the vine; you are the branches. If a man remains in me and I in him, he will bear much fruit; apart from me you can do nothing. If anyone does not remain in me, he is like a branch that is thrown away and withers; such branches are picked up, thrown into the fire and burned. If you remain in me and my words remain in you, ask whatever you wish, and it will be given you. This is to my Father's glory, that you bear much fruit, showing yourselves to be my disciples" (John 15:5-8).

"For we know that our old self was crucified with him so that the body of sin might be done away with, that we should no longer be slaves to sin – because anyone who has died has been freed from sin. Now if we died with Christ, we believe that we will also live with him. For we know that since Christ was raised from the dead, he cannot die again; death no longer has mastery over him. The death he died, he died to sin once for all; but the life he lives, he lives to God. In the same way, count yourselves dead to sin but alive to God in Christ Jesus" (Rom 6:6-11).

Repeat after me: Through the power of Holy Spirit, Who indwells my spirit, Jesus – my Lord and Savior, and

Father God; in Whom I live and dwell and have my being; and Who live within me: *"I will not let sin control the way I live; nor give in to sinful desires. I will not let any part of my body become an instrument of evil to serve sin. Instead, giving myself completely to God, for – I was dead, but have now been given new life. So I will use my whole body as an instrument to do what is right [an instrument of righteousness] for the glory of God"* (Rom 6:12-14).

Now, with your eyes still closed, return with me to the heavenly realms, into the Temple, in Holy of Holies. Seated alongside Christ Jesus, your Lord and Savior, see the apostle, Paul join the two of you. Hear him tell you:

"Of this [Gospel] I was made a minister according to the gift of God's free grace (undeserved favor) which was bestowed on me by the exercise (the working in all its effectiveness) of His power.

"To me, though I am the very least of all the saints (God's consecrated people), this grace (favor, privilege) was granted and graciously entrusted: to proclaim to the Gentiles the unending (boundless, fathomless, incalculable, and exhaustless) riches of Christ [wealth which no human being could have searched out],

"Also to enlighten all men and make plain to them what is the plan [regarding the Gentiles and providing for the salvation of all men] of the mystery kept hidden through the ages and concealed until now in [the mind of] God Who created all things by Christ Jesus. **[The purpose is] that through the church the complicated, many-sided wisdom of God in all its infinite variety and innumerable aspects might now be made known to the angelic rulers and authorities (principalities and powers) in the heavenly sphere.**

"This is in accordance with the terms of the eternal and timeless purpose which He has realized and carried into effect in [the person of] Christ Jesus our Lord, In Whom, because of our faith in Him, we dare to have the boldness (courage and confidence) of free access [an unreserved approach to God with freedom and without fear.] So I ask you not to lose heart [not to faint or become despondent through fear" (Eph 3:7-13).

Who are these rulers and authorities in the heavenly realms that Paul is speaking of? And what is the manifold wisdom of God that is to be made known to them by the church – by you and I! Paul answers these questions a bit later in his letter to the Ephesians, saying: *"Finally, grow powerful in union with the Lord, in union with his mighty strength! Use all the armor and weaponry that God provides, so that you will be able to stand against the deceptive tactics of the Adversary.*

"For we are not struggling against human beings, but against the rulers, authorities and cosmic powers governing this darkness, against the spiritual forces of evil in the heavenly realm. So take up every piece of war equipment God provides; so that when the evil day comes, you will be able to resist; and when the battle is won, you will still be standing.

"Therefore, stand! Having the belt of truth buckled around your waist, put on righteousness for a breastplate, and wear on your feet the readiness that comes from the Good News of shalom. Always carry the shield of trust, with which you will be able to extinguish all the flaming arrows of the Evil One. And take the helmet of deliverance; along with the sword given by the Spirit, that is, the Word of God; as you pray at all times, with all kinds of prayers and requests, in the Spirit, vigilantly and persistently, for all God's people" (Eph 6:10-18 CJB).

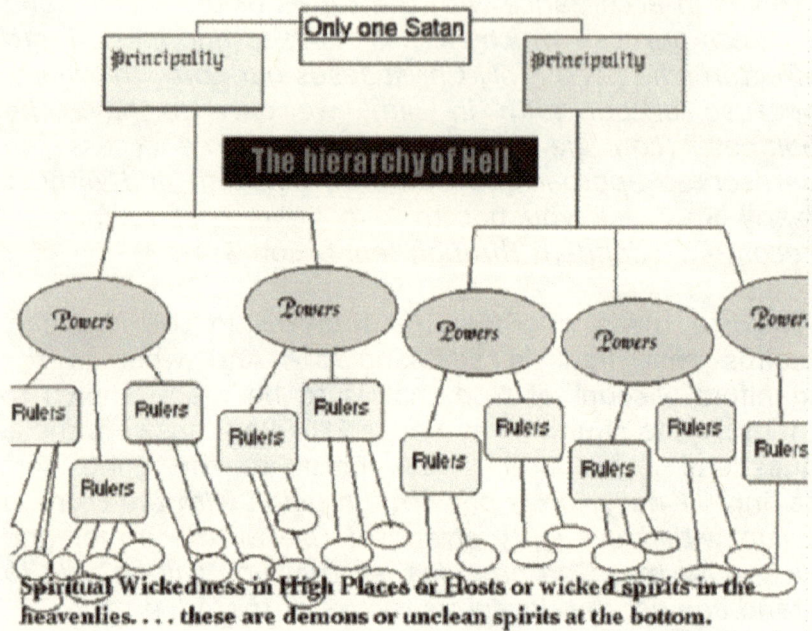

Finally – says Paul – *"pray for [the leaders and] me, too, that whenever I open my mouth, the words will be given to me to be bold in making known the secret of the Good News, for which I am an ambassador in chains. Pray that I may speak boldly, the way I should"* (Eph 6:19-20 CJB). ... *"May God the Father and the Lord Yeshua the Messiah give you love and trust. Grace be to all who love our Lord Yeshua the Messiah with undying love"* (vs 23-24 CJB).

~ Questions, Concerns & Key Points ~

1. how many internal organs does a man have?

2. How many muscles do we have, and which one is the strongest?

3. The brain makes up what percentage of one's weight?

4. How many thoughts each day does the average person have?

5. What is the Reticular Formation?

6. What is the Enteric Brain, and the Amygdala?

7. Where do our deepest thoughts originate?

Chapter 15 The Power of Imagination: Part 1

Introduction:
In a previous chapter, we introduced the concept of imagination, demonstrating its connection with faith – the 'unseen substance – mentioned in Hebrews 11:1. In this chapter, we will begin to investigate the power of imagination – a a power that God has created within us, through which we can transcend the reality of our five senses.

Reflections:
Consider for a moment, the power of imagination as evidenced in the lives of some of the Patriarchs of old. We find several examples described within the Book of Hebrews. For instance: "**By faith**, Noah, after receiving divine warning about things as yet unseen, was filled with holy fear and built an ark to save his household. **Through this faith**, he put the world under condemnation and received the righteousness that comes from trusting" (Heb 11:7).

"**By faith**, Abraham obeyed, after being called to go out to a place which God would later give him as a possession; indeed, **he went out without knowing where he was going**. By faith, he lived as a temporary resident in the Land of the promise, as if it were not his, staying in tents with Isaac and Jacob, who were to receive what was promised along with him. For **he was looking forward to the city with permanent foundations, of which the architect and builder is God**" (Heb 11:8-10 CJB).

"**By faith**, Moses, after he had grown up, refused to be called the son of Pharaoh's daughter. He chose being mistreated along with God's people rather than enjoying the passing pleasures of sin. He had come to regard abuse suffered on behalf of the Messiah as greater riches than the treasures of Egypt, for **he kept his eyes fixed on the reward**. **By faith**, he left Egypt, not fearing the king's anger; **he persevered as one who sees the unseen**. **By faith**, he obeyed the requirements for the Passover, including the smearing of the blood, so that the Destroyer of the firstborn would not touch the firstborn of Israel" (Heb 11:24-28 CJB).

Moses scorned the riches of Egypt because he had his eyes fixed on the reward – God's promise that the meek would inherit the earth. In his first recorded public sermon – the Sermon on the Mount – Jesus declared: *"Blessed are the meek, for they will inherit the earth"* (Matt 5:5); apparently quoting the words of the Psalmist, who penned: *"A little while, and the wicked will be no more; though you look for them, they will not be found. But the meek will inherit the land and enjoy great peace"* (Ps 37:10-11).

Moses relied on these promises and crafted his lifestyle to claim them. It was recorded of Moses, *"The man Moses was very meek or humble, more than any man who was on the face of the earth"* (Num 12:3). Moses did not consider rejecting the riches of Egypt a sacrifice. He had caught a vision of what it would be like to be an inheritor – along with Yeshua Messiah – of the world and its riches. Compared to them, the riches of Egypt were nothing. In faith, he scorned them and committed his life to fulfilling the condition for receiving God's promised inheritance.

These Patriarchs of old – and many others, whose lives have been recorded as examples – grasped the power inherent in the fusion through faith of man's imagination with the promises of God. Satan is fully aware of the tremendous power of imagination; and comprehending its potential, he seeks to distort, if not destroy, man's visionary, creative ability. What does Satan know that we do not – or have known and forgotten? Come with us – back to the dawn of creation.

Before we take this journey through the realm of the principalities, powers and rulers of darkness – the powers of the heavens – let's ask God's protection. With our eyes closed, but with the eye of our soul – our imagination – fully awake, come away with me to the heavenly realms, where, encased within Christ, we are seated with him there (Eph 2:6).

As we enter the heavenly temple, passing through the gates into the Holy of Holies, to stand before the Throne of Grace; stop and look down – beneath your feet, into the heavenly realms where the powers of darkness dwell, joining me in prayer as we bind every satanic and demonic power.

In the Name, and through the blood, of Yeshua Messiah, I now bind you Satan, all Principalities, Powers, Rulers and Cosmic Forces of evil, together with every demonic practice engaged in by mankind. By binding you, I make you impotent and ineffective in my life. Through the authority transferred to me by Jesus Christ, I command you to leave my presence – both my physical presence on earth, and my spiritual presence in the heavenlies. I forbid you to distort the Truth of God; or to create or cause, confusion or chaos. In Jesus' Name, I command you to begone – now!

Father God, as I stand before your Throne of Grace, clothed in the Righteousness of Christ, and as your forgiven beloved child, I beseech you now, in the Name of Your Beloved Son, Yeshua Messiah, to assign holy angels to guard me, to protect me, and everything your have given me stewardship over. Open my spiritual eyes and ears that the information presented in this lesson on imagination will go down deep into my spirit, correcting any misconception and/or misinterpretation I may have held. "Create in me, O my God, a pure heart, and renew a steadfast spirit within me" (Ps 51:10).

Don Doyle, one of the founders of Yoke-fellows International, shared with me (Doc) a meaningful motto that has guided their ministry and is worthwhile including here, as we seek God's guidance for our own life: *"God formed me; Satan deformed me; man may reform me; but only God can transform me."*

When God Created Man:
In Genesis one, we read about mankind's creation: *"Then God said, "Let us make humankind in our image, in the likeness of ourselves; and let them rule over the fish in the sea, the birds in the air, the animals, and over all the earth, and over every crawling creature that crawls on the earth. So God created humankind in his own image; in the image of God he created him: male and female he created them. God blessed them: God said to them, "Be fruitful, multiply, fill the earth and subdue it"* (Gen 1:26-28 CJB).

Reading this, we catch just a glimpse of the initial part of mankind's creation – his design – performed by and through the imagination of Almighty God. Here the Elohiym [a plural word in Hebrew, meaning the Almighty Ones but translated in the singular, as God] says:

*"Let **us** make [Hebrew aw-saw (meaning to fashion or design)] humankind, in **our image** [Hebrew tseh-lem (meaning an illusion, or exact representation)] in the likeness [Hebrew dem-ooth (meaning similitude or sameness)] of **ourselves**." So God [Elohiym] created [Hebrew baw-raw (meaning to fashion – indicative of a formative process)] in His own image [Hebrew tseh-lem (meaning an illusion)], in the image of (a representative illusion of) God [Elohiym]; He (They) created [Hebrew baw-raw (meaning to form them)] male and female."*

This brief snippet of Scripture introduces us to two very important aspects and tools of creation: 1) imaginative design (being carefully fashioned; and 2) a process of purposeful formation (or construction). The first aspect employed the first tool – imagery, or creative design through imagination; the second aspect was a carefully pursued formative process, that was carried out by God, calling forth features, characteristics, traits and talents – speaking them into existence.

God spoke [commanded – Hebrew aw-mar (meaning to declare or command)]; and it was so. Thus, the second 'tool' employed in the creative process was speech.

In the Image and Likeness of The Elohim:
Mankind was created in the image and likeness of God [(plural) – both male and female], through God's careful employment of imagination and speech (calling them into existence); declaring the details of his form, shape and purpose. As such, mankind is himself a creator – designed by the Master Creator to create things within the dominion, or realm, placed under his rule.

Man was given the commission (Gen 1:28) to replenish [Hebrew maw-lay (meaning to fill)] the earth. This command was not merely to procreate his species, as some have contended; but was a directive to fill the earth with whatever was needed and purposeful. Man was also told to multiply [Hebrew raw-baw' (meaning to expand in whatever direction or respect needed, and to expand his authority to exercise dominion over all that he created. Thus, the earth, and everything thereon, was to a great extent, left to mankind to design and create.

Spirit Begets Spirit:
Created in God's image – Who is Spirit – man is spirit, and was originally clothed in God's Shekinah glory (Ps 8:5). Sinning, mankind exchanged this covering of glory with shame (Ps 4:2). Subsequent to his rebellion and fall, God's Shekinah glory departed and, becoming disembodied spirits, they felt naked, shamed and filled with fear, anxiety and panic (Gen 3:10). God, in divine mercy, covered them with skin – providing them an overcoat as it were, since the Hebrew word employed, refers to an outer-garment.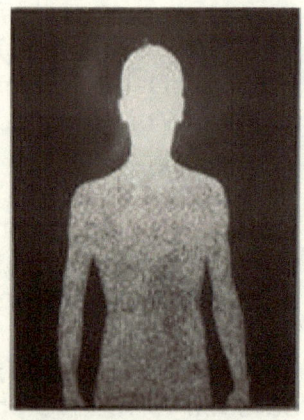

Unlike mankind's original covering, this one was formed [Hebrew yaw-tsar (meaning to mold, like a Potter)]; created from the elements of the earth (Gen 2:7). Thus mankind, in the image and likeness of his Creator, would now call forth and form, from the elements of the earth, those things he imagined. It was a plan ordained by the God of all creation, to involve mankind – His beloved children – in the process of creation. Nothing could have honored His children more.

However, Lucifer [now Satan], created to direct God's holy angels in the care of, and ministry to, God's family, learning of God's plan to bring children into the world, rebelled: he would not care for and minister to – let alone worship – another created being! As a result, we enter the long saga of God's plan of redemption – His plan to buy them back from their bondage to Satan, through the blood of His First Begotten, His Unique Beloved Son, Yeshua:

"For God so loved the world that he gave his only and unique Son, so that everyone who trusts in him may have eternal life, instead of being utterly destroyed. For God did not send the Son into the world to judge the world, but rather so that through him, the world might be saved" (John 3:16-17 CJB).

Satan understood that God had created the entire cosmos, including planet earth, and everything on it, by employing the combination of imagination and speech. Therefore, he knew that if he could inhibit, distort, or restrict either of these, he could inhibit the creative powers and processes of mankind. Understanding that once a thing is envisioned in one's imagination, it will most likely be declared to another, and through this speaking it out, giving it power, motivating one to form or fashion it, completing the creative process.

As Solomon declared: *"The tongue has the power of life and death, and those who love it will eat its fruit"* (Prov 18:21). To ensure that the 'fruit' [the product] of man's speech would tend toward death, rather than toward life, Satan set about to attack mankind's imaginative processes; and his attack was horribly effective. We see its effect in the lives of the Antediluvian world [that time prior to Noah's Flood.]

They had participated in the unthinkable – cohabiting and interbreeding with the Watchers [the Guardian Angels sent to watch over them, guide them and protect them from the attacks of the Evil One – Satan. "The Nephilim were on the earth in those days – and also afterward – when the Watchers went in to the daughters of men and had children by them" (Gen 6:4).

"Adonai saw that the people on earth were very wicked, that all the imaginings of their hearts were always of evil only. Adonai regretted that he had made humankind on the earth; it grieved his heart" (Gen 6:6 CJB).

To counteract this great evil, God sent a flood upon the earth – the flood of floods, that destroyed everything on the earth – except for those few, who being in Noah's Ark, survived. This included a single human family: Noah, his three sons, Shem Ham and Japheth, and their wives; together with one pair of every species of animals, plus an additional number of those that were to be used for sacrifices and those that here to be used for man's food.

Exiting the Ark, Noah and his family, discovered a drastically changed planet. The fountains of the great deep – the earth's circulatory system – had broken up; the windows of heaven had opened, breaking apart the moisture barrier in the heavens [the waters above the sky (Gen 1:7)]; two changes that brought to an end the terrarium effect that had protected man, animals and plants from harmful ultra-violet light and radiation.

Then too, mankind's diet was materially altered. In the Garden of Eden, man had dined from the Tree of Life; after their rebellion and fall, they had been expelled from Eden and had to till the ground to produce their food, and by God's direction, they added vegetables and grains to their diet. Now – following the devastations brought on by the flood – for the first time in the history of the earth, man was provided with meat (Gen 9:1-3).

With the majority of the fauna – including the fruit and nut bearing trees, the vegetables, and grains – gone from the face of the earth for a season; this was necessary, but there was a tremendous cost. Mankind's lifespan – which before the flood averaged just short of 1,000 years – was now shortened to 120 years: just 12% of that enjoyed in the Antediluvian world.

"Adonai said, *"My Spirit will not live in human beings forever, for they too are flesh; therefore their life span is to be 120 years"* (Gen 6:3-4 CJB). At the same time, there was – from God's perspective – a major benefit to mankind having a shortened lifespan. His imagination was still bent toward evil [*"The people on earth were very wicked – all the imaginings of their hearts were always of evil only"* (Gen 6:5)]; but what man could achieve in a shortened lifetime was now limited.

Throughout the Old Testament, God guided mankind through dreams and visions: *"I, Adonai, make myself known to him in visions, I speak with him in dreams"* (Num 12:6-7 CJB); and He promised to continue to guide mankind, declaring: *"I will pour out my Spirit on all humanity. Your sons and daughters will prophesy, your old men will dream dreams, your young men will see visions"* (Joel 3:1 CJB).

Joel's prophecy was not fulfilled until the Day of Pentecost, se as of fir ut th he int he lat se of

Parables rely on the use of imagination. The transition to this form of teaching was spoken of in the Old Testament: *"I spoke to the prophets, gave them many visions and told parables through them"* (Hos 12:10). Concerning Jesus' ministry, it is recorded that he taught primarily through parables (Mk 4:2); and when asked why, he said:

"Here is why I speak to them in parables: they look without seeing and listen without hearing or understanding. That is, in them is fulfilled the prophecy of Isaiah which says, 'You will keep on hearing but never understand, and keep on seeing but never perceive, because the heart of this people has become dull – with their ears they barely hear, and their eyes they have closed, so as not to see with their eyes, hear with their ears, understand with their heart, and repent, so that I could heal them'" (Matt 13:13-15 CJB). ... *"This was to fulfill what had been spoken through the prophet, "I will open my mouth in parables, I will say what has been hidden since the creation of the universe"* (Matt 13:35 CJB).

Satan's initial plan, to contaminate mankind's imagination was thwarted, but he had no intention of giving up. Over time – down through the ages, and even in our day – he has influenced many, both theologians and laymen in the church, to consider mankind's imagination something evil, in and of itself. To intentionally visualize something, became among large segments of the church, evil – even demonic or satanic. However, the same people who declared man's imagination evil, made use of their own on a regular basis.

One cannot plan out anything without engaging their imagination. Try designing a landscape plan for your home without visualizing it; or, if you are a homemaker, try looking through one of your favorite cookbooks to select a desert you'd like to make for friends who are coming to visit, without engaging your imagination. One cannot even budget his or her finances or time without imagining the outcome.

If one is honest with themselves, they will soon discover that everything we create, construct, build or assemble, exists first in our imagination. Then, as we speak it out – if only to ourselves – we become motivated to form it [giving it form and substance]; resulting in our imaginations becoming a manifest part of our physical reality.

So, imagination is the act of creating something that is not, out of things that are not [or nothingness]; these things becoming real, or manifest, only when our imagination is linked with our speech and carrying out the formative process – in the likeness of Father God. Mankind's most profound likeness, or similarity, to Father God, is seen in the process of creation: we create things in our imagination, then speak them out – often even recording them on paper; after which we carefully form, or craft them, bringing that which we imagined into physical existence and reality.

Years after Noah's Flood, when the descendants of Noah's youngest son, Ham, once more rebelled. Not content, as God's children, to carry out His commission to 'go into all the world and take dominion,' they decided to settle in the Plain of Shinar, build cities, and make a name for themselves. *"They said, "Come, let us build ourselves a city, with a tower that has its top reaching up into heaven, so that we may make a name for ourselves and not be scattered over the face of the whole earth"* (Gen 11:4 CJB).

But God was watching. *"Adonai came down to see the city and the tower the people were building. Adonai said, "Look, the people are united, they all have a single language, and see what they're starting to do! At this rate, nothing they set out to accomplish will be impossible for them! Come, let's go down and confuse their language, so that they won't understand each other's speech." So from there Adonai scattered them all over the earth, and they stopped building the city. For this reason it is called Babel [meaning confusion] – because it was there that Adonai confused the language of the whole earth, and from there Adonai scattered the people all over the earth"* (Gen 11:5-9 CJB).

In further recognition of mankind's ability to carry out whatever he imagined; God took another step to ensure that mankind could not reunite: He altered the earth's structure, breaking its substructure into various parts that we now refer to as the Tectonic Plates. We know through geophysical evidence, when this took place; the timing coinciding with God's intervention.

It is recorded in Scripture that Eber, one of Noah's descendants, had two sons – Joktan and Peleg. And of Peleg, the Scriptural record states: "One was named Peleg [meaning division], because during his lifetime the earth was divided" (Gen 10:25; 1 Ch 1:19). Why would God take such drastic action? Because, He created mankind in His own image, and thus, He knew our full potential – potential for good or for ill. He, himself, said of us – that united – nothing we undertake is impossible to accomplish.

Solomon, writing under the inspiration of Holy Spirit, said that man's speech has in it the power of life and death. Through the combined use of our imagination and speech, we can bless and create; or curse and destroy.

Of mankind, it is recorded: *"I know that whomever you bless is in fact blessed, and whomever you curse is in fact cursed"* (Num 22:6 CJB).

Satan is also knowledgeable of mankind's creative potential, and is committed to see that it is used for evil and not for righteousness. Jesus, drawing a parallel between Satan's plan for humanity, and God's plan, said: *"Yeshua said to them again, "Yes, indeed! I tell you that **I am the gate for the sheep. All those who have come before me have been thieves and robbers**, but the sheep didn't listen to them. I am the gate; if someone enters through me, he will be safe and will go in and out and find pasture. **The thief comes only in order to steal, kill and destroy; I have come so that they may have life, life in its fullest measure.***

*"**I am the good shepherd. The good shepherd lays down his life for the sheep**. The hired hand, since he isn't a shepherd and the sheep aren't his own, sees the wolf coming, abandons the sheep and runs away. **Then the wolf drags them off and scatters them.** The hired worker behaves like this because that's all he is, a hired worker; so it doesn't matter to him what happens to the sheep. I am the good shepherd; I know my own, and my own know me – just as the Father knows me, and I know the Father – and I lay down my life on behalf of the sheep. Also I have other sheep which are not from this sheep-pen; I need to bring them, and they will hear my voice; and there will be one flock, one shepherd"* (John 10:7-16 CJB).

Unfettered, mankind's imagination – combined with his lust – guides him into the pathways of evil. God said: *"Pay attention to what I say. Then I will be your God, and you will be my people. In everything, live according to the way that I order you, so that things will go well for you.' But they neither listened nor paid attention, but lived according to their own plans, in the stubbornness of their evil hearts, thus going backward and not forward"* (Jer 7:23-25 CJB).

~ Questions, Concerns & Key Points ~

1. Consider the power of faith combined with imagination – or hope.
   - Abram left his homeland journeying to an unknown land.
   - Moses scorned the treasures of Egypt, keeping his eyes focused on God's promised reward.

2. Consider carefully the motto of Yoke-fellows International:
   - **God formed us,**
   - Satan deformed us,
   - Man can reform us,
   - Only God can transform us.

3. Identify the creative tools God has entrusted to man, by which he can – and does – alter his world?

4. Describe the changes that took place in man as a result of his rebellion and fall:
   - Spiritual
   - Soulish [thoughts, feelings, beliefs, attitudes]
   - Physical
   - Environmental
   - Relational

5. Describe the changes God wrought in the earth after the Great Flood – Noah's Flood:

6. In what way has God directed mankind using man's imagination:
   - Old Testament
   - New Testament

Chapter 16 The Power of Imagination: Part 2

A Divine Remedy:
Even while Israel was rebelling against God, worshiping idols and sacrificing to the false gods of the nations surrounding them, God provided them a remedy. He told them He was sending them into captivity in the nations whom gods they served; but promised them:

"There you will serve gods which are the product of human hands, made of wood and stone, which can't see, hear, eat or smell. However, from there you will seek Adonai your God; and you will find him if you search after him with all your heart and being. In your distress, when all these things have come upon you, in the acharit-hayamim, you will return to Adonai your God and listen to what he says; for Adonai your God is a merciful God. He will not fail you, destroy you, or forget the covenant with your ancestors which he swore to them" (Deut 4:28-31 CJB).

Unlike Saul, his predecessor, and those who would follow him, King David listened. He asked God to show him his heart and help him correct his wayward ways. He prayed:

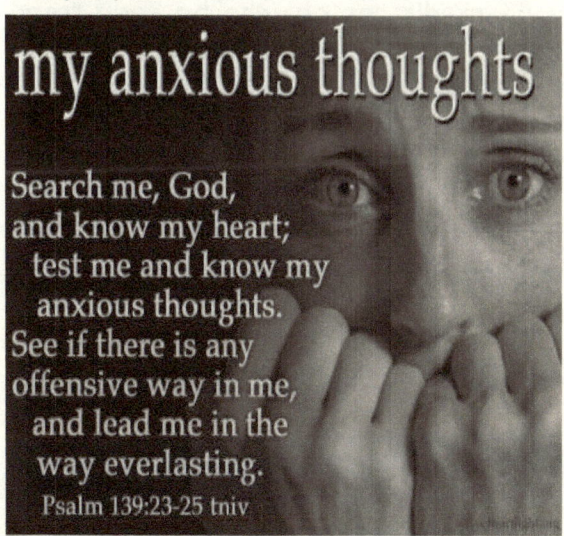

"Examine me, O God, and know my heart; test me, and know my anxious thoughts. See if there is in me any offensive, hurtful way within me, and lead me in the way everlasting" (Ps 139:23-24).

David had obvious read, and taken to heart, the words of Joshua, Israel's great leader after the death of Moses. Joshua counseled the people to: *"keep this book of the Torah [Law] on your lips, and meditate on it day and night, so that you will take care to act according to everything written in it. Then your undertakings will prosper, and you will succeed. Haven't I ordered you, 'Be strong, be bold'? So don't be afraid or downhearted, because Adonai your God is with you wherever you go"* (Josh 1:8-9 CJB).

God's promise, that if one would meditate on the [Torah] Book of the Law, their undertakings would prosper and they would succeed, directed David's kingly reign. Listen to David's own words: *"How blessed are those who reject the advice of the wicked, don't stand on the way of sinners or sit where scoffers sit! Their delight is in Adonai's Torah; on his Torah they meditate day and night. They are like trees planted by streams – they bear their fruit in season, their leaves never wither, everything they do succeeds"* (Ps 1:1-3 CJB).

David's understanding of the power of imagination and speaking out what one meditates on, can be seen from the following Scriptures. *"God, **within your temple we meditate on your grace**. God, your praise, like your name, extends to the ends of the earth. Your right hand is filled with righteousness"* (Ps 48:10-11 CJB). ... *"I will remember the works of the Lord: surely I will remember thy wonders of old. **I will meditate also of all thy work, and talk of thy doings**"* (Ps 77:11-12).

The Psalmists who followed David's footsteps commitment to meditation is equally evident. *"**I will meditate on your precepts** and keep my eyes on your ways. **I will find my delight in your regulations**. I will not forget your word"* (Ps 119:15-16 CJB". ... *"Open my eyes, so that I will see the wonders from your*

Torah. Though I'm just a wanderer on the earth, don't hide your mitzvot [commandments] from me. **I am continually consumed with longing for your rulings**" (Ps 119:18-20 CJB).

"Even when princes sit and plot against me, **your servant meditates on your laws**. Also your instructions are my delight; they are my counselors" (Ps 119:23-24 CJB). ... "I told you of my ways, and you answered me; teach me your laws. Make me understand the way of your precepts, and **I will meditate on your wonders**" (vs. 26-27 CJB).

"I will delight myself in your mitzvot [commandments], which I have loved. I will lift my hands to your mitzvot [commandments], which I love; and **I will meditate on your laws**" (vs. 47-48 CJB). ... "Let the proud be ashamed, because they wrong me with lies; as for me, **I will meditate on your precepts**. Let those who fear you turn to me, along with those who know your instruction. Let my heart be pure in your laws, so that I won't be put to shame" (vs. 78-80 CJB).

"**How I love your Torah! I meditate on it all day**. I am wiser than my foes, because your mitzvot are mine forever. I have more understanding than all my teachers, because **I meditate on your instruction**. I understand more than my elders, because I keep your precepts" (vs. 97-100 CJB).

"**Your word is a lamp for my foot and light on my path**. I have sworn an oath and confirmed it, that I will observe your righteous rulings" (vs. 105-106 CJB). ... "I take your instruction as a permanent heritage, because it is **the joy of my heart**" (vs. 111 CJB). ... "Your instruction is a wonder; this is why I follow it. **Your words are a doorway that lets in light,** giving understanding to the thoughtless" (vs. 129-130 CJB).

"Wholeheartedly I am calling on you; answer me, Adonai; I will keep your laws. I am calling on you; save me; and I will observe your instruction. I rise before dawn and cry for help; I put my hope in your word. **My eyes are open before the night watches, so that I can meditate on your promise**" (vs. 145-148 CJB).

Unfortunately, the aspirations of these psalmists never came to fruition. Generation after generation, the Children of Israel rebelled – departing further and further from God – until at last God withdrew His protection and their kingdom was captured, the people disbursed throughout the nations. But, God did not forget His promise to them. In his first public sermon – the Sermon on the Mount – Jesus referred to that promise, saying:

"And **why be anxious** about clothing? **Think about the fields of wild irises, and how they grow**. They neither work nor spin thread, yet I tell you that not even Solomon in all his glory was clothed as beautifully as one of these. If this is how God clothes grass in the field – which is here today and gone tomorrow, thrown in an oven – won't He much more clothe you? What little faith you have!

"So **don't be anxious**, asking, 'What will we eat?,' 'What will we drink?' or 'How will we be clothed?' For it is the pagans who set their hearts on all these things. Your heavenly Father knows you need them all. But seek first his Kingdom and his righteousness, and all these things will be given to you as well. **Don't worry about tomorrow** – tomorrow will worry about itself! Today has enough worries of its own already!" (Matt 6:28-34).

"Keep asking, and it will be given to you; keep seeking, and you will find; keep knocking, and the door will be opened to you. For everyone who keeps asking receives; he who keeps seeking finds; and to him who *keeps knocking, the door will be opened. Is there anyone here who, if his son asks him for a loaf of bread, will give him a stone? or if he asks for a fish, will give him a snake? So if you, even though you are bad, know how to give your children gifts that are good, how much more will your Father in heaven keep giving good things to those who keep asking him!"* (Matt 7:7-11 CJB).

These words of Jesus call upon the listener – or reader – to engage his or her imagination; seeking God's Kingdom and righteousness; asking God for whatever one needs, demands one to visualize, Jesus knew, and sought to reveal to us, the secret of effecting change and realizing God's promised blessings. Jesus is both fully human and divine. He was a participant in creation and knew that imagination plus speech motivates one to action – action that manifests one's imagination as physical reality. The principle is God's principle of creation. It still works – if we will learn to work the principle.

From of old, God guided and instructed His people through dreams and visions given the patriarchs and prophets – dreams and visions – that were action invoking commands. For example, consider the command given Abram when: *"He brought him outside and said, "Look up at the sky, and count the stars – if you can count them! Your descendants will be that many! "He believed in Adonai, and he credited it to him as righteousness"* (Gen 15:5-6 CJB).

Then also, there is the example of Elijah, who – trusting in God's Word – called together his enemies to witness God answering his prayer for rain, after three and one-half years of drought. After embarrassing the prophets of Baal – who had been praying all day for fire to consume their sacrifice; Elijah placed his sacrifice to God on the altar and soaked it with water. Then he prayed.

"At the time of sacrifice, the prophet Elijah stepped forward and prayed: "O Lord, God of Abraham, Isaac and Israel, let it be known today that you are God in Israel and that I am your servant and have done all these things at your command. Answer me, O Lord, answer me, so these people will know that you, O Lord, are God, and that you are turning their hearts back again." Then the fire of the Lord fell and burned up the sacrifice, the wood, the stones and the soil, and also licked up the water in the trench. When all the people saw this, they fell prostrate and cried, "The Lord-he is God! The Lord-he is God!" (1 Kings 18:36-39).

After praying, and in faith holding onto God's Word, *"Elijah said to Ahab"* [the king intent on Elijah's' destruction], *"Go, eat and drink, for there is the sound of a heavy rain"* (1 Kings 18:41).

Having sent the king on his way, *"Elijah climbed to the top of Carmel, bent down to the ground and put his face between his knees."* [Apparently to thank God for hearing and answering his prayer.] *"Go and look toward the sea,"* he told his servant. And he went up and looked. *"There is nothing there,"* he said. Seven times Elijah said, "Go back." The seventh time the servant reported, "A cloud as small as a man's hand is rising from the sea." Elijah said, "Go and tell Ahab, 'Hitch up your chariot and go down before the rain stops you.'" (1 Kings 18:42-44).

Did Abram's and Elijah's imagination have anything to do with the outcome of their situations? Let Scripture speak for itself: *"In the beginning God created the heavens and the earth. The earth was unformed and void [a vacuum], darkness was on the face of the deep, and the Spirit of God hovered over the surface of the water.* **Then God said, "Let there be light"; and there was light.** *God saw that the light was good, and God divided the light from the darkness. God called the light Day, and the darkness he called Night. So there was evening, and there was morning, one day"* (Gen 1:1-5 CJB).

The word translated as 'light' in Genesis 1:3 is a word translated into Greek as photon, which is the basic unit of the universe – of all matter and antimatter. So, from a scientific viewpoint, when God said, "Light be!" That was the 'Big Bang!' At that moment, God spoke the basic unit of all matter and antimatter into existence. From that moment on, God called many other creative features into existence (Gen 1:6-25); Scripture each time stating that God was pleased with His creation, pronouncing it good.

After preparing planet earth as a home for his children, *"God [Elohiym (plural) said: "Let us make humankind in our image, in the likeness of ourselves; and let them rule over the fish in the sea, the birds in the air, the animals, and over all the earth, and over every crawling creature that crawls on the earth." So God created humankind in his own image; in the image of God he created him: male and female he created them"* (Gen 1:26-27 CJB). ... *"Then Adonai, God, formed a person [Hebrew: Adam] from the dust [elements] of the ground*

[Hebrew: adamah (red earth)] *and breathed into his nostrils the breath of life, so that he became a living being"* (Gen 2:7-8 CJB).

In these Scriptures, God imagined, God spoke, and God carried out the formative processes necessary – from mater [photon] cerated earlier – to manifest, in the physical realm, his imagination.

Mankind was not given dominion over the spiritual [antimatter] features of the cosmos – he was given dominion over only the physical realm [matter] on planet earth. The earth and all that there was thereon, was placed under man's dominion and remained under his rule until he acquiesced his dominion to Satan. So, when God called the Sons of the Morning together and Satan appeared among them, representing earth (Job 1:6-7; 2:1-2), he was the rightful ruler.

But, in the fullness of time, Christ came to earth, waged a victorious battle against Satan, and after entering the netherworld to proclaim his victory over all satanic and demonic forces, he restored the dominion of earth to the rule of mankind. The fact that we are unaware of this, does not negate its reality. Whether one knows it or not is the difference between whether one is walking by sight, or walking in faith. Scripture – both Old and New Testaments – declare that the just shall live by faith.

Regarding those who live by faith, Habakkuk wrote: *"Look at the proud: he is inwardly not upright; but the righteous will attain life through trusting faithfulness"* (Hab 2:4 CJB). The apostle Paul wrote: *"For I am not ashamed of the Good News, since it is God's powerful means of bringing salvation to everyone who keeps on trusting, to the Jew especially, but equally to the Gentile. For in it is revealed how God makes people righteous in his sight; and from beginning to end it is through trust - as the law puts it, "The person who is righteous will live his life by faith"* (Rom 1:16-17).

"Now it is evident that no one comes to be declared righteous by God through legalism, since "The person who is righteous will attain life by trusting and being faithful." Furthermore, legalism is not based on trusting and being faithful, but on [a misuse of] the text that says, "Anyone who does these things will attain life through them." The Messiah redeemed us from the curse pronounced in the Torah [Law] by becoming cursed on our behalf; for the Tanakh says [it is written], "Everyone who hangs from a stake comes under a curse" (Gal 3:11-13 CJB).

The author of the Book of Hebrews states the case for righteousness by faith so succinctly: *"There is so, so little time! The One coming will indeed come, he will not delay. But the person who is righteous will live his life by trusting [faith], and if he shrinks back, I will not be pleased with him." However, we are not the kind who shrink back and are destroyed; on the contrary, we keep trusting [exercising faith] and thus preserve our lives! Trusting [faith] is being confident of what we hope for, convinced about things we do not see. It was for this that Scripture attested the merit of the people of old"* (Heb 10:37-11:2 CJB).

We live in a two-dimensional reality: 1) the phenomenal, or physical [outer] dimension – lived in and through our body' and 2) the pneumenal, or spiritual [inner] dimension – lived in and through our soul and spirit. In our outer dimension, that is limited to our immediate environment, our focus is on our physical needs – air, water, food, clothing, shelter and sexual fulfillment.

In our inner dimension, which transcends all time and space, our focus is on our spiritual, emotional and intellectual needs. It is here – in our inner-being – that we spend the greater part of life. It is within our inner-being that we develop our self-concept, or self-image, our beliefs, values, attitudes, principles, etc. It is our subconscious that serves as the filter we see the world through; that directs our decisions and controls our behavior. It is the content of our subconscious that is manifest in and through our outer dimension, or body.

It is also within our inner-being, or subconscious, that we have experienced the most disabling wounds, and developed life-controlling problems, It is, however, within our power, through salvation in Christ Jesus, and the resulting indwelling of Holy Spirit, to heal our core-being. Being born-again, thereby entering the process of salvation, our spirit is quickened, transforming us from a two-dimensional being into a three-dimensional being [physical, psychological and spiritual.]

This transformation alters our self-concept, values, beliefs, attitudes and principles; providing us a new outlook on life. From this point forward in life, our inner-thoughts will emanate from our spirit – governed by Holy Spirit, rather than from our wounded soul, controlled by past hurts and unrequited pain, that guides us back into hurtful relationships and situations.

The apostle Paul described this difference, saying: "You used to be dead because of your sins and acts of disobedience. You walked in the ways of the worldly culture and obeyed the Ruler of the Powers of the Air, who is still at work among the disobedient. Indeed, we all once lived this way — we followed the passions of our old nature and obeyed the wishes of our old nature and our own thoughts. In our natural condition we were *headed for God's wrath, just like everyone else. But God is so rich in mercy and loves us with such intense love that, even when we were dead because of our acts of disobedience, he brought us to life along with the Messiah – it is by grace that you have been delivered"* (Eph 2:1-5). ... *"Therefore, if anyone is in Christ, he is a new creation; the old has gone, the new has come!"* (2 Cor 5:17).

Once born-again [born from above] in Christ, we are – once again – spirit beings, indwelled by Holy Spirit. Jesus, explaining this to Nicodemus, said: *"Indeed, I tell you that unless a person is born from water and the Spirit, he cannot enter the Kingdom of God. What is born from the flesh is flesh, and what is born from the Spirit is spirit"* (John 3:5-7 CJB).

Spirits operate according to spiritual laws, not physical or soulish [psychological] laws. Therefore, if we – being born-again – are to function effectively as a three-dimensional being [body, soul and spirit], we must begin to study God's Word, to search out His immutable, universal laws, that if lived by, will enable us to enjoy an abundant life in the earthly, physical realm, have peace within our soul [the psychological realm], and enjoy eternal life within the spiritual realm.

Jesus said: *"The thief comes only in order to steal, kill and destroy; [But] I have come so that they may have life, life abundantly in its fullest measure"* (John 10:10) ... *"Everyone who believes and trusts in him may have eternal life"* (John 3:15).

Most Christians have again and again, opened their Bibles and read these words: *"In the beginning, God"* – without ever comprehending their full significance – that everything originates in God. The spiritual realm is the causal realm, as Jesus declared in his model prayer: *"Our Father in heaven!May your Name be kept holy. May your Kingdom come.* **May your will be done on earth as it is in heaven"** (Matt 6:9-10).

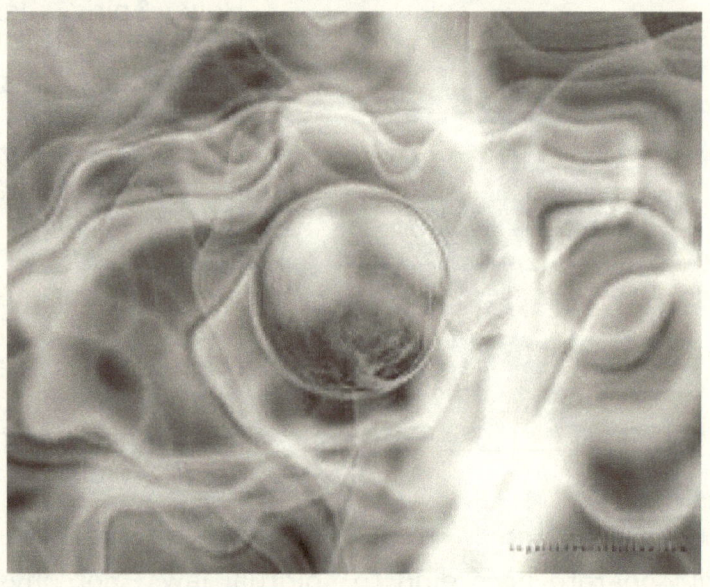

God's will is already being done in heaven. Since the spiritual realm is the casual realm, it is imperative that we understand how this realm operates; and how its operation affects the earthly realm – the soulish and physical realm that we inhabit. Our failure to understand how the spirit realm functions will keep us from hearing God's voice, preventing any real change, resulting in our being immature, impotent Christians.

Paul warned of this saying: *"But mark this: There will be terrible times in the last days. People will be lovers of themselves, lovers of money, boastful, proud, abusive, disobedient to their parents, ungrateful, unholy, without love, unforgiving, slanderous, without self-control, brutal, not lovers of the good, treacherous, rash, conceited,* **lovers of pleasure rather than lovers of God – having a form of godliness but denying its power**. *Have nothing to do with them. They are the kind who worm their way into homes and gain control over weak-willed women, who are loaded down with sins and are swayed by all kinds of evil desires,* **always learning but never able to acknowledge the truth**" (2 Tim 3:1-8).

To these, the Gospel seems veiled, or obscured. And Paul, speaking of these, said: **"If the gospel is veiled, it is veiled to those who are perishing. The god of this age has blinded the minds of unbelievers, so that they cannot see the light of the gospel of the glory of Christ, who is the image of God**. *For we do not preach ourselves, but Jesus Christ as Lord, and ourselves as your servants for Jesus' sake. For* **God, who said, "Let light shine out of darkness," made his light shine in our hearts to give us the light of the knowledge of the glory of God in the face of**

Christ. And we have this treasure in jars of clay to show that this all-surpassing power is from God and not from us" (2 Cor 4:3-8).

Our soul [our intellect, emotions, beliefs, attitudes, values, etc.] guides – and is manifest in and through – our body. The eternal question we must answer, is: Who controls my soul? As much as we would like to consider ourselves to be self-controlled, all the evidence in Scripture is contrary to this.

Joshua, preparatory to taking the Children of Israel across the Jordan River into Canaan, the Promised Land, assembled the people and challenged them to examine themselves, saying: *"Fear Adonai, and serve him truly and sincerely. Put away all the gods your ancestors served beyond the [Euphrates] River and in Egypt, and serve Adonai! [But] If it seems bad to you to serve Adonai, then* **choose today whom you are going to serve!** *Will it be the gods your ancestors served beyond the River? or the gods of the Emori, in whose land you are living? As for me and my household, we will serve Adonai!"* (Josh 24:14-15 CJB).

Joshua did not challenge them to be self-controlled; he said, "choose today whom you are going to serve." Our choice is – and always has been – to serve the Lord Our God as an obedient child; or to serve Satan as a slave. We may imagine ourselves to be self-controlled, but the apostle Paul, made it abundantly clear that self-control is a spiritual gift, bestowed on those who are born-again and spirit-filled.

Describing the difference between one governed by the flesh as opposed to one governed by the indwelling Holy Spirit; Paul set forth the evidence of those controlled by Satan, comparing them with one who is born-again and spirit-filled, which he identified as the 'fruit of the Spirit.'

"So I say, live by the Spirit, and you will not gratify the desires of the sinful nature. For the sinful nature desires what is contrary to the Spirit, and the Spirit what is contrary to the sinful nature. They are in conflict with each other, so that you do not do what you want. But if you are led by the Spirit, you are not under law.

"The acts of the sinful nature are obvious: sexual immorality, impurity and debauchery; idolatry and witchcraft; hatred, discord, jealousy, fits of rage, selfish ambition, dissensions, factions and envy; drunkenness, orgies, and the like. I warn you, as I did before, that those who live like this will not inherit the kingdom of God.

"But the fruit of the Spirit is love, joy, peace, patience, kindness, goodness, faithfulness, gentleness and self-control. Against such things there is no law. **Those who belong to Christ Jesus have crucified the sinful nature with its passions and desires. Since we live by the Spirit, let us keep in step with the Spirit**" (Gal 5:16-25).

Since self-control is a gift – or manifestation – of the indwelling Holy Spirit guiding our life, fallen human beings are not, and cannot be, self-controlled. Someone – either Holy Spirit, or Satan – is always guiding, governing – controlling, if you please – our soul; and through our soul, our body.

Satan and the demons under his command would love to have man worship them, viewing them as gods. Ancient Babylon embraced them, becoming the sponsor of the mystery religions that have engulfed the globe. The children of Israel were seduced by them; giving in to worshiping them and sacrificing to them – even to sacrificing their own sons and daughters!

In the Hellenistic culture of the first century, the Greeks worshiped a pantheon of gods, which the early church fathers identified as demons. The worship of demons was so common during that era, the Apostle Paul cautioned the church concerning them, saying: *"The Spirit clearly says that in later times some will apostatize [abandon] the faith and follow deceiving spirits and things taught by demons. Such teachings come through hypocritical liars, whose own consciences have been seared as with a hot iron"* (1 Tim 4:1-2).

The deceptive teachings promoted by those controlled by demons, will – Jesus warned – *"fool even the chosen, if possible"* (Mt 24:24). How then, are the saints – you and I – to discern the difference between the spirits, to prevent satanic and demonic forces from indwelling our spirits and corrupting our souls? The apostle Paul provided a clear, sure preventive measure, available to every born-again believer.

Paul said: *"This is my prayer: that your love may abound more and more in knowledge and depth of insight, so* **that you may be able to discern what is best and may be pure and blameless until the day of Christ, filled with the fruit of righteousness that comes through Jesus Christ** – *to the glory and praise of God"* (Phil 1:9-11).

In his letter to the Corinthians, Paul provided this assurance to those who are filled with righteousness that comes through Jesus Christ, saying: **"he who unites himself with the Lord is one with him in spirit"** (1 Cor 6:17).

Explaining this further, Paul wrote: *"The Torah [Law] of the Spirit, which produces this life in union with Messiah Yeshua, has set me free from the Torah [Law] of sin and death"* (Rom 8:2-3 CJB). ... And, *"God's peace, passing all understanding, will keep your hearts and minds safe in union with the Messiah Yeshua"* (Phil 4:7-8).

It may help you better comprehend what Paul is describing, if you view your soul as a computer. Now, imagine that your computer [your soul] has two operating systems installed: the Law of God; and the Law of Sin and Death. Also loaded on your computer [soul] are many programs that can be operated in either operating system – [programs such as beliefs, tenets, attitudes, values, principles, ethics, taboos, etc.].

Prior to being born-again, we had only one operating system through which the programs identified could function – the Law of Sin and Death – meaning that all program functions, had one, and only one, outcome: sin and death. As born-again Christians, we have – through the indwelling Holy Spirit – a second operating system installed: the Law of God. However, the old operating system – the Law of Sin and Death – is still resident in our soul. Therefore, for the output of my computer [my behavior] to be different than before my salvation, new instructions must be given and a new data-base developed from which to operate.

This is essentially what Paul describes as the 'transformation of the soul.' In his letter to the Christians in Rome he wrote: *"In other words, do not let yourselves be conformed to the standards of the 'olam hazeh [present world culture]. Instead, keep letting yourselves be transformed by the continual renewing of your minds; so that you will know what God wants and will agree that what he wants is good, satisfying and able to achieve"* (Rom 12:2 CJB).

Although indwelled by Holy Spirit, our wounded soul still needs to be healed, or transformed. That, which prior to our salvation seemed impossible, now becomes possible – those things that were beyond our ability to achieve, are now achievable – all because of the indwelling Holy Spirit. Solomon, grasped this potential and wrote: **"The human spirit is the lamp of Adonai; it searches one's inmost being"** (Prov 20:27 CJB). Solomon's father, King David, who recognized the importance of this, wrote: **"For you, Adonai, light my lamp; Adonai, my God, lights up my darkness"** (Ps 18:29 CJB).

Jesus, employing this same metaphor, said: *"No one who has kindled a lamp hides it or places it under a bowl; rather, he puts it on a stand, so that those coming in may see its light.* **The lamp of your body is the eye.** *When you have a 'good eye,' [that is, when you are generous,] your whole body is full of light; but when you have an 'evil eye,' [when* *you are stingy,] your body is full of darkness.* **So take care that the light in you is not darkness! If, then, your whole body is filled with light, with no part dark, it will be wholly lighted, as when a brightly lit lamp shines on you"** (Luke 11:33-36 CJB).

Inner-Healing:
Inner-healing equates to a combination of Inner-seeing [imagination], plus inner-speaking [self-talk or inner-dialog], plus inner-hearing [hearing the voice of God]. This equates to imaginatively creating life; or walking in the Spirit by faith, in the light of God, which will promote health and well-being of body, soul and spirit.

The apostle Paul, who admonished us to be transformed by the continual renewal of our mind (soul); providing us the guidance necessary both to achieve inner-healing and to walk in the Spirit. He says, *"So if you were raised along with the Messiah, then seek the things above, where the Messiah is sitting at the right hand of God. Focus your minds on the things above, not on things here on earth. For you have died, and your life is hidden with the Messiah in God. When the Messiah, who is our life, appears, then you too will appear with him in glory!*

"Therefore, put to death the earthly parts of your nature – sexual immorality, impurity, lust, evil desires and greed (which is a form of idolatry); for it is because of these things that God's anger is coming on those who disobey him. True enough, you used to practice these things in the life you once lived; but now, put them all

away ... because you have stripped away the old self, with its ways, and have put on the new self, which is continually being renewed in fuller and fuller knowledge, closer and closer to the image of our Creator" (Col 3:1-11 CJB).

Elaborating on this idea in his letter to the Christians in Rome, Paul wrote: *"For those who identify with their old nature **set their minds** on the things of the old nature, but those who identify with the Spirit **set their minds** on the things of the Spirit. **Having one's mind controlled by the old nature is death, but having one's mind controlled by the Spirit is life and shalom [peace]**. For **the mind controlled by the old nature is hostile to God**, because it does not submit itself to God's Torah — indeed, it cannot. Thus, those who identify with their old nature cannot please God.*

"But you, you do not identify with your old nature but with the Spirit – provided the Spirit of God is living inside you, for anyone who doesn't have the [indwelling] Spirit of the Messiah doesn't belong to him. However, if the Messiah is in you, then, on the one hand, the body is dead because of sin; but, on the other hand, the Spirit is giving life because God considers you righteous. And if the Spirit of the One who raised Yeshua from the dead is living in you, then the One who raised the Messiah Yeshua from the dead will also give life to your mortal bodies through his Spirit living in you" (Rom 8:5-11 CJB).

The word 'mind' highlighted in the text above, is translated from the Greek word, *'phren'*, pertaining to one's feelings, or sensitive nature, which are aspects or functions, or one's subconscious, including one's imagination. It is that portion of our soul that is occupied and controlled by either: the powers of darkness, whose intent are to steal, kill and destroy; or by Holy Spirit, that lights our candle [lamp of our soul]; illuminating both soul and spirit [our entire inner-being].

In other words, whatever, or whomever, controls our subconscious [our imagination and emotions] will control our entire being and become manifest in our behavior – defining our reality.

Our next chapter will examine what Scripture reveals about how we can use our imagination to change our life, our relationships, and the world. We will also reveal exciting new scientific discoveries that confirm the Word of God, providing us additional tools that we can use to pull down the strongholds of the Enemy, and build up the Kingdom of God.

~ Questions, Concerns & Key Points ~

1. How did God use captivity, or bondage, together with man's imagination, to spiritually restore Israel?

2. Does God still use bondage – addictions – together with imagination, to restore men?

3. Scripture says the heart of man is deceitfully wicked, beyond our comprehension. How then, can we discover what God sees in our heart (spirit and soul)?

4. What can man do – in cooperation with God – to correct the deviancy within our soul?

5. Describe the function of visualization in effecting change; and in realizing God's blessings?

6. Identify some of the biblical examples of an individual employing visualization to effect change and/or realize God's blessings?

7. What is the limit, or scope, of man's ability to alter his environment?

8. What change is effected in this scope by our being born-again?

9. Describe your understanding of the words of Matt 6:9-10.

10. How can man develop self-control?

11. Identify the components of inner-healing?

Chapter 17 The Power of Imagination – Part 3

A change in our imaginations = A Change in our life and Changing our life = Change in our World: both our inner-world and our outer-world.

As we mentioned in the closing paragraphs of our last lesson; whoever, or whatever, controls our subconscious mind [our imaginations, beliefs, values and emotions] will also control our intellect, thus directing our behavior; thereby becoming our manifest reality.

Winner of Inner-Conflicts:
Whenever our will and our imaginations are in conflict with one another, our imaginations will win. This is serious since **it is our imagination that forms our beliefs, values and attitudes; our self-concept, or self-image; our world-view; our concept of those who we relate to; and most importantly, our concept of God**. Formed in our imagination, these concepts are then stored in our memory, which – in conjunction with our Reticular Formation – will govern what we will accept as truth, or reject as falsehood; and will thus govern our decisions. In fact, our subconscious mind consistently overrides our conscious mind, defeating our intellect and reason in fulfilling our desires. This, no doubt, is why the apostle Paul, said: *"Clothe yourselves with the Lord Yeshua the Messiah; and don't waste your time thinking about how to provide for the sinful desires of your old nature"* (Rom 13:14 CJB).

1 Picture = 1,000 words:
How can our subconscious mind have such power? As the old cliché pictured at the right declares, "A Picture is Worth a Thousand Words." And, while our intellect operates on an alphanumeric

analytical basis; our subconscious mind processes information as pictures – according to size, shape, color, arrangement, etc.; together with associated sounds, smells, taste and feel. What we see, together with its associated sensory information, we experience, and what we experience, we are far more likely to remember than what we analytically determine to be true based on facts we have received.

Therefore, what controls our imagination – our inner-imagery – truly controls our life. As Solomon wrote many, many years ago: *"As a man thinks in his inner-being, so he is, or will be"* (Pro 23:7). Understanding this, prompted him to write:

"My son, pay attention to what I say; listen closely to my words. Do not let them out of your sight, keep them within your heart; for they are life to those who find them and health to a man's whole body. **Above all else, guard your heart, for it is the wellspring of life**" (Prov 4:20-23 NIV). Notice that while Solomon said that there is life in his words, he says '**do not let them out of your sight**,' and above, or beyond, these words, guard your heart.

The word translated 'heart' in this text is the Hebrew word, 'libekaa' referring to one's inner-being, and more often translated as feelings, or understanding. It is the power of our subconscious that prompted the apostle Paul to counsel us: *For though we live in the world, we do not wage war as the world does.*

"The weapons we fight with are not the weapons of the world. On the contrary, they have divine power to

demolish strongholds. We demolish arguments and every pretension that sets itself up against the knowledge of God, and we **take captive every thought to make it obedient to Christ**" (2 Cor 10:5 NIV).

While the words of Solomon, and his father, King David, brought life, they were – being based on the Law given Moses, to be surpassed in glory. The apostle Paul speaks of this, saying: *"Now if the ministry that brought death, which was* **engraved in letters on stone***, came with glory, so that the Israelites could not look steadily at the face of Moses because of its glory, fading though it was, will not the ministry of the Spirit be even more glorious? If the ministry that condemns men is glorious, how much more glorious is the ministry that brings righteousness! For what was glorious has no glory now in comparison with the surpassing glory. And if what was fading away came with glory, how much greater is the glory of that which lasts!*

"Therefore, since we have such a hope, we are very bold. We are not like Moses, who would put a veil over his face to keep the Israelites from gazing at it while the radiance was fading away. But their minds were made dull, for **to this day the same veil remains when the old covenant is read. It has not been removed, because only in Christ is it taken away***. Even to this day when Moses is read, a veil covers their hearts. But* **whenever anyone turns to the Lord, the veil is taken away***.*

*"Now the Lord is the Spirit, and where the Spirit of the Lord is, there is freedom. A***nd we, who with unveiled faces all reflect the Lord's glory, are being transformed into his likeness with ever-increasing glory, which comes from the Lord, who is the Spirit**" (2 Cor 3:7-18 NIV).

Under the Old Testament, believers lived their lives according to prescriptive Law; a law that served as a veil, preventing them from beholding the full glory of God; but through Christ, our Savior, this veil has been removed, and we can – in spirit-to-spirit union with Christ, enter the Holy of Holies and stand before the Throne of Grace. True, we cannot yet behold Him as He is. Like Balaam of old, we must say: *"I see Him, but not now; I behold Him, but not near"* (Num 24:17). Only in our imagination – our 'inner-seeing' can we in this present time gaze into His eyes.

But, *"since we are children of God,* **we shouldn't suppose that God's essence resembles gold, silver or stone shaped by human technique and imagination**. *"In the past, God overlooked such ignorance; but now he is commanding all people everywhere to turn to him from their sins"* (Acts 17:29-30 CJB). As the apostle Paul declared: *"Dear friends, now* **we are children of God, and what we will be has not yet been made known. But we know that when he appears, we shall be like him, for we shall see him as he is**. *Everyone who has this hope in him purifies himself, just as he is pure"* (1 John 3:2-3 NIV).

Co-creators:
Like our heavenly Father, and our elder brother, Jesus, we are creators. As Christians, we have – through the power of Holy Spirit, Who indwells our spirit – the ability to create things that bring ourselves and others life; yet, we must never forget that the old man of sin still lies resident within our soul, and will if resurrected, create things that minister death; both to ourselves and to others. Like our heavenly Father and elder Brother, we create by making a declaration of our imaginations. *"The tongue has the power over life and death, and those who indulge it, or love it, must eat its fruit"* (Prov 18:21 CJB).

Jesus clarified the deciding factor between whether our tongue produces life or death, saying: *"If you make a tree good, its fruit will be good; and if you make a tree bad, its fruit will be bad; for a tree is known by its fruit."* [To the Pharisees who were challenging him, he said:] *"You snakes! How can you who are evil say anything good? For the mouth speaks what overflows from the heart. The good person brings forth good things from his store of good, and the evil person brings forth evil things from his store of evil. ... by your own words you will be acquitted, and by your own words, you will be condemned"* (Matt 12:33-36 CJB).

The Seedbed of Life:
"Jesus told ... another parable: "The kingdom of heaven is like a man who sowed good seed in his field. But while everyone was sleeping, his enemy came and sowed weeds among the wheat, and went away. When the wheat sprouted and formed heads, then the weeds also appeared. "The owner's servants came to him and said, 'Sir, didn't you sow good seed in your field? Where then did the weeds come from?' "An enemy did this,' he replied. "The servants asked him, 'Do you want us to go and pull them up?'

*"'No,' he answered, 'because while you are pulling the weeds, you may root up the wheat with them. Let both grow together until the harvest. At that time I will tell the harvesters: First collect the weeds and tie them in

bundles to be burned; then gather the wheat and bring it into my barn'" (Matt 13:24-30 NIV). ... "Then he left the crowd and went into the house. His disciples came to him and said, "Explain to us the parable of the weeds in the field."

"He answered, "The one who sowed the good seed is the Son of Man. The field is the world, and the good seed stands for the sons of the kingdom. The weeds are the sons of the evil one, and the enemy who sows them is the devil. The harvest is the end of the age, and the harvesters are angels. "As the weeds are pulled up and burned in the fire, so it will be at the end of the age. The Son of Man will send out his angels, and they will weed out of his kingdom everything that causes sin and all who do evil. They will throw them into the fiery furnace, where there will be weeping and gnashing of teeth. Then the righteous will shine like the sun in the kingdom of their Father. He who has ears, let him hear" (Matt 13:36-43).

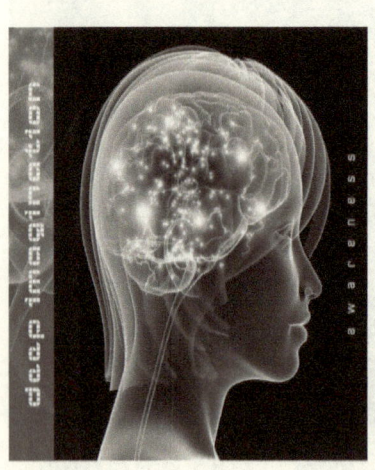

Our imagination is the seedbed that contains both good and bad seeds – the good planted by God and His agents [godly parents, teachers, clergy, etc.], and the bad by Satan and his agents [demoniacally influenced people and demons themselves]. God and His agents sow seeds of truth, since God is true. "*For the word of the Lord is right and true; he is faithful in all he does*" (Ps 33:4 NIV). In contrast, Satan and his agents sow seeds of error, since he is a liar. "*He was a murderer from the beginning, not holding to the truth, for there is no truth in him. When he lies, he speaks his native language, for he is a liar and the father of lies*" (John 8:44-45 NIV).

Satan is the arch-deceiver *"that age-old serpent, who is called the Devil and Satan, he who is the seducer (deceiver) of all humanity the world over"* (Rev 12:9 AMP). His seeds are – like the tares sown among the wheat in Christ's parable – counterfeits: lust in place of love; jealousy in place of loving care; power and control in place of nurture; greed in place of generosity; slavery in place of servitude; etc.

As we grow, the seeds – both the good and the bad – germinate; and at first, it is very hard to tell them apart, because they have yet to produce any fruit. But as they mature and begin to bear fruit, the difference between the genuine – God-breathed seed, and Satan's counterfeit seed is striking.

"The acts of the sinful nature are obvious: *sexual immorality, impurity and debauchery; idolatry and witchcraft; hatred, discord, jealousy, fits of rage, selfish ambition, dissensions, factions and envy; drunkenness, orgies, and the like. I warn you, as I did before, that those who live like this will not inherit the kingdom of God. But the fruit of the Spirit is love, joy, peace, patience, kindness, goodness, faithfulness, gentleness and self-control. Against such things there is no law"* (Gal 5:19-23 NIV).

Different seeds not only produce different looking plants [people]; they not only produce different fruit [behavior]; the final disposition of the plants is different – the good seed producing, as it were perennial plants, and the bad seed, annual plants. Explaining his parable of the field sown with good seed and bad, Jesus explained to his disciples that, *"The harvest is the end of* the age, and the harvesters are angels. As the weeds are pulled up and burned in the fire, so it will be at the end of the age. The Son of Man will send out his angels, and they will weed out of his kingdom everything that causes sin and all who do evil. They will throw them into the fiery furnace, where there will be weeping and gnashing of teeth. Then the righteous will shine like the sun in the kingdom of their Father. He who has ears, let him hear" (Matt 13:39-43 NIV).

"**All of us ... at one time**" [were controlled by the seeds of wrath], "*gratifying the cravings of our sinful nature and following its desires and thoughts. Like the rest, we **were by nature objects of wrath**. But because of his great love for us, God, who is rich in mercy, made us alive with Christ even when we were dead in transgressions*" (Eph 2:3-5 NIV). ... [But] "*God raised us up with Christ and seated us with him in the heavenly realms in Christ Jesus, in order that in the coming ages he might show the incomparable riches of his grace, expressed in his kindness to us in Christ Jesus*" (Eph 2:6-8 NIV).

Through Jesus' substitutionary death for our sins, "*God placed all things under his feet and appointed him to be head over everything for the church, which is his body, the fullness of him who fills everything in every way*" (Eph 1:22-23 NIV). Through his substitutionary death, a doorway was opened, enabling us, who were once objects of wrath, to become reconciled with God.

"*Therefore, brothers, since **we have confidence to enter the Most Holy Place by the blood of Jesus, by a new and living way opened for us through the curtain [veil], that is, his body**"* (Heb 10:19-21 NIV); "Ask and it will be given to you; seek and you will find; **knock and the door will be opened to you**. For everyone who asks receives; he who seeks finds; and **to him who knocks, the door will be opened**" (Matt 7:7-8 NIV).

This doorway through the veil, into the Holy of Holies provides us access to Father God, and His Throne of Grace; but the *"**gospel is veiled, it is veiled to those who are perishing**; [for] the god of this age has blinded the minds of unbelievers, so that they cannot see the light of the gospel of the glory of Christ, who is the image of God"* (2 Cor 4:3-5 NIV).

What is this veil? Remember, Satan is a cunning deceiver, a counterfeiter; thus he uses – or rather, misuses -- what most believe is right – the Law, or legalism.

The apostle Paul, reminds us that when Moses came down from Mt. Sinai carrying the Decalogue, they put a veil over his face because the glory of God emanating from his face sent fear through the Israelites. Then, after laying his foundation, he said: *"to this day the same veil remains when the old covenant is read. It has not been removed, because only in Christ is it taken away. Even to this day when Moses [the Law] is read, a veil covers their hearts. But **whenever anyone turns to the Lord, the veil is taken away**"* (2 Cor 3:14-16 NIV).

In contrast to the legalism that hung over Israel, and in keeping with his parable about the good seed and bad, Jesus, in his last comments to his disciples, said: *"My children, I will be with you only a little longer. You will look for me, and just as I told the Jews, so I tell you now: Where I am going, you cannot now come. "**A new command I give you: Love one another. As I have loved you, so you must love one another. By this all men will know that you are my disciples, if you love one another**"* (John 13:33-35 NIV).

*"You did not choose me, but **I chose you and appointed you to go and bear fruit — fruit that will last**. Then the Father will give you whatever you ask in*

*my name. **This is my command: Love each other**"* (John 15:16-17 NIV). *"Remain in me, and I will remain in you. No branch can bear fruit by itself; it must remain in the vine. Neither can you bear fruit unless you remain in me. "I am the vine; you are the branches. **If a man remains in me and I in him, he will bear much fruit; apart from me you can do nothing**"* (John 15:4-6 NIV). *"This is to my Father's glory, that you **bear much fruit**, showing yourselves to be my disciples"* (John 15:8 NIV).

The apostle Paul, bringing to a conclusion, the difference between the Old Covenant based on the Decalogue, and the New Covenant based on love, said: *"So, my brothers, you also died to the law through the body of Christ, that you might **belong to another**, to him who was raised from the dead, in order that we might **bear fruit to God**. For **when we were controlled by the sinful nature, the sinful passions aroused by the law were at work in our bodies, so that we bore fruit for death**. But now, by dying to what once bound us, we have been released from the law so that we serve in the new way of the Spirit, and not in the old way of the written code"* (Rom 7:4-6 NIV).

What makes the difference in which seeds germinate, grow and bear fruit to God? Reverting once again to Solomon, we read again: *"For as a man thinks in his heart [his inner-being], so he is [so it will be]"* (Pro 23:7). if Satan can control our thoughts, he can – and will – control us. Understanding this, Paul wrote: *"For although we do live in the world, we do not wage war in a worldly way; because the weapons we use to wage war are not worldly. On the contrary, they have God's power for demolishing strongholds. We demolish arguments and every arrogance that raises itself up against the knowledge of God; we **take every thought captive and make it obey Yeshua the Messiah**"* (2 Cor 10:3-6 CJB).

By taking our thoughts – our imaginations and emotions – captive, we nullify and/or eradicate, demonic imagery that would otherwise set itself up as a stronghold against the truth, in arrogance, creating arguments and disputing the knowledge of God. Consider the power of negative thoughts, or imaginations. The Patriarch Job, after being assailed by Satan, declared: *"My sighing serves in place of my food, my groans pour out in a torrent; for the very thing I feared has overwhelmed me, what I dreaded most has happened to me"* (Job 3:23-24).

Could Job's negative thoughts really have such power? Employing the graphical depiction of known wavelengths in the universe, inserted below, imagine that the seen spectrum shown in the lower bar, were to represent the Voice of America – the strongest radio wave on earth. The human brain emits a radio wave, in its frequency that would far exceed the limits of wavelength represented by the top bar! Moreover, how a person thinks – whether positive or negative – determines which end of the band he or she operates in.

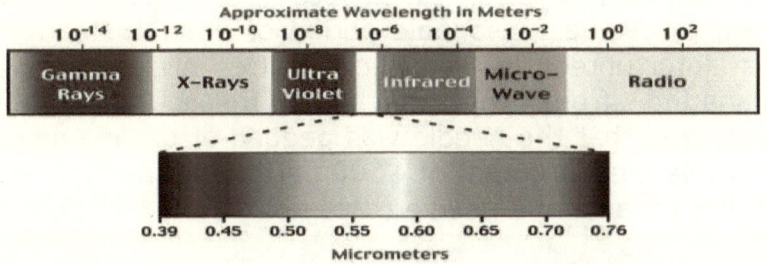

Our brains are continually broadcasting – sending our thoughts, both intellectual and emotional, over the air waves in a frequency band far outside our ability to see, hear or feel them, but nevertheless, they are real and can be transformed into tangible form in the same manner that radio waves can be transformed to music, and T.V. signals can be transformed into pictures and sound. In each case, they need only a receiver; and in the case of brain waves, others' brains form the receivers.

Dr. Jerome Stowell, a NASA scientist, developed an extremely sensitive electronic device to measure waves emanating from the brain. By agreement, he set up an experiment at a local hospital, in the ward treating the terminally ill to see if there were any discernible difference in the brain waves of those thinking positive thoughts, compared with those focused on the negative. His research findings were beyond his expectations.

Case Number One:
In one instance, he set up his instrument outside the room of an elderly woman who was worshiping and praising the Lord. After setting up the instrument, he settled back, waiting to collect the results of her thoughts over a reasonable period of time. Instead, he was interrupted by a 'click, click, clicking' noise emanating from the machine. Inspecting it, he discovered that the needle was pegged at the maximum allowable measurement of +500 parts. The machine was clicking because the needle could not go any higher.

Case Number Two:
Following what he thought to be very unusual results obtained in case # 1; the scientist set his equipment up outside the room of a man who had been identified by the nurses as 'negative.' He was easily angered and when his needs were not immediately met, he would yell, scream and curse the nurses, even taking the Lord's name in vain to add emphasis. Once again the scientist set up his equipment and settled back in a chair to collect his data. Almost immediately, the man began yelling and cursing; and once again the machine began clicking; 'Click, click, click'; but when the scientist inspected it, the needle was pegged this time at the opposite end – at a -500 parts – the highest it could go.

With Dr. Stowell was a group of research scientists, all of whom were astonished, since they had previously measured the output of a 50,000 watt radio station, that had registered a mere +9 parts on the dial! These cases, said Dr. Stowell, 'made me think seriously about my spiritual condition.' Later, when a fellow scientist shared with him about our Lord and Savior, Jesus Christ, telling him that Christ had died for his sins, Dr. Stowell became a believer, acknowledging Christ Jesus as his Lord and Savior.

We are constantly broadcasting our thoughts, imaginations, attitudes and emotions, creating our own environment, and influencing the environment of others. Depending on the content of the data transmitted, we contribute to an atmosphere of light, attracting God's holy angels; or an atmosphere of darkness, attracting the principalities and powers of darkness – the rulers of evil in the heavenly realms. It is our choice who and what we invite into our presence: God's angels and His blessings, or the Adversary's demons and their attacks.

Each person's brain waves are unique – much like our fingerprints, our DNA, or the cornea of our eyes. Like data that is transmitted over the Internet encrypted, our thoughts, in a unique pattern, are broadcast into the ether. It is mathematically and electronically impossible to duplicate the rhythmic pattern of a single thought, let alone trying to duplicate an individual's thought pattern.

The Life You Create

By J. V. Potter

You are building the life you will live; tis yours to make right or to mar;

By the power of thought you are building, each block, be it a stone or a star;

Dark stones from the earth, or bright stars from the sky; Which form the walls of your soul?

Is your life broken like stones from a cistern or gleaming like stars from the sky?

Or made of blocks that were hewed from God's quarry, each one cut so precisely, so square;

Then, fit into the walls of His temple, with His own loving nurture and care?

The Power of Our Broadcasts:

It is one thing to grasp the fact that we are constantly broadcasting information of an almost unimaginable strength within our brain frequency; it is an entirely different matter when one begins to comprehend the effects of the data broadcast, both on ourselves and on others.

The Effect on Ourselves:
Our Thoughts ~ Few people think what they think they are thinking. Think about it: do you really know what you are thinking about most of the time? Our thoughts are revealed by the kind of life we lead. If you are happy and successful, you have been thinking thoughts of happiness and success. If you are wading through an endless stream of problems and finding life painful to bear, it is caused by your own thoughts of doubt, failure, anger, helplessness, incompetence, and pain. In other words, whether you think life is miserable or great, you're correct, for life is whatever you think it is. Solomon knew precisely what he was talking about when he penned: *"For as a man thinks in his heart, so he will be"* (Pro 23:7).

Our Emotions ~ To understand the impact of our emotions upon ourselves, we need to first look at the etiology, or origin, of the word emotion. It is a contraction of three words – *'energy-in-motion.'* When we receive sensory information, [i.e., what we see, hear, taste, touch and/or smell], it disturbs our electrochemical homeostasis (balance). This in turn, triggers the production within our body, of certain hormones or other chemicals; and their release, which is designed to restore our electrochemical balance. In some instances, such as when one becomes angry, this chemical balancing act can take up to seventy-two (72) hours!

This activity takes place within our subconscious mind. Therefore, we don't think our emotions, we feel them. What we are feeling is the imbalance in our electrochemical makeup; and the greater the imbalance, the stronger our emotions. Unlike our intellectual thoughts, they are not expended externally; but are dissipated over time, within our own body. This affects our autonomic nervous system, that regulates numerous body functions including: heart rate, breathing, blood pressure, digestion, urinary tract and bowels, pancreas, gallbladder, etc.

This in turn, creates additional problems – spiritual ones. For example; the apostle Paul warned: *"Be angry, but don't sin — don't let the sun go down before you have dealt with the cause of your anger; otherwise you leave room for the Adversary"* (Eph 4:26-27 CJB). The question most ask, is "How can my emotions – the imbalance in my electrochemical homeostasis – provide a doorway for the Adversary?' The answer is relatively simple.

Anger, worry, embarrassment, shame, depression, and other strong emotions, do two things: they give rise to strong, negative imaginations; and they open the Reticular Formation in the brain. Our imaginations are created through a combination of sensory information received (18%), and our subconscious interpretation of that information (82%). In other words, our experience – every experience – is comprised of 18% sensory data (emotions), and 82% interpretation of that data.

Relying on an old, but well proven theory called, **Rational Emotive Therapy** (RET), one can begin to see the effect. RET postulates that our behavior is based on the A,B,C's of reacting, which stand for the following:

- A = The **Activating Event** ~ what happened that triggered an emotional arousal?

- B = Our **Belief Systems** ~ what we believe about the event, based on the sensory data received.

- C = The **Consequences** of our interpreting the activating event through our beliefs, which may or may not be true.

Applying this to the action or inaction of another person that triggers an emotional arousal that remains unresolved when we retire; another function of our subconscious mind, closely associated with our imaginations, is triggered. Sound asleep, our inner-imagery – our dream-world – takes over, in an effort to resolve the unresolved, which caused the emotional arousal we went to sleep with. Asleep, and unaware of our unconscious thought-processing – our inner-imagery (or imaginations) now expressed in dreams – replays the activating event over and over.

Each time the event is replayed, our subconscious mind senses our emotional arousal (the 18% mentioned above), and sets about interpreting it through our internal-imagery (the 82% referenced above. Thus, each time our subconscious mind replays the event, the emotional impact becomes greater and greater, causing one to spiral downward into the emotional pit. Each time the activating event is replayed, the associated emotional arousal increases, opening our Reticular Formation, allowing information we would normally reject, to enter the Amygdala – the deep recess of our memory – where we store our foundational beliefs and life-commandments.

Then, after a fitful night's sleep, we awake, totally unaware that as we slept unholy entities with ungodly directives entered our soul. We awake, often feeling worse than when we laid down, and usually, more angry at the person or persons we believed were responsible for the injustice we suffered; or more worried at the circumstances we face; or more ashamed than ever before. Going to sleep with unresolved issues, we have indeed, provided an open doorway for the powers of darkness, to enter and take control of our soul.

The Effect on Others
The power of the brain is infinite. Your subconscious mind works on the information provided it through inner-seeing, inner-feeling, and inner-saying (inner dialog). Once your subconscious mind has formulated an well imagined solution to whatever problem you are facing, it attempts to connect you with the people and events needed to create that reality. It accomplishes this by transmitting the imagery developed (your imagination) to your intellectual thought processes, and as you consider the imagined possibilities, you broadcast these to others.

What you think about in your subconscious – even as you sleep – will either draw people and events to you, or repel them from you, as a result of their reactions to your thoughts that are broadcast through the ether. The same concept [the A,B, C principle] described above works – your broadcast thought, once received by others, being the activating event. Your subconscious mind is not concerned about the morality of the solution envisioned. It functions merely to help create your reality by formulating messages and sending them to your conscious mind where they can be called into existence, completing two-thirds of the creative process.

Everything action you take, word you say or thought you believe emanates from your subconscious mind. Just thinking you can do or achieve something does not make it happen. It simply creates a positive awareness that begins to be manifest in how you think, feel and act. These messages are sent out to those you encounter and they too, begin to see the possibilities – good or bad.

Whatever your subconscious mind can imagine, it can bring into your conscious awareness, ways to make that happen. Your subconscious mind works to develop the reality imagined, and will – unconsciously – attempt to impose that reality on yourself and others. Moreover, if one's subconscious mind is left unguarded, by reason of an open Reticular Formation, the reality it now attempts to impose may well be ungodly – even demonic.

The Remedy:
There was a time when many, particularly within the church, thought that using one's imagination might be evil; but God created our subconscious thought processes as well as our conscious ones. They are God-given faculties, that if used for good, can help win the world for Christ. Remember, it was God who inspired Solomon to write: *"For as a man thinks in his heart, so he (it) will be"* (Pro 23:7). It was also Solomon who, by inspiration wrote: *"Above all else, guard your heart [your subconscious mind], for it is the wellspring of life"* (Pro 4:23).

It was he who wrote: *"The tongue has the power of life and death, and those who love it will eat its fruit"* (Pro 18:21); and instructed man to *"Put away perversity from your mouth; keep corrupt talk far from your lips. Let your eyes look straight ahead, fix your gaze directly before you. Make level paths for your feet and take only ways that are firm. Do not swerve to the right or the left; keep your foot from evil"* (Pro 4:24-27).

Winning the Battle"
Imagination will consistently rule over our will power; but our imagination bows to our intellect – our conscious mind – *"For as a man thinks in his heart, so it will be"* (Pro 23:7).

By changing our mind, we change our imaginations; and by changing our imaginations, we alter the messages broadcast into the ether; thereby altering the effect we have on ourselves and others. Paul wrote: *"take every thought captive and make it obedient to Christ"* (2 Cor 10:5).

What we think, we will speak out [or prophesy a self-fulfilling prophecy], calling forth life or death [creating] (Pro 18:21). Our imagination + our speaking it out = our action (our volition or will), when engaged, creates our manifest reality. Thus – as Scripture declares – whatever we confess with our mouth becomes our reality. *"If you confess with your mouth, "Jesus is Lord," and believe in your heart that God raised him from the dead, you will be saved. For it is with your heart that you believe and are justified, and it is with your mouth that you confess and are saved"* (Rom 10:9-11). ... *"Let us therefore hold fast our confession [of faith in Him]"* (Heb 4:14).

To illustrate the battle we must win, consider how many times you, and/or those you know, have confessed, "Jesus, by your stripes, I am healed", while in our imagination, we visualize the disease we suffer from. When such conflict exists, our imagination will win every time. It is our imagination that triggers our autonomic nervous system and the enteric brain, thus effecting our immune system; and it is our immune system that, when functioning properly, prevents the onset of disease.

To win this battle, we *must* get our imagination and our speech (our confession of faith) aligned. Achieving harmony between our imagination and confession of faith is the key that unlocks the door to an altered reality. Merely parroting God's Word, i.e., 'Your Word says *"by Your stripes I am healed,"* so, therefore, I am healed,' will not change the reality of the situation.

We must be in union with Jesus Christ [unified in spirit, thought and imagination]. Only such oneness will enable us to realize God's promised provision, protection and healing. Trying to achieve this state of oneness by reading and re-reading Scripture – as many do – can result in a mind-over-matter ritual, rather than a spirit-over-matter reality.

A spirit-over-matter reality can be achieved only as I surrender self, meditate on God's Word; engage my imagination to visualize God's will; and allow indwelling Holy Spirit to impart God's will for my life, at this moment in time. When we are in God and God is in us God [Elohiym ~ Father, Son and Holy Spirit] (Jn 14:20; 17:21); God will direct our spirit; to direct our soul (our subconscious mind); to direct our intellect; to govern our body; to manifest what we are meditating on. God is the source – He is all in all – and He will make things happen; converting spiritual realities into physical manifestations, when our will is in agreement with His. Jesus, in the model prayer he gave his disciples, prayed: *"may thy will be done on earth as it is in heaven"* (Matt 6:10).

When our will becomes aligned with God's marvelous things happen. We call them miracles, but for the most part, they were God's will all along; He is merely waiting until we can surrender self to allow His will to be done on earth, as it is in heaven. David understood this and declared: *"Delight yourself in Adonai, and he will give you your heart's desire. Commit your way to Adonai; trust in him, and he will act. He will make your vindication shine forth like light, the justice of your cause like the noonday sun"* (Ps 37:4-6 CJB).

The prophet Isaiah also grasped the concept, saying: *"I have spoken and will bring it about; I have made a plan, and I will fulfill it. Listen to me, you stubborn people, so far from righteousness: I am bringing my justice nearer, it is not far away; my salvation will not be delayed, I will place my salvation in Zion, for Israel my glory"* (Isa 46:11-13 CJB). The prophet Amos wrote: *"Can two journey together, except they be in agreement?"* (Amos 3:3).

James, the brother of Jesus, gave us a practical application of this, saying: *"Now if any of you lacks wisdom, let him ask God, who gives to all generously and without reproach; and it will be given to him. But let him ask in trust, doubting nothing; for the doubter is like a wave in the sea being tossed and driven by the wind. Indeed that person should not think that he will receive anything from the Lord, because he is double-minded, unstable in all his ways"* (James 1:5-8 CJB).

The apostle Paul wrote: *"I [we] have not stopped giving thanks for you, remembering you in my [our] prayers. I [we] keep asking that the God of our Lord Jesus Christ, the glorious Father, may give you the Spirit of wisdom and revelation, so that you may know him better. I [we] pray also that the eyes of your heart may be enlightened in order that you may know the hope to which he has called you, the riches of his glorious inheritance in the saints, and his incomparably great power for us who believe.*

"That power is like the working of his mighty strength, which he exerted in Christ when he raised him from the dead and seated him at his right hand in the heavenly realms, far above all rule and authority, power and dominion, and every title that can be given, not only in the present age but also in the one to come" (Eph 1:16-22 NIV).

I asked God to give me happiness.
God said, "No. I give you blessings.
Happiness is up to you."
I asked God to spare me pain.
God said, "No.
Suffering draws you apart from worldly cares
and brings you closer to me."
I asked God to make my spirit grow.
God said, "No. You must grow on your own,
but I will prune you to make you fruitful."
I asked for all things that I might enjoy life.
God said, "No.
I will give you life so that you may enjoy all things."
I asked God to help me help those weaker than
myself.
God said... "Ahhhha,
At last, you're beginning to get the idea."

~ Questions, Concerns & Key Points ~

1. When our imagination and will are in conflict, which will win over the other?

2. Fill in the blank: "What controls our _____ controls our life."

3. What are the weapons used in spiritual warfare?

4. As Co-creators with God, how – other than having children – do we exercise our creative ability?

5. What is the "seedbed" that contains both good and evil seeds that Jesus spoke of in Matt 13?

6. What determines which type of seed – good or bad – germinates, grows and bears fruit?

7. There is scientific proof that our thoughts effect others as well as ourselves? [ ] True ~ [ ] False

8. In Rational Emotive Therapy [RET] what do the letters: A, B & C stand for?

9. Is our imagination spontaneous, or can one control their imagination?

10. Explain the difference between, "mind-over-matter" and "spirit-over-matter" and the effect each has on one's experienced reality?

Chapter 18 ~ Interior Redecorating

Introduction:
When Nehemiah, the Israelite returned from exile and discovered Jerusalem, the beloved city of the Lord, decimated and the wall broken down, he set about to restore them. The first thing he did was to inspect the damage. Next, he and his countrymen removed the rubble; after that they reconstructed the walls – completing the repairs in just fifty-two days. When the walls were complete, they reset the gates and bars. After that there was just one more task to complete – a very important task – redecorating the interior of a room within the wall.

Nehemiah's record says: *"Malkiyah, one of the goldsmiths, made repairs as far as the house of the temple servants and the merchants, opposite the Mustering Gate and on to the upper room at the corner. Finally, between the upper room at the corner and the Sheep Gate the goldsmiths and merchants made repairs"* (Neh 3:31-32 CJB).

317

This room they believed to be the abode of Holy Spirit and they took great care in redecorating it; covering the walls and ceiling with gold-leaf, and furnishing it with the finest upholstered furnishings – all in royal purple – fit for the king. It was here – many believe – that Jesus ate the Last Supper and here, where the 120 disciples waited for that which he had promised them: the baptism of the Holy Spirit on Pentecost.

Our Inner-room:
Pursuing this spiritual pattern given us; and employing our imagination, we have surveyed the damage, removed the rubble, restored our walls – the walls of our soul – and set the gates. Now, it is time to redecorate our inner-room – our soul and spirit.

In the last two chapters, we have examined the power of imagination, and saw that by speaking out our imagination, we give it life, so that what we envisioned, we create, since it becomes a manifest part of our reality. We saw that this fulfills both the wisdom of Solomon who said that, "as a man thinks in his heart, so it will be" (Pro 23:7); and the words of Christ, who said, "out of the overflow of the heart the mouth speaks" (Matt 12:34), warning that *"The good man brings good things out of the good stored up in him, and the evil man brings evil things out of the evil stored up in him"* (vs. 35-36).

We learned that the word 'heart' used in these Scriptures refers to our soul – that part of our being which the apostle Paul tells us, needs to to be transformed (Rom 12:2). Paul says that this transformation must take place through the renewing, renovation, or redecorating, of our mind – our deep, subconscious mind – including our imaginations, beliefs, attitudes and emotions. He says that *"all of us, with faces unveiled, see as in a mirror the glory of the Lord; and we are being changed into his very image (transformed into his likeness) from one degree of glory to the next, by Adonai (the Lord), the Spirit"* (2 Cor 3:18).

We know, that as born-again Christians, *"our citizenship is in heaven. And we eagerly await a Savior from there, the Lord Jesus Christ, who, by the power that enables him to bring everything under his control, will transform our lowly bodies so that they will be like his glorious body"* (Phil 3:20-21); *"In a moment, in the twinkling of an eye, at the last trumpet call, we shall be changed [transfigured]"* (1 Cor 15:52). But, while our body is to be transformed, or transfigured upon Christ's return; the transformation of our soul, is to take place here and now – prior to his return.

Interior Decorating:
Since we are to be changed into the Lord's very image and likeness, we need to understand what this means and how to achieve it. King David, the Psalmist, described the Lord's image, saying: *"Just one thing have I asked of Adonai; only this will I seek: to live in the house of Adonai all the days of my life, to see the beauty of Adonai and visit him in his temple"* (Ps 27:4). The prophet Isaiah, concurred with this description, saying: *"Your eyes will see the king in his beauty"* (Isa 33:17).

The apostle Peter wrote: *"Though you have not seen him, you love him; and even though you do not see him now, you believe in him and are filled with an inexpressible and glorious joy"* (1 Peter 1:8-9). And, although we have not yet seen him, we – his children – will know him. As John, the beloved apostle, said: *"We are God's children now; and it has not yet been made clear what we will become. We do know that when he appears, we will be like him; because we will see him as he really is"* (1 John 3:2 CJB).

In order that we may become like him, it was necessary that he first, become one like us. The author of the Book of Hebrews verifies this, saying: *"For in bringing many sons to glory, it was only fitting that God, the Creator and Preserver of everything, should bring the Initiator of their deliverance to the goal through sufferings. For both Yeshua, who sets people apart for God, and the ones being set apart have a common origin – this is why he is not ashamed to call them brothers when he says, "I will proclaim your name to my brothers; in the midst of the congregation I will sing your praise."*

Also, *"I will put my trust in him, . . ."* and then it goes on, *"Here I am, along with the children God has given me."* Therefore, since the children share a common physical nature as human beings, he became like them and shared that same human nature; so that by his death he might render ineffective the one who had power over death (that is, the Adversary) and thus set free those who had been in bondage all their lives because of their fear of death" (Heb 2:10-15 CJB).

Jars of Clay:

Jeremiah lamented: *"How the precious sons of Zion, once worth their weight in gold, are now considered as pots of clay, the work of a potter's hands!"* (Lam 4:2). Originally created as children of light, God's children were – after their rebellion and fall – wrapped in outer-garments made of the elements of the earth. These garments were symbolically referred to as bodies of clay; the Potter being Yeshua, our Lord. Employing this same metaphor, the prophet Isaiah wrote: *"O Lord, you are our Father. We are the clay, you are the potter; we are all the work of your hand"* (Isa 64:8).

Relying on this metaphor, God gave the prophet Jeremiah a vision illustrating the future redemption of fallen man. *"This is the word that came to Jeremiah from the Lord: "Go down to the potter's house, and there I will give you my message." So I went down to the potter's house, and I saw him working at the wheel. But the pot he was shaping from the clay was marred in his hands; so the potter formed it into another pot, shaping it as seemed best to him.*

"Then the word of the Lord came to me: "O house of Israel, can I not do with you as this potter does?" declares the Lord. "Like clay in the hand of the potter, so are you in my hand" (Jer 18:1-6). The redemptive plan symbolized by the potter's reconstruction of the vessel he was crafting – which we refer to as salvation – is both corporate and yet individual; that is, Christ died once for all mankind, yet each person must individually accept Jesus Christ (Yeshua Messiah) as our Lord and Savior. Some of the Scriptures that speak of this include the following:

"He has appeared once for all at the end of the ages to do away with sin by the sacrifice of himself. Just as man is destined to die once, and after that to face judgment, so Christ was sacrificed once to take away the sins of many people; and he will appear a second time, not to bear sin, but to bring salvation to those who are waiting for him" (Heb 9:26-28).

"Unlike the other high priests, he does not need to offer sacrifices day after day, first for his own sins, and then for the sins of the people. He sacrificed for their sins once for all when he offered himself" (Heb 7:27-28). ... *"We have been made holy through the sacrifice of the body of Jesus Christ once for all"* (Heb 10:10).

The apostle Paul said: *"Christ died for sins once for all, the righteous for the unrighteous, to bring you to God"* (1 Peter 3:18). ... *"The death he died, he died to sin once for all; but the life he lives, he lives to God. In the same way, count yourselves dead to sin but alive to God in Christ Jesus"* (Rom 6:10-12). ...

*"For God, who said, "Let light shine out of darkness," made his light shine in our hearts to give us the light of the knowledge of the glory of God in the face of Christ. But **we have this treasure in jars of clay** to show that this all-surpassing power is from God and not from us"* (2 Cor 4:6-8).

From Jars of Clay to Children of Light:
While Adam and Eve's fall brought the effects of sin onto all mankind, resulting in God's Children of Light becoming as it were, Jars of Clay; through Jesus' substitutionary sacrifice and its redemptive power; we will once again be like him! Explaining this, the Apostle Paul said:

"There is also a spiritual body. So it is written: "The first man Adam became a living being"; the last Adam, a life-giving spirit. The spiritual did not come first, but the natural, and after that the spiritual. The first man was of the dust of the earth, the second man from heaven. As was the earthly man, so are those who are of the earth; and as is the man from heaven, so also are those who are of heaven. And just as we have borne the likeness of the earthly man, so shall we bear the likeness of the man from heaven.

"I declare to you, brothers, that flesh and blood cannot inherit the kingdom of God, nor does the perishable inherit the imperishable. Listen, I tell you a mystery: We will not all sleep, but we will all be changed – in a flash, in the twinkling of an eye, at the last trumpet. For the trumpet will sound, the dead will be raised imperishable, and we will be changed. For the perishable must clothe itself with the imperishable, and the mortal with immortality" (1 Cor 15:44-53).

We shall see Jesus, King of Kings and Lord of Lords in his beauty; and he will see us. More importantly, we will know each other, for being like him, we will see him as he is. And, since He is beautiful, and we shall see him as he is, one can deduce that we too will be beautiful. The beauty we shall share with him now – in this dimension, as part of the Body of Christ – is not external but internal. The apostle Peter, writing about this, said: *"Your beauty should not consist in externals such as fancy hairstyles, gold jewelry or what you wear; rather, let it be the inner character of your heart, with the imperishable quality of a gentle and quiet spirit. In God's sight this is of great value"* (1 Peter 3:3-5).

Children of Light in a Dark World:
While we will one day be transfigured, exchanging these jars of clay for imperishable, immortal bodies; we are – in Christ – to be Children of Light, while still living in this dark, sin-filled, world. Paul described the life we are to live in his letter to the Ephesian church, saying: *"Be imitators of God, therefore, as dearly loved children and live a life of love, just as Christ loved us and gave himself up for us as a fragrant offering and sacrifice to God. … For you were once darkness, but now you are light in the Lord.*

"Live as children of light (for the fruit of the light consists in all goodness, righteousness and truth); and find out what pleases the Lord; have nothing to do with

the fruitless deeds of darkness, but rather expose them; For it is shameful even to mention what the disobedient do in secret. But everything exposed by the light becomes visible, for it is light that makes everything visible. ... Be very careful, then, how you live – not as the unwise, but as the wise, making the most of every opportunity, because the present age is evil" (Eph 5:1-2 & 8-16).

Out With the Old and In With the New:
Returning to Jeremiah's metaphor of salvation, we read: – *"Go down to the potter's house, and there I will give you my message." So I went down to the potter's house, and I saw him working at the wheel. But the pot he was shaping from the clay was marred in his hands; so the potter formed it into another pot, shaping it as seemed best to him"* (Jer 18:2-4).

God created mankind as a triune being to reflect the image and likeness of the Godhead – Father, Son and Holy Spirit – being in nature, body, soul and spirit. Our spirit interacts with the spiritual realm, communicating with God spirit-to-spirit, since *"God is spirit and His worshipers must worship Him in spirit and in truth"* (Jn 4:24). Our soul – the fusion of God's Spirit with our physical body (Gen 2:7) – represented mankind before the fall; his physical body indwelled by, or fused with, Holy Spirit.

"The Lord God formed the man from the dust of the ground and breathed into his nostrils the breath of life, and the man became a living being, or soul" (Gen 2:7); our was spirit formed within us, as the residence of Holy Spirit. *"Adonai, who stretched out the heavens, laid the foundation of the earth and formed the spirit inside human beings"* (Zech 12:1CJB). Our soul, which includes our intellect, our imaginations, our emotions our beliefs and attitudes, comprises our unique person-hood; and is the bridge between the spiritual realm and the physical realm; governing the manner in which we think, the

beliefs we develop, our emotions, and elected behavior. Through our soul, we interact in the soulish realm – with others, on a day-to-day basis.

Our body – originally of light, but now of clay – is the vehicle through which our chosen behavior is manifest in the physical realm. Our body is the bridge between our spirit and soul, and the material universe; receiving information through our five senses and sending information through our words, the inflection in our voice, and our physical acts. It is the vehicle of expression for our internal person-hood; enabling us to interact with the person-hood of others, as we develop and maintain relationships.

At the moment of our salvation, our spirit is renewed; indwelled once again by Holy Spirit; therefore, spiritually, we are a brand new creation. From that moment on – if we permit and cooperate – our soul is transformed through the indwelling Holy Spirit. Peter said, *"Even though you have not seen him, you love him. Though you do not see him now, you believe in him. You are filled with a glorious joy that can't be put into words. You are receiving the salvation [or transformation] of your souls; the result of your faith"* (1 Peter 1:8-9 NirV).

The physical body, designed only for the physical realm, will [...] ood can [...] the per [...] and as [...] the gra [...] ule ove [...] the gra [...]

The soul will dominate, governing the behavior of our body, instead of Holy Spirit governing it through our spirit, if it is allowed. The apostle Paul described this inner-conflict in his letter to the Christians in Rome, writing: *"Those who live according to the sinful nature have their minds set on what that nature desires; but those who live in accordance with the Spirit have their minds set on what the Spirit desires.*

"The mind of sinful man is death, but the mind controlled by the Spirit is life and peace; the sinful mind is hostile to God. It does not submit to God's law, nor can it do so. Those controlled by the sinful nature cannot please God. You, however, are controlled not by the sinful nature but by the Spirit, if the Spirit of God lives in you. And if anyone does not have the Spirit of Christ, he does not belong to Christ. But if Christ is in you, your body is dead because of sin, yet your spirit is alive because of righteousness. And if the Spirit of him who raised Jesus from the dead is living in you, he who raised Christ from the dead will also give life to your mortal bodies through his Spirit, who lives in you" (Rom 8:5-11).

This inner conflict – the battle between the soul and the spirit, for the control of our body – is a battle of inestimable importance with eternal consequences. Describing this battle and its gravity, Paul said: *"For if you live according to the sinful nature, you will die; but if by the Spirit you put to death the misdeeds of the body, you will live, because those who are led by the Spirit of God are sons of God. For you did not receive a spirit that makes you a slave again to fear, but you received the Spirit of sonship. And by him we cry, "Abba, Father." The Spirit himself testifies with our spirit that we are God's children. Now if we are children, then we are heirs — heirs of God and co-heirs with Christ, if indeed we share in his sufferings in order that we may also share in his glory"* (Rom 8:13-17).

Recognizing the eternal gravity of the outcome of this inner-conflict, Paul penned: *"I don't think the sufferings we are going through now are even worth comparing with the glory that will be revealed to us in the future. The creation waits eagerly for the sons of God to be revealed; for the creation was made subject to frustration – not willingly, but because of the one who subjected it. But it was given a reliable hope that it too would be set free from its bondage to decay and would enjoy the freedom accompanying the glory that God's children will have.*

"We know that until now, the whole creation has been groaning as with the pains of childbirth; and not only it, but we ourselves, who have the first-fruits of the Spirit, groan inwardly as we continue waiting eagerly to be made sons – that is, to have our whole bodies redeemed and set free. It was in this hope that we were saved. But if we see what we hope for, it isn't hope – after all, who hopes for what he already sees? But if we continue hoping for something we don't see, then we still wait eagerly for it, with perseverance" (Rom 8:18-25 CJB).

While we share in this hope that Paul mentions, we do suffer in these decaying jars of clay; a major cause of our suffering being misalignments between our spirit, our soul and our body. To comprehend these misalignments, we need to understand the links between our body, soul and spirit.

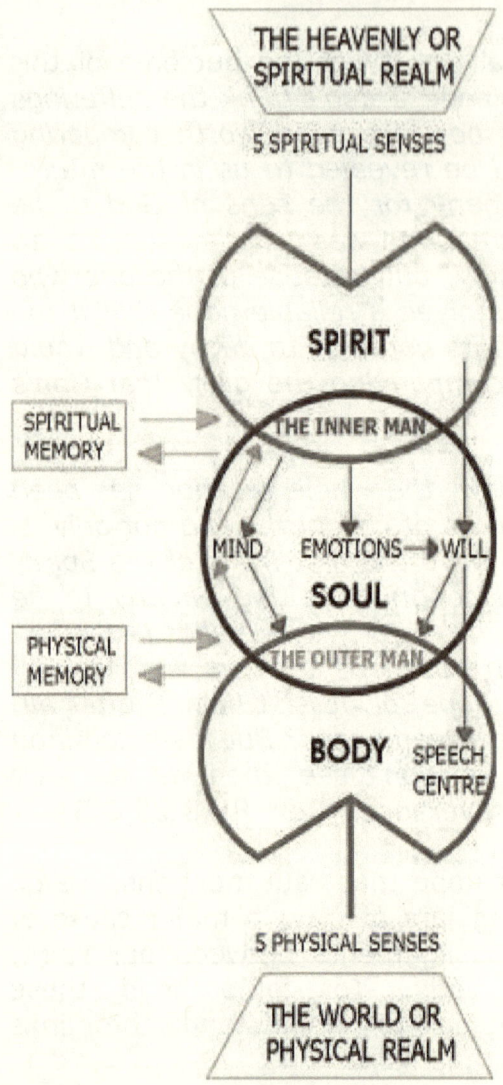

The link between the spirit and the body is our will, demonstrated in the solid line running from the spirit down to the outer man and the speech center in the adjacent graphic. This link, referenced numerous times in Scripture, such as in the following text:

*"Then **Choose for yourselves** this day whom you will serve"* (Jos 24:15); *"I call heaven and earth as witnesses against you that I have set before you life and death, blessings and curses. **Now choose life**, so that you and your children may live"* (Deut 30:19-20);

*"**As for me, I will declare** this forever; **I will sing** praise to the God of Jacob"* (Ps 75:9); *"The Spirit and the bride say, "Come!" And let him who hears say, "Come!" Whoever is thirsty, let him come; and **whoever wishes**, let him take the free gift of the water of life"* (Rev 22:17). It is with our will that we choose whether or not to accept salvation and whether or not to obey God.

The tongue is the link between the soul and the body, as illustrated in the previous graphic. It is the primary output media of the soul. There are numerous Scriptures referencing this. For example, David said: *"You removed my sackcloth and clothed me with joy, Adonai, **so that my inner-being can praise you and not be silent**; Adonai my God, I will thank you forever!"* (Ps 30:11-12); *"**The tongue has power over life and death**; those who indulge it must eat its fruit"* (Prov 18:21).

The apostle James declared: *"For we all stumble in many ways; if someone does not stumble in what he says, he is a mature man who can bridle his whole body. If we put a bit into a horse's mouth to make it obey us, we control its whole body as well. And think of a ship – although it is huge and is driven by strong winds, yet the pilot can steer it wherever he wants with just a small rudder. So too **the tongue is a tiny part of the body, yet it boasts great things**"* (James 3:2-5).

The combination of the will and the tongue provide the link between spirit and soul. Some of the Scriptures referencing this link include the following: *"**Someone who speaks in a(n) [unknown] tongue should pray for the power to interpret**. For **if I pray in a tongue, my spirit does pray, but my mind is unproductive**"* (1 Cor 14:13-14);

*"**The word is near you; it is in your mouth and in your heart**," that is, the word of faith we are proclaiming: That if you confess with your mouth, "Jesus is Lord," and believe in your heart that God raised him from the dead, you will be saved"* (Rom 10:8-9);

"It is written: ***"I believed; therefore I have spoken."*** ***With that same spirit of faith we also believe and therefore speak****"* (2 Cor 4:13-14).

The human spirit can express itself through the body directly [through the speech center] without engaging our intellect to effect interpretation and gain understanding; however our freewill must be exercised in order to permit this. My freewill and the words I speak determine whether I give the Lord dominion over my life, or whether I allow Satan and the demons under his command to have dominion over my body. My imagination, linked with my will, is the deciding factor. When I obey God, I facilitate the harmonious functioning of my body, soul and spirit, supporting its functioning as a fully integrated being, as Jesus did while, being on the earth, he was in the flesh.

Origin of Body-Soul-Spirit Misalignments, Personality Disorders and Physical Illness: Misalignments of spirit, soul and body – having our spirit out of line -- or off-line as it were – is the origin of most psychological, physiological, relational and even financial and environmental problems.

When our imagination and our tongue are not in agreement – not aligned by our spirit – it allows the Powers of Darkness to gain a foothold [doorway or passage] into our soul, which if not corrected, will develop into a spiritual stronghold. These spiritual strongholds include those things we commonly refer to as addictions, obsessions, compulsivities and other life-controlling problems.

Conditions Contributing to Misalignments:
You may wish to envision these strongholds as lies and/or misinformation inscribed upon your soul as memories – spiritual or physical, as illustrated in the graphic on a previous page. There are several conditions

that contribute to these lies and the resulting misalignments of spirit, soul and body, and include:

1. **Genetic Predispositions** ~ "I punish the children for the sin of their parents. I punish the grandchildren and great-grandchildren of those who hate me" (Ex 20:5-6; 34:7; Num 14:18; Dt 5:9; NirV).

2. **Occult Involvement** ~ Including residual effects of past involvement in the occult, including things such as astrology, spiritualism, necromancy, lithomancy, numerology, Ekankar (out-of-body experiences), Ouija boards, etc.

3. **Death Wishes** ~ Expressing things such as: "I would be better off dead!" "I wish I were dead" or "I wish I could just die." "I just can't take it any more."

4. **Physical Trauma** ~ accidents or illnesses resulting in a period of unconsciousness, and/or major surgery during which a full-body anesthetic was administered.

5. **Emotional Trauma** ~ Particularly any severe or prolonged emotional trauma during your formative years (birth to fifteen); during which you experienced a sense of despair, being fractured, shattered or wrenched apart.

6. **Chemical Abuse** ~ The abuse of toxic chemicals, including alcohol, mood- altering drugs, inhalants, refrigerants, sufficient to impair your functionality.

7. **Hypnotism** ~ Specifically stage hypnosis and regression experiments other than medically controlled or supervised clinical hypnotherapy, during which you yielded the control of your mind to another person.

Nearly everyone has experienced at least one or two of these contributing factors, and many people have experienced many if not all of them.

Symptoms of Misalignment:
Symptoms of spirit, soul, body misalignments include, but are not limited to, the following:

1. **Spiritual lethargy or apathy** ~ This includes: neglect of God's work that you have been called to; being content with your spiritual condition, no longer pursuing spiritual growth; lack of participation and excuse-making; fear of man rather than fear of God; pride; Denominationalism and/or Ecumenism; Secret Disbelief.

2. **Emotional disassociation or numbness** ~ Often includes a sense of being distant, emotional detachment, the inability to connect with others, being removed from presenting problems, removed from the immediate environment, depression, post-traumatic stress flashbacks.

3. **Mental impairments** ~ There is a myriad of mental impairment problems, but those most closely associated with spirit, soul misalignment, include: thought-blocking (losing one's thoughts while talking); circumstantial or tangential thinking (start talking in one direction and then go off on a tangent in a totally different direction (tangential thinking), or go into way too much detail about what you're talking about but eventually getting back to the main point (circumstantial thinking); memory impairment (often resulting from deficient levels of the essential reward hormones – Dopamine, Acetylcholine, GABA and Serotonin).

4. **Personality disorders** ~ Personality disorders, formerly referred to as character disorders, are a class of personality types and behaviors that the defined by "an enduring pattern of inner experience and behavior that deviates markedly from the expectations of the culture of the individual exhibiting it. Associated behaviors can result adopting maladaptive coping skills, which may lead to personal problems that induce extreme mood disorders, such as anxiety, distress and depression. Some of the more common personality disorders that are generally considered trauma-induced, include:

   - **Antisocial** ~ a pervasive disregard for the law and the rights of others

   - **Avoidant** ~ social inhibition, feelings of inadequacy, overly sensitive, avoidance of social interactions.

   - **Borderline** ~ extreme 'black and white' polarized thinking, instability in relationships, and fear of rejection or abandonment.

   - **Dependent** ~ pervasive pathological dependence on other people

   - **Histrionic** ~ pervasive attention-seeking, approval-seeking behavior, including inappropriate sexual advances and exaggerated emotions.

   - **Narcissistic** ~ a pervasive pattern of grandiosity, need for admiration, a lack of empathy and compassion

- **Obsessive-Compulsive** ~ rigid conformity to rules, moral codes, excessive cleanliness, orderliness, etc.

5. **Glandular malfunctions** ~ any malfunctions of the adrenals, thyroid, pituitary, ovaries or testes, spleen, pancreas, etc., give rise to various, often debilitating physical illness. The most common cause of glandular malfunctions is stress and internalized anger.

These symptoms may stem from other causes, however, misalignment will exacerbate them, while restoring proper alignment often negates the need for other remedies, but nearly always makes other remedies more effective.

Restoring Alignment:
God directed Jeremiah to: *"Go down to the potter's house, and there I will give you my message." So I went down to the potter's house, and I saw him working at the wheel. But* **the pot he was shaping from the clay was marred in his hands; so the potter formed it into another pot, shaping it as seemed best to him**. *Then the word of the Lord came to me: "O house of Israel,* **can I not do with you as this potter does?"** *declares the Lord.* **"Like clay in the hand of the potter, so are you in my hand"** (Jer 18:2-6).

"The god of this age has blinded the minds of unbelievers, so that they cannot see the light of the gospel of the glory of Christ, who is the image of God. For we do not preach ourselves, but Jesus Christ as Lord, and ourselves as your servants for Jesus' sake. For God, who said, "Let light shine out of darkness," made his light shine in our hearts to give us the light of the knowledge of the glory of God in the face of Christ. But we have this treasure in jars of clay to show that this all-surpassing power is from God and not from us" (2 Cor 4:4-8).

Preparing for Re-alignment:
During the prayer that follows for the realignment of our Spirit, Soul and Body, we will be depending solely upon Holy Spirit to assign ministering spirits to minister to each one, in exactly the manner needed. But before praying, there is preparatory work that must be completed through soul-cleansing prayer. Pray with me, and modify the following to comply with the specific spiritual strongholds in your life:

Father God, in spirit-to-spirit union with Yeshua Messiah, encased within him, I now enter the Heavenly Holy of Holies, and at your invitation, I approach your Throne of Grace. In the Name of Yeshua Messiah, and relying on the interpretation of Holy Spirit, Who indwells my spirit, I take authority over every Principality and Power of the kingdom of darkness, commanding you to leave our presence and go into outer darkness. I ask You, Father God, to commission holy angels to surround us with warring angels to protect us against any attack or harassment, and to prevent them from hearing my confessions and using them against me at a later time.

Now, Father:
1. *I embrace the genetic stream that You chose to place me in – both my biological mother's lineage and my biological father's lineage; and in Jesus' Name and through the empowerment of*

indwelling Holy Spirit, I cut-off every negative genetic predisposition (naming all that you are aware of); and understanding that in Your grace, you limited the impact of evil to three or four generations in most cases, but imposed no limit on the good, I now embrace the positive traits and characteristics of my genetic heritage.

2. Father, I Repent of any involvement in the occult (naming them specifically, i.e., astrology, fortunetelling, crystal-ball or palm-reading, Ouija board, Taro cards, etc.) and any abuse of mood-altering chemicals or experiences (naming them specifically, including Marijuana, Alcohol, Nicotine, pornography, etc,). I renounce each and every one of these Father, and make a renewed commitment to avoid these things through the empowerment of Holy Spirit, Who indwells my spirit, in Jesus name.

3. Father, I repent of any death wish I have made (identifying the specific words you have used); and I now renounce, cancel and nullify the power of those words through the indwelling power of Holy Spirit, in Yeshua Messiah's name; and Father God, I now choose life, and chose to live in this body, to fulfill Your will and purpose for my life, until You call me home in Your perfect timing.

4. Father, I forgive any and all persons, organizations, corporations or agencies that were in any way responsible for the physical trauma that I have experienced, including (name all of the physical trauma you are aware of); I repent from any bitteness and resentment against them, or feelings of vengeance and retribution; and I ask You, Holy Spirit, to blot out their sin record, in Jesus' name.

5. Father, I forgive each and every person who has caused emotional trauma and pain, including (identify all you are aware of); I ask you to forgive them also Father God; and forgive me for any bitterness and resentment against them; and any feelings of vengeance and retribution; and I ask You, Holy Spirit, to blot out their, and my own, sin record, in Jesus' name; and to insure that my name is recorded in the Lamb's Book of Life.

6. Father, I repent of any experiences where I played with hypnosis, mystical experiences, extra-sensory perception, out-of-body experiences, or other experiences wherein I may have yielded my mind to another person; I renounce all such behavior; and I covenant with you that, with the empowerment of Holy Spirit, I shall avoid all such experiences in the future.

Prayer for Re-alignment of Spirit, Soul and Body:

Sitting with your feet together – but not crossed – and your hands palm down on your knees (to prevent electromagnetic confusion), close your eyes (merely to avoid environmental distractions). Pray with me:

"Father God; in Jesus' name, and through the power of indwelling Holy Spirit; I now ask that the ministering angels that You assigned me, to pull my inner man (my soul and spirit) into this body, completely, even now, as I pray.

[Some people report that they literally 'feel the pull' around their ankles or legs, even though no human being is touching them; however not all experience these sensations, so don't be concerned, whether you do or not. Simply trust Holy Spirit, and cooperate with whatever is necessary to insure that your spirit and soul are properly aligned within your body. And, now, whether you feel anything or not, continue to pray with me ...]

I Command my spirit, soul and body to come into perfect alignment, according to Father God's sovereign design – His blueprint – for my life, in Jesus' name. In Jesus' name, I break every demonic link between my spirit and soul, and my soul and body; and I ask you Father God, in the name of Jesus, and through the power of indwelling Holy Spirit, to establish Godly links between my body and soul, my soul and my spirit, and between my spirit, Holy Spirit, Yeshua Messiah, and You.

Father God, I ask you to commission holy angels to minister to me – touching the front and back of my head, setting the electromagnetic polarity of my body, soul and spirit aright – normalizing it, according to your perfect design. Thank you Father God for your amazing love, care and nurture as You have ministered to me this morning/evening.

[Once again, some will sense a definite touch as Holy Spirit and holy angels minister to them. Some sense an inner-being adjustment, some do not, however, be assured that God has heard your prayer and in His faithfulness, has corrected whatever needed correcting. You may not feel anything immediately, but may – in the days ahead – sense a change, such as increased clarity of thought and focus, or clearer sense of purpose and direction – God knows exactly what you need.]

Harmonic Brain Balance:
To function harmoniously, we need balance between our brain's right and left hemispherical thought processing. Each hemisphere of the brain is dominant for specific behaviors. For example, in the vast majority of people, the right hemisphere is dominant for our spatial abilities, face recognition, visual imagery, and music; and is generally referred to as our subconscious mind, in that we do not use it analytically; whereas the left hemisphere is more dominant for calculations, math, logic and other analytical capabilities, as well as articulating words and sounds. A few, left-handed individuals have the hemispherical functions reversed – the right side being their intellectual side, and the left being their subconscious.

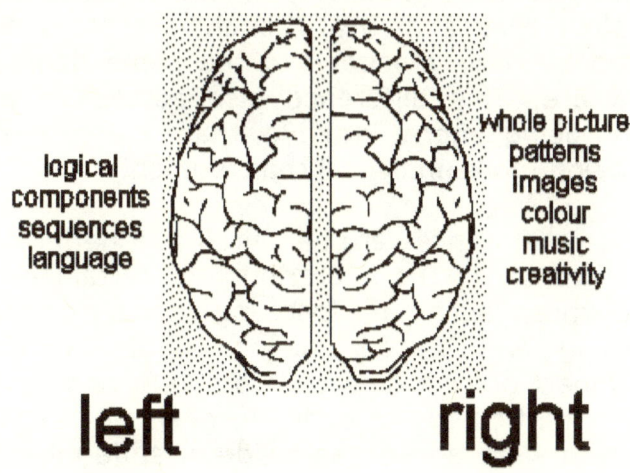

Most individuals have one hemisphere, whose thought processing is more dominant, resulting in that person relying more on the thought processing of that hemisphere. For example, if one's left hemispherical thoughts dominate, one will tend to rely more on their intellect than on their emotions; or if their right hemispherical thoughts dominate, one will give greater credence to their emotions and imagination. The cerebral hemispheres are divided right down the middle into a right hemisphere and a left hemisphere. The hemispheres communicate with each other through a thick band of about 200 to 250 million nerve fibers called the corpus callosum. There is also a smaller band of nerve fibers called the anterior commissure connects parts of the cerebral hemispheres.

The number of nerve fibers in the corpus callosum in men are up to two-thirds fewer, and much smaller in diameter than those in women; men also have far fewer anterior commisures, or nerve fibers, connecting the two hemispheres of their brain than women. These differences allow women to interpret the world to their children through word pictures as they mature from developmental stage to developmental stage; and enable men to more effectively mentor teens and young adults, since their analytical thought processes are not influenced by their emotions to the same degree that women's are. This difference also results in women generally being more intuitive than men, and men usually being more analytical than women.

While these differences are beneficial in a perfect world; in our fallen state, they contribute to certain negative characteristics, such as fostering gender prejudice, stereotyping and biased opinions. These differences greatly impact one's memory – women having far better memories, particularly of early-life events – resulting in women who were abused as children, suffering deeper, more profound, soul wounds than men who were similarly abused. These differences likewise impact the amount and depth of emotional healing needed to overcome soul wounds.

Thoughts from both hemispheres are integrated through the corpus callosum – which serves as sort of a communication bridge for our inner-dialog. Thought processes from left and right hemispheres are mediated by a combination of attractive and repulsive signals made possible by some very specialized cells that reside at the mid-line of the corpus callosum (also referred to as the synaptic cleft) – which serves also as the mid-line of the body's nervous system. [This is, of course, a overly simplistic description of the workings of each hemisphere and their interaction but it provides a general idea.]

Soul wounding can, and does, disrupt the delicate balance between hemispherical functions resulting in anomalies such as males having diminished levels of emotional sensitivity and females having diminished analytical abilities. The damage may be far more profound than this, contributing to: racing thoughts giving rise to anxiety; dyslexia and other learning disabilities; attention deficit and attention deficit hyperactive disorders; by-polar disorders; confusion and impaired decision-making abilities; marked inner conflict between intellectual and emotional thoughts; sexual adjustment and sexual identity issues.

Restoring hemispherical balance allows God's sovereign design to govern, enabling both men and women to use their God-given talents and traits to the fullest; enhancing their ability to receive dreams and visions without soulish interference and misinterpretation. Restoring brain balance and harmony facilitates soul-healing, helping to resolve the disorders identified earlier.

Restoring Brain Balance and Harmony:
Close your eyes and imagine that you were with Jeremiah when God directed him to go down to the Potter's House. Imagine watching the Potter work his clay, forming an earthen pot, according to his envisioned design. Now, as you watch him, imagine that you were there, with Jeremiah, when the Potter discovered there

was a flaw in the vessel he was creating. Imagine that you are that vessel, and God – the Master Potter – has discovered flaws in your soul.

Imagine being placed once again onto the Potter's Wheel, as God – the Master Potter – begins to reform you, restoring you to His Sovereign pattern for your life. As the Potter's Wheel spins round and round, allow all the impurities in your life to come up and out – moving ever closer to the edge of the Wheel, as it continues spinning around and around.

As the Wheel continues to spin, feel the impurities fall off the Potter's Wheel, leaving you a lump of pure clay in the Master Potter's hands. With your eyes still closed, feel the Master's hands, as he gently forms you, shaping you into a vessel fit for the purpose He created you to fulfill. Feel His love, His nurture and care, as He forms you gently – never being in a hurry – far more interested in how you turn out, than how fast you mature.

As the wheel continues to spin, see if you can determine which direction it is spinning in – is it spinning to the left, or is it spinning to the right? Feel the Master's hands now, very gently smoothing your surface, expressing His approval, His pleasure over your shape, your form, your finish. Now, as the Potter's Wheel continue to spin, sense the increasing oneness – the spirit-to-spirit union – between yourself, Father God, Holy Spirit and Yeshua Messiah, as you allow them to inhabit your soul, becoming one with you.

Hear Yeshua Messiah (Jesus Christ) whisper in your ear: *"Because I live, you also will live. ... I am in my Father, and you are in me, and I am in you"* (John 14:19-21). ... *"If anyone loves me, he will obey my teaching. My Father will love him, and we will come to him and make our home with him"* (John 14:23-24).

"Remain in me, and I will remain in you. No branch can bear fruit by itself; it must remain in the vine. Neither can you bear fruit unless you remain in me. "I am the vine; you are the branches. If a man remains in me and I in him, he will bear much fruit; apart from me you can do nothing. ... If you remain in me and my words remain in you, ask whatever you wish, and it will be given you" (John 15:4-8).

"I pray also for those who will believe in me through their message, that all of them may be one, Father, just as you are in me and I am in you. May they also be in us so that the world may believe that you have sent me" (John 17:20-22). ...

"Peace be with you! As the Father has sent me, I am sending you" (John 20:21).

Now, feel the Master Potter – Father God – gently remove you from the Potter's Wheel and place you in the kiln, the refining fire.

"For God is like a refiner's fire ... He shall sit as a refiner of silver; and purify [His[sons, purging them as gold and silver, that they may offer unto the Lord an offering in righteousness ... then shall [their] offering ... be pleasant unto the Lord, as in the days of old, and as in their former years" (Mal 3:2-3).

"Delight yourself in the Lord and he will give you the desires of your heart. Commit your way to the Lord; trust in him and he will do this: He will make your righteousness shine like the dawn, the justice of your cause like the noonday sun. Be still before the Lord and wait patiently till he comes" (Ps 37:4-7). "Do not offer the parts of your body to sin, as instruments of wickedness, but rather offer yourselves to God, as those who have been brought from death to life; and offer the parts of your body to him as instruments of righteousness" (Rom 6:13-14).

"Awake, awake, O [children of] Zion, clothe yourself with strength. Put on your garments of splendor" (Isa 52:1). ... "I tell you, open your eyes and look at the fields! They are ripe for harvest. Even now the reaper draws his wages, even now he harvests the crop for eternal life, so that the sower and the reaper may be glad together. Thus the saying 'One sows and another reaps' is true. I sent you to reap what you have not worked for. Others have done the hard work, and you have reaped the benefits of their labor" (John 4:35-38).

~ Questions, Concerns & Key Points ~

1. When Nehemiah directed the reconstruction of the city walls, what was the crowning act of restoration?

2. Holy Spirit's indwelling of man's spirit was foretold by what symbolism within old Jerusalem?

3. The transformation of our souls was symbolically foretold by what within old Jerusalem?

4. The potter's reshaping of the vessels mentioned in Jeremiah 18, symbolically speaks of what?

5. What is the treasure in jars of clay spoken of in 2 Corinthians 4:6-8.

6. The crowning act of salvation is the restoration of our physical bodies to make them fit for heaven?
   [ ] True ~ [ ] False

7. Identify the following links:
   1. Between our spirit and body?
   2. Between our soul and body?
   3. Between our spirit and soul?

8. Identify the conditions that contribute to body-soul-spirit misalignments?

9. Identify the symptoms of this misalignment?

10. Hoe does one go about restoring this alignment?

11. Explain 'harmonic brain balance'?

Chapter 19 ~ Restoring Balance & Harmony

Introduction:
Last week, we introduced an application of the Potter's Wheel, mentioned in Jeremiah 18, where Jeremiah watched as the potter reformed the pot he had been creating, eliminating weaknesses and faults that had surfaced. We noted that God asked Jeremiah, "Can I not do with you as this potter does?" ... "Like clay in the hand of the potter, so are you in my hand" (Jer 18:6); and we witnessed – as we prayed – God coming into our midst and reforming some of us. Perhaps some of you even have testimonies of additional reforming that God has performed since we were last together? If so, please share with us.

Handedness and Brain Harmony:
Another type of soul wounding that causing neurological imbalance often occurs when one's natural pattern of handedness (the hand one uses for things like eating, writing, etc.), is disrupted. This may have happened when one born neurologically left-handed was encouraged as a child to use their right hand, making them believe they are right-handed; or when a person born neurologically right-handed injured their right hand or arm, resulting in them developing a habitual pattern of left-handedness.

To test for birth neurological handedness – regardless which hand you are accustomed to using – extend your arms out to the side; then without looking down at your hands, bring them together in front of you and clasp them together. Next, check to see which of your thumbs is on top –

for example, in the preceding picture, the man's right thumb is on top.

Whichever thumb is on top indicates your neurological handedness. If your neurological handedness is opposite from your habitual handedness, this may cause inner-confusion; and can even contribute to dyslexia and other learning disabilities.

Problems with balance are another characteristic symptom of the conflict between neurological handedness and habitual pattern handedness. When the problem with one's balance cannot be attributed to some genetic malformation, such as having one leg shorter than the other; or having suffered injuries to one's hip, knee, leg ankle or foot; it is likely due to Vestibular (or inner-ear) dysfunction, then one should suspect the conflict described above.

There is a simple self-test you can perform to determine whether or not your have balance problems that originate in the inner-ear. Before we address this, however, let's pray for God's healing for any who do have a genetic malformation, or uncorrected damage, to their lower-back, hips, legs, knees, ankles and/or feet.

Healing Prayer:
Father God, we enter the heavenly Holy of Holies, and humbly approach Your Throne of Grace in the Name of Your Beloved Son, Yeshua Messiah. According to His instruction, and anointing, we now ask You to commission ministering spirits – Your righteous angels – to minister healing to everyone within the sound of my voice, who suffers from any genetic malformation, any injury or disease, affecting their lower-back, their hips, legs, knees, ankles and/or feet. In Jesus' Name, touch them, restoring every injury, correcting every genetic malformation, and strengthening every bone, nerve, ligament, tendon and joint. According to Your sovereign

plan for each of our lives, let it be so, Father God – Amen!

Balance-Test:
Stand up for a moment, balancing your weight on both feet; standing until you feel well balanced. Now, close your eyes.

Now, stand on your left leg, lifting your right leg slightly. If you feel a bit wobbly, like you might lose your balance, your right ear, and the right-hemisphere of your brain needs some alignment. Now, with your eyes still closed, stand on your right leg, and lift your left leg slightly. If you feel a bit wobbly, like you might lose your balance, your left ear, and the left-hemisphere of your brain needs alignment. If this little self-test revealed any lack of hemispherical alignment affecting your balance and hearing, make a note of it – identifying which side and the degree of your imbalance – i.e., slight, moderate, or significant (causing me to lose my balance).

Now, take your seat again and record any imbalance you felt. The Vestibular (or inner-ear) dysfunction causing this imbalance – other than a genetic anomaly – can have one of several causes:

- Spirit – Soul – Body misalignment

- Neurological damage

- Demonic oppression

- Infection – bacteriological, viral or parasitic

Spirit, Soul, Body Misalignment:
To address any spirit, soul, body misalignment, let's close our eyes, and in our imagination, let's return to the Potter's House (Jer 18), as you – in your imagination -- once again, watch the potter's wheel spinning round and round.

Envision placing yourself at the middle of the wheel. Once again, sense the rotation of the wheel, as it spins around and around. Now, as the wheel continues spinning, repeat after me, the following prayer, as you visualize what I am describing:

Father God, in spirit-to-spirit union with Yeshua Messiah, encased within Him; covered with His Robes of Righteousness; I enter the heavenly Holy of Holies, humbly approaching Your Throne of Grace. Father God, I ask You to restore the balance within my inner-man – my spirit, soul and body alignment – in accordance to your sovereign plan for my life. Restore perfect balance between the left and right hemispheres of my brain, between left and right hemisphere cognitions; between the left and right auditory nerves; restoring perfect balance – body, soul and spirit. Father God, I ask this in the Name of your Beloved Son, Yeshua Messiah, and through the enabling power of Holy Spirit – Amen.

Neurological Damage:
If you have any known, or suspected, neurological damage – affecting your hearing and/or your balance – pray with me, for God to supernaturally restore all damage.

Father God, standing before your Throne of Grace, covered by Christ Jesus' Robes of Righteousness; and in His Name, I ask You to restore all neurological damage, and to create any features needed to correct any genetic anomaly, and strengthen any neurological weakness, through the power of Holy Spirit, Who indwells my spirit, in the name of Your Beloved Son, Yeshua Messiah – Amen.

Demonic Oppression:
If you have any past involvement in the occult, have reason to believe that anyone has cursed you, or that you may have spoken a curse over yourself, giving the powers of darkness a foothold in your life, which may have – by this time in your life – developed into a stronghold, then join me, putting on the full armor of God (Christ's Robe of Righteousness, the Belt of Truth, the Breastplate of Righteousness, and Shoes fitted out with the Gospel of Peace); as we enter the heavenly Holy of Holies.

Standing beside our Lord and Savior, take up the Shield of Faith, with which you can extinguish every flaming arrow of the Adversary; putting on the Helmet of Salvation, pick up the Sword of the Spirit – the Word of God – as you look down beneath your feet that are shod with the Gospel of Peace, into the spiritual forces of evil in the heavenly realms (Eph 6:12-17).

Declare with me: *Satan, principalities, princes, magistrates, and other powers of the dark world of evil in the heavenly realm, and demons on and underneath the earth: I address you in the Name of Yeshua Messiah, and through his blood offered on calvary, by* which He established his victory and your defeat; 'Being put to death in the body, but made alive in the Spirit, through whom he declared to you his victory and your defeat' (1 Pe 3:18-19); understand that this same Jesus has anointed me to 'drive out demons' (Mt 10:8); therefore in his name I command that you break every assignment in and over my life; that you loose yourselves from my soul, and that you be made a part of the footstool of Jesus Christ, until he return to pronounce final judgment upon you. I declare this in the name of Yeshua Messiah, my Lord and Savior.

Now, put your hands over your ears and temples and declare: *"In Jesus Name, I now pull out every fiery dart of the enemy – from my ears, from my inner-ears, and from my mind [Now begin pulling out Satan's fiery darts – which, although unseen, have infested your life. With your hands make a strong pulling motion – Pull, pull, pull]. I command every dysfunction to come out, in Jesus' Name!*

Infection – Bacteriological, Viral and Parasitic:
Understanding – based on God's Word – that all disease is the work of the powers of darkness; and that Jesus anointed us to *"Heal the sick, raise the dead, cleanse those who have leprosy, and drive out demons"* (Mt 10:8); *I command you Satan, and every demonic force, to break off every assignment on my life. I command you every adversary of my body, soul and spirit, to depart and become a part of the footstool of Jesus Christ, until he return to pronounce final judgment upon you. I declare this in the name of Yeshua Messiah, my Lord and Savior.*

In the name of Yeshua Messiah, I now declare null and void the power of every infection – whether bacteriological, viral or parasitic – in my body; and in the name of Yeshua Messiah, and through the power of Holy Spirit, Who indwells my spirit, I now declare that this body, which was redeemed by, and is now the *property of, my Lord and Savior, is healed – Amen, Amen!*

Holy Hands:

What is the significance of using your hands to pull out unseen fiery darts of the Adversary? The apostle Paul said: **"It is my wish that when men pray, no matter where, they should lift up hands that are holy** — *they should not become angry or get into arguments"* (1 Tim 2:8).

Why would Paul say this – unless he was aware of something that we have forgotten: the power of symbolism.

Following the great flood, God told Noah, *"The fear and dread of you will fall upon all the beasts of the earth and all the birds of the air, upon every creature that moves along the ground, and upon all the fish of the sea;* **they are given into your hands**" (Gen 9:2-3). The power of God, expressed through holy men's hands is recorded again and again throughout Scripture.

God met Moses at the burning bush in the wilderness and directed him to return to Egypt and confront Pharaoh, assuring him He would be with him. Moses resisted saying, *"What if they do not believe me or listen to me and say, 'The Lord did not appear to you'?"* Then the Lord said to him, **"What is that in your hand**?" *"A staff,"* he replied. The Lord said, *"Throw it on*

the ground." Moses threw it on the ground and it became a snake, and he ran from it. Then the Lord said to him, *"**Reach out your hand** and take it by the tail." So Moses reached out and took hold of the snake and it turned back into a staff in his hand. This,"* said the Lord, *"is so that they may believe that the Lord, the God of their fathers — the God of Abraham, the God of Isaac and the God of Jacob — has appeared to you"* (Ex 4:1-5).

Next God said: *"**Put your hand inside your cloak**." So Moses put his **hand** into his cloak, and when he took it out, it was leprous, like snow. "Now put it back into your cloak," he said. So Moses put his **hand** back into his cloak, and when he took it out, it was restored, like the rest of his flesh. Then the Lord said, "If they do not believe you or pay attention to the first miraculous sign, they may believe the second. But if they do not believe these two signs or listen to you, take some water from the Nile and pour it on the dry ground. [Using his **hands**] The water you take from the river will become blood on the ground"* (Ex 4:6-9).

Still doubtful, Moses told God he could not speak well, and although God assured him He would give him the ability; He also directed Moses elder brother Aaron to go to the wilderness to let his brother know that those seeking his life were all dead and that it was safe to return to Egypt. Still Moses faltered, saying: *"Since I speak with faltering lips, why would Pharaoh listen to me?"* (Ex 6:30). God replied saying: *"See, I have made you like God to Pharaoh, and your brother Aaron will be your prophet"* (Ex 7:1-2).

As Moses and Aaron prepared to confront Pharaoh, *"The Lord said to Moses and Aaron, "When Pharaoh says to you, 'Perform a miracle,' then say to Aaron, '**Take your staff and throw it down before Pharaoh**,' and it will become a snake"* (Ex 7:8-9). I'm sure that you all know the story. *"Moses and Aaron went to Pharaoh and did* *just as the Lord commanded.* **Aaron threw his staff down** *in front of Pharaoh and his officials, and* **it became a snake***. Pharaoh then summoned wise men and sorcerers, and* **the Egyptian magicians also did the same things by their secret arts***: Each one threw down his staff and it became a snake.* **But Aaron's staff swallowed up their staffs**" (Ex 7:10-13).

Take note of the symbolism employed in these and the following Scriptures. Pharaoh refused to let the Israelites leave so God said to Moses: *"Tell Aaron, 'Take your staff and* **stretch out your hand over the waters** *of Egypt — over the streams and canals, over the ponds and all the reservoirs' —* **and they will turn to blood**" (Ex 7:19). ... *"Moses and Aaron did just as the Lord had commanded. He* **raised his staff** *in the presence of Pharaoh and his officials and* **struck the water of the Nile***, and all the* **water was changed into blood**" (vs 20).

Next, God told Moses: *"Tell Aaron,* **'Stretch out your hand with your staff** *over the streams and canals and ponds, and make frogs come up on the land of Egypt.'" So Aaron* **stretched out his hand** *over the waters of Egypt, and the frogs came up and covered the land"* (Ex 8:5-7). ... *"Then the Lord said to Moses, "Tell Aaron,* **'Stretch out your staff** *and strike the dust of the ground,' and throughout the land of Egypt the dust will become gnats." They did this, and when Aaron* **stretched out his hand** *with the staff and struck the dust of the ground, gnats came upon men and animals. All the dust throughout the land of Egypt became gnats"* (Ex 8:16-18).

Next, the Lord told Moses: *"Go to Pharaoh and say to him, 'This is what the Lord, the God of the Hebrews, says: "Let my people go, so that they may worship me." If you refuse to let them go and continue to hold them back,* **the hand of the Lord will bring a terrible plague** *on your livestock in the field"* (Ex 9:1-3).

Still Pharaoh balked, so God said to Moses and Arron: *"Take **handfuls of soot** from a furnace and have Moses toss it into the air in the presence of Pharaoh. It will become fine dust over the whole land of Egypt, and festering boils will break out on men and animals throughout the land. So they took soot from a furnace and stood before Pharaoh. Moses **tossed it into the air**, and festering boils broke out on men and animals"* (Ex 9:8-10).

Pharaoh still resisted so God said to Moses: *"**Stretch out your hand** toward the sky so that hail will fall all over Egypt – on men and animals and on everything growing in the fields of Egypt." When **Moses stretched out his staff toward the sky**, the Lord sent thunder and hail, and lightning flashed down to the ground. So the Lord rained hail on the land of Egypt; hail fell and lightning flashed back and forth. It was the worst storm in all the land of Egypt since it had become a nation"* (Ex 9:22-25). ... Then, when Pharaoh seemingly relented, *"Moses left Pharaoh and went out of the city. **He spread out his hands toward the Lord**; the thunder and hail stopped, and the rain no longer poured down on the land"* (Ex 9:33-34).

Once more, Pharaoh recanted his word, and once more, God directed Moses to stretch his hands out over Egypt. *"The Lord said to Moses, "**Stretch out your hand over Egypt** so that locusts will swarm over the land and devour everything growing in the fields, everything left by the hail."*

*So **Moses stretched out his staff** over Egypt, and the Lord made an east wind blow across the land all that day and all that night. By morning the wind had brought the locusts; they invaded all Egypt and settled down in every area of the country in great numbers. Never before had there been such a plague of locusts, nor will there ever be again"* (Ex 10:12-15).

Seemingly it seemed, this would be enough to convince Pharaoh to release the Israelites, but he was a man with a hard, hard heart. So, he hardened his heart the more and would not let the Israelites go (Ex 10:20). In response, "*The Lord said to Moses, "**Stretch out your hand toward the sky** so that darkness will spread over Egypt – darkness that can be felt." So **Moses stretched out his hand toward the sky**, and total darkness covered all Egypt for three days. No one could see anyone else or leave his place for three days. Yet all the Israelites had light in the places where they lived"* (Ex 10:21-23).

As you know, Pharaoh resisted the Lord until it finally cost him the life of his first-born son, and then his army and his chariots that were all buried beneath the waters of the Reed Sea. But, Israel had other enemies to conquer, and as they undertake this task, we once more see the importance of holy hands.

*"Moses said to Joshua, "Choose some of our men and go out to fight the Amalekites. Tomorrow **I will stand on top of the hill with the staff of God in my hands.**" So Joshua fought the Amalekites as Moses had ordered, and Moses, Aaron and Hur went to the top of the hill.*

*"**As long as Moses held up his hands, the Israelites were winning, but whenever he lowered his hands, the Amalekites were winning**. When **Moses' hands grew tired**, they took a stone and put it under him and he sat on it. **Aaron and Hur held his hands up** — one on one side, one on the other — so that **his hands remained steady till sunset**"* (Ex 17:9-13). ...
And, *"Moses built an altar and called it The Lord is my Banner. 16 He said, "For **hands were lifted up to the throne of the Lord**"* (Ex 17:15-16).

Transference of Sins:
We also see the significance of one's hands in the sacrificial system. *"The elders of the community are to **lay their hands on the bull's head before the Lord,** and the bull shall be slaughtered before the Lord. ... **In this way the priest will make atonement for them, and they will be forgiven. ... This is the sin offering for the community**"* (Lev 4:15-21). By laying their hands on the bull's head, they were symbolically transferring the people's sins to the bull.

OFFERINGS

We see this again on the annual day of atonement. *"When Aaron has finished making atonement for the Most Holy Place, the Tent of Meeting and the altar, he shall bring forward the live goat. **He is to lay both hands on the head of the live goat and confess over it all the wickedness and rebellion of the Israelites** — all their sins — and put them on the goat's head. ... The goat will carry on itself all their sins to a solitary place"* (Lev 16:20-22).

Hand, Head, Heart Connection:
The Decalogue (the ten commandments) were to be tied as symbols on the Israelites foreheads and hands (Dt 6:8; 11:18) symbolizing that one's thoughts and behavior were to be governed by God's Ten Words. *"Fix these words of mine in your hearts and minds;* **tie them as symbols on your hands** *and bind them on your foreheads"* (Deut 11:18).

Recognition of Sovereignty:
King David, prayed to God, crying: *"Hear my cry for mercy as I call to you for help, as* **I lift up my hands toward your Most Holy Place**" (Ps 28:2). Then, demonstrating the symbolic significance of the use of our hands in worship, David says: *"If we had forgotten the name of our God or* **spread out our hands to a foreign god**, *would not God have discovered it, since he knows the secrets of the heart?"* (Ps 44:20-21). To insure that all recognize God's sovereignty, the Sons of Korah, who were appointed by David to lead worship, said: *"***Clap your hands, all you nations***; shout to God with cries of joy. How awesome is the Lord Most High, the great King over all the earth!"* (Ps 47:1-2).

David speaks of the use of hands during prayer, saying: *"When I was in distress, I sought the Lord; at night* **I stretched out untiring hands** *and my soul refused to be comforted. ... I remembered my songs in the night. My heart mused and my spirit inquired"* (Ps 77:2 & 6). This was repeated by the Sons of Korah for use in times of grief. *"My eyes are dim with grief. I call to you, O Lord,* **every day; I spread out my hands to you**. [Asking] *"Do you show your wonders to the dead? Do those who are dead rise up and praise you?"* (Ps 88:9-10).

When King Solomon dedicated the temple, he – like those before him – lifted holy hands toward the throne of God. *"Then Solomon stood before the altar of the*

Lord in front of the whole assembly of Israel, **spread out his hands toward heaven**" (1 Kings 8:22-23). Dedicating the temple as a physical reminder of God's Temple in heaven, Solomon declared: *"When a prayer or plea is made by any of your people Israel – each one aware of the afflictions of his own heart, and* **spreading out his hands toward this temple** *– then hear from heaven, your dwelling place. Forgive and act; deal with each man according to all he does, since you know his heart (for you alone know the hearts of all men)"* (1 Kings 8:38-40).

The Psalmists had a great deal to say about the use of our hands in worship. Following are but a few selected Scriptures: "**Lift up your hands in the sanctuary and praise the Lord**" (Ps 134:2). ... *"May my prayer be set before you like incense;* **may the lifting up of my hands be like the evening sacrifice**" (Ps 141:2). *"***I spread out my hands to you***; my soul thirsts for you like a parched land"* (Ps 143:6).

Lazy Hands ~ Lazy Life:
Solomon also speaks of the negative use of one's hands, saying: "**Lazy hands make a man poor**, *but* **diligent hands bring wealth**" (Prov 10:4). ... "**Diligent hands will rule**, *but laziness ends in slave labor"* (Prov 12:24). ... *"A little sleep, a little slumber,* **a little folding of the hands to rest** *– and poverty will come on you like a bandit and scarcity like an armed man"* (Prov 24:33-34). ... "**The fool folds his hands and ruins himself**" (Eccl 4:5).

Preparations for Battle:
David had a great deal to say about the use of our hands symbolically preparing for battle: "**He trains my hands for battle**; *my arms can bend a bow of bronze"* (Ps 18:34). ... *"Praise be to the Lord my Rock, who* **trains my hands for war, my fingers for battle**" (Ps 144:1). ... *"May the praise of God be in their mouths and* **a double-edged sword in their hands**, *to inflict*

vengeance on the nations and punishment on the peoples, to bind their kings with fetters, their nobles with shackles of iron, to carry out the sentence written against them. This is the glory of all his saints" (Ps 149:6-9).

Another instance in the annals of the Israelites demonstrates the power of symbolism in the use of our hands. [When] *"Elisha was suffering from the illness from which he died. Jehoash king of Israel went down to see him and wept over him. "My father! My father!" he cried. "The chariots and horsemen of Israel!" Elisha said, "Get a bow and some arrows," and he did so.* **"Take the bow in your hands**,*" he said to the king of Israel. When he had taken it, Elisha put his hands on the king's hands. "Open the east window," he said, and he opened it.* **"Shoot!" Elisha said, and he shot**. *"***The Lord's arrow of victory, the arrow of victory over Aram!" Elisha declared***. "You will completely destroy the Arameans at Aphek."*

"Then he said, "Take the arrows," and the king took them. Elisha told him, **"Strike the ground." He struck it three times and stopped**. *The man of God was angry with him and said, "You should have struck the ground five or six times; then you would have defeated Aram and completely destroyed it. But now you will defeat it only three times"* (2 Kings 13:14-19). History tells us of the accuracy of these words – Israel won three times and then was defeated.

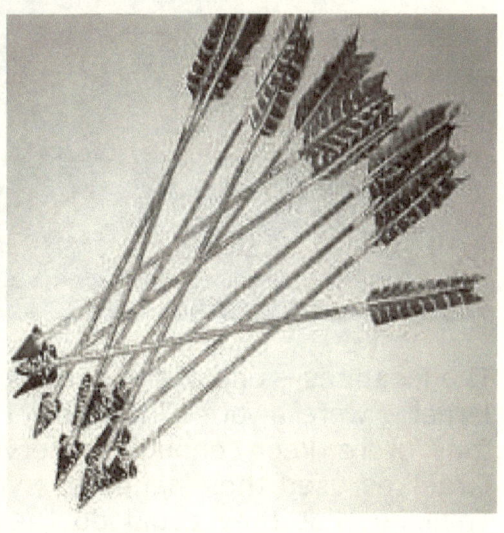

Symbols of Covenant Relationship:
As important as the use of one's hands to symbolize power is, this seems to be limited to those in covenant relationship with God. The prophet Isaiah, warned Israel of this, saying: *"When you **spread out your hands in prayer**, I will hide my eyes from you; even if you offer many prayers, I will not listen. Your hands are full of blood; wash and make yourselves clean. Take your evil deeds out of my sight! Stop doing wrong, learn to do right!"* (Isa 1:15-17).

The Moabites – one of the nations that sought to destroy Israel – were aware of the power of God Almighty; and they were keen enough observers to note that the Israelites used their hands as symbols of God's power. Thinking that they could do the same, and call God's power down for their own purposes, they tried emulating the Israelites' hand movements. But, they were not in covenant relationship with God, Who said of them:

"Moab will be trampled under him [Judah] as straw is trampled down in the manure. **They will spread out their hands in it, as a swimmer spreads out his hands to swim**. *God will bring down their pride despite the cleverness of their hands. He will bring down your high fortified walls and lay them low; he will bring them down to the ground, to the very dust"* (Isa 25:10-12).

Symbol of Guilt/Innocence:
Pilate, who tried unsuccessfully to save Jesus from crucifixion understood the significance of the symbolism in the use of one's hands. *"When Pilate saw that he was getting nowhere, but that instead an uproar was starting,* **he took water and washed his hands in front of the crowd. "I am innocent of this man's blood," he said. "It is your responsibility!"** (Matt 27:24).

Sign of Authority:
Throughout the Old Testament the outcome of battles were described as the conquered being **given into the hand of the conquerer** – a reminder of what the Lord told Noah, repeating it to others with whom He cut a covenant, telling them that everything was placed in their hands. It is a term we still employ today.

Healing Hands:
Long ago, Job declared: *"For he wounds, but he also binds up; he injures, but* **his hands also heal"** (Job 5:18).

Most of Christ's miracles speak of the use of his hands: *"He took the blind man by the hand and led him outside the village. When he had spit on the man's eyes and* **put his hands on him**, *Jesus asked, "Do you see anything?" He looked up and said, "I see people; they look like trees walking around." Once more Jesus* **put his hands on the man's eyes**. *Then his eyes were opened, his sight was restored, and he saw everything clearly"* (Mark 8:23-25).

"*He took the children in his arms, **put his hands on them and blessed them***" (Mark 10:16). "*When the sun was setting, the people brought to Jesus all who had various kinds of sickness, and **laying his hands on each one, he healed them**"* (Luke 4:40-41).

"*On a Sabbath Jesus was teaching in one of the synagogues, and a woman was there who had been crippled by a spirit for eighteen years. She was bent over and could not straighten up at all. When Jesus saw her, he called her forward and said to her, "Woman, you are set free from your infirmity."* **Then he put his hands on her, and immediately she straightened up and praised God**" (Luke 13:10-13).

When Jesus anointed his disciples, commissioning them to go and minister in his name, he said: "**They will place their hands on sick people**, and they will get well" (Mark 16:18). We read of the fulfillment of these words in the Book of Acts.

Shipwrecked on an island, Paul was used by God, through healing – to bring the gospel to the people: *"There was an estate nearby that belonged to Publius, the chief official of the island. He welcomed us to his home and for three days entertained us hospitably. His father was sick in bed, suffering from fever and dysentery. Paul went in to see him and, **after prayer, placed his hands on him and healed him**. When this had happened, the rest of the sick on the island came and were cured"* (Acts 28:7-10).

Symbol of Commissioning: The use of hands to commission one stems back nearly to the beginning of the Old Testament. When God established the Levitical Priesthood, the priests were to be thus recognized. *"Bring the Levites to the front of the Tent of Meeting and assemble the whole Israelite community. You are to bring the Levites before the Lord, and the Israelites are to **lay their hands on them**. Aaron is to present the Levites before the Lord as a wave offering from the Israelites, **so that they may be ready to do the work of the Lord**"* (Num 8:9-11).

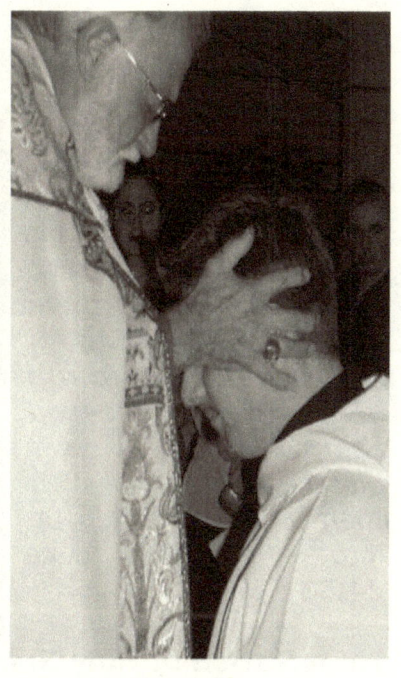

*"Moses did as the Lord commanded him. He took Joshua and had him stand before Eleazar the priest and the whole assembly. Then **he laid his hands on him and commissioned him, as the Lord instructed**"* (Num 27:22-23).

*"**Joshua son of Nun was filled with the spirit of wisdom because Moses had laid his hands on him**. So the Israelites listened to him and did what the Lord had commanded Moses"* (Deut 34:9).

*"In the church at Antioch there were prophets and teachers: Barnabas, Simeon called Niger, Lucius of Cyrene, Manaen (who had been brought up with Herod the tetrarch) and Saul. While they were worshiping the Lord and fasting, the Holy Spirit said, "Set apart for me Barnabas and Saul for the work to which I have called them." So after they had fasted and prayed, **they placed their hands on them and sent them off**"* (Acts 13:1-3).

Symbol of Blessing:
Closing his earthly ministry, Christ once again employed his hands symbolically. *"When he had led them out to the vicinity of Bethany, **he lifted up his hands and blessed them**. While he was blessing them, he left them and was taken up into heaven"* (Luke 24:50-52).

Impartation of Holy Spirit:
In addition to blessing his disciples, Christ commissioned them to go unto others, teaching them those things he had taught them. *"Jesus came to them and said, "All authority in heaven and on earth has been given to me. Therefore go and make disciples of all nations, baptizing them in the name of the Father and of the Son and of the Holy Spirit, and teaching them to obey everything I have commanded you. And surely I am with you always, to the very end of the age"* (Matt 28:18-20).

The Apostles carried out Christ's commission to the fullest. Not only did they teach them Christ's words, in the spirit of the anointing He had laid on them, they anointed others, imparting the baptism of Holy Spirit onto them.

*"Then Peter and John **placed their hands on them, and they received the Holy Spirit**"* (Acts 8:17). ... *"Ananias went to the house and entered it. **Placing his hands on Saul**, he said, "Brother Saul, the Lord-Jesus, who appeared to you on the road as you were coming here — has sent me so that you may see again and be **filled with the Holy Spirit**." Immediately, something like scales fell from Saul's eyes, and he could see again. He got up and was baptized, and after taking some food, he regained his strength"* (Acts 9:17-19).

*"While Apollos was at Corinth, Paul took the road through the interior and arrived at Ephesus. There he found some disciples and asked them, "Did you receive the Holy Spirit when you believed?" They answered, "No, we have not even heard that there is a Holy Spirit." So Paul asked, "Then what baptism did you receive?" "John's baptism," they replied. Paul said, "John's baptism was a baptism of repentance. He told the people to believe in the one coming after him, that is, in Jesus." On hearing this, they were baptized into the name of the Lord Jesus. When **Paul placed his hands on them, the Holy Spirit came on them, and they spoke in tongues and prophesied**. There were about twelve men in all"* (Acts 19:1-7).

Paul admonished his understudy, Timothy, that these gifts were to continue being imparted to those worthy of the calling, by the laying on of hands. *"Do not neglect your gift, which was given you through a **prophetic message when the body of elders laid their hands on you**"* (1 Tim 4:14) ... *"Do not be hasty in **the laying on of hands**, and do not share in the sins of others"* (1

Tim 5:22) ... *"I remind you to fan into flame **the gift of God, which is in you through the laying on of my hands**. For God did not give us a spirit of timidity, but a spirit of power, of love and of self-discipline"* (2 Tim 1:6-7).

This act – the impartation of the baptism of Holy Spirit – which has become a thing of the past for much of the Body of Christ, and considered a bit esoteric by those who practice it, was considered one of the elementary teachings of the first century church. The author of the Book of Hebrews summed this up, saying: *"Therefore let us leave the elementary teachings about Christ and go on to maturity, not laying again the foundation of repentance from acts that lead to death, and of faith in God, **instruction about baptisms, the laying on of hands**, the resurrection of the dead, and eternal judgment. And God permitting, we will do so"* (Heb 6:1-3).

Symbols of Victory:

When Jesus entered Jerusalem riding on a donkey, fulfilling the words of the prophet: *"as it is written, "Do not be afraid, O Daughter of Zion; see, your king is coming, seated on a donkey's colt"* (John 12:14-15). ... [And] *"the great crowd that had come for the Feast heard that Jesus was on his way to Jerusalem.* ***They took palm branches and went out to meet him, shouting, "Hosanna!" "Blessed is he who comes in the name of the Lord!" "Blessed is the King of Israel!"*** (John 12:12-13).

Likewise, as Yeshua Messiah enters the new Jerusalem – the heavenly City of Zion – it is prophesied *"After this I looked and there before me was a great multitude that no one could count, from every nation, tribe, people and language, standing before the throne and in front of the Lamb. They **were wearing white robes and were holding palm branches in their hands**. And they cried out in a loud voice: "Salvation belongs to our God, who sits on the throne, and to the Lamb"* (Rev 7:9-10).

~ Questions, Concerns & Key Points ~

1. Explain how one van determine their thought-process hemispherical dominance and neurological dominant handedness?

2. Describe a simple self-assessment one can perform to determine their hemispherical brain balance, and any impairment therein?

3. Describe the significance in the use of one's hands in spiritual warfare, and in ministry – such as in healing, ordinations, etc.

4. Describe the "hand – head – heart connection."

5. Identify the various uses of one's hands mentioned in Scripture.

Chapter 20 ~ Power in Our Hands

All of the Scriptures about hands, cited in the previous chapter, are but a fraction of those recorded. Why cite so many to prove a point? Normally this would not be necessary, however, there is an old, very valuable proverb which says that a good teacher should know at least ten times as much about any subject than what they intend to teach. Since we are not only ministering to you in this course, but teaching you to minister, it is important that you have ready access to far more Scripture than you will use in your ministry. As the apostle Peter counseled long ago: *"Always be prepared to give an answer to everyone who asks you to give the reason for the hope that you have"* (1 Peter 3:15).

Holy Hands:

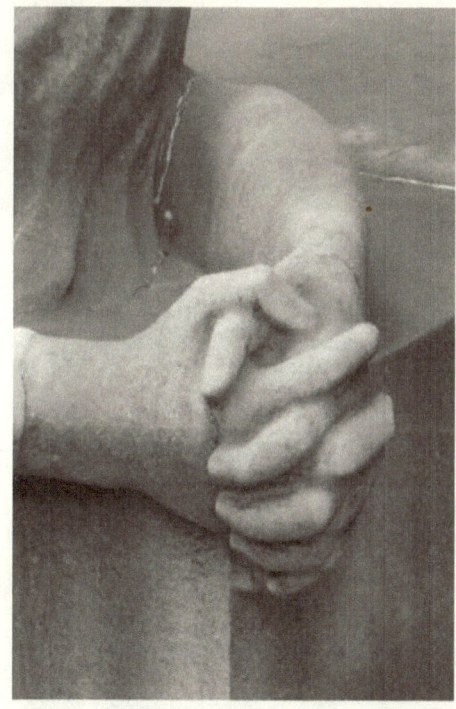

Is all this mention of hands mere picturesque speech, or is there some power in the use of our hands that most no longer understand? If so, what is this power? Assuming there is some latent power in our hands, how can we recover the knowledge concerning its use that the ancients apparently understood? To answer these questions, we need first to validate -- or invalidate -- the idea of there being some power in our hands: power to heal, power to bless, to curse, to win battles, worship effectively, etc. Words themselves can hardly provide an indisputable answer – but experience can.

To experientially grasp the significance of the use of our hands, close your eyes, sit back with your feet flat on the floor, your hands resting on your knees; take a few deep breaths, relax, and engage your imagination. Before we begin our exercise, let's pray, seeking God's protection from the powers of darkness.

Father God, in spirit-to-spirit union with our elder brother Yeshua Messiah, we now approach Your Throne of Grace; and from Your Throne Room, we look down to where we are assembled this moment. We take authority, in the Name of Yeshua Messiah, over every principality and power – every demonic force – commanding you to depart our presence and be made a part of the footstool of our Lord and Savior, until He come to meet out your final punishment. Now Father God, we ask that You commission holy angels to surround us as we enter into this exercise; and that You Holy Spirit, guide our imagination and thoughts, according to the will of The Father; in Jesus Name we pray – Amen.

Recollections and Reflections:

Now, protected within the covering shield of God's holy angels, allow Holy Spirit to guide your imagination back – further and further – to one of the happiest, most joyful experiences in your life. Perhaps it is an early birthday party; a Christmas morning when you opened your presents to find just what you had been hoping for; a picnic by the beach or in your favorite park. Holy Spirit knows just where to take you.

As you begin to sense where Holy Spirit has taken you, take a few moments to get in touch with your surroundings. Now, answer the following question to yourself: Where are you? What kind of a day is it – sunny, cloudy, windy or calm? Who is there with you? Take in as much detail of what you are seeing as possible. What are you hearing? Are you eating anything? If so, what does it taste like? Can you smell the food, the perfume people are wearing? Is anyone touching you, or are you touching anyone or anything?

As you begin to get in touch with this sensory information, take your neurologically dominant hand – the one identified by having its thumb on top in our earlier experiment – and begin to rub your thumb and index finger together gently. As you rub them together, try to get more fully in touch with the sensory information of the experience you have recalled. Now, as you become more fully aware of this sensory information, rub your thumb and index finger together a bit stronger. Continue this – getting in touch with your sensory information and increasing the pressure between your thumb and finger – until you seem to have reached the peak of your emotions.

Continue rubbing them together for a few moments, enjoying the pleasant experience brought up in your inner-imagery – what you are seeing, hearing, smelling, tasting and touching. In the future, whenever you experience stress or conflict, you will be able to recall this pleasant moment and re-experience it.

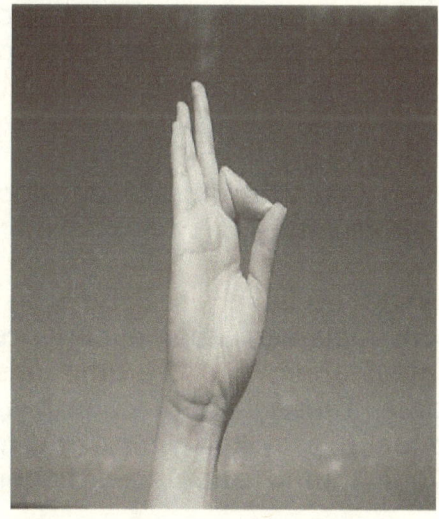

To understand how this is possible, take a few moments to gradually return to the present moment in time – experience feeling the chair you are sitting on; feel the floor beneath your feet; now, becoming more aware of the sounds surrounding you, slowly open your eyes.

Neurolinguistic Anchors and Links:
What you have done in this little walk through your imaginations is to develop a positive neurolinguistic anchor. The word, *'neurolinguistic,'* refers to the language of the nerves. The term, *positive anchor*, means that you have developed a neurological anchor to a positive experience. To understand the benefit of this, take a few moments to reflect on the most recent conflict you have experienced – it may have been a conflict with your spouse, a child, a brother or sister, a fellow employee, neighbor or shopkeeper. It really doesn't matter whom the conflict was with or what it was about; just allow yourself to feel the feelings that you experienced during the conflict.

As you become fully in touch with your emotions surrounding that conflict; rub your thumb and index finger, on your neurologically dominant hand, together lightly. Experience the slight change in your emotions? If you were successful in building a positive neurological anchor, you will sense your conflictual emotions beginning to subside and will begin to notice a sense of peace and tranquility come over you. How many of you can sense the change? If you do not sense the change, then take the time to develop this when you have the opportunity.

What you have just done is to establish a neurolinguistic link between the experience you recalled in your imagination, and the emotions you experienced at that time. These links function bi-directionally – that is, it is equally easy for your hand-movements [e.g., rubbing your thumb and index finger together] to create an imagination, as it is for an imagination to create a hand-movement. God has created us in such a way that when we move our hands, it triggers mental imagery; and our mental imagery triggers our hands. Moreover, when we speak out our imaginations, it triggers our will, or volition, which will move us to carry out our imagination.

It is this phenomena that the following Scripture is based on: *"Hear, O Israel: The Lord our God, the Lord is one. Love the Lord your God with all your heart and with all your soul and with all your strength. These commandments that I give you today are to be upon your hearts. Impress them on your children. Talk about them when you sit at home and when you walk along the road, when you lie down and when you get up. Tie them as symbols on your hands and bind them on your foreheads. Write them on the door frames of your houses and on your gates"* (Deut 6:4-9).

In this Scripture we see portrayed the neurological link from the hand, to the head (mind or soul) to the heart (spirit); and the outworking thereof, as they become manifest to others (written on the door frames of our houses and on our gates). As Christ told the Pharisees, *"The mouth speaks what overflows from the heart. The good person brings forth good things from his store of good, and the evil person brings forth evil things from his store of evil"* (Matt 12:34-36).

Prepared for Battle:
Grasping the significance of this neurological link between our hands (the symbolic motions we make), our heads (our soul – particularly our imaginations), our hearts (spirits – including our will and volition) and our

actions, consider the imagery expressed in the following words of King David:

"As for God, his way is perfect; the word of the Lord is flawless. He is a shield for all who take refuge in him. For who is God besides the Lord? And who is the Rock except our God? **It is God who arms me with strength** *and makes my way perfect.* **He makes my feet like the feet of a deer; He enables me to stand on the heights. He trains my hands for battle; my arms can bend a bow of bronze**.

"You give me your shield of victory, and your right hand sustains me; you stoop down to make me great. You broaden the path beneath me, so that my ankles do not turn. I pursued my enemies and overtook them; I did not turn back till they were destroyed. I crushed them so that they could not rise; they fell beneath my feet. **You armed me with strength for battle**; *you made my adversaries bow at my feet.*

"You made my enemies turn their backs in flight, and I destroyed my foes. They cried for help, but there was no one to save them – to the Lord, but he did not answer. I beat them as fine as dust borne on the wind; I poured them out like mud in the streets" (Ps 18:30-42). ... *"Praise be to the Lord my Rock, who* **trains my hands for war, my fingers for battle**. *He is my loving God and my fortress, my stronghold and my deliverer, my shield, in whom I take refuge, who subdues peoples under me"* (Ps 144:1-2).

God continues to prepare us for battle – the great spiritual conflict of the cosmos – the battle against the powers of darkness. Christ, in his commissioning of his disciples, implemented the use of our hands in winning this war. He said: *"****Go into all the world*** *and* ***preach the good news to all creation***. *Whoever believes and is baptized will be saved, but whoever does not believe will be condemned. And these signs will accompany* *those who believe: In my name* **they will drive out demons; they will speak in new tongues; they will pick up snakes with their hands**; *and when they drink deadly poison, it will not hurt them at all;* **they will place their hands on sick people, and they will get well**" (Mark 16:17-18).

Most stop reading at the end of Christ's commissioning act of his disciples; but in doing so, they miss an important element – Mark's validation of Jesus' words. The last few words of Mark's Gospel provides this validation. *"After the Lord Jesus had spoken to them, he was taken up into heaven and he sat at the right hand of God.* **Then the disciples went out and preached every- where, and the Lord worked with them and confirmed his word by the signs that accompanied it**" (Mark 16:19-20).

In Christ, we are spiritually positioned in heaven. *"Because of his great love for us, God, who is rich in mercy, made us alive with Christ even when we were dead in transgressions – it is by grace you have been saved. And God raised us up with Christ and seated us with him in the heavenly realms in Christ Jesus"* (Eph 2:4-7). Yet, like Christ – and because we have become one with him in – spirit-to-spirit union – we are spiritually in heaven and simultaneously, physically on earth.

"We are God's workmanship, created in Christ Jesus to do good works, which God prepared in advance for us to do" (Eph 2:10). These good works – as we have seen – include the work of our hands, the involvement of our minds (souls), and the commitment of our hearts (spirits); all prepared in advance by God, that we might be enabled to carry out the Great Commission.

One thing that stops many from carrying out the ministry that they have been called to is their own soul wounding – the work of the Adversary of our souls. However, this need not be so. In our next lesson, we will demonstrate how to use your hands – your own hands – to resolve your inner-conflict and facilitate the healing of your soul.

Assignment:
Before proceeding to the next lesson, there are several very important techniques you must master in order to gain the maximum benefit from this lesson.

First, re-read this lesson, committing to memory, as many of the Scriptures about the use of one's hands in ministry, that you possibly can.

Second, practice using your positive anchor until you can feel a meaningful change in your emotions whenever you employ it. You can accomplish this by getting in touch with as many positive experiences as possible, while you are rubbing your thumb and index finger on your neurologically dominant hand together. This is called 'stacking' and will add strength to your positive anchor.

Third – but not necessarily in this order – ask, and then trust, Holy Spirit to bring those positive experiences you have had to your conscious mind. You may think that they are beyond your recall, but remember – Jesus promised that *"the Comforter, which is the Holy Spirit, whom the Father will send in my name, shall bring all things to your remembrance"* (Jn 14:26).

~ Questions, Concerns & Key Points ~

1. How much more than one's student should a good teacher know about his/her subject?

2. What are Neurolinguistic Anchors and Links?

3. What is their purpose, or function?

4. How does one go about creating these?

5. Which of the following statements is true?
   - Moving our hands triggers mental imagery
   - Our mental imagery triggers hand-movements
   - Both

6. Describe how one can be both here on earth and seated with Christ in heavenly places, as stated by Paul in Eph 2:6?

Chapter 21 ~ Resolving Inner-Conflicts

Introduction:
In our last lesson, on restoring inner-balance and harmony, you learned how to develop a positive neurological anchor – an anchor, which if used, can re-center you emotionally in times of stress, helping you change your focus from negative things to those that are more positive, more nurturing to your soul. If you practiced using it, as was assigned, you will have noticed that the more you use it,  the stronger it becomes, and the less time it takes to settle your emotions and draw your mind to positive memories.

Think of your positive anchor as fulfilling the apostle Paul's directives, to:

1. *Take your thoughts captive* ~ *"We take every thought captive and make it obey the Messiah"* (2 Cor 10:5); and

2. *Refocus on the positive* ~ *"Focus your thoughts on what is true, noble, righteous, pure, lovable or admirable, on some virtue or on something praiseworthy"* (Phil 4:8-9).

Thought-stopping and Thought-substitution:
This is referred to in clinical terms as thought-stopping [taking your thoughts captive]; and thought-substitution [refocusing on the positive'.

In this lesson, our first task will be to develop a negative anchor. Why a negative anchor? Certainly we don't want to anchor our soul to the negative – quite the contrary –

we want to prevent this, and a negative neurological anchor, used correctly, can help us accomplish this.

A strong, negative neurological anchor will provide you one more tool in your toolbox, that you can employ to help take your negative thoughts captive and focus on the positive.

Moreover, since *"as a man thinks in his heart, so he will be"* (Pro 23:7); the use of these tools – both the positive and the negative anchors – can help you overcome obsessive-compulsive behavior patterns, addictions and other life-controlling problems.

These are the strongholds mentioned by Paul in the following Scripture. *"Although we do live in the world, we do not wage war in a worldly way; because* **the weapons we use to wage war are not worldly. On the contrary, they have God's power for demolishing strongholds. We demolish arguments and every arrogance that raises itself up against the knowledge of God**; *we take every thought captive and make it obey the Messiah"* (2 Cor 10:3-5 CJB).

In contrast to these strongholds – those things that take us captive and make us slaves, God wants to be our stronghold, insuring our freedom. **"The Lord is my rock**, **my fortress** *and my deliverer; my God,* **my rock**, *in whom I take refuge. He is* **my shield**, *the power that saves me,* **my stronghold***"* (Ps 18:2).

Constructing A Negative Anchor:
Once again, as in our last lesson, before we begin our exercise, let's pray, seeking God's protection from the powers of darkness.

Father God, in spirit-to-spirit union with our elder brother Yeshua Messiah, we now approach Your Throne of Grace; and from Your Throne Room, we look down to where we are assembled this moment. We take authority, in the Name of Yeshua Messiah, over every principality and power – every demonic force – commanding you to depart our presence and be made a part of the footstool of our Lord and Savior, until He come to meet out your final punishment. Now Father God, we ask that You commission holy angels to surround us as we enter into this exercise; and that You Holy Spirit, guide our imagination and thoughts, according to the will of The Father; in Jesus Name we pray – Amen.

Recollections and Reflections:

Make yourself as comfortable as possible and sit back and close your eyes. Now, protected within the covering shield of God's holy angels, allow Holy Spirit to guide your imagination back – further and further – to focus on one of the most disgusting, most revolting things you have ever experienced. It may have been your discovery of a dead, decomposing animal; coming onto a wreck where people were seriously injured; some picture that is truly disgusting to you. Holy Spirit knows just where to show you.

As you begin to sense what Holy Spirit is showing you, take a few moments to get in touch with your surroundings. Now, answer the following questions to yourself: Where are you? What kind of a day is it – sunny, cloudy, windy or calm? Is anyone there with you? If so, who? Take in as much detail of what you are seeing as possible. What are you hearing? Are you eating anything? If so, what does it taste like? What are you smelling? Is anything touching you, or are you touching anything?

As you begin to get in touch with this revolting sensory information, take your neurologically non-dominant hand – the one identified by having its thumb underneath in our experiment in the last lesson – and begin to rub your thumb and index finger together gently. As you rub  them together, try to get more fully in touch with the sensory information of the disgusting, revolting thing brought to mind. Now, as you become more fully aware of this sensory information, rub your thumb and index finger together a bit stronger. Continue this – getting in touch with your sensory information and increasing the pressure between your thumb and finger – until you seem to have reached the peak of your emotions.

Continue rubbing them together for a few moments, as long as you can tolerate the negative sensory information brought up in your inner-imagery – i.e., what you are seeing, hearing, smelling, tasting and touching. As you continue rubbing your thumb and forefinger together, recognize how you want to turn away from, or escape, the thing or experience creating your negative emotions. In the future, whenever you need to say 'NO' to something that is tempting, or to change your focus from something or someone, you need only employ this negative anchor; and in an instant, you will be able to recall the disgusting, revolting thing you have been focusing on, and turn away, or withdraw from it.

Now, as you did after creating your positive anchor, take a few moments to gradually return to the present moment in time – experience feeling the chair you are sitting on; feel the floor beneath your feet; now, becoming more aware of the sounds surrounding you, slowly open your eyes.

Neurolinguistic Anchors and Links:
In this little walk through your imaginations, you have developed a neuolinguistic negative anchor. Remember, the word, *'neurolinguistic,'* refers to the language of the nerves; and the term, *negative anchor*, means that you have developed a neurological anchor to a negative experience. To fully comprehend the benefit of this, briefly allow yourself to get in touch with one of the strongholds in your life. For example: if you struggle with alcohol, drugs, tobacco, pornography, overeating, gambling – or whatever your strong temptation is – imagine that you are about to indulge in that besetting sin.

Allow yourself sufficient time to fully get in touch with your emotions surrounding this struggle. For instance: if your struggle is with alcohol, imagine pouring yourself a drink and bringing the glass up to your lips. Now, rub your thumb and index finger, on your neurologically non-dominant hand, together firmly, while you simultaneously tell yourself, "No!" "I will not indulge my passions or give in to this temptation again."

Do you feel a slight change in your emotions? If you were successful in building a positive neurological anchor, you will sense the strong, temptation begin to subside and will begin to notice feeling disgusted – perhaps even feel a bit nauseated – and have a desire to get rid of the drink (or whatever tempting thing you have been focusing on). How many of you sensed a change in your emotions?

You have just established a neurolinguistic link between rejecting the tempting thing you recalled in your imagination, and the negative emotions you experienced. Remember, these links function bi-directionally – that is, it is equally as easy for your hand-movements (rubbing your thumb and index finger together) to create an imagination, as it is for an imagination to create a hand-movement.

God has created us in such a way that when we move our hands, it triggers our mental imagery; then, when we speak out our imaginations, it triggers our will, or volition, moving us to carry out what we imagined. In other words, suppose that your struggle is with smoking. You can employ this negative anchor to help yourself say "NO" to your cravings; and then, as you speak out your new resolve, i.e., "I do not need to smoke and will not", your body will begin to respond. Remember, what we imagine and speak out, we empower ourselves to create – which in this case is positive change.

Combining Positive & Negative Anchors:
It might at first seem that combining our positive and negative anchors would merely cancel out their effectiveness; but, if combined correctly, this is not the case. Their use can be combined in such a way that they actually reinforce one another. For example: if you struggle with compulsive overeating, the next time your craving calls; use your  negative neurological anchor to call up your negative, disgusting, revolting emotions; and when you begin to feel them; tell yourself, "These feelings are caused from overeating. I do not need to give in to them; quite the contrary, I am leaving the kitchen, and will go, listen to some enjoyable music."

After leaving the kitchen, turn on some music that you enjoy; and as you sit back in your comfortable chair;

reward yourself for making this decision by using your positive neurological anchor, which will enhance the pleasure being derived from your music, and will help you re-center your emotions. Combining your positive and negative anchors in this manner can help you break down those negative strongholds in your life; enabling you to experience the protection of God's stronghold – his deliverance, protection and peace.

Operant Conditioning:
The combined use of our positive and negative neurolinguistic anchors, correlates with a psychological concept referred to as Operant Conditioning. **Operant conditioning** occurs when an individual intentionally modifies the occurrence and form of their own behavior by associating that behavior with a particular stimulus.

Reinforcement and punishment – which are the core tools of operant conditioning – may be either positive [delivered following a response], or negative [withdrawn following a response]. This creates a total of four basic consequences, with the addition of a fifth procedure known as extinction [i.e. there is no change in consequences following a response.]

It is important to note that the actors are not spoken of as being reinforced, punished, or extinguished; it is their actions that are reinforced, punished, or extinguished. Additionally, reinforcement, punishment, and extinction are not terms whose use is restricted to the laboratory. Naturally occurring consequences can also be said to reinforce, punish, or extinguish behavior and are not always delivered by people.

- **Reinforcement** is a consequence that causes a behavior to occur with greater frequency.

- **Punishment** is a consequence that causes a behavior to occur with less frequency.

- **Extinction** is the lack of any consequence following a behavior. When a behavior is inconsequential [i.e., producing neither favorable nor unfavorable consequences] it will occur with less frequency. When a previously reinforced behavior is no longer reinforced with either positive or negative reinforcement, it leads to a decline in the response.

Scientific Footnotes:
Research scientists have established that what we do with our hands sends signals to our brain. This is called the 'ascending reticular formation' meaning that the reticular formation is opened by signals generated by the movement of our hands and/or feet, that ascend up the spinal column into the brain; opening the reticular formation. Just as when an emotional arousal opens our reticular formation in a descending fashion, allowing new information to be stored in the deepest parts of our memory; so when ascending signals open the reticular formation, the hand movement and associated imaginations are stored away in our memory. When this happens, certain neuro-chemicals are created and a new neurolinguistic link is established. From this time on – unless the link is broken – a similar touch automatically retrieves one's associated imaginations & intent.

Biblical Examples:
We have already mentioned the story of Moses and Aaron and the use of the staff and their hands before Pharaoh (Ex 5-8); and the story of Elisha directing Jehoash to strike the earth with the arrows. There are many others – for example, the story of Joshua defeating the city of Ai. *"The Lord said to Joshua, "Hold out toward Ai the javelin that is in your hand, for into your hand I will deliver the city." So Joshua held out his javelin toward Ai. As soon as he did this, the men in the ambush rose quickly from their position and rushed forward. They entered the city and captured it and quickly set it on fire"* (Josh 8:18-19).

We would be remiss not to mention the Israelites crossing of the Reed Sea. God guided the Israelites out of Egypt, along the desert road that came to a dead end at the shores of the Sea of Reeds. Pharaoh pursued them and the people became terrified. *"Then the Lord said to Moses, "Why are you crying out to me? Tell the Israelites to move on. Raise your staff and stretch out your hand over the sea to divide the water so that the Israelites can go through the sea on dry ground"* (Ex 14:15-17). ... *"Moses stretched out his hand over the sea, and all that night the Lord drove the sea back with a strong east wind and turned it into dry land. The waters were divided, and the Israelites went through the sea on dry ground, with a wall of water on their right and on their left"* (vs. 21-22).

This miraculous deliverance is recorded again and again throughout Scripture, since it was, truly a miracle; but it begs the question – "Would Moses have had the confidence to order approximately 2,000,000 people to march forward into the sea, had he not previously received training in the symbolic use of the rod and hands, and had already witnessed the power of God.

There are important lessons to be learned from these examples:

- They all included the symbolic use of one's hands and weaponry,

- They all required the individual to hear the voice of God,

- They all required faith (imagination + will + speech).

Using Anchors to Resolve Inner-Conflicts:
*"Yeshua said to them [the Pharisees], **"Every kingdom divided against itself will be ruined, and every city***

or household divided against itself will not survive. If Satan drives out Satan, he is divided against himself; so how can his kingdom survive?" (Matt 12:25-27 CJB).

Another pertinent Scripture contains the words of Solomon, who said: **"Unless the Lord builds the house, its builders labor in vain***. Unless the Lord watches over the city, the watchmen stand guard in vain. In vain you rise early and stay up late, toiling for food to eat – for he grants sleep to those he loves"* (Ps 127:1-2).

These Scriptures unquestionably are referencing one's physical home, or residence, but none the less, they set forth a principle – that divided we fall, but united we stand. Our inner-being – our spirit and soul – is the house, or temple of the Lord. As Paul said in his letter to the Christians in Corinth: *"**Know ye not that ye are the temple of God, and that the Spirit of God dwelleth in you**?"* (1 Cor 3:16).

*"What fellowship can light have with darkness? What harmony is there between Christ and Belial? What does a believer have in common with an unbeliever? What agreement is there between the temple of God and idols? For **we are the temple of the living God**. As God has said: "I will live within them and walk among them, and I will be their God, and they will be my people"* (2 Cor 6:14-16).

Origins of Inner-conflict:
Is there any lack of harmony within your soul? – Are you aware of any inner-conflict, or turmoil? Inner-conflict and turmoil destroys internal harmony, creating self-sabotaging defense-mechanisms. These self-defeating defense-mechanisms are subconscious – operating below the level of our consciousness, in the darkness of our inner-being. For example: When our imaginations and emotions choose one path, our intellectual thoughts

choose another, blocking the manifestation of our imaginations so that they never become fully realized. Job describes such inner-conflict, saying: *"Though I cry, 'I've been wronged!' I get no response; though I call for help, there is no justice.* ***He has blocked my way so I cannot pass; he has shrouded my paths in darkness****"* (Job 19:7-8).

Inner-Conflicts and Confusion:
We may on the one hand earnestly desire to follow God; even imagine seeing ourselves serving Him on the mission field, teaching in a seminary, or standing in the pulpit; but in our intellect we do not consider ourselves worthy of this calling. On the other hand, we may intellectually commit ourselves to serve the Lord, while our imaginations and emotions drive us to serve self – doing our own thing, or serving the flesh.

This confusion and conflict between our imaginations and emotions on the one side; and our analytical rationale on the other, is evidence of soul wounding. This soul-wounding results in the misalignment of our spirit, soul and body; which were designed to work harmoniously to achieve God's purpose for which we were created. Thus, our own wounded, contaminated soul blocks God's blessings, aborting His sovereign plan for our life.

This, of course, is Satan's precise plan – to steal our blessings, destroy God's plan for our life, and ultimately to kill us. After all, as Jesus warned us, *"The thief comes only to steal and kill and destroy"* (Jn 10:10). Satan, and the demons he commands, entice us to serve the flesh instead of serving God, leaving us afterward feeling naked – exposed – as Adam and Eve declared; empty and full of shame.

The woman Jesus met at the well in Samaria was experiencing this emptiness and shame. *"When a Samaritan woman came to draw water, Jesus said to her, "Will you give me a drink?" – His disciples had gone into the town to buy food. – The Samaritan woman said to him, "You are a Jew and I am a Samaritan woman. How can you ask me for a drink?" – For Jews do not associate with Samaritans. – Jesus answered her, "If you knew the gift of God and who it is that asks you for a drink, you would have asked him and he would have given you living water."*

"Sir," the woman said, "you have nothing to draw with and the well is deep. Where can you get this living water? Are you greater than our father Jacob, who gave us the well and drank from it himself, as did also his sons and his flocks and herds?" "Jesus answered, "Everyone who drinks this water will be thirsty again, but whoever drinks the water I give him will never thirst. Indeed, the water I give him will become in him a spring of water welling up to eternal life."

"The woman said to him, "Sir, give me this water so that I won't get thirsty and have to keep coming here to draw water" (John 4:7-15).

She was filled with shame for, the next few verses describe her lifestyle – living with numerous men without being married. Jesus promised to take her shame; beyond this, he promised to give her a source of inner joy that would well up inside of her, insuring her eternal life.

Shortly before his crucifixion, Jesus repeated this promise – only this time to a crowd of people. *"On the last and greatest day of the Feast, Jesus stood and said in a loud voice, "If anyone is thirsty, let him come to me and drink. Whoever believes in me, as the Scripture has said, streams of living water will flow from within him." By this he meant the Spirit, whom those who believed in him were later to receive. Up to that time the Spirit had not been given, since Jesus had not yet been glorified"* (John 7:37-39).

God desires to release blessings in our lives. His Word says: *"If you fully obey the Lord your God and carefully follow all his commands ... the Lord your God will set you high above all the nations on earth. All these blessings [those enumerated in the following texts] will follow after you, come upon you and accompany you if you obey the Lord your God"* (Deut 28:1-2). ... *"However, if you do not obey the Lord your God and do not carefully follow all his commands and decrees ... all these curses [those enumerated in the following texts] will come upon you and overtake you"* (Deut 28:15).

Our Heavenly Father, has promised us unlimited blessings; "God's power has given us everything we need for life and godliness, through our knowing the One who called us to his own glory and goodness. By these he has given us valuable and superlatively great promises, so that through them you might come to share in God's nature and escape the corruption which evil desires have brought into the world" (2 Peter 1:3-4 CJB).

Jesus [Yeshua Messiah] died to redeem mankind out of the hand of Satan, and provide us a way back to the Father. He said: *"I am the way and the truth and the life. No one comes to the Father except through me"* (John 14:6-7). Returning to his Father, Jesus and Father God sent us another Comforting Counselor, Holy Spirit. Jesus said: *"If you love me, you will keep my commands; and I will ask the Father, and he will give you another comforting Counselor like me, the Spirit of Truth, to be with you forever"* (John 14:15-17).

If we have been born-again [that is born-from-above] Holy Spirit indwells our spirit, ready to release within us, the rivers of blessings Father God promised; but we have damned up the channels! The dams, blockades and barricades are all of our own creation; we constructed them, and we can destroy them – releasing once more, the promised streams of living waters.

The same Scripture that pronounced a curse for rebellion, provides a remedy – a blessing for repentance: *"If they will confess their sins and the sins of their fathers – their treachery against me and their hostility toward me, which made me hostile toward them ... I will remember my covenant with Jacob and my covenant with Isaac and my covenant with Abraham, and I will remember their land"* (Lev 26:40-43).

This promise is reiterated in the New Testament. *"This is the message we have heard from him and declare to you: God is light; in him there is no darkness at all. If we claim to have fellowship with him yet walk in the darkness, we lie and do not live by the truth. But if we walk in the light, as he is in the light, we have fellowship with one another, and the blood of Jesus, his Son,* purifies us from all sin. ... **"If we confess our sins, he is faithful and just and will forgive us our sins and purify us from all unrighteousness"** (1 John 1:5-9).

Once we resolve our inner-conflicts, to remove the dams that we have constructed, God's unlimited blessings will just naturally flow again – providing us physical, emotional, spiritual blessings, financial sufficiency, as well as relational and environmental healing – health and wholeness. King David, the Psalmist, declared: *"Praise be to the Lord, who has given rest to his people ... just as he promised. Not one word has failed of all the good promises he gave .... May the Lord our God be with us as he was with our fathers; may he never leave us nor forsake us"* (1 Kings 8:56-58).

God stands ready to fulfill His promises – waiting for us to remove the dams of our own construction – an act described as simply opening the door to our heart. The Lord says: *"Those whom I love I rebuke and discipline. So be earnest, and repent.* **Here I am! I stand at the door [of your heart] knocking. If anyone hears my voice and opens the door, I will come in and eat [fellowship] with him, and he with me**. *And I will let him who wins the victory sit with me on my throne, just as I myself also won the victory and sat down with my Father on His throne"* (Rev 3:19-21).

Dams, Barricades and Blockades:
To remove these dams, barricades and blockades, we must first identify them. After all, some of them have

been in place so long, we have come to consider them part of God's design for our life; and their effect – the blocking of God's promised blessings – as normal. This idea is certainly not consistent with God's declared intent according to John the Beloved: *"Beloved, I wish above all things that thou mayest prosper and be in health, even as thy soul prospereth"* (3 John 2). God wants us to experience prosperity and good health; but notice – our realization thereof is tied to the prosperity [the well-being] of our soul.

Those things that diminish the prosperity of our soul may be hidden to us. As Jeremiah the prophet said: *"The heart is more deceitful than anything else and mortally sick. Who can fathom it?* (Jer 17:9). He then answers this vital question, saying: "I Adonai [the Lord], search the heart; I test inner motivations" (vs. 10). Through this same prophet, Adonai [the Lord] says, *"Call out to me, and I will answer you – I will tell you great things, hidden things of which you are unaware … I will bring health and healing; I will heal them and reveal to them peace and truth in plenty. … I will cleanse them from all their sins, through which they offended and rebelled against me"* (Jer 33:3, 6 & 8).

Understanding God's mercy and His willingness to reveal the contamination of our soul, and heal it; David prayed: *"Examine me, God, and know my heart; test me, and know my thoughts. See if there is in me any hurtful way, and lead me along the eternal way"* (Ps 139:23-24). James reiterates this concept in the New Testament, writing: *"If any of you lacks wisdom, he should ask God, who gives generously to all without finding fault, and it will be given to him"* (James 1:5-6).

Following are some of the dams, barricades and blockades common to man – inner-conflicts that contaminate our soul, blocking or drying-up the channels of God's blessings. Take time to go through this list carefully and prayerfully, allowing Holy Spirit to illuminate those that are preventing you from realizing God's best, that He has planned for you. Check all those that apply. Holy Spirit may show you others – outside of this list – and if so, jot them down in the space provided below:

Envisioned Desires	Fears & Intellectual Block
A desire to serve God in Ministry	Fear that family will not approve
Desiring oneness with your spouse	Withdraw fearing control
A desire to trust God completely	Fear of financial inadequacy or ruin
A desire for success & prosperity	Thinking that you do not deserve this
A desire to lose weight	Fear of losing armor/transparency
A desire for physical healing	Fear of losing associated benefits
A desire to pay tithe	Fear that God won't take care of me
A desire for my spouse to change	Fearful of putting them in God's hands
A desire for a godly spouse	Fear that you don't deserve one
A desire for eternal life	Fear you've committed to many sins
Allowing God to provide all my needs	Believing God only does what I can't
Trusting God to watch over my kids	Fearing that He won't
Desiring intimacy with God	Fearful of God
A desire to step out in faith	A fear of failure & embarrassment
A desire to 'let go and let God'	A fear He won't do what I want

Envisioned Desires	Fears & Intellectual Block
A desire to let-go of my children	Fear they can't take care of themselves
Desiring a deserved raise/promotion	Fear of being turned down
Wanting to be 'the apple of God's eye	Seeing myself as His step-child at best
Wanting God's approval	Fear of family disapproval
Desiring to express emotions	Fearing rejection or shaming

~ Questions, Concerns & Key Points ~

1. Explain 'thought-stopping' and thought-substitution' and the biblical support for each.

2. What is the purpose and function of neurolinguistic anchors and links?

3. What are some of the benefits one can achieve by emplpying a combination of positive and negative neurolinguistic anchors?

4. What is the purpose of speaking-out our imaginations, dreams and visions?

5. What is 'Operant Conditioning' and how does it work?

6. What is one of the primary origins of inner-conflict?

7. What is the relationship between inner-conflict and soul-wounding?

8. How can one's own shame be blocking God's intended blessings?

9. What is the remedy for shame?

Chapter 22 ~ Restoring Inner-Peace

Introduction:
We closed our last lesson with an assignment – to set aside time to identify our inner-conflicts: those things that serve as dams, blockades and barricades in our life. Take a few minutes to review the list; adding other inner-conflicts that Holy Spirit may have illuminated.

Envisioned Desires	Fears & Intellectual Block
A desire to serve God in Ministry	Fear that family will not approve
Desiring oneness with your spouse	Withdraw fearing control
A desire to trust God completely	Fear of financial inadequacy or ruin
A desire for success & prosperity	Thinking that you do not deserve this
A desire to lose weight	Fear of losing armor/transparency
A desire for physical healing	Fear of losing associated benefits
A desire to pay tithe	Fear that God won't take care of me
A desire for my spouse to change	Fearful of putting them in God's hands
A desire for a godly spouse	Fear that you don't deserve one
A desire for eternal life	Fear you've committed to many sins
Allowing God to provide all my needs	Believing God only does what I can't
Trusting God to watch over my kids	Fearing that He won't
Desiring intimacy with God	Fearful of God

Envisioned Desires	Fears & Intellectual Block
A desire to step out in faith	A fear of failure & embarrassment
A desire to 'let go and let God'	A fear He won't do what I want
A desire to let-go of my children	Fear they can't take care of themselves
Desiring a deserved raise/promotion	Fear of being turned down
Wanting to be 'the apple of God's eye	Seeing myself as His step-child at best
Wanting God's approval	Fear of family disapproval
Desiring to express emotions	Fearing rejection or shaming

Soul Fragmentation:
These conflicts, in addition to serving as dams, blockades and barricades, preventing us from realizing God's promised blessings; also serve to fragment our soul since one part of our inner-being is telling us to do one thing, and another part, another thing. Unless resolved, this contributes to our becoming a double-minded [double-souled] person, unstable in all our ways (James 1:8).

God's Remedy:
If this describes you, God has a remedy! *"Come close to God, and he will come close to you. Clean your hands, sinners; and purify your hearts, you double-minded people! ... Humble yourselves before the Lord, and he will lift you up"* (James 4:8-10 CJB).

For each of the inner-conflicts enumerated above – as well as others, specific to you, that you have added – God's Word provides abundant answers. For example: if we have self-identity issues, we need to remember that we are God's children (John 1:12). However, it is not be one's intent to engage these inner-conflicts – since confronting them with Scripture often serves to strengthen these self-sabotaging defense-mechanisms.

Instead of triggering the strengthening of these defense-mechanisms, we want to see them removed through the power of God. As the apostle Peter said: *"May grace (God's favor) and peace (which is perfect well-being, all necessary good, all spiritual prosperity, and **freedom from fears and agitating passions and ... conflicts be multiplied to you** in the full, personal, precise, correct, knowledge of God and of Jesus our Lord. For His divine power has bestowed upon us all things that [are requisite and suited] to life and godliness, through the [full, personal] knowledge of Him Who called us by and to His own glory and excellence (virtue)"* (2 Peter 1:2-3).

The apostle Paul declared: *"We are God's workmanship, created in Christ Jesus to do good works, which God prepared in advance for us to do"* (Eph 2:10); but, the blockages within our soul – unless removed – will prevent us from doing those good works. We must, therefore, remove these dams, barricades and blockades, so that we can effectively carry out the ministry of reconciliation that God has commissioned us for.

Our Spiritual Assignment:
Remember, *"If anyone is in Christ, he is a new creation; the old has gone, the new has come! All this is from **God, who reconciled us to himself through Christ and gave us the ministry of reconciliation**: that God*

*was reconciling the world to himself in Christ, not counting men's sins against them. And **he has committed to us the message of reconciliation. We are therefore Christ's ambassadors, as though God were making his appeal through us**"* (2 Cor 5:17-20).

Like Moses of old, we have been given the assignment of liberating those held in bondage by the Adversary. Like Moses, we often feel inadequate because of wounds within our soul. But with the staff of the Lord in our hands, nothing is impossible. Remember, when the Adversary's representatives threw down their staffs [representing the power of Satan]; Aaron threw down his [representing the power of God]; and his staff swallowed up their staffs.

The Staff of the Spirit:
Moses was used of God to manifest signs and wonders within the physical realm; in contrast, we have been called of God, and anointed by His Spirit, to manifest signs and wonders within the spiritual realm. After describing our spiritual battlefield – the struggle *"against the rulers, against the authorities, against the powers of this dark world and against the cosmic forces of evil in the heavenly realms"* (Eph 6:12); he identifies our staff.

He admonishes us to put on the full armor of God (vs 11), and then tells us to: *"Take the helmet of salvation [deliverance] along with **the sword given by The Spirit, which is the word of God**"* (Eph 6:17). Then, once equipped with this sword [or staff] provided by The Spirit, Paul advises us how to wage this war in the spirit realm. He says: *"pray at all times, with all kinds of prayers and requests, in the*

Spirit, vigilantly and persistently, for all God's people" (Eph 6:18).

Power in the Word:

The sword given us by the Spirit – the Word of God – is powerful, having capabilities that are beyond our imagination. *"For the word of God is living and active. Sharper than any double-edged sword, it penetrates even to dividing soul and spirit, joints and marrow; it judges the thoughts and attitudes of the heart. Nothing in all creation is hidden from God's sight. Everything is uncovered and laid bare before the eyes of him to whom we must give account"* (Heb 4:12-13).

God's power can swallow up everything the Adversary of our souls throws at us. Even death – Satan's ultimate weapon – has been swallowed up in victory! *"We will not all sleep, but we will all be changed – in a flash, in the twinkling of an eye, at the last trumpet. For the trumpet will sound, the dead will be raised imperishable, and we will be changed. For the perishable must clothe itself with the imperishable, and the mortal with immortality.*

"When the perishable has been clothed with the imperishable, and the mortal with immortality, then the saying that is written will come true: **"Death has been swallowed up in victory**." *"Where, O death, is your victory? Where, O death, is your sting?" The sting of death is sin, and the power of sin is the law. But thanks be to God! He gives us the victory through our Lord Jesus Christ"* (1 Cor 15:51-57).

Swallowing Up the Works of Evil:
God's power will swallow up every work of the Adversary. His Word says: "***Do not be afraid** of the people of the land, because **we will swallow them up**. Their protection is gone, but **the Lord is with us. Do not be afraid of them**"* (Num 14:9). ... *"Your hand will lay hold on all your enemies; your right hand will seize your foes. At the time of your appearing you will make them like a fiery furnace. In his wrath **the Lord will swallow them up, and his fire will consume them**"* (Ps 21:8-9).

*"He will destroy the shroud that enfolds all peoples, the sheet that covers all nations; **he will swallow up death forever**. The Sovereign Lord will wipe away the tears from all faces; he will remove the disgrace of his people from all the earth. The Lord has spoken"* (Isa 25:7-8).

Gaining Victory Over Inner-Conflicts:
To experience God's victory over the works of Satan in your life – to experience God's kingdom of light, swallowing up Satan's kingdom of darkness – close your eyes, sit back in your chair and relax. Take a few deep breaths and exhale slowly, relaxing more and more with each breath. ... Now, join me, repeating the following prayer as we seek God's protection and guidance.

Father God, in spirit-to-spirit union with Jesus, my Lord and Savior, I now enter the heavenly Holy of Holies and approach Your Throne of Grace. Seated with Christ (Eph 2:6), and looking down into the physical realm, I command you – every principality and power of the kingdom of darkness – to leave my physical presence – now! – in Jesus' name. In His Name, I command you to be made a part of his footstool until he return to execute judgment upon you.

Now Heavenly Father, I ask You to commission your holy angels – ministering spirits – to put a guard around me [and those with me]; and I ask You, Holy Spirit, to guide me through the following exercise, according to my Father's will, in the name of Yeshua Messiah – Amen.

Exercise:
Now, with your eyes still closed, hold your non-dominant hand – the one whose thumb was underneath in the handedness test -- out in front of you, palm up and open. Now, employing your memory and your imagination, reflect on the list of inner-conflicts that you identified.

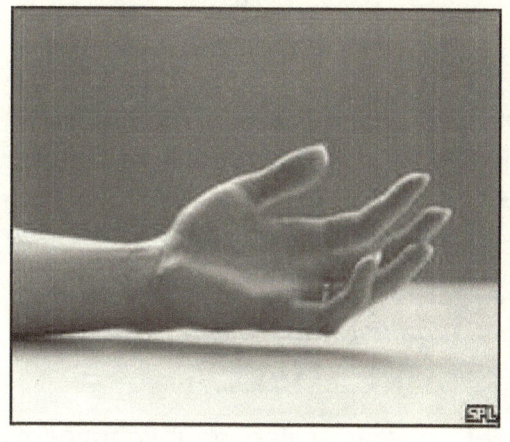

As each memory floats to the surface in your memory, visualize placing that inner-conflict in your open palm; now, allow all your repressed emotions surrounding that conflict; to come up – out of your inner-being; up – out through your arm, and into your open palm. In your imagination, see every person associated with that inner-conflict, and visualize placing them in your open palm, along with the inner-conflict and its associated emotions.

Allow Holy Spirit – Who brings all things to our remembrance – to guides you from this inner-conflict to the next; now, repeat the process: using your imagination, place the inner-conflict; all associated repressed emotions; and all the people associated with this inner-conflict, out into your open palm. Take your time - you have as much time as needed - to get in touch with each inner-conflict that you identified. Visualize each and every one, coming up and out of you – out into your open palm, of your non-dominant hand.

Relax and trust Holy Spirit to search your inner-being and guide you through this process. Trust in what you are shown. God's Word says He will *"tell you great and unsearchable things you do not know ... [to] bring health and healing .. so that you can enjoy abundant peace and security. [He has promised to] cleanse you from all sins you have committed against Him, and forgive you all your sins of rebellion against Him"* (Jer 33:3,6, & 8).

Capturing Your Conflicts:
When all of your inner-conflicts – all the negative emotions associated with them, that you have repressed; and all the people connected with these inner-conflicts, are in the palm of your open hand; close your hand tightly over them, making a fist. As you close your hand, squeeze it tightly, and begin to visualize them as the demons responsible:

"For our struggle is not against human beings, but against the rulers, the authorities and cosmic powers governing this darkness, against the spiritual forces of evil in the heavenly realm" (Eph 6:12).

Keeping your fist closed tightly, raise your dominant hand and hold it up to God, asking Him to fill it with His victorious power, His love, light, truth, blessings, provision, protection, healing, and everything else you may need. Allow God's assurance of victory over the dark forces – and His power – to enter your hand.

Now, begin to visualize your dominant hand as representing the serpent of the Lord – the serpent that Aaron's rod turned into when he threw it down in front of the Adversary – when it consumed all of the enemy's serpents. None of your adversaries – none of your inner-conflicts – can escape God's consuming power.

God's Word says: *"Though they hide themselves on the top of Carmel, there I will hunt them down and seize them. Though they hide from me at the bottom of the sea, there I will command the serpent to bite them. Though they are driven into exile by their enemies, there I will command the sword to slay them"* (Amos 9:3-4).

God – Holy Spirit – has illuminated your inner-being searching out every inner-conflict in your soul; they are captured, and the Lord is now ordering the serpent [His serpent – hidden in the palm of your dominant hand] – to bite the negative serpents, herding them into exile, killing them there, and swallowing them up.

Trusting in God's healing power, put your closed fist – your non-dominant hand – out in front of you and visualize it becoming the serpent of Satan who has been responsible for the creation of all your inner-conflicts. Now, bring your other hand – your dominant hand – out in front of you, and visualize it becoming the serpent Aaron's rod turned into; with its mouth wide open.

Keeping your eyes closed, continue to visualize your non-dominant closed fist –the one containing your inner-conflicts – as the serpent of Satan; and your open dominant hand, as the serpent under the Lord's command. Bring them slowly toward each other, as though they are two mortal enemies stalking each other. Slowly, very slowly, bring them closer toward each other, as you continue to visualize in your mind, a mortal combat about to take place – a battle between Satan [represented by your non-dominant closed fist], and Yeshua Messiah [represented by your open hand].

Envision this combat taking place as Satan, facing off with the Lord. Now, as they slowly approach one another; suddenly bring your dominant hand down over your non-dominant hand, closing it tightly. Squeeze it tight, allowing God's victory to swallow up every inner-conflict that you have had trapped in subconscious and is now in your fist.

Envision them being swallowed up, together with all associated negative emotions and all the people connected with them, who caused you hurt of pain. Continue to hold your dominant hand [representing God's victory] tight over your non-dominant hand, as you repeat after me, the following prayer.

Holy Spirit, in Jesus' Name, and in accord with the will of Father God, register this victory – the victory of Christ over Satan – over every inner-conflict he and his demons have instigated in my life – register this victory down, into the deepest part of my brain; down into the amygdala, where it will continually declare victory over every inner-conflict in my life, that I have been set free; allowing me to fulfill Father God's sovereign plan and purpose for my life. Thank You Father God, Holy Spirit and Yeshua Messiah [my Lord and Savior] for setting me free from my inner-conflicts, and healing my inner-being this very day – Amen, Amen!

Restoring Peace:
As we envisioned this struggle between our inner-conflicts and the healing power of God, giving God the ultimate victory; we were sending neurological signals back and forth across the corpus callosum – the bridge between the left and right hemispheres of our brain. This begins to create harmony between our intellectual [alphanumerical and analytical] and our affective [imaginative, creative and emotional] thought processes. When we endeavor to do this ourselves, the

more we struggle to restore harmony, the faster the neurological signals race back and forth, back and forth.

Over time, this accelerated mode of thinking can create a pattern – a very destructive pattern – one that produces stress and anxiety, while simultaneously diminishing the body's ability to produce specific reward hormones that are designed to provide us a sense of well-being, peace and contentment. These racing thoughts – racing traffic, as it were – can create headaches, confusion, stomachaches, cause difficulty concentrating, and even create manic episodes.

Slowing Racing Thoughts:
If you are experiencing, or have experienced, any of these symptoms, raise your dominant hand – the one whose thumb was on top in our 'hand-dominance' experiment – above your head. Now, lift it up to the Lord; and with your hand lifted high, pray the following prayer with me.

Father God, I come before Your Throne of Grace in the Name of Yeshua Messiah, Your Beloved Son; and in the power of indwelling Holy Spirit. Heavenly Father, You know precisely what I need for my thought processes to become balanced; and I ask You now, in Jesus' Name, and through Holy Spirit, Who indwells my spirit, to anoint my hands, my mouth and tongue, that Your healing virtue will be released – and that Yeshua Messiah, who took all my diseases to the cross – might now undertake supernatural healing in my brain. Thank You Father, Son – Yeshua Messiah – and Holy Spirit – Amen.

Now, place your dominant hand over your head vertically with your little finger up and your thumb facing backwards, similar to that pictured in the adjacent photo.

Now, bring your dominant thumb down and rest it over the center of your head – over your soft spot – which is at the center of your corpus callosum illustrated in detail on the following page. This is a place often referred to as the primary synaptic cleft, since more neuron endings meet here than at any other place in the body.

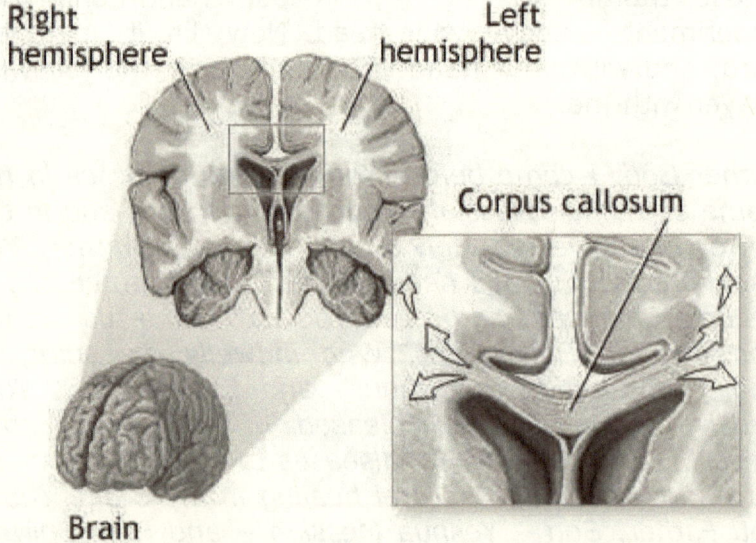

Now, as you begin to visualize your thoughts as traffic crossing over a bridge in a very orderly fashion, repeat after me, the following prayer:

In Jesus' Name; through the power of Indwelling Holy Spirit; and in accord with the will of Father God, Who desires that I experience excellent health; I now command any excessive chatter, all racing thoughts, and all chaotic thoughts, to cease. I command my thought processes to become normalized. I command all erratic thoughts, all unhealthy and all unholy thoughts to cease and leave my brain and my body, which are the property of my Lord and Savior, Yeshua Messiah. I command any demonic spirit that has contributed to confusing, erratic thoughts, to be gone – now – in Jesus' name.

Holy Spirit, I ask you to come now and adjust the width of my corpus callosum – the bridge between my intellectual thoughts and my imaginations and emotions – making it the precise width necessarily to control the speed of my thoughts, to be in accord with Father God's perfect, sovereign plan for my life. Father God, move through Your Spirit, to bring perfect balance in my brain – balance between left and right hemisphere thoughts – enabling me to function according to Your perfect will, I ask these things Father, in the Name of Your Beloved Son, Yeshua Messiah.

Now, begin to visualize your racing thoughts slowing – watching as it were traffic, moving over the bridge between left and right hemispheres of your brain – slowing, more and gradually becoming more orderly and manageable.

[You may feel a slight pressure just above your ears – over your temples – as this divine adjustment takes place. Women have approximately three times the number of connecting neurons in the corpus callosum than men, so the time this process of adjustment takes may vary between genders. The process may take several hours – perhaps even a day or more – so be patient and continue to speak out your positive confession, that, *"This will bring health to my body and nourishment to my bones,"* according to God's Word. (Prov 3:8),]

Restoring Harmony:
God has promised: *"I will bring health and healing; I will heal my people and will let them enjoy abundant peace and security"* (Jer 33:6); and, *"we have the mind of Christ"* (1 Cor 2:1).

To operate in the mind of Christ, we need to invite God to bring harmony between our imaginative and creative; and our analytical thoughts; and to remove everything that would prevent us from thinking as Christ would think. This means inviting God to destroy the works of the devil with His consuming fire – destroying any scars, tumors, parasites, genetic malformations – everything that is not in accord with God's sovereign design for my life.

Now, raise both hands to the Lord, and join me as we ask God to empower our hands for healing and restoration. *Father God, as I lift my hands toward Your heavenly Throne of Grace, I ask – in the Name of Your Beloved Son, Yeshua Messiah – that You empower my hands through indwelling Holy Spirit, and release Your healing power and carry out Your sovereign will – Amen.*

Now, place both of your hands – palms open – over your ears and temples; and repeat after me, as you visualize perfect harmony; *"I command any incongruence, any dissonance or dis-harmony, between my left and right hemispheres to cease, in Jesus' Name;*

*I command the underlying origin of all inner-conflicts, all disharmony to cease; and I ask you Heavenly Father, to restore perfect harmony. I speak perfect peace, harmony, integration and congruence between my left and right hemispherical thought processes, in Jesus' Name.*

Continue to pray with me: *Heavenly Father, I receive your promise that "We [I] have the mind of Christ" (1 Cor 2:16); that my attitudes are governed by being in spirit-to-spirit union with the Messiah Yeshua (Phil 2:5); and that by his anointing, I am to "speak your word with great boldness, stretching out my hand to heal and perform miraculous signs and wonders through the name of your holy servant, Jesus (Acts 4:30)."*

Now, in accordance with God's Word, operating in the mind of Christ, I say to my left and right hemispheres of my brain: *"Be healed! Be brought into perfect balance and harmony."* Now, repeat with me, the following prayer:

Father God, Your "Word is alive and active! It is at work and is sharper than any double-edged sword – cutting right through to where soul meets spirit and joints and marrow; it is quick to judge the inner reflections and attitudes of the heart. Before You, God, nothing created is hidden – all things are naked and open before you" (Heb 4:12-13).

Touch me father with Your light – aim it as a double-edged sword and remove every negative thing in my brain, restoring it to perfect balance and harmony in Jesus' name. By Your sovereign power, and according to Your sovereign will, adjust all of the chemistry and neurotransmitters within my brain and my central nervous system, neutralizing any excessive or toxic chemicals, and providing any missing or deficient chemicals, as You normalize the electrochemical balance within my brain and central nervous system, in Jesus' name – Amen!

Restoring Mental Health:
If you have suffered from any symptoms of manic-depression – have severe mood-swings; any tendency to disassociate, any tendency to create an alternate reality, any impulse-control problems, any obsessive-compulsive thoughts and behaviors, or seizures; it is possible that your hippo-campus and hypothalamus may need to be adjusted to line up with God's perfect design.

If this applies to you, place the palm of your dominant hand lightly on your forehead; and the palm of your non-dominant hand on the back of your head. [This complete, or close, an internal electrochemical feedback circuit within the limbic system of the cerebellum.]

Recognizing that you have asked Father God to anoint your hands for healing, repeat after me the following prayer: *In Jesus Name and according to His anointing and direction, I command you brain – be adjusted, and align with God's sovereign plan for my life! ... Father*

God, I thank you for Your healing, through the blood of Jesus and the indwelling power of Holy Spirit – Amen.

Restoring Hormonal Balance:
Now, place the index finger of your dominant hand on the tip of your nose and slide it slowly up your nose until you feel the spot where the cartilage in your nose meets the bony structure. Holding your index finger gently against that spot, repeat after me, the following prayer:

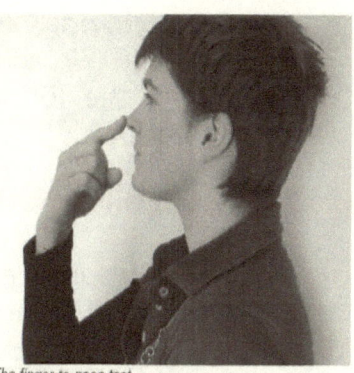
The finger-to-nose test.

In Jesus Name and according to His anointing and direction, I now command every organ in my body to come into perfect functioning order – every chemical secretion and/or electrochemical stimulus of every organ, to come into perfect accord, with Father God's sovereign design for my life. I speak health and healing into my immune and auto-immune systems, in Jesus' Name.

Father God, I continue to thank you for Your healing, through the blood of Jesus and the indwelling power of Holy Spirit; and for perfect health, according to Your expressed will (3 John 2); and I renew my vow – offering to You, my body as a living sacrifice, as my spiritual act of worship – which I pray is, through our spirit-to-Spirit union, holy and pleasing to You Father – Amen.

Student Charge:
"And now [brethren]," according to the words of the apostle Paul, "I commit you to God [I deposit you in His charge, entrusting you to His protection and care]. And I commend you to the Word of His grace [to the commands and counsels and promises of His unmerited favor]. His Word is able to build you up and to give you

[your rightful] inheritance among all God's set-apart ones (those consecrated, purified, and transformed of soul" – [Amen] (Acts 20:32).

~ Questions, Concerns & Key Points ~

1. Explain the origin and manifestation of soul-fragmentation?

2. Explain the remedy for soul-fragmentation?

3. For what purpose – according to the Apostle Paul – was mankind created?

4. What is the primary difference in the battlefield Moses was commissioned to display God's power in, vs. the battlefield where we are to display His power through signs and wonders?

5. How can one use the combined power of God's Word, our imagination, our hands and our voice, to heal inner-wounds and gain victory over inner-conflicts?

6. Explain the concept of using our hands to capture and destroy our inner-conflicts?

7. Describe how one can use their hands to slow their racing thoughts?

8. Explain how one can use their hands to restore congruence and harmony between their left and right hemisphere thought-processes?

9. Explain how one can use their hands, together with prayer, to restore mental health?

10. Explain how one can use their hands, together with prayer, to restore hormonal balance?

Chapter 23 ~ Receive Ye The Holy Spirit

Introduction:
During the last several chapters, we have reviewed what Scripture says about physical healing and about the healing, restoration and transformation of our soul. What we have not spoken of at any depth, is what Scripture says concerning the renewing of our spirit.

We have reviewed the Scriptures which show that mankind is a spirit-being who was originally indwelled by Holy Spirit; and that when man rebelled, Holy Spirit departed. And we know what Scripture says about our once again being indwelled by Holy Spirit after we have accepted Christ as our Lord and Savior. What we have not discussed is what Scripture says about the process, or procedure.

King David, after sinning with Bathsheba, cried out to the Lord, *"Do not cast me from your presence or take your Holy Spirit from me. Restore to me the joy of your salvation and grant me a willing spirit, to sustain me"* (Ps 51:11-12). ... *"Into your hands I commit my spirit; redeem me, O Lord, the God of truth"* (Ps 31:5). Notice that David plead, *"Create in me a pure heart, O God, and renew a steadfast spirit within me"* (Ps 51:10).

"On the evening of that first day of the week, when the disciples were together, with the doors locked for fear of the Jews, Jesus came and stood among them and said, "Peace be with you!" After he said this, he showed them his hands and side. The disciples were overjoyed when they saw the Lord.

*"Again Jesus said, "Peace be with you! As the Father has sent me, I am sending you." And with that **he breathed on them and said, "Receive the Holy Spirit**"* (John 20:19-22 NIV).

The King James' Version translates the highlighted phrase as: *"And when he had said this, **he breathed on them, and saith unto them, Receive ye the Holy Ghost**"*; similarly, the Weust Version has it as: *"And having said this, **He breathed on them and says to them, Receive at once the Holy Spirit**"* (vs 22 Weust). The Greek text is noticeably different.

The Greek:
I'm fairly confident that most of our readers are not fluent in Greek, but for those of you who are, and for those of you who wish to do your own word study on this, the following is from the Greek New Testament.

"Oús¢s oún opsías t¢i h¢méra ekeín¢ t¢i miá sabbátœn kaí tœin thurœin kekleisménœn hópou ¢isan hoi math¢taí diá tón phóbon tœin Ioudaíœn, ¢ilthen ho I¢soús kaí ést¢ eis tó méson kaí légei autoís: eir¢in¢ humín. kaí toúto eipœin édeixen tás cheíras kaí t¢in pleurán autoís. echár¢san oún hoi math¢taí idóntes tón kúrion. eípen oún autoís [ho I¢soús] pálin: eir¢in¢ humín: kathœis apéstalkén me ho pat¢ir, kagœi pémpœ humás. kaí toúto eipœin enephús¢sen kaí légei autoís: lábete pneúma hágion: án tinœn aph¢ite tás hamartías aphéœntai autoís, án tinœn krat¢ite kekrát¢ntai."

Translating this, it would read: *"And He breathed ('emphusao') [a derivative of ('emphutos', meaning to implant), and saith [put-forth, showing] unto them, "Receive [catch, accept, take hold of] Most Holy Spirit."*

There are a few of the translations, or versions, that have picked up on this noticeable and important difference. The Darby Version states it as: *"[Jesus] said therefore again to them, Peace [be] to you: as the*

Father sent me forth, I also send you. And having said this, **he breathed into [them], and says to them, Receive [the] Holy Spirit.**" Another version that follows the Greek text, is the Message.

The Message translates the phrase as: *"Then* **he took a deep breath and breathed into them. "Receive the Holy Spirit,***" he said."* To resolve this seemingly minor, but nonetheless important discrepancy, of whether Jesus breathed on his disciples or into them, come with me to Pentecost.

The Upper Room & Pentecost:
Few people ever associate the incident when Jesus breathed into them, saying: "Receive Most Holy Spirit" and the Day of Pentecost. However, they are intimately connected. Jesus had told his disciples to go to Jerusalem and wait for that which He had promised. Then, twice before Pentecost, He appeared in their midst. It was on one of these occasions that he breathed into them, telling them to receive Most Holy Spirit. Then – shortly thereafter – Most Holy Spirit came into their midst, falling upon them, and baptizing them all with the Spirit and Fire, entering and indwelling their spirits.

"When the day of Pentecost came, they were all together in one place. Suddenly a sound like the blowing of a violent wind came from heaven and filled the whole house where they were sitting. They saw what seemed to be tongues of fire that separated and came to rest on each of them. **All of them were filled with the Holy Spirit** *and began to speak in other tongues as the Spirit enabled them"* (Acts 2:1-4).

"And when the day of Pentecost was now accomplishing, they were all together in one place. And there came suddenly a sound out of heaven as of a violent impetuous blowing, and filled all the house where they were sitting. And there appeared to them parted tongues, as of fire, and it sat upon each one of them. And **they were all filled with [the] Holy Spirit***, and began to speak with other tongues as the Spirit gave to them to speak forth"* (Acts 2:1-4 Darby).

This was the fulfillment of the words of John the Baptist, who said: *"I baptize you with water for repentance. But after me will come one who is more powerful than I, whose sandals I am not fit to carry. He will baptize you with the Holy Spirit and with fire"* (Matt 3:11-12). ... *"John answered them all, "I baptize you with water.

But one more powerful than I will come, the thongs of whose sandals I am not worthy to untie. He will baptize you with the Holy Spirit and with fire" (Luke 3:16-17).

In this, we see once again, the importance of symbolism and imagination. In the translation, 'he breathed *on* them,' the symbolism is lost. But, in the translation, 'he breathed *into* them, saying: "Receive Most Holy Spirit," we see the symbolism of our being indwelled by Holy Spirit. Jesus had promised them that when the Comforter came, the Spirit – Whom had been **with** them, would now be **within** them (Jn 14:17-19).

Here Biblical symbolism is of the greatest significance: we are not merely to be influenced by, but to be indwelled by, Most Holy Spirit. It is this, and this alone enables us to be *"transformed from glory to glory; so that we may share His sufferings and be continually transformed in spirit into His likeness"* (Php 3:10). Only through the indwelling of Holy Spirit is this possible.

Spiritual Manifestations:
We are accustomed in today's church to hearing a great deal about spiritual gifts. It is fairly common for churches to encourage their staff and members to take one of the many Spiritual Gifting Assessments; in order to determine the gift or gifts one is most likely to operate in. This seems to be consistent with Scripture on the subject which says:

"Now there are different kinds of gifts, but the same Spirit gives them. Also there are different ways of serving, but it is the same Lord being served. And there are different modes of working, but it is the same God working them all in everyone" (1 Cor 12:4-7 CJB).

Most teachings approach the subject of Spiritual Gifts as though they are something that are bestowed upon one – something external – perhaps associated with the ordination of the laying on of hands when being commissioned or ordained. This, however, is *not* what Scripture says. Let's read what the apostle Paul said carefully, and you will grasp the significance of the symbolism Christ used when he said: "Receive the Holy Spirit."

SPIRITUAL GIFTS

Paul wrote: "Moreover, **to each person is given the particular manifestation of the Spirit** that will be for the common good. To one, through the Spirit, is given a word of wisdom; to another, a word of knowledge, in accordance with the same Spirit; to another, faith, by the same Spirit; and to another, gifts of healing, by the one Spirit; to another, the working of miracles; to another, prophecy; to another, the ability to judge between spirits; to another, the ability to speak in different kinds of tongues; and to yet another, the ability to interpret tongues.

"One and the same Spirit is at work in all these things, distributing to each person as he chooses. For just as the body is one but has many parts; and all the parts of the body, though many, constitute one body; so it is with the Messiah. For **it was by one Spirit that we were all immersed into one body**, whether Jews or

Gentiles, slaves or free; and **we were all given the one Spirit to drink**" (1 Cor 12:7-13 CJB).

Note the highlighted phrases: 1) **'to each person is given the particular manifestation of the Spirit'**; 2) **'by one Spirit that we were all immersed into one body'**; and 3) **'we were all given the one Spirit to drink'**.

The spiritual gifts are not something bestowed upon one; but are manifestations of something [more precisely someone] who is internal – the indwelling Holy Spirit. We – the members of Christ's Body [the church] were immersed into Holy Spirit, becoming part-and-parcel, one in spirit-to-Spirit union with Christ, Father God and Holy Spirit. And, we were all given the Spirit to drink – another symbolism of it becoming something that is internal, not external. Holy Spirit is internal – we are immersed and indwelled – not bestowed upon.

Spiritual gifts are therefore – as Paul stated – manifestations of the indwelling Holy Spirit. They are not something that we can develop, as some have taught. Quite the contrary – they are developed within us by Holy Spirit, and become manifest, or evident, as we yield our lives to God – becoming a living sacrifice; after which Holy Spirit will transform us from glory to glory; until we with unveiled faces reflect the Lord's glory (Rom 12:1-2; 2 Cor 3:18).

There are, of course, certain gifts that are bestowed – as opposed to those that are manifest from within. These bestowed gifts are the gifts Christ gave the church, which we read of in Paul's letter to the Ephesians.

"Each one of us, however, has been given grace to be measured by the Messiah's bounty. This is why it says, "After he went up into the heights, he led captivity captive and he gave gifts to mankind."

"Now this phrase, "he went up," what can it mean if not that he first went down into the lower parts, that is, the earth? The one who went down is himself the one who also went up, far above all of heaven, in order to fill all things.

"Furthermore, he gave some people as emissaries, some as prophets, some as proclaimers of the Good News, and some as shepherds and teachers. Their task is to equip God's people for the work of service that builds the body of the Messiah, until we all arrive at the unity implied by trusting and knowing the Son of God, at full manhood, at the standard of maturity set by the Messiah's perfection" (Eph 4:7-13 CJB).

Ordination for Ministry:
These gifts are more external – bestowed by Holy Spirit, but usually made evident through the laying on of hands and prayer when one entering the ministry is ordained or commissioned. This act of ordination or commissioning is – according to Paul – to be reserved for those who already evidence the manifestation of those spiritual gifts that come from our being indwelled by Holy Spirit, and yielding our life to the Lord.

Recognizing the importance of this, Paul gave specific directions concerning the life-style standards of those who serve in ministry. And, in his letter to Timothy, he speaks specifically concerning the ordinance of the laying on of hands.

*"Before God, the Messiah Yeshua and the chosen angels, I solemnly charge you to observe these instructions, not prejudging and **not doing anything out of favoritism**. Do not be hasty in granting s'mikhah [Hebrew for Ordination] to anyone, and do not share in other people's sins – keep yourself pure"* (1 Tim 5:22 CJB).

You will note that I have highlighted, in the preceding Scripture, the phrase *"**not doing anything out of favoritism.**"* There was a problem within the first century church that still prevails today – those seeking ordination for recognition or to make a profit from ministry. Scripture clearly condemns this practice.

Most notable was the incident when Simon blatantly approached the apostles, seeking to buy the spiritual abilities that he witnessed them exercising.

"When Simon saw that the Spirit was given at the laying on of the apostles' hands, he offered them money and said, "Give me also this ability so that everyone on whom I lay my hands may receive the Holy Spirit." Peter answered: "May your money perish with you, because you thought you could buy the gift of God with money! You have no part or share in this ministry, because your heart is not right before God. Repent of this wickedness and pray to the Lord. Perhaps he will forgive you for having such a thought in your heart. For I see that you are full of bitterness and captive to sin" (Acts 8:18-23).

The apostle Paul, in his letter to Timothy, dealt specifically with this concern. **"If anyone teaches**

false doctrines and does not agree to the sound instruction of our Lord Jesus Christ *and to godly teaching, he is conceited and understands nothing. He has an unhealthy interest in controversies and quarrels about words that result in envy, strife, malicious talk, evil suspicions and constant friction between men of corrupt mind, who have been* **robbed of the truth and who think that godliness is a means to financial gain***.*

"But godliness with contentment is great gain. For we brought nothing into the world, and we can take nothing out of it. But if we have food and clothing, we will be content with that. **People who want to get rich fall into temptation and a trap and into many foolish and harmful desires that plunge men into ruin and destruction. For the love of money is a root of all kinds of evil.** *Some people, eager for money, have wandered from the faith and pierced themselves with many griefs. But you, man of God, flee from all this, and pursue righteousness, godliness, faith, love, endurance and gentleness"* (1 Tim 6:3-11).

Again and again, in his letters to the various churches, Paul warned of those who desired to be teachers, elders, deacons or bishops for the purpose of dishonest gain.

Spiritual gifts can be neither bought nor sold – whether one is thinking of those manifest gifts most often referred to as "the Gifts of the Spirit," or those bestowed Spiritual Gifts to the Church," referenced as specific ministries within the church; they are all distributed by Holy Spirit, or at the direction of Holy Spirit, as we the case with the ordination of Paul and Barnabus.

"In the church at Antioch there were prophets and teachers: Barnabas, Simeon called Niger, Lucius of Cyrene, Manaen (who had been brought up with Herod the tetrarch) and Saul.

Paul & Barnabas on Missionary Trip:

While they were worshiping the Lord and fasting, the Holy Spirit said, "Set apart for me Barnabas and Saul for the work to which I have called them." So after they had fasted and prayed, they placed their hands on them and sent them off" (Acts 13:1-3).

Receive Ye Most Holy Spirit:
If you have misunderstood the baptism and infilling of Holy Spirit; or failed to comprehend that the gifts of the Spirit are manifestations of the transforming work of Holy Spirit indwelling your spirit, join me in embracing the spiritual symbolism the Bible portrays. Lift your hands toward God's heavenly Throne of Grace, and inhaling deeply, invite Holy Spirit to indwell your spirit, as you join me in the following prayer:

Father God, I come before You this moment petitioning you as David did long ago. "Into Your hands I commit my spirit; redeem me, O Lord, the God of truth (Ps 31:5); Create in me a pure heart, O God; renew a steadfast spirit within me. Do not cast me from Your presence or take Holy Spirit from me (Ps 51:10-11); Teach me to do your will, because you are my God. Let your Holy Spirit guide me ... For your name's sake, Adonai, preserve my life" (Ps 143:10-11).

Father God, through the sacrifice of Your Beloved Son, Yeshua Messiah, I approach Your Throne of Grace; I commit my body to You, a living sacrifice and I invite You, Holy Spirit, to indwell my spirit, to write on my heart, the Laws of God; to transform my soul; and to manifest Yourself through me, according to Your will; Fill me Holy Spirit; use me as You see fit; And, Father God, pour out You love into my heart by Holy Spirit, Whom You have given; that I might go forth fulfilling Christ's command to love others as You, Your Beloved Son, Jesus, and Holy Spirit, have loved me; in Jesus Name, Amen.

~ Questions, Concerns & Key Points ~

1. The profound significance of one's hands is noted in Jesus' last prayer: *"Father, **into Your hands** I commit my spirit."*
2. What is the difference and significance in whether Jesus breathed *on* his apostles, or *into* them, when he imparted Holy Spirit unto them?
3. Which of the following statements is most correct?
   - Spiritual gifts are bestowed upon one
   - Spiritual gifts can be developed through practice
   - Spiritual gifts are the manifestation of indwelling Holy Spirit
   - Some spiritual gifts are bestowed upon one, while others are manifest from the Spirit within
4. Are the gifts Christ gave the church [Apostles, Prophets, Evangelists and Teaching-shepherds] gifts that are bestowed upon one, or manifest from within?
5. Ordination should not be bestowed upon one who shows favoritism, teaches heresy, has an unhealthy interest in controversies, semantics, theological debates, or ministry for financial gain.

Chapter 24 ~ Releasing Emotional Baggage

Introduction:

Is your burden to heavy to bear? Jesus said, *"If you are tired from carrying heavy burdens, come to me and I will give you rest. Take the yoke I give you. Put it on your shoulders and learn from me. I am gentle and humble, and you will find rest. My yoke is easy to bear, and My burden is light"* (Matt 11:28-30 CEV).

The pathway of life is difficult enough without being burdened down, or wearing a yoke that is not ours. Many may not even grasp the full significance of Christ's promise – since we have never used a yoke. The kind of yoke this Scripture is referring to is a wooden beam that fits between a pair of oxen, allowing them to pull a load. Oxen nearly always work in pairs. A pair of oxen is also called a *yoke of oxen*, and yoke is also used as a verb: "to *yoke* a pair of oxen."

If my burden is heavy and my yoke tight or ill-fitting, I need to examine two things: 1) Who I am yoked to; and 2) What I am carrying. Jesus calls the yoke His; inferring that I should be yoked to him; and since His burden – the one He is giving me – is light; then, if my burdens are weighting me down, they are not from Him. Is this is the case, we need to let it go.

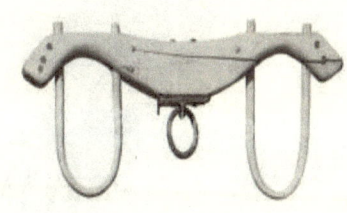

The Prophet Isaiah commented long ago on our being yoked with Christ, as compared to being yoked to another, however, due to inaccuracies in translation, the full meaning of his message has been lost in time. We refer to the following Scripture which most are familiar with: *"Those who hope in the Lord will renew their strength. They will soar on wings like eagles; they will run and not grow weary, they will walk and not be faint"* (Isa 40:31 NIV).

In reality, the original Hebrew text says something quite different. It reads: *"Those whose hearts are entwined with Adonai's will renew their strength, shall experience a mighty increase in strength, substance and wealth; they will ascend spiritually, soaring aloft as with eagles' wings; they will rush like eagles, neither becoming exhausted nor weary on their journey."*

Entwined Spiritually

Take a moment or two to meditate on this Scripture. If our heart is entwined with Christ's – yoked to Him in spirit-to-spirit union – we will experience a mighty increase in strength, substance and wealth in the physical realm [here on earth]; and we will ascend spiritually, soaring aloft as on eagle's wings [enabling us to see things from God's perspective, rather than from our weary, physical path.] Thus energized, we will be able to rush like an eagle, becoming neither exhausted, discouraged, nor weary, in our journey through life.

Effortless Soaring:
Eagles, when soaring aloft, expend almost no energy; they are carried aloft on uplifting air currents called thermals. Soaring silently, effortlessly, they can, not only see their prey from astounding distances, they can, while keeping their eye fixed on them, swoop down – descending upon them at speeds in excess of 200 miles per hour – to capture and kill them!

Similar to soaring eagles, we are spiritually enabled to ascend effortlessly – being in spirit-to-Spirit union, entwined with Christ, and lifted by the power of Holy Spirit into the heavens – and on into the Holy of Holies, to stand before the Throne of Grace.

Paul assures us that *"God raised us up with Christ and seated us with him in the heavenly realms in Christ Jesus"* (Eph 2:6). From this perspective, we can look down on all our enemies – the principalities, rulers, authorities and cosmic forces of evil in the heavenly realms (Eph 6:12).

Seated with Christ in Father God's throne room, we can – like the eagle – look down and easily identify the enemies of our soul; and, empowered by Father God, Christ Jesus and Holy Spirit, who indwell us, we can swoop down, as it were, to capture them, cast them out of our life, and make them part of the footstool of Jesus Christ (Lk 20:43).

Back in the physical realm, airplanes – much like eagles – depend on the principle of soaring, or being carried aloft by thermal air currents. Heavier than air, they defy gravity through the application of a higher law – the law of aerodynamics. Aerodynamics is our one "exception" for the law of gravity. The law of aerodynamics says (among other, far more complicated things) that the law of gravity can be *counteracted* if the right variables are applied.

The Law of Aerodynamics:
Simplistically, if you combine the right shape, with the right speed, and the right weight; the law of aerodynamics will counteract the law of gravity and you will fly [or soar] rather than falling to the ground. What a wonder! Applying these variables, flight is now an achievable possibility within the human experience. There is, however, a downside.

This law of aerodynamics ceases to counteract the law of gravity when any *one of the* variables ceases to fall within certain prescribed limits. If this happens, the plane will come tumbling out of the sky to an ugly end.

To help prevent such disasters, all pilots and airlines have adopted flying standards – rules, if you please – concerning just how much fuel the plane can carry and how much baggage one can bring aboard.

Traveling Light:
Hoping they will not need to penalize anyone, airlines usually offer incentives – such as early boarding – for passengers who travel light. This sounds a lot like the instructions Jesus gave His disciples before sending them out to exercise His authority over evil spirits.

"He called together his twelve apostles and sent them out two by two with power over evil spirits. He told them, "You may take along a walking stick. But don't carry food or a traveling bag or any money. It's all right to wear sandals, but don't take along a change of clothes" (Mark 6:7-10 CEV). In other words, to accomplish the work He was appointing them so, they needed to travel light.

Excess Baggage & Unnecessary Weight:
Likewise, if we are to effectively carry out the assignment He has given us, we need to shed ourselves of all unnecessary weight – all burdensome baggage. Imagine that you are about to board a plane, weighted down with luggage – things you may believe you really need to hang onto – when you suddenly hear a voice – a voice you recognize; that still, small voice inside.

It is saying: *"Humble yourselves, then, under God's mighty hand, so that he will lift you up in his own good time. Leave all your burdens with him, because he cares for you"* (1 Peter 5:6-7 TEV).

You aren't even thinking about your burdens; your mind is on your destination – heaven – but suddenly you become aware that your boarding pass has been stamped, "Excess Baggage." What's more important to you now – the baggage you have so carefully packed away – or your ultimate destination?

To help you make up your mind, you hear the voice of the apostle Paul, assuring you: *"The Holy Spirit, Who will give you life in union with Christ Jesus has set you free from the law of sin and death"* (Rom 8:2).

Spiritual Gravity – The Law of Sin and Death:
In other words, the law of sin and death [the law of gravity] is still in effect; but so is another law. In spirit-to-Spirit union with Christ, you are set free [liberated from] that spiritual law of gravity through the indwelling Holy Spirit [the spiritual law of aerodynamics.]

The Parable of the Vine and Branches:
Employing another parable – the form of teaching Christ most relied on – recall him saying: *"I am the vine and you are the branches. Those who stay united within me, and I within them, are the ones who bear much fruit; because apart from me you can't do a thing. Unless a person remains united within me, he is thrown away like a severed branch and dries up. Such branches are gathered and thrown into the fire, where they are burned up.*

"If you remain united within me, and my words within you, then ask whatever you want, and it will happen for you. This is how my Father is glorified – in your bearing much fruit; this is how you will prove to be my disciples" (John 15:5-8 CJB).

Listen to what Jesus is saying: If we continue to abide in Him, we will bear much fruit. Experiencing Christ's abiding presence is essential. Fruit is not produced immediately – the branch must abide [or remain] in the vine. Similarly, we must continue in spirit-to-Spirit union with Christ. The author of Hebrews said, *"The Word of God is living and operative – sharper than any two-edged sword"* (Heb 4:12).

As branches off the true vine, we must still be pruned and nurtured to mature. Then, after enduring the test of time, we will produce [bear] much fruit. In this way – and only in this way – can we, through God's testing and pruning, prove to the world, that we are His disciples.

God's Tests:
Remember the girl climbing the trail, pictured on the first page of this lesson? She, the eagle, and the airplane we have alluded to, all require effort to ascend. The following Scriptures illustrate this: *"Delight yourself in Adonai, and he will give you your heart's desire. Commit your way to Adonai; trust in him, and he will act. He will make your vindication shine forth like light, the justice of your cause like the noonday sun. Be still before Adonai; wait patiently till he comes"* (Ps 37:4-7 CJB).

"All a man's ways are pure in his own view, but Adonai weighs the spirit. If you entrust all you do to Adonai, your plans will achieve success" (Prov 16:2-3 CJB). ... *"Let all who run to you for protection always sing joyful songs. Provide shelter for those who truly love you and let them rejoice. Our Lord, you bless those who live right, and you shield them with your kindness"* (Ps 5:11-12 CEV).

The Valley of Baca:
The Psalmist wrote: *"Blessed are those whose strength is in you, who have set their hearts on pilgrimage. As they pass through the Valley of Baca [the desert], they [build dams to catch the heavy rains] making it a place of springs"* (Ps 84:5-6).

Notice, that the sojourners were the ones who built dams – doing the possible – while depending on God for what seemed to them impossible – heavy rains in the desert. When doing our part – the possible – one can confidently say to the Lord: *"Test me, O Lord, and try* me, examine my heart and my mind; for your love is ever before me, and I walk continually in your truth"* (Ps 26:2-3).

God never tests our heart to condemn or belittle us. In fact, He assures us that *"There is no condemnation [no adjudging of guilt or wrong] for those who are within Christ Jesus"* (Rom 8:1). He tests our heart because *"The heart is more deceitful than anything else and mortally sick. Who can fathom it?"* (Jer 17:9 CJB).

Understanding this, the Psalmist cried to the Lord: *"Examine me, O my God, and know my heart; test me, and know my thoughts. See if there is in me any hurtful way, and lead me along the eternal way [the Way everlasting]"* Ps 139:23-24 CJB).

Emotional Baggage:
Deep within our heart – beyond our ability to discern them – there may be things creating a mortal illness within our soul, weighing us down like excess baggage – baggage sufficient to keep us from boarding a plane, or ascending spiritually to heavenly realms.

Sources of Soul-wounding:

Soul-wounding sufficient to create such excess baggage and mortal illness of the soul stems from one of the following:

1. Unforgiven sins,

2. Unresolved – past – wounding experiences, and associated emotions

3. Misbeliefs and misguided life-commandments,

4. Unrealized expectations and unmet needs,

5. Unrequited anguish and grief,

6. Ungodly and cherished thoughts, emotions, attitudes, beliefs, values, opinions and behavior,

7. A failure to embrace God's Word, receive Salvation through Christ, and/or Invite Holy Spirit to indwell our spirit.

Scientific research suggests that eighty percent (80%) of all our activities, as adults, are motivated by repressed anger, fear, guilt, shame, sensual drives, unmet needs and damaged emotions, that are tucked away – hidden deep within our subconscious. In fact, one study conducted by the American Medical Association in the early 90's suggested that as high as 90% of all hospital beds were filled due to internalized anger and unforgiveness!

Paul counsels us: *"Do not let yourselves be conformed to the standards of the present age and culture. Instead, keep letting yourselves be transformed by the continual renewing of your minds; so that you will know what God wants and will agree that what he wants is good, satisfying and able to achieve"* (Rom 12:2 CJB).

Any of us who have begun this process, knows that it is an ever-present, ongoing struggle – that can, at times, be very discouraging. However, it need not be this difficult – there is a better way!

Divine Editing of Our Soul:
King David, who sought God's editing of his soul, said: *"Sacrifice and offering you did not desire, but my ears you have pierced; burnt offerings and sin offerings you did not require. ... "Here I am, I have come – it is written about me in Your scroll [of my life"* (Ps 40:6-7).

Please pray the following Scripture with me: *"Lord God,"* according to Your Word in (Collosians 3:3-4), *"I have died in Christ, and my life is now hidden with Christ in You. [I know] When Christ, who is my life, appears, then I also will appear with Him in glory."* [Amen]

Ancient Israel's sins were displayed in the midst of the heavens on a flying scroll – for all to see (Zech 5:1); and John the Revelator suggests that this will be the case for the lost, as they surround the Holy City, New Jerusalem (Rev 18-20). But, *"You died, and your life is how hidden with Christ in God. [And] when Christ, who is your life, appears, then you also will appear with him in glory"* (Col 3:3).

Now, with your eyes closed, pray with me: *"I thank You that my sins are hidden with Christ in You, Father God, and in Jesus' Name, I come before Your Throne of Grace today, requesting that as I invite Holy Spirit to inspect my soul – as though it were a scroll – or an audio-video tape – that; and ask that You allow Holy Spirit to edit my lifeline scroll; removing the memory, or the sting* associated with the memory, of: any unforgiven sins; all unresolved – past – wounding experiences, and associated emotions; all misbeliefs and misguided life-commandments; all unrealized expectations and unmet needs; any unrequited anguish and grief; all ungodly and cherished thoughts, emotions, attitudes, beliefs, values, opinions and behaviors; every past failure to embrace Your Word, receive Salvation through Christ, and/or Invite Holy Spirit to indwell my spirit – in Christ Jesus' Name – Amen.

Now, with your eyes still closed, envision yourself standing alongside Christ Jesus in the Heavenly Holy of Holies. In your imagination, ask Christ Jesus and Father God, to allow you to review, with them, the detailed audiovisual record of your life-experience.

Envision the time-line of your life being unrolled before you – your past, present and future. Since God is not limited by time or space; imagine that you can not only see and hear what is recorded thereon, you can also smell, taste, and feel, everything from the past – you can once again experience all the sensory information in an instant of time.

As your lifeline audio-visual record is rolled out, you need not look at it, nor examine any of those things you identified. Father God, Christ Jesus and Holy Spirit know exactly what those things are, and they will be doing the review and the editing. All they need is your permission and presence; your presence is merely so you can experience the reality of the divine editing process.

With your permission, The Majestic, Supreme Ones [Father, Son and Holy Spirit], will fast-rewind your lifeline tape, editing out all of those things you have identified; then, They will fast-forward the time-line of your life, editing new information back in – replacing all those things removed – with God's fruit of the Spirit:

love, joy, peace, patience, goodness, faithfulness, gentleness and self-control.

Entering the Casual Realm:
This may seem difficult for some of you to even imagine, but remember – only for humans is time is unidirectional -- [moving constantly forward.] God dwells outside of time – in the casual realm – beyond the dimensions of time and space; therefore, He can move in any direction He so chooses. And, since we are in Christ Jesus – and through Him, in Father God and Holy Spirit; and, through this spirit-to-Spirit union, They are in us; we can also – through faith and prayer – enter into this casual realm.

Jesus said: *"I tell you the truth, anyone who has faith in me will do what I have been doing. He will do even greater things than these, because I am going to the Father. And I will do whatever you ask in my name, so that the Son may bring glory to the Father. You may ask me for anything in my name, and I will do it"* (John 14:12-14).

When Jesus told His disciples this, he was himself, limited to the same bounds that we are subject to – the four dimensions of the physical realm – width, height, depth, and time. But now, Christ Jesus is with the Father, in the eternal, casual realm; and within Jesus, we also can enter this realm. Entering this realm – in our imagination – we can begin to understand what Adonai meant when he said to Moses, *"I Am Who I Am; What I Am; [and] I Will Be What I Will Be"* (Ex 3:14).

Now, as Holy Spirit guides you, in your imagination, see yourself standing in the heavenly Holy of Holies (Eph 2:5-6), hidden in Christ, through spirit-to-Spirit union (Gal 3:27); see yourself *"approach the throne of grace with confidence, so that [you] may receive mercy and find grace to help in [your] time of need"* (Heb 4:16).

Seated in heavenly places – where time does not exist – join with Christ as he declares: *"I saw Satan fall like lightning from heaven."* [I now hear Christ assuring me] *"I have given you authority to trample on snakes [the serpent Satan] and scorpions [demons]; indeed to overcome all the enemy's forces [cosmic and human]; nothing will harm you"* (Luke 10:18-20).

Standing in the casual realm, take hold of the authority the Lord Jesus has given you, and declare with me: *Satan, every Principality, Ruling Power, Cosmic Force, and humans under their influence ~ I command you to leave the place where my physical being is located – Now! in the Name of Yeshua Messiah – I command you to become a part of the footstool of Christ* (Lk 20:43).

The Divine Editing Process: Now, with your lifespan rolled out in the heavens [either North and South or East and West – it makes no difference], and looking down from the Throne Room; invite Holy Spirit to begin the editing – guiding you back, back, backwards in time. As your time-line is fast rewound, see your whole life in a single glance; watch as the ministering angels who God has commissioned, begin to mark those places that Holy Spirit points out to them.

They may be using different colored markers, one for each of the seven areas described above; or they may be marking them all with the same color – it really doesn't matter.

Just relax, as you envision your ministering angels unroll your time-line – going back, back, back, further and further in time – marking each and every thing that either needs to have  the memory thereof removed, or the sting and pain of the memory blotted out -- [Holy Spirit knows which is best, and will instruct the angels assigned you.]

Imagine watching the years of your life fly by – racing past in reverse – going back, back, back – all the way back to the moment of your conception, when the Spirit of God entered into your mother's womb.

 When your ministering angels have guided you all the way back to the womb – to the moment of conception – visualize the time-line of your soul slowing down and coming to rest, right at that moment when you were conceived.

Since you are now in the casual realm – outside the normal physical limitations – Invite Holy Spirit to join you as you watch the ministering angels cut-off, or disconnect all the neurological links to all the emotional trauma you experienced, resulting from your in utero and/or birthing experience wounds. Notice the angels marking all those things that may have inhibited your emotional development, and are perhaps even affecting you now – even in your adult years.

Experiencing the Editing:
As Holy Spirit and your ministering angels disconnect these neurological links, you may very briefly experience a sense of being unwanted, rejected or abandoned; you may experience your mother's fear, anger or confusion. There may even have been thoughts of abortion that you need healing from. Once your have briefly experienced whatever Holy Spirit would have you experience to give you understanding – and your emotions have settled down again – join me as we pray.

Father God, thank You for allowing me to share this experience with You. Thank You for cooperating with Holy Spirit, to mark all those places in my soul that need edited. I pray now, Father God, for my unborn inner-child. Through the Blood of Jesus, Your Beloved Son, cancel, nullify, and disconnect all the neurological links between my mother's wounded soul and mine. Heal my inner-child from all of this trauma, I pray.

I also command any demon – any spirit of the kingdom of darkness – who attached to my soul while in my mother's womb, to disconnect, and depart, becoming part of the footstool of Jesus Christ – Now! – Amen, Amen.

Father, I also ask that you cancel all generational curses that have entered my family lifeline, whether on my mother's side or my fathers; I ask, in Jesus' Name, and through His blood, that these be broken and edited out of my DNA.

I command all familial spirits who have tracked my family lineage, to break every assignment against me, and/or against my children; and to leave – my life and theirs – now!, becoming part of the footstool of Christ Jesus.

Father God, I forgive all who have knowingly or unknowingly sinned against me in any way – including sins against my ancestry: all who wounded me physically or emotionally; injured me, disregarded my personal boundaries, imposed ungodly limits on me, demeaned my identity and/or creativity, abused me in any manner, as well as those who have told lies, or gossiped about me.

I forgive them all Father. Now, in Jesus' Name and in the power of Indwelling Holy Spirit, I remit their sins and release them, understanding that – according to (John 20:23) – they will be forgiven by You. Father, Lord Jesus, Holy Spirit – I ask that you move sovereignly to sever all ties between their spirits and mine.

Divine Inspection & Restoration:
Recognizing that all we have done – all that is hidden within our soul – is written in God's scroll, join me as we share David's prayer: *"I desire to do your will, O my God; your law is within my heart"* (vs. 8). ... *"Wash me thoroughly [and repeatedly] from my iniquity and guilt and cleanse me and make me wholly pure from my sin!* (Ps 51:2).

"Surely I was sinful at birth, sinful from the time my mother conceived me. Surely you desire truth in the inner parts; you teach me wisdom in the inmost place. Cleanse me with hyssop, and I will be clean; wash me, and I will be whiter than snow. Let me hear joy and gladness; let the bones you have crushed rejoice. Hide your face from my sins and blot out all my iniquity. Create in me a pure heart, O God, and renew a steadfast spirit within me" (Ps 51:1 & 5-10).

Forgive me of all my sins – including my ungodly thoughts, cherished ungodly emotions, ungodly reactions and ungodly life-commandments. Thank You Father God, Lord Jesus, Holy Spirit – I receive Your forgiveness – and in humility, I forgive myself. As you edit my soul, erase my sin record from your book of remembrance, according to Your Word that:

"I, even I, am he who blots out your transgressions, for my own sake, and remembers your sins no more" (Isa 43:25);l "He forgave us all our sins, having canceled the written code, with its regulations, that was against us [me] and that stood opposed to us [me]; he took it away, nailing it to the cross" (Col 2:13-15).

Destroying Satan's Record:
Father, I also ask that you eradicate from Satan's Record, all my sins and besetting weaknesses; and that from this moment henceforward, that neither he nor his demons have any foothold in my soul, and no grounds for accusing me.

Father, repair the walls of my soul. I claim Your promise: "I will make your battlements of rubies, your gates of sparkling jewels, and all your walls of precious stones" (Isa 54:12).

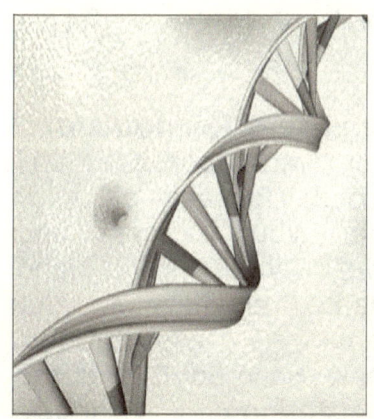

Now, as we pray together the following prayer, imagine once again, the audio-video tape, containing the time-line of your soul; and see Holy Spirit and the assigned ministering angels, remove all the markers they placed on the time-line of your soul – healing your DNA -- as your time-line is fast-rewound.

See them collect these markers and place them on the cross of Christ – who died to remove every sin, every disease, all pain, suffering, poverty and shame.

"Surely He has borne our griefs – our (sicknesses, weaknesses, and distresses) and carried our sorrows and pains [of punishment], yet we [ignorantly] considered Him stricken, smitten, and afflicted by God [as if with leprosy]. But He was wounded for our transgressions, He was bruised for our guilt and iniquities; the chastisement [needful to obtain] peace and well-being for us was laid upon Him, and with the stripes [that wounded] Him we are healed and made whole.

"All we like sheep have gone astray, we have turned every one to his own way; and the Lord has made to light upon Him the guilt and iniquity of us all. He was oppressed, [yet when] He was afflicted, He was submissive and opened not His mouth; like a lamb that is led to the slaughter, and as a sheep before her shearers is dumb, so He opened not His mouth" (Isa 53:4-7 AMP).

Release & Relinquish:
Now, with your eyes still closed; Release all your pain, your sadness and grief, your guilt and shame, relinquish all your unrealized expectations. Allow Holy Spirit and the ministering angels assigned you to take them – removing their effect from your soul.

"The Spirit of the Sovereign Lord is on me ... the Lord has anointed me to preach good news to the poor. He has sent me to bind up the brokenhearted, to proclaim freedom for captives and release from darkness for prisoners, to proclaim the year of the Lord's favor ... to comfort all who mourn, and provide for those who grieve ... to bestow on them a crown of beauty instead of ashes, the oil of gladness instead of mourning, and a garment of praise instead of a spirit of despair" (Isa 61:1-3).

Returning once again to the heavenly Holy of Holies, seated by Jesus, your Lord and Savior, see your physical being far below – in the present moment of time. See yourself now taking your place on the audio-visual record of your life.

Making All Things New:

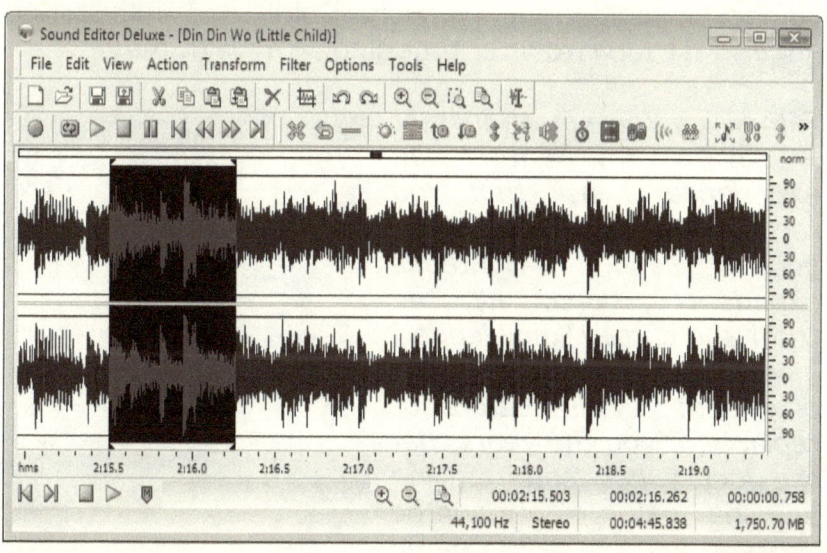

"And he that sat upon the throne said, Behold, **I make all things new. And he said unto me, Write: for these words are true and faithful. And he said unto me, It is done.** I am Alpha and Omega, the beginning and the end. I will give unto him that is athirst of the fountain of the water of life freely. He that over-cometh shall inherit all things; and I will be his God, and he shall be my son" (Rev 21:5-7).

Praying with me: *Father God, in spirit-to-Spirit union with Yeshua Messiah, Your Beloved Son, and through Him, enjoying spirit-to-Spirit union with You and Holy Spirit; I ask you to direct ministering angels to minister to me, restoring my soul. I trust in Your Word, that "The Law of Adonai is perfect, restoring the inner-person [soul]" (Ps 19:7).*

Now, as you envision your audiovisual time-line being fast-forwarded, pray with me: *I pray, Father God, that in place of every marker removed from the time-line of my soul, You will direct Your Holy Angels to edit-in – filling every void – with "the fruit of the Spirit: ... love, joy, peace, patience, kindness, goodness, faithfulness, gentleness and self-control" (Gal 5:22-23).* Editing-in, editing-in, editing-in, as Holy Spirit and ministering angels fast-forward your time-line. Pray with me:

Father, as You –in an instant – review my entire life experience, I ask that You reconnect and enhance all my good and righteous experiences; and, all the truth and correct knowledge I have learned. Lord, You promised: "I will restore or replace for you the years that the locust has eaten ...And you shall eat in plenty and be satisfied and praise the name of the Lord, your God, Who has dealt wondrously with you. And My people shall never be put to shame" (Joel 2:25-26 AMP).

Now, see the audio-visual record of your life gently slowing down and finally coming to rest at the present moment. Remembering that all time is all present before God; and now, in spirit-to Spirit union with Christ, turn the eyes of your soul toward the future, as you hear the Lord say: *"I know the plans I have for you ... plans to prosper you and not to harm you, plans to give you hope and a future"* (Jer 29:11-12).

Your Revised Record:
Allow God to show you – perhaps symbolically – the future He has planned for you. See now the revised audiovisual record of your life – the one He describes, saying: *"Then those who feared the Lord talked with each other, and the Lord listened and heard.* **A scroll of remembrance was written in his presence concerning those who feared the Lord and honored his name**.

"They will be mine," says the Lord Almighty, "in the day when I make up my treasured possession. I will spare them, just as in compassion a man spares his son who serves him. And you will again see the distinction between the righteous and the wicked, between those who serve God and those who do not" (Mal 3:16-18).

"So don't be ashamed of bearing testimony to our Lord. ... On the contrary, accept your share in suffering disgrace for the sake of the Good News. God will give you the strength for it, since he delivered us and called us to a life of holiness as his people. It was not because of our deeds, but because of his own purpose and the grace which he gave to us who are united [spirit-to-Spirit] with the Messiah Yeshua. He did this before the beginning of time, but made it public only now through the appearing of our Deliverer, the Messiah Yeshua, who abolished death and, through the Good News, revealed life and immortality.

"I am not ashamed, because I know him in whom I have put my trust, and I am persuaded that he can keep safe until that Day what he has entrusted to me. Follow the pattern of the sound teachings you have heard from me, with trust and the love which is yours in the Messiah Yeshua. Keep safe the great treasure that has been entrusted to you, with the help of Holy Spirit, who lives within us" (2 Tim 1:8-14 CJB).

Conclusion:
"This is what the Lord says: "Stand at the crossroads and look; ask for the ancient paths, ask where the good way is, and walk in it, and you will find rest for your souls" (Jer 6:16);

"The Lord will guide you always; he will satisfy your needs in a sun-scorched land and will strengthen your frame. You will be like a well-watered garden, like a spring whose waters never fail. Your people will rebuild the ancient ruins and will raise up the age-old foundations; you will be called Repairer of Broken Walls, Restorer of Streets with Dwellings" (Isa 58:11-12).

Your New Assignment:
"And Jesus came and spoke to them, saying, "All authority has been given to Me in heaven and on earth. Go therefore and make disciples of all the nations, baptizing them in the name of the Father and of the Son and of the Holy Spirit, teaching them to observe all things that I have commanded you; and lo, I am with you always, even to the end of the age. Amen" (Matt 28:18-20).

Ask what you can do to help accomplish the mission of Jesus. What is this mission? And what can you do?

"If anyone is in Christ, he is a new creation; the old has gone, the new has come! All this is from God, who reconciled us to himself through Christ and gave us the ministry of reconciliation: that God was reconciling the world to himself in Christ, not counting men's sins against them. And he has committed to us the message of reconciliation. We are therefore Christ's ambassadors, as though God were making his appeal through us. We

implore you on Christ's behalf: Be reconciled to God" (2 Cor 5:17-21).

~ Questions, Concerns & Key Points ~

1. To identify our emotional baggage, what two things need we examine?

2. Explain the meaning and significance of Isaiah 40:31

3. Carefully consider the concept and import of being entwined – in spirit-to-Spirit union within Christ.

4. What is our one 'out' or 'exception' to the Law of Gravity?

5. Explain the Law of Aerodynamics – its components, and the consequences of any of these failing to be within the prescribed limits?

6. What must we do to rid ourselves – our soul – of excess baggage and unnecessary weight?

7. What physical law symbolically represents spiritual gravity?

8. Explain Jesus' parable of the Vine and Branches, and its applicability to our spiritual well-being and ministry?

9. Explain David's parable of The Valley of Baca?

10. Why does God test our hearts?

11. Identify the varied sources of soul-wounding?

12. How destructive is internalized anger and unforgiveness?

13. Explain the concept of divine editing?

14. Explain the various dimensions – the physical, soulish, spiritual and casual realms?

15. What should one do if they begin to experience negative emotions during the divine editing process?

16. As a result of the divine editing process, what record is destroyed?
    - God's record of my sins
    - Satan's record of my sins
    - My record of my sins
    - Both God's and Satan's records
    - Both Satan's and my own record

17. What is our role in the divine editing process?

18. Which of the following is accomplished through divine editing?
    - The negative things of the past are edited-out
    - New information is edited-in
    - Both

19. Once the divine editing of our soul is complete, what are we then equipped to carry out?

~ Bibliography ~

Following are the resources that we have referred to in writing this book. We honor each one mentioned here by name, and many others, whose names we may have forgotten, who have contributed to the wisdom we have sought to convey to you. Of course, most of all, we thank Father God for life; our Lord and Savior, Jesus Christ, for redeeming our souls; and for Holy Spirit Who indwells our spirits, Who guides and directs, through inspiration as we write; and for God's holy angels – ministering spirits – conveying our petitions to God and bringing us His responses.

Sandford, John and Paula
Horman, Aiko, Ph.D.
Payne, Leanne, M.Div.
Thompson, Bruce
Ballard, Larry and Vi
Richard and Phyllis Arno

~ About the Authors ~

James V. Potter, Ph.D., and Paula M. Potter, MA – husband and wife – are Christian Authors, Educators, Pastoral Counselors and Ordained Ministers. Dr. and Paula Potter make their home in Northern California, where they retired in 2003 after decades in clinical pastoral counseling practice. Prior to their move to Northern California, they resided in Hawaii, on the Big Island.

There, they served on the staff of the Family Ministry School, University of the Nations, a Division of Youth With A Mission; As Associate Pastors with the Gospel of Salvation Churches and the New Covenant Church; and were engaged in private Clinical Pastoral Counseling.

Dr. James and Paula Potter, founded the Hawaii Family Care Centers – a network of community based, Christian Counseling Centers, serving at-risk individuals and families, ministering to substance abusers, addicts, domestic violence perpetrators and victims, and individuals struggling from various mood and personality disorders. Returning to California in 1995, Dr. Potter and Paula founded Agape Family Care Services and the Alliance Recovery Service, carrying on the clinical practice they had begun while in Hawaii.

After retiring from clinical practice in 2003, Dr. Potter and Paula founded Advocare Ministries, and its divisions: Advocare Publishing Co., to publish Christ-centered counseling resources, self-help guides and spiritual guidance materials; and Advocare Family Skills Institute, to carry on the work of training and equipping Christian Counselors.

Through their affiliations with Vision Bible College and Vision International University, Dr. Potter and Paula mentor students in their bachelor and masters studies worldwide, through on-line instruction.

Dr. Potter and Paula are Certified Christian Marriage and Family Therapists; Certified Clinical Pastoral Counselors; Certified Domestic Violence and Abuse Prevention and Treatment Specialists; Certified Substance Abuse and Addiction Prevention and Treatment Specialists; and Certified Prepare/Enrich Counselors and Trainers.

Dr. Potter has been listed in numerous directories, including: Marquis, Who's Who in America, Who's Who in the World, Who's Who in Religion, and Who's Who in Education; Men of Achievement; the International Biographical Centre; Association for Christian Therapists; and the National Christian Counselors Association.

Dr. Potter is a member of the World Association for Online Education, and both Dr. Potter and Paula Potter serve as adjunct faculty for Vision International University, and teach in the Bonneyview Road Christian Center, Educational Programs, Redding, California.

~ Other Titles ~

Other titles by these authors you might find enjoyable and rewarding, include:

- God's Precious Promises: A Guide to Appropriating As Your Own, God's 8,000 + Promises
- Mysteries of The Bible: The Primeval Era ~ A Story of the Time When Giants Roamed the Earth
- Mysteries of the Bible: Armageddon ~ Christ & His Bride vs. The Antichrist & His Concubines [Iran with Gog & Magog; Radical Islam; MS-13 & MS-18]
- The Divine Exchange: Life for Life ~ Soul for Soul
- Our Spiritual Authority: Restoring the Power & Authority of the 1st. Century Church
- Waging Winning War in the Spirit Realm

- Soul Care: An Introduction to Pastoral Care
- Counseling Addicts & Offenders: A Guide to Criminal Justice Counseling

- Mastery Over Anger: Healing Relationships Through Constructive Conflict-Resolution
- Conquistando La Ira (Spanish Mastery Over Anger)
- Assertiveness, Individuation & Autonomy
- Conquering Codependency
- Jekyll & Hyde: Arrested Development & Personality Disorders
- Healing Inner-Child Wounds: Breaking Life Commandments
- Growing Beyond Our Genetics: Adolescence & Beyond
- Affair-Proofing Your Marriage: Bonding vs. Relationship Bondage

- Toxic Shame & The Journey Out
- Substances of Abuse: An ID & Symptom Guide

www.ingramcontent.com/pod-product-compliance
Lightning Source LLC
Chambersburg PA
CBHW032013230426
43671CB00005B/70